Getting straight "A"s doesn't have to be a mystery...

these practical, concise, and affordable study guides will tell you how!

VISIONS OF THE

CANADIAN
ABORIGINAL
ISSUES

DAVID ALAN LONG
The King's University College, Edmonton

OLIVE PATRICIA DICKASON
University of Alberta

HARCOURT
BRACE
CANADA

Harcourt Brace & Company, Canada

Toronto Montreal Fort Worth New York Orlando
Philadelphia San Diego London Sydney Tokyo

Requests for permission to make copies of any part of the work should be mailed to: Permissions, College Division, Harcourt Brace & Company, Canada, 55 Horner Avenue, Toronto, Ontario M8Z 4X6.

Every reasonable effort has been made to acquire permission for copyright material used in this text, and to acknowledge all such indebtedness accurately. Any errors and omissions called to the publisher's attention will be corrected in future printings.

Canadian Cataloguing in Publication Data

Main entry under title:

Visions of the heart

ISBN 0-7747-3382-9

1. Native peoples — Canada.*   I. Long, David Alan,
1958-   . II. Dickason, Olive Patricia, 1920-   .

E78.C2V5 1996   971'.00497   C95-933010-0

Publisher: Heather McWhinney
Senior Acquisitions Editor: Christopher Carson
Projects Manager: Liz Radojkovic
Developmental Editor: Laura Paterson Pratt
Director of Publishing Services: Jean Davies
Editorial Manager: Marcel Chiera
Supervising Editor: Semareh Al-Hillal
Production Editor: Laurel Parsons
Production Manager: Sue-Ann Becker
Production Co-ordinator: Sheila Barry
Copy Editor: Jim Lyons
Cover Design: Opus House
Interior Design: Dave Peters, revised by Opus House
Typesetting and Assembly: IBEX Graphic Communications Inc.
Printing and Binding: Kromar Printing Ltd.

Cover Art: Jane Ash Poitras, *In Our Dreams the Spirits Tell Us Things*, 1991. Private Collection, Toronto. Reproduced with permission.

This book was printed in Canada.

1 2 3 4 5   00   99 98 97 96

PREFACE

The contributors to *Visions of the Heart* share the conviction that many people in Canada want to engage in hopeful, unifying dialogue. We also believe that such conversation between people in Canada will cultivate a just and unifying vision to the extent that there is critical reflection on both the admirable and the ignoble aspects of this country's history. A conversation such as this, involving a handful of Cree from the Treaty Six Confederacy in central Alberta, a francophone from Quebec, and a number of anglophone Edmontonians, took place in Edmonton not long after the constitutional discussions at Meech Lake. At one point, Laurent Gagnon from Quebec stated that there had been little room for hope in the constitutional talks because their success depended on everyone having to make concessions. He noted that the unifying vision that a people need if they are to flourish was sorely lacking in discussions at Meech Lake. Although some people assert that there continues to be a lack of vision in Canada, it is precisely Native peoples' commitment to the visions of their hearts that has enabled them to survive, and to seek justice, healing, and reconciliation. Our contribution to unifying dialogue in *Visions of the Heart* is therefore twofold: to examine critically past and present sources of oppression of Native life in Canada, and to explore ways in which aboriginal people in Canada have sought to realize the visions of their hearts.

However, unifying dialogue does not imply sameness of experience and oneness of voice. In order to understand the diverse ways in which aboriginal people have attempted to realize their visions, contributors to *Visions of the Heart* have explored Canadian aboriginal issues from a variety of methodological angles and theoretical perspectives. Regardless of whether the brushstrokes of contributors have resulted in relatively abstract, generalized pictures or intimate, highly detailed portraits, we agree that meaningful academic discourse on Canadian aboriginal issues honours differences in experience and perspective. The contributors to this collection also agree that as we approach the 21st century, academics who give account of the contents, meanings, and socio-historical implications of people's lives and visions must take seriously their role as the new storytellers. They recognize that just as storytellers of the past gave expression to a myriad of experiences, the invitation of difference into academic and non-academic conversations is the lifeblood of genuine, visionary dialogue. In *Visions of the Heart* we invite readers to explore aboriginal peoples' visions, and the efforts of these people and their supporters to attain them. Our hope is that readers will appreciate that even though it can take a brief historical moment for a nation to fall, the heart of genuine visions that seek justice, reconciliation, and healing is difficult if not impossible to eradicate.

ACKNOWLEDGEMENTS

Editing *Visions of the Heart* has been a rewarding experience, due in large part to those I worked and lived with who helped bring it to fruition. Undoubtedly, my editorial task would have been much more difficult had not Chris Carson and Laura Paterson Pratt from Harcourt Brace shared both my vision and my enthusiasm for the book from the outset. Much that is positive about the paths this book takes in relation to contemporary Native issues also reflects the skill and effort of its writers and reviewers. I appreciate both the insights and the diligence that the contributing authors brought to their work, and for their patience in working with a first-time editor. Moreover, constructive review comments of the proposal, as well as the working and final drafts of each chapter, contributed significantly to this shared project. I am also grateful to my colleagues John Hiemstra, Heather Looy, and Carol Everest at The King's University College, who contributed to this book through their willingness to listen to my ideas and challenge me to wrestle with the philosophical and literary dimensions of scholarship that are often ignored by sociologists. My final collegial note of appreciation is addressed to Olive, whom I wish to thank for quite unselfconsciously serving as my mentor by challenging me to put my often taken-for-granted sociological, and sometimes not-so-sociological, preconceptions to the test.

On a more personal note, I am privileged to receive support, encouragement, and joy from Karen, and from our children, Jennica, Bethany, and Sarah. This project would have been much more onerous if my family had not continuously brought everyday renewal and hope into my life. Finally, it is an understatement to say that it is unfortunate that issues such as these are a part of Canadian life. I therefore feel greatly indebted to the many Native people who had the courage and trust to disclose very personal thoughts and experiences to those of us committed to listening to their stories and to giving them an academic voice. Without the contributions of Native people young and old, it would be impossible to address the complexity of relations involving Native and non-Native people in a manner that promises healing and delivers hope.

David Alan Long

A Note from the Publisher

Thank you for selecting *Visions of the Heart: Canadian Aboriginal Issues*, by David Alan Long and Olive Patricia Dickason. The authors and publisher have devoted considerable time to the careful development of this book. We appreciate your recognition of this effort and accomplishment.

We want to hear what you think about *Visions of the Heart: Canadian Aboriginal Issues*. Please take a few minutes to fill in the stamped reader reply card at the back of the book. Your comments and suggestions will be valuable to us as we prepare new editions and other books.

CONTENTS

INTRODUCTION

Shared vision lies at the heart of every flourishing human community, and has long been communicated through stories passed from generation to generation. These stories have been spoken aloud, chiselled onto stone tablets, etched with ochre onto papyrus leaves, woven into wampum belts, enscribed in ornate, highly formalized manuscripts, and typed into internationally accessible data banks. People have also commemorated their heart-felt visions in many ways, from the slaughtering of sacrificial lambs by Hebrew priests during Passover to signify cleansing, to Plains Amerindian males engaging in self-mutilation to induce personal and communal visions in their version of the Sun Dance, to gay and lesbian adaptations of Canada Day parades. Regardless of how they are embodied, genuine communal visions invite a people to contemplate, lament, and celebrate the vagaries of human experience. Moreover, shared vision cultivates hope by enabling a people to plan their common future together. The contributors to this collection acknowledge that Native people in Canada have long expressed such heart-felt visions, or, as we call them, *Visions of the Heart*.

Unfortunately, not all visions of the heart seek peace, justice, and harmony among different peoples. Human history is rife with attempts by people with certain visions to control and destroy the visions of their enemies, presumably since without a vision the enemy is said to perish. A disquieting message from much of human history is that even shared visions that leave a path of human misery and destruction in their wake can and do flourish. For example, European explorers and colonizers had a particular vision for Canada. Because the colonizers regarded the aboriginal inhabitants of this land as inferior, they implemented policies and legislation with the intent of isolating or assimilating them. Most of the chapters that follow examine ways in which European colonialism represented a shared, albeit oppressive, vision imposed on aboriginal people living in Canada. Together, the chapters offer a depiction of the multifaceted relationship between European colonization and the physical, cultural, and structural aspects of Native life in Canada. The result, depending on one's perspective, can be a less than pretty socio-historical picture.

Since roughly the early 1960s, there have been significant changes in the experiences of Canada's aboriginal people and in writing by and about them. Before that time, acculturation theory supported the idea that social disorganization, cultural conflict, and feelings of inferiority reflected an inability on the part of certain groups of people to adjust to rapid social and cultural change. Promoters of this perspective further assumed the superiority of dominant groups and societies. Consequently, aboriginal people were blamed for having inadequate skills, a lack of understanding in relation to European ways, and a general unwillingness to commit themselves to alleviating their widespread personal and social problems. Apparent support for acculturation theory was found in aboriginal peoples' high rates of physical and mental illness, suicide, homicide, incarceration, and unemployment and in their relatively impoverished standards of living. In other words, little could be done to help aboriginal people in Canada because not only were they seen to be responsible for their own problems, they also lacked adequate skills and commitment to address their problems in constructive ways.

Beginning in the mid-1960s, internal colonialism theory was offered as an alternative way of making sense of who or what was to blame for the personal and social problems experienced by Native people in Canada. According to this perspective, the process of colonization operates at a number of different levels. At the structural level, colonizers formally reorganize all aspects of indigenous life through the enforcement of policies and legislation that reflect the colonizers' perspective and serve the colonizers' interests. At the intergroup and interpersonal levels, the homogenizing cultural ways and means of colonizers gradually displace the diverse ways and means of indigenous cultures.

Although most contributors to *Visions of the Heart* have made use of internal colonialism theory to explore connections between the policies and practices of European colonization and many problematic aspects of Native life, we have kept in mind that human beings are creative social agents who experience, interpret, and adapt to social life in many different ways for many different reasons. According to critics of Indian residential schools, for example, the violent, oppressive character of these institutions is directly responsible for the personal, familial, and economic problems experienced by many of the Native people who attended them. While acknowledging that the residential system was harmful in certain respects, others point out that there are also many "successful," well-adjusted Native people who attended these schools. Understanding the past and present significance of residential schooling thus means much more than critically examining the personal and cultural experiences of students and their families, tallying up how many people were negatively or positively affected, or exploring the evolution of educational policies and practices. Fundamentally, we understand residential schooling and other social phenomena to the extent that we are open to a variety of perspectives in their historical, structural, cultural, and interpersonal dimensions. Readers should therefore keep in mind that while the application of internal colonialism theory contributes to a critical understanding of relations between aboriginal and non-aboriginal peoples in Canada, the theory does not enable us to understand these relationships fully.

In *Visions of the Heart*, we invite readers to explore and reflect critically on the relationships between European colonization and, among other things, the loss of elder leadership, the creation of elected band council systems of Native government, the control or outright banning of certain religious and cultural ceremonies, the grouping of aboriginal people into different categories with different rights and responsibilities, the establishment of reserves and residential schools, the widespread removal of children from their families and communities under the guise of child welfare concerns, the fragmentation of health-related services and provisions, and the culturally blind practices of those representing the Canadian criminal justice system. As you read and think about these and other phenomena, we ask that you attempt to walk in the shoes of the colonizers as well as the colonized.

This collection is thus a conscious attempt to challenge and enable readers to put their theoretical perspective on Native life in Canada to the test. It provides support for the view that academic descriptions and analyses, along with offering insight, ought to raise a number of questions for discussion and debate. To encourage dialogue beyond this book, questions specific to each contribution are included at the end of each chapter. Beyond these specific questions, we wish to encourage readers to reflect on the more general questions of who should be responsible for changing current conditions of Native life "for the better," and how those who are responsible for bringing about change and healing should go about their tasks. The efforts undertaken by Native and non-Native people to address the issues raised in this book illustrate the responses by certain people to these questions. *Visions of the Heart* is therefore intended as more than a collection of articles by individuals writing on a common theme in their areas of expertise. Together, these chapters illustrate the value of discussion that involves people with different experiences and perspectives. This type of discussion also challenges those who esteem unity of literary or methodological style and oneness of voice.

Although academics and others have written about the lives of Native peoples in this country since the days of first contact, the writers represented in this book share the conviction that there have been relatively few attempts to examine Canadian Native issues in a systematic and comprehensive manner. Certainly, there have been national and provincial task forces, non-government organizations, and individual researchers who have analyzed many aspects of aboriginal life in Canada, but studies offering a "big-picture," social-scientific perspective on contemporary aboriginal issues have been few and far between. In their analyses, Norris, Long and Fox, Fleras, Voyageur, Barman, Peters, Monture-Angus, Brascoupé, and Long and Bordeau seek to fill part of this gap in our understanding. The data included in their research come from a large number and variety of sources: submissions to the Royal Commission on Aboriginal Peoples (RCAP), national, provincial, and territorial task forces, Statistics Canada data from virtually every federal and provincial ministry, government and non-government studies, and numerous other reports and discussion papers. Nonetheless, social scientists can easily fall prey to relying on aggregate data drawn from regions, cities, reserves and settlements with vastly different economies, cultures, and structures for the simple reason that it is economical to do so. Even Norris, who provides a national-level, statistically precise analysis of past, present, and future demographic trends involving Native people in Canada, cautions readers who would quickly generalize from such data to all First Nation, non-registered, Métis, or Inuit people in this country.

As valuable as big-picture studies are, researchers recognized during the mid-1980s that generalized research findings needed to be augmented by more nuanced pictures of Native life. Consequently, researchers began examining the interpersonal and community-level perspectives, experiences, and initiatives of Native people and their supporters. This type of research is well represented in the contributions of McFarlane, Irwin and Farrell, Long and Fox, Peters, Barman, Monture-Angus, and Long. By drawing out the diverse and subtle character of aboriginal life in Canada, these authors challenge us to reflect on the validity of sweeping generalizations.

All the contributors to this book readily acknowledge that giving account of Native social issues is a highly interpretive act. Moreover, they all support the social justice perspective that informs *Visions of the Heart*, a perspective that maintains that academics ought to do more than describe social circumstances and name particular visions that legitimize the oppression of outsiders. Their fundamental concern is to challenge and enable readers to think beneath and beyond descriptions of conditions, to ask informed critical questions, and to engage in humble, visionary dialogue in relation to contemporary aboriginal issues. Given the inclusive character of this collection, our most difficult editorial task was to encourage contributors to articulate a shared vision for this book while enabling them to maintain their own voice.

Together, the chapters highlight a number of significant issues in research involving aboriginal peoples. Perhaps the most basic of these is that much contemporary social science provides a rather impersonal, detached approach to understanding social life in Canada. We recognize that writers and readers hold a variety of views on the relationship between researchers and researched, and that we undoubtedly have different reasons for viewing the relationship the way we do. Constructive dialogue therefore depends on having a sense of how and why we view the relationship in particular ways. This does not necessarily mean having to tell our own personal story every time we speak or write. Rather, it means openly reflecting on certain fundamental methodological issues in research involving human subjects. The issues that the contributors to *Visions of the Heart* reflected on included: (1) their academic role; (2) different experiences, concerns, and perspectives of aboriginal and non-aboriginal people in relation to the lives of aboriginal peoples, perhaps also including differences among aboriginal (or non-aboriginal) people; (3) general difficulties in cross-cultural research; (4) the benefits and drawbacks of using certain types of data (ethnographic, oral history, interview, survey, archival, etc.); (5) problems with studying dependent populations; (6) dilemmas confronted in conveying the inner workings of societies based on oral traditions to literate audiences; and (7) the personal, interpretive, and politically charged issues surrounding voice appropriation, all of which are fundamentally a question of the appropriateness and validity of telling another's story. Not all authors articulate their position on all of these issues in their chapters, and indeed some authors apparently choose not to engage very many of them. We nonetheless offer the different styles of writing and various methodological approaches represented throughout *Visions of the Heart* as a strength of this collection.

One major theme that runs throughout the book concerns the relationship between past experiences and present circumstances involving aboriginal people in Canada. Many of the chapters — notably those by Dickason and Smillie on the relationship between historians and Native history, Couture on elders, Voyageur on Native women, Fleras on bureaucratization, McFarlane on leadership, Barman on residential school education, Long and Fox on health and healing, Monture-Angus on criminal justice, Peters on urban Native life, and Long on the Native social movement — place the development of issues and activities involving aboriginal people in historical context. Furthermore, Dickason, Smillie, Fleras, Brascoupé, and Long and Bourdeau all underscore that Canadian aboriginal issues do not merely involve high-profile Native and non-Native leaders, but also a multitude of interactions through which socially diverse actors support or oppose one another in interpersonal, communal, national, and international contexts.

In contrast to the socio-historical character of the chapters mentioned above, Couture, Irwin and Farrell, Voyageur, Fox, Peters, Brascoupé, and Monture-Angus invite readers to reflect on the experiences of Native people from everyday, grass-roots perspectives. Couture's reverent account of the re-emergence of Native elders and Fox's oral historical account of health in Stoney Country together illustrate that wisdom can only be gained from experience. Irwin's and Farrell's decision to not provide a linear historical account reflects their desire to distance themselves from precontact histories, which they believe have largely been interpreted through European eyes. Finally, Peters's challenging vision of the role of Native people in urban areas, Brascoupé's account of Native economic development, and Monture-Angus's analysis of Native criminal justice demonstrate that meaningful dialogue and constructive social change depend at root on people's openness to different perspectives and visions. Unlike most social-scientific accounts of Native life in Canada, these chapters invite us to listen to interpretations of Native life from the perspective of Native people themselves. By breaking down the socially constructed barriers between researchers and researched, these writers offer an alternative, more personal view of social science.

Concerning the historical aspect, the standard western approach to history has been broadening and deepening as a result of the aboriginal challenge. Faced with the problem of tracing out the histories of peoples without writing, historians are having to resort to an interdisciplinary approach, one that draws from geology, archaeology, anthropology, linguistics, and oral traditions, each providing insights that in various combinations can lead to different answers from those offered in the past. In treating the Native factor within a narrow focus, and dismissing it as a relic of the past, historians and others have impoverished Canadian history. However, there is more to re-assessing the evidence than simply keeping the Native factor in mind. As Couture, Irwin and Farrell, Fox, Peters, Monture-Angus, and Brascoupé demonstrate, historians and other social scientists need to make the effort to understand Native concerns and, above all, to appreciate Native perceptions. Indeed, each chapter in *Visions of the Heart* shows that the Native contribution to the formation of modern Canada has been both much greater and more multifaceted than has ever been generally acknowledged, and that Natives actively contribute to Canadian society today. The contributors to this collection share the conviction that in taking up the challenge to understand the historical role of Native people in Canada, academics and non-academics alike will contribute to more hopeful, unifying dialogue.

CHAPTER 1

Toward a Larger View of Canada's History: The Native Factor[1]

Olive Patricia Dickason

A major lesson of the Oka confrontation of 1990 for most Canadians was the startling realization of how little they knew about their own history. For many, it was a revelation to learn that the conflict, far from being a flash in the pan, had roots that go deep into our national past — easily to the first meetings between Amerindians and Europeans, and by extension even beyond, if the attitudes that both sides brought with them are included. There was nothing in our standard national histories that prepared Canadians for this. The accepted historical approach, at least until recently, has been to begin with the voyages of Jacques Cartier, give a brief summary of his relations with the Amerindians of the St. Lawrence Valley, go on to discuss the fur trade and missionary activity, which were described as radically altering the Amerindian way of life, and perhaps to include something about the role of Amerindians in the colonial wars of the seventeenth and eighteenth centuries. Once launched into the political and constitutional development of our country, historians have habitually left the Amerindians far behind as picturesque but irrelevant relics of the past. Not even mentioned are the numbered treaties of the west and north, by which the federal government acquired enormous areas of Amerindian lands for white settlement and industrial development, paving the way for the creation of the Canadian confederacy. Until well into the twentieth century, Canadian historians habitually depicted Natives as barbarians much in need of the civilizing influence of whites. There was little, if any, serious attempt to examine the Amerindian side of the story.[2]

HISTORY AS DEFINED IN THE WESTERN WORLD

History as developed in the western world during the nineteenth century is based upon written documentation, particularly when derived from official sources (Dickason, 1992, p. 11). Further, until the past few decades, the emphasis was almost exclusively on public affairs where the powerful and important dominated; not only were the rank and file who made up the bulk of society largely excluded, but preliterate or tribal societies were almost completely ignored. Such societies were labelled prehistoric or per-haps protohistoric; the best they could hope for was to become historic by extension, when they came into contact with literate societies. Since this meant that history began with the arrival of Europeans, Canadians consid-ered theirs a young country, a land of much geography and little history.[3] As H.H. Trevor-Roper, regius professor of modern history at Oxford Univer-sity, maintained when discussing Africa, the period before the arrival of Europeans "is largely darkness, like the history of pre-European, pre-Columbian America. And darkness is not a subject of history" (*The Rise of Christian Europe*, cited in Krech, 1991, p. 345).

In the case of Canada, the meeting of French and Amerindians on the north Atlantic coast in the sixteenth century was very poorly documented, because with few exceptions (principally Jacques Cartier, who made three official voyages, 1534–42), early visitors came over on their own initiative, attracted by the profits to be made from fishing and whaling. Keeping records was not a concern, except perhaps for commercial reasons, and the survival rate of those records has reflected their low official impor-tance. It should also be remembered that these meetings were not a first, neither for the French nor for the Natives. The French had been trading with Amerindians in Brazil for nearly a century before they began seriously to develop the northern fur trade toward the end of the sixteenth century. By that time, northern Amerindians and Inuit had been dealing with Basques and Breton fishermen for almost as long, and before that may have encountered Norse. The earliest accounts we have indicate prior familiarity on both sides (except perhaps for the Norse); nowhere in the documented Canadian experience do we find Amerindians reacting toward Europeans as they did in the Caribbean toward the Spanish, whom they at first regarded as returning spirits. The closest approximation of this that has been recorded for Canada was Cartier's reception by the people upriver on the St. Lawrence above Stadacona (today's Quebec City), especially at Hochelaga (today's Montreal). There is some indication that they regarded Cartier as a shaman, with curing powers; however, their joy seems to have been mainly inspired by the French breach of Stadacona's control of the river, and the consequent prospect of direct trade with the French. Known documentary sources about these contacts, patchy as they are, in most cases have not been thoroughly searched by historians with Native history in mind. Surviving records, early published material, and Native traditions all need to be re-examined with this in view. A point to remember is that written accounts, no matter how objec-tive they may seem, are always influenced by the attitudes and beliefs of the writer. Sorting out the biases from facts is rarely simple, no matter what the source of the information.

TOWARD A BROADER CONCEPTION

Despite such difficulties, this century has seen a move toward a broader view of history, a move which has meant that, among other things, historians have begun to pay more attention to tribal nations. Because those nations were oral rather than literate peoples (even those who did possess a form of writing had not developed it into a widely shared form of communication), reconstructing their precontact history in the western sense of the term is a daunting task. The inadequacy of written sources means that researching such a history calls for an interdisciplinary approach, one that draws from geology, archaeology, anthropology, linguistics, oral traditions, and the arts. Each provides insights that when pieced together with whatever documentary evidence exists help to fill in the picture. A principal problem for this approach has been the development of critical techniques to evaluate the information; cross-checking can be difficult, if possible at all. On top of that, the type of information provided by oral history does not necessarily fit the requirements of western-style history.[4]

Before delving into research methods, two questions should be answered: why is an understanding of prehistory important, and why should historians concern themselves about first contacts if the information is so difficult to come by? To begin with the last question, first contacts set the pattern for what was to follow in Amerindian–white relationships. The first impressions of Europeans — that Amerindians were "a remarkably strange and savage people, without faith, without law, without religion" (Thevet, 1878, p. 135) — crystallized into attitudes that determined patterns of relationships, which in turn influenced policies.

It is comparatively simple to trace out this sequence in today's sometimes problematic relations between First Nations and mainstream society. Two clear examples of this are the confrontation at Oka in 1990 over land that the Mohawk claim to be theirs since time immemorial, and Justice Allan McEachern's rejection in 1991 of the Gitksan and Wet'suwet'en claim to 57 000 square kilometres of traditional lands in northern British Columbia, a resource-rich area about the size of Nova Scotia. Justice McEachern denied the existence of aboriginal rights of ownership and jurisdiction,[5] drawing on arguments that had been developed originally from the sixteenth through the eighteenth centuries to justify the European takeover of aboriginal lands. According to these arguments, a sedentary lifestyle based on farming within a nation-state was a prerequisite for proprietary and sovereign rights; since hunter/gatherers were without settled abodes, they had no legitimate claims to either. In the case of the Mohawk, they are facing the added challenge of proving that they were the first, and continuous, occupants of the lands they are claiming. From these examples, it should be clear why it is important to understand the nature and history of precontact societies in Canada, at least as far as we are able. As Renaissance Europe had debated, were these fully formed societies, although of models very different from those of Europe?

Or were they living according to nature, and thus with no more property rights (or rights of any kind, for that matter) than panthers or bears, to use a nineteenth-century journalistic expression?

WHAT GEOLOGY HAS TO SAY

Geology is included among the disciplines that contribute to our knowledge about our First Nations, because it tells us what the ecological conditions were, and so when and where humans could survive. Since Canada was largely ice-bound until about 10 000 to 14 000 years ago, human habitation appears to have been first confined to the few areas that escaped glaciation, such as the Yukon. In regions south of the glaciers, it has been estimated that ecological conditions have been suitable for human habitation for about 50 000 years or more. It is widely believed that Amerindians first crossed over from Siberia on foot during periods when intensification of the glaciation lowered the sea level, transforming Bering Strait into a grassy steppe some 2000 kilometres wide (Dickason, 1992, pp. 21, 23). Geologists inform us that this land bridge, called Beringia, emerged several times during the late Pleistocene geological age (the Wisconsin stage) between about 75 000 and 14 000 years ago (Young, 1988). It provided a rich habitat for such animals as mammoth, mastodon, giant bison, saiga antelope, and the predators that preyed upon them. That the herds attracted human hunters is a reasonable assumption supported by archaeological evidence from both sides of the Bering Strait.

However, the presence of land game does not necessarily imply that that the rich marine life off the coasts was ignored. Nor did the convenience of the pedestrian route mean that it was the only one that was used. In fact, the evidence is to the contrary; early camp sites tend to be by sea coasts and waterways, probably because of the comparative ease of harvesting marine resources, not to mention that of water travel. The Japanese Current, sweeping straight eastward across the Pacific to the Americas, provided a natural aquatic highway that would not have presented any great problems. We know that sea voyages were being undertaken as early as 50 000 years ago, as that was the time that humans reached the island continent of Australia. The argument that Arctic conditions were too dangerous for early seagoing technology is tenuous at best; the seagoing Beothuk canoe, for example, was well adapted for use among the ice floes.

ARCHAEOLOGY LENDS A HAND

Archaeology has been history's principal ally in tracing out the first settling of the Americas. But here also difficulties abound. Because bones do not preserve well in New World soils, the evidence of very early human presence has been based on artifacts rather than skeletal remains, a situation unique to the Americas (Dillehay, 1991, p. 13). Rather than providing sure answers, dates established so far for human habitation have given rise to more questions, as the oldest ones have come out of unglaciated South America, and the most recent ones for precontact migration have come from the ice-bound Arctic. This, of course, argues for first arrival by sea. Attempts to prove an American genesis for modern Amerindians on archaeological evidence have not been successful.[6] For most Amerindians, this is not important, because scientific evidence is not needed to convince them that this is the land of their origin.

Archaeology has been described as "simply another process for understanding the past" (Devine, 1991, p. 21). No more than other types of knowledge does it give us final answers; what it does do is provide fresh insights as new data and new dating and interpretive techniques become available, which they are doing at an increasing rate (Trigger, 1985, p. 52). Dating, and especially interpretation, have always been particular problems for archaeologists, who even under the best of circumstances must work with non-perishable material remains, a tiny percentage of the data that would have been available from the site when it was active. It is extremely rare for sites to be preserved as they were used — Pompeii, buried under a volcanic eruption in A.D. 63, is probably the best known; in the Americas, there is Ozette, a Makah village on the Olympic Peninsula in the state of Washington, that was buried under a mud slide about 500 years before Columbus. Since Makah still live in the area, archaeologists have been able to work with the people to reconstruct the village's lifestyle. More often there is little, if any, apparent connection between ancient sites and present-day inhabitants. The best that can usually be hoped for is to be able to deduce the broad outlines of the social dynamics of the communities that once occupied them. As Bruce Trigger has observed (1985, p. 52), archaeology studies what humans made or used; while such data can sometimes suggest what people thought and did, they are inadequate for fleshing out the intricacies of social interactions. Nor, where writing is absent, can archaeology pinpoint languages, except perhaps in very general terms.

That said, however, archaeology is still our main source of information about the distant past; for one thing, it can reveal much about trade patterns by tracing the sources of non-local plants, as well as non-local materials used in the manufacture of such items as tools. For another, it can tell us much about the tools themselves. Tools as such do not reveal methods or systems of use; but, as archaeologists learned when they began to involve Native communities in their projects, knowledge of these ancient technological systems has not entirely disappeared. An example of what can happen through such co-operation was recently illustrated when archaeologists and villagers of the Koani Pampa in the Bolivian altiplano co-operated to reconstruct and put into practice ancient agricultural techniques for growing potatoes, and were rewarded with a dramatic increase in yields.[7] In this case, recovering an ancient technology brought material benefits to the natives concerned, and satisfaction to the archaeologists for having proved a point. In Canada as well, co-operation between archaeologists and the Native communities affected by their work has already brought benefits, not the least of which is a much wider and deeper understanding of the complexity and creativity of our aboriginal societies, and consequently of ourselves as a multicultural nation.

ANTHROPOLOGY'S CONTRIBUTION

Anthropology, as a discipline, is closely connected to both archaeology and history. In the widest sense, anthropology is the science of humans in their myriad diversities. Where history looks for its evidence principally in documents, and archaeology to artifacts and material remains, anthropology relies mainly on direct observation of living societies; it is the study of humans in terms of their time and place. History and archaeology are concerned with the past, anthropology with the present, although within the framework of what went before. Physical anthropology illustrates one type of linkage with both history and archaeology. Since physical characteristics are influenced by cultural behaviour, skeletal remains can tell us something about ways of life: height, for instance, can be influenced by nutrition, diet can affect jaw conformity and the condition of teeth, diseases can affect bones, and injuries can point to occupational hazards or war.

Each of these approaches to the study of humans is supplementary to the other, as was seen in the case of archaeology. Historians are capitalizing more and more upon anthropology as they look for information to help them understand Native behaviour as reported in the documents. Some call this partnership between anthropology and history "ethnohistory," but the term is not universally accepted; history is history, say some historians, even if in some cases they have to turn to other than documentary evidence. The term "ethnohistory" came into use in the 1950s, following a proposal by anthropologist William N. Fenton, to the Institute of Early American History and Culture, that ethnologists and historians collaborate on the "common ground" of Indian–white relations to enhance our understanding of the past (Merrell, 1989, p. 94). That historians were slow to respond reflected, at least in part, hesitancies about entering unknown territory.

LANGUAGE, ORAL TRADITION, AND THE ARTS

Still another discipline that contributes to this holistic approach to history is that of language. Studies have shown that prehistorically unglaciated North America contained by far the greatest number of languages, 93 percent, along with a higher degree of differentiation than did the glaciated areas (Dickason, 1992, p. 25). The two most widely diffused languages in the prehistoric Americas were Cree, in the once-glaciated north, and Inuktitut, in the ice-bound Arctic. The latter still shows clear traces of its Asiatic connections. Of the 500 or so languages spoken in North America, the greatest concentrations were in California and on the coast of the Gulf of Mexico; in South America, the number totalled more than 1500. It has been proposed that such a wealth of languages was more likely to have evolved in many localities over a very long span of time than to have been brought in by separate migrations (Gruhn, 1988, pp. 77–79). It has even been theorized that all Amerindian languages, except for Na-Dene (Athapaskan) and Eskimo-Aleut, developed from a single prototype called Amerind. This highly controversial hypothesis postulates three founding migrations, the first of which brought Amerind, by far the largest, most widespread, and most diversified of the three proposed basic groups (Greenberg, 1987, pp. 331–37). Such theorizing has received some support from recent genetic studies that suggest that all Amerindians have descended from four primary maternal lineages, although this is vigorously disputed by advocates of a multiplicity of migrations (Schurr et al., 1990).[8]

Finally, the oral traditions of Native peoples are receiving more acceptance by ethnohistorians as a source of evidence, particularly for the recent past. More controversial is such evidence for the distant past, particularly when there are different versions of the same event. In that case, independent confirmation is needed. Myths are in another realm; with their different conception of time and nature, they deal with the interconnecting patterns of the spiritual and material worlds, whereas history deals with humans within the time and space of the material world. Myths tell us about a people's view of themselves, and how they relate to the world around them; history records the actions by which humans work out their destiny. Mythic descriptions of how humans came to be here are many and varied, abounding in metaphors; what these stories have in common is their emphasis and confirmation of the peoples' place in the web of the universe as well as their fundamental attachment to the land. Their underlying message is clear: however and whenever Amerindians came to be here, this is their homeland; they have no bonds with any other.

Besides myths and storytelling, rituals and the visual arts also have roles in explicating and recording these relationships. Orally and visually, they are all part of the dialogue by which peoples create their cultural contexts and thus define themselves.

POINTS OF DEPARTURE

Obviously, undertaking a history of Canada's aboriginal peoples is not a simple matter. Two points of departure suggest themselves. First, despite the rich variety of their cultures, there is an underlying commonality in

Amerindian worldviews, evident in their myths.[9] Similarly, the wide disparities in their societal developments notwithstanding, they still shared
many underlying assumptions, so that their cultures fit into a hemisphere-
wide pattern; like Europeans on the other side of the Atlantic, they shared
a basic civilization. The "formidable originality" of these civilizations has
led some scholars to place them on a par with those of the Old World, the
Han, the Gupta, and the Hellenistic age (Needham and Gwei-Djen, 1985,
p. 64). Canada was in the northern zone of a hemispheric civilization, just
as the American hemisphere would later be on the western periphery of
European civilization.

Second, it is important to keep in mind the fundamental importance of
the early encounters between Europeans and Amerindians. As already
noted, these set the pattern for Amerindian–white relationships and have
influenced policies to this day. The general sixteenth-century European
impression that Amerindians were "sans foi, sans loi, sans roi" stemmed
from first reports that New World men lacked churches and marketplaces,
and lived according to nature "like beasts in the woods." Columbus, for
one, could not see that Amerindians had government, because in warm
latitudes they wore little, if any, clothing. When he spoke with an elderly
cacique "who seemed respectable enough although he wore no clothes,"
Columbus was surprised to observe "sound judgment in a man who went
naked" (Anghiera, 1912, pp. I:102–3). Leading European thinkers concluded that Aristotle's doctrine "that some men are by nature free and
others servile" applied to Amerindians; in other words, that they were not
yet fully developed as human beings, although capable of becoming so,
like children. The custom of referring to Amerindians as children or, even
worse, as "savages" endured until well into the second half of the twentieth century. Such a people were obviously not qualified to run their own
affairs; besides, the rights of Christians had priority over those of non-
Christians. On both these counts, Europeans had no doubts about their
right to claim New World lands for themselves. As we learn more about
Amerindian societies, it is becoming clearer all the time how wrong these
European impressions were; that New World societies met individual and
community needs very well, and had worked out solutions to problems of
living that are still viable today.

Lack of official documentation for the early contact period, at least as
far as Canada was concerned, was offset to some extent by the publicity
to which the discoveries gave rise. Columbus's letter making his sensa-
tional announcement was disseminated with unheard-of speed, thanks to
the new technology of the printing press. This heralded new fashions in
literature: cosmographies, particularly popular during the last half of the
sixteenth and first part of the seventeenth centuries, and travel tales,
much in vogue during the seventeenth and into the eighteenth centuries,
until they were overtaken by explorers' accounts, which hit their stride
during the eighteenth century and continued through to the early twentieth century. Cosmographers, as their name indicates, set themselves the

task of describing the whole world and everything in it, particularly its peoples and their societies; travel accounts concentrated more on adventure, while those of explorers developed a scientific bent, particularly during the nineteenth and twentieth centuries. This literature is invaluable for the researcher, because it opens a window onto the type of information that was being disseminated, as well as reactions to the wonders of worlds previously unknown to Europeans. For the student of Amerindian–white relations, this literature is in some ways more useful than official records, because it reflects more clearly the general level of knowledge of the time. As always, however, caution must be exercised, particularly when generalizing.

EARLY INTERACTIONS

What this literature reveals, although not always directly, is the highly charged nature of so many early interactions. Far from overwhelming simple savages, Europeans often found themselves in complex and difficult negotiations from which they did not always emerge the winners. Recollet friar Gabriel "Theodat" Sagard (fl. 1614–36) tells of one such confrontation at Tadoussac, which occurred when a chief felt himself to be insulted by inappropriate gifts offered by the French during pretrade ceremonies. He told his people to help themselves to whatever French trade goods they wanted, paying what they wished. Although the French were not in a position to resist, the Amerindians, on thinking the matter over, later brought extra furs to make up the value of what had been taken. Both sides agreed to forget the incident, and "to continue always in their old friendship." As Sagard saw it, the French were more concerned about offending the Amerindians than the Amerindians were of antagonizing the French (Sagard, 1939, pp. 45–46; Dickason, 1992, p. 105). Both the seventeenth-century entrepreneur Nicholas Denys (1598–1688) and the eighteenth-century Jesuit historian Pierre-François de Charlevoix (1682–1761) reported that some sagamores took a haughty tone when dealing with the French; in the words of Charlevoix, they made it clear "they were honoring the Great Sagamo of the French by treating him as an equal" (Charlevoix, 1744, p. I:128; Denys, 1908, pp. 195–96).

An important factor that has been overlooked all too often by historians was the role of religion in these early encounters. Ritual was traditionally very important to Amerindians, whose most respected leaders were also shamans. A major factor in the success of the French with their Amerindian alliances was their identification of the centrality of religion in Amerindian leadership, and their enlistment of these sentiments in their favour. This was of considerable consequence to the role of the missionaries, who, besides functioning in their evangelical capacity, also operated as agents of the state. In this, the French conformed to Amerindian political reality; as one eighteenth-century colonial governor observed, "It is only these men [the missionaries] who can control the Savages in their duty to God and the King."[10] Without an appreciation of how spiritual sensibilities shaped Amerindian politics, it is not possible to understand Native behaviour in relation to Europeans or, for that matter, in any other field of action.

Recent confrontations between Amerindians and the dominant society, of which Oka is but the most spectacular example, and the rise of Amerindian participation in the constitutional debates give witness to the continuing strength of Native cultures. In treating the Native factor within a narrow focus, and dismissing it as a relic of the past, historians have impoverished Canada's history. However, when re-assessing the evidence, particularly for the early period, historians will have to do more than just keep the Native factor in mind: rather, they will have to make the effort to understand Native concerns and, above all, to appreciate Native perceptions, and internalize these as part of Canadian history. The Native contribution to the formation of modern Canada has been both much greater and more multifaceted than has ever been acknowledged. Native peoples are also an active part of our society today. For just one example, Amerindians have been in the forefront of the environmental movement. Canada's First Nations are a vital part of our national persona, both present and future. The challenge that faces historians is to take a broader and deeper view of Canada's past, which will not only change our understanding of our history, but also enormously enrich it. Because our sense of history is fundamental to our sense of ourselves, both as individuals and as a nation, it arms us for the formidable task of working out solutions to the social and political problems that are developing as a result of our rapidly evolving technology. As the ante rises, so does the importance of history.

NOTES

1. An earlier version of this chapter appeared in Riewe and Oakes (1993, pp. 1–10), and some of its material is drawn from Dickason (1992, particularly chapter 1).

2. See James W. St. G. Walker's pioneering study, "The Indian in Canadian Historical Writing" (Walker, 1971). See also his follow-up article (Walker, 1983).

3. On June 18, 1936, William Lyon Mackenzie King, Liberal prime minister of Canada 1921–26, 1926–30, and 1935–48, observed in the House of Commons "that if some countries have too much history, we have too much geography" (Colombo, 1974, p. 306).

4. Some of these problems are described by Rowley (1993).

5. "Land Claim Dismissed," *The Edmonton Journal*, March 8, 1991; "Judge Heard 100 Witnesses, Read 10,000 Documents," *The Edmonton Journal*, March 8, 1991; "Natives Hit Another Dead End," *The Edmonton Journal*, March 17, 1991; "A Stunning Blow to Native Rights," *The Montreal Gazette*, March 13, 1991.

6. See, for example, Goodman (1981). Some of the various approaches to the study of early man in the Americas are found in Laughlin and Harper (1979).

7. "Archaeology Makes Edible Impact," *The Christian Science Monitor*, October 9, 1991, p. 12. Not only did potato yields rise from 2.5 tons to 70 tons per hectare, but weather damage to crops was minimized. All this was achieved without the use of artificial fertilizers or large infusions of capital.

8. For a different interpretation of the evidence, see Milford H. Wolpoff's article in Trinkaus (1989).

9. Claude Levi-Strauss (1988; 1981) is particularly strong on this point.

10. National Archives of Canada, Archives des Colonies, C11B 12:37v, Saint-Ovide à Maurepas, 25 novembre 1731.

DISCUSSION QUESTIONS

1. Outline the attitudes that have given rise to the saying that Canada is a young country of much geography and little history.

2. Why were the first meetings of Europeans with Canada's aboriginal peoples so poorly documented?

3. Describe the role of archaeology in tracing out Canada's early history.

4. How important were first impressions in the development of European attitudes toward Amerindians? What was the effect on subsequent policies?

5. What can geology tell us about the early presence of humans in the Americas?

6. What is "ethnohistory"? Would you put it in a separate category from standard history?

FURTHER READINGS

Chiappelli, Fredi, ed. 1976. *First Images of America*, 2 vols. Berkeley: University of California Press. A wide-ranging collection of essays on first contacts between Europeans and Amerindians throughout the Americas.

Honour, Hugh. 1975. *The European Vision of America*. Cleveland: Cleveland Museum of Art. A catalogue of European reactions to the Americas were expressed in visual representations from the days of first meetings through to the late nineteenth century.

Josephy, Alvin M., Jr. 1992. *America in 1492*. New York: Alfred A. Knopf. This hemispheric-wide survey brings into sharp focus the high level of achievement and rich variety of New World cultures on the eve of the European arrival.

McGhee, Robert. 1941. *Ancient Canada*. Ottawa: Canadian Museum of Civilization. Archaeologist McGhee reconstructs selected scenes from Canadian precontact history, and in the process examines some unsolved mysteries. Why, for example, was an adolescent buried with great ceremony on the Labrador coast 7000 years ago? And what is the explanation for those hilltop fortresses in British Columbia? Answers are still being sought.

Weatherford, Jack. 1991. *Native Roots*. New York: Crown Publishers. Exploring the inability (or unwillingness) of sixteenth-century Europeans to appreciate, or even to see, the civilizations of the Americas, Weatherford concludes that modern North American cultural roots lie buried in ancient archaeological sites. Although he deals specifically with the United States, his observations also apply to Canada.

REFERENCES

Anghiera, Pietro Martire d'. 1912. *De Orbe Novo*, 2 vols., tr. Francis Augustus MacNutt. New York: Putnam's.

Charlevoix, Pierre-François. 1744. *Histoire et description generale de la Nouvelle France*, 3 vols. Paris: Giffart.

Colombo, John Robert, ed. 1974. *Colombo's Canadian Quotations*. Edmonton: Hurtig.

Denys, Nicolas. 1908. *The Description and Natural History of the Coasts of North America* (Acadia), ed. William F. Ganong. Toronto: Champlain Society.

Devine, Heather. 1991. "The Role of Archaeology in Teaching the Native Past: Ideology or Pedagogy?" *Canadian Journal of Native Education* 18(1): pp. 11–22.

Dickason, Olive Patricia. 1992. *Canada's First Nations: A History of Founding Peoples*. Toronto: McClelland and Stewart.

Dillehay, Tom D. 1991. "The Great Debate on the First Americans." *Anthropology Today* 7(4): pp. 12–13.

Goodman, Jeffrey. 1981. *American Genesis*. New York: Summit Books.

Greenberg, Joseph H. 1987. *Language in the Americas*. Stanford: Stanford University Press.

Gruhn, Ruth. 1988. "Linguistic Evidence in Support of the Coastal Route of Earliest Entry into the New World." *Man* (N.S.) 23(2): pp. 77–100.

Krech, Shepard, III. 1991. "The State of Ethnohistory." *Annual Review of Anthropology* 20: pp. 345–75.

Laughlin, William S. and Albert B. Harper, eds. 1979. *The First Americans: Origins, Affinities and Adaptation*. New York and Stuttgart: Gustav Fischer.

Levi-Strauss, Claude. 1981. *The Naked Man*, tr. J. and D. Weightman. New York: Harper and Row.

———. 1988. *The Jealous Potter*, tr. Bénédicte Chorier. Chicago and London: University of Chicago Press.

Merrell, James H. 1989. "Some Thoughts on Colonial Historians and American Indians." *William and Mary Quarterly* (3rd ser.) 46(1): pp. 94–119.

Needham, Joseph and Lu GweiDjen. 1985. *Trans-Pacific Echoes and Resonances: Listening Once Again.* Singapore and Philadelphia: World Scientific.

Riewe, Rick and Jill Oakes, eds. 1993. *Human Ecology Issues in the North*, vol. II. Edmonton: Canadian Circumpolar Institute.

Rowley, Susan. 1993. "Frobisher Miksanut: Inuit Accounts of the Frobisher Voyages." Pp. 27–40 in *Archaeology of the Frobisher Voyages*, ed. William W. Fitzhugh and Jacqueline S. Olin. Washington, D.C. and London: Smithsonian Institution.

Sagard, Gabriel. 1939. *The Long Journey to the Country of the Hurons*, tr. H.H. Langton. Toronto: Champlain Society.

Schurr, Theodore G., et al. 1990. "Amerindian Mitochondrial DNA Have Rare Asian Mutations at High Frequencies, Suggesting They Derived from Four Primary Maternal Lineages." *American Journal of Human Genetics* 46: pp. 613–23.

Thevet, André. 1878. *Les singularitez de la France Antarctique*, ed. Paul Gaffarel. Paris: Maisonneuve. (Reprint of 1558 edition.)

Trigger, Bruce. 1985. *Natives and Newcomers.* Kingston and Montreal: McGill-Queen's University Press.

Trinkaus, Erik, ed. 1989. *Emergence of Humans: Biocultural Adaptations in the Late Pleistocene.* Cambridge: Cambridge University Press.

Walker, James W. St. G. 1971. "The Indian in Canadian Historical Writing." *Canadian Historical Association Historical Paper 1971:* pp. 21–51.

———. 1983. "The Indian in Canadian Historical Writing, 1971–1981." Pp. 340–61 in *As Long as the Sun Shines and Water Flows*, ed. Ian A.L. Getty and Antoine S. Lussier. Vancouver: University of British Columbia Press.

Young, Steven B. 1988. "Beringia: An Ice-Age View." Pp. 106–10 in *Crossroads of Continents: Cultures of Siberia and Alaska*, ed. William W. Fitzhugh and Aron Crowell. Washington, D.C.: Smithsonian Institution.

CHAPTER 2

The Missionary Vision of the Heart

Benjamin G. Smillie

PERSONAL BIOGRAPHY

I am a son of a missionary. The missionary outlook is very much in my bones. I was born in India. My father was an educational missionary, the principal of a residential school. The mission residential school for boys was founded by a Canadian Presbyterian missionary following the terrible famine in India in 1897–99. The legacy of the famine was a large number of infant babies, mostly orphans, who were left on the doorstep of the mission homes. To meet the need, a school for boys called Rasalpura was started in 1901. The boys were encouraged to develop skills so that they would have a trade when they graduated. Underlying the philosophy of the school was an emphasis on the dignity of labour, when the Indian society of the time relegated manual work to the lower castes. J.T. Taylor, a missionary historian, described the school: "Faith in Jesus, who was not ashamed to be a carpenter in Nazareth, must bring in its training an entire revolution in India's idea of manual labour" (Taylor, 1916, p. 1073).

My father was well suited for this work. He came from a farm background in Huron County, Ontario, so he had practical skills to combine with his academic work when he went to India. The vocational school gave boys training in academic subjects, motor mechanics, welding, carpentry, tailoring, and printing. The school registrants were indigent boys. My mother, a trained nurse from Edinburgh, who had been night superintendent of Edinburgh Infirmary in Scotland before she married my father, ran the school hospital. She also taught English. As in Canadian missions among Native people, we missionary kids did not go to the school where our parents taught. In fact, I went to a British school in the hills away from the heat of Bhopal province in central India.

THE MISSIONARY VISION OF THE HEART

Many Native people who have gone to residential schools have met my parents — kindly, dedicated, forgoing of a lot of the privileges that were open to their colleagues back home in Canada. They would have the option of returning home if they could not stand the life in India but most stayed to tough it out. My family suffered many hardships. For example, my sister, aged four, died of a goiter, and my aunt (my father's first wife) died in a flu epidemic in India when she was seven months' pregnant. My family's vision of the heart was to see all people converted to a new society centred on Christ and the church. "Go into all the world and preach the gospel" meant doing practical deeds with the preaching.

My father and other educational missionaries rationalized our privileges by saying that the education our schools provided became a base for the leaders of independence. Our protégés had advanced missionary education. But the East Indians and North American Indians would see that the persons trained by the missionary were trained for discontent. The Indian graduates would never get advancement like the missionary because their skin was not white. After Indian independence in 1947, events precipitated rapid change, as Indians took leadership, but it had been a long struggle for educational autonomy, given the paternalism of white Christian leadership. In hindsight, the Indians would not be blinded by our family's hardships, because they have heard that story before. We, as a missionary family, suffered little compared with Indian people. We lived in a large bungalow with five servants, including an *ayah* (nanny), and had the ability to travel, get further education — in fact all the privileges that the Indians could only dream about.

But the vision of the heart of the missionary could not be questioned for its intensity and commitment. James Evans of Norway House in Manitoba and Robert Rundle of Alberta represent a page in Canadian history that will not be forgotten. In fact, Canada has benefited from the commitment of these missionaries and their families.

MY VISION OF THE HEART

I am very aware "Where there is no vision the people perish" (Prov. 29:18). But my vision of the heart has been shaped by my missionary past, which has a mixture of good and bad influences on my vision. First, I have to acknowledge that because I was born in India, it is my birthright to see an international vision of one world as multiracial. I visualize a peaceable realm of God, beautifully expressed in Isaiah's vision:

> The wolf shall live with the lamb,
> the leopard shall lie down with the kid,
> the calf and the fatling together,
> and a little child shall lead them. . . .

> They will not hurt or destroy in all my holy mountain;
> for the earth will be full of the knowledge of God
> as the waters cover the sea. (Isa. 11:6–9)

The debate over the missionary's complicity in the sins of racism, particularly of the residential schools, still goes on in me and leaves me embarrassed, because to an eleven-year-old boy living in India in the 1930s, the racism that was going on was covered over by an aura of pride. I was sure all missionaries were doing God's work and I had not developed eyes to see.

But I have to say there is a problem of "present mindedness" in the critics in interpreting the work of missionaries and residential schools. There is a tunnel outlook that sees the faults and thinks the missionaries should carry the blame, because in a self-professing way, they were supposed to be different, when in fact their outlook reflected the mores of the period. But there is also a fallacious assumption that the critics' outlook would have been different, given the advantage of hindsight.

J.R. Miller, a perceptive historian who has studied criticism of residential schools, points out that Native leaders put the blame squarely on governments for their parsimonious outlook on native education — governments that left missionaries to carry the burden, while being underfunded and understaffed — whereas academics and newspaper reporters concentrate their criticism on missionaries. Miller says:

> It is difficult to know which is greater, the myopia or the hypocrisy of these non-Native critics. The attraction of a myopia that enables critics to perceive only the missionary as culpable is in part rooted in secularists' feeling of distance from the institutional church. Critics' tendency to blame a social institution with which they feel little involvement is perhaps understandable. But there is more to it than that. If, like Fred Loft and Andrew Paull [Native leaders], critics shifted their gaze to the government and its officers, they would have to deal with a morally unsettling fact. That reality is that in a democracy it is the citizenry that ultimately has to accept the responsibility for what its government does. If people in a democracy get the government they deserve, then in the ultimate sense the Native policy that emerges is their responsibility, too. (Miller, 1994, p. 32)

But as soon as I get involved in taking the side of the missionary, it makes me uneasy because every excuse becomes a form of self-justification.

MY ROLE AS A HINTERLAND THEOLOGIAN IN INTERPRETING ABORIGINAL HISTORY

My vision of the heart cannot accept the status quo as an adequate vision of the heart. I have to try and put myself in a more critical role than I have inherited. To do this I have taken the viewpoint of a hinterland theologian, who has been very much influenced by God's preferential option for the poor.[1]

Laundering History

The bias of my writing, while I come from the wealthy one-third of the world's privileged, is to realize that the writings of white Anglo-Saxon males making comments on aboriginal history have to have some correction. This involves me in recording church history from the perspective of those whose memoirs are not recorded on the monuments celebrating great events with the heroes of power. I look for those buried under the monuments — indigenous people who have left no mark on the hinterland because they have been shunted from the prestigious position of metropol power. They live in the frozen north or the northern parkland, in many cases confined to reserves where Indian agents have circumscribed the rules for living. When the annals of history have described the life of indigenous people, their stories have been written by historians who have been "launderers of history" (Drache, 1978). The term "launderers" is used by economic historian Daniel Drache to expose economic historians who wash out class conflict in their recording of history. As I examine the work of church historians, I find they are tempted to do the same laundering.

For example, George Ladd, a United Church historian, describes this laundering in the writing of church historian John Webster Grant. Grant explains that in 1902 when the Peguis people were surrendering their land rights and accepting the cloistered life at St. Peter's Reserve in Manitoba, John Semmons was a trusted Methodist minister on the reserve. On the occasion of the surrender, Semmons acted as inspector of Indian agencies and schools. His strategic function was to shout at exactly the right moment: "Keyawaw tatoo kakatch mitatoomitanow tatopisk ke natawayisayakook nata itska itootah," which is Cree for "All you that want $90 go to that side" (Ladd, 1986, pp. 14–15). Semmons belonged to the British-Ontarian Protestant society that attempted to create a monoculture in Manitoba by excluding or assimilating "foreign" cultures. Missionaries like Semmons engaged in a type of racism different from that of the land speculator or the company agent. Ladd explains:

> Semmons' [racism] was high-minded and condescending. Though he too was a shareholder in a local land investment company, he really did want the reserve surrendered for the Indians' own good. Surrendering their land would remove them to a safe place where they would not be exposed to the irresistible temptation of strong drink. (Ladd, 1986, pp. 15–16)

John Webster Grant, in the *Moon of Wintertime* (1984, pp. 251–58), claims an ameliorating role for the missionaries, in that they protected Native people from alcoholism and economic exploitation by encouraging them to give up their land and move onto the reserves. Ladd suggests, to the contrary, that the missionaries' actions were a form of betrayal, precisely because they were trusted by the Native people (Ladd, 1986, pp. 13–15).

Hinterland theology can avoid the trap of laundering by combining the roles of the social scientist and the historical theologian. The methodology includes a need to do a class analysis, using empirical data to assess the scene accurately. It follows the emphasis of liberation theology in God's preferential option for poor people who live marginalized lives in the hinterland. Hinterland theology, through the insights of feminist theology, deals with the sexism in patriarchical interpretations of the Bible, which then reinforces the oppression of women. The Bible is used as an instrument to canonize the power of men in society. The third ingredient of hinterland theology is the emphasis on Native spirituality, in its concern for all creation.

DIFFERENCES IN ABORIGINAL AND NON-ABORIGINAL PERSPECTIVES

Doctrine of Creation

Native spirituality stands as a corrective to the Judeo-Christian tradition, which has used the creation story in Genesis 1 to legitimize the plundering of nature:

> Be fruitful and multiply, and replenish the earth and subdue it: and have dominion over the fish of the sea, and over the fowl of the air and every living thing that moveth upon the earth. (Gen. 1:28)

In contrast to the Biblical vision of creation is a vision of harmony with creation that is in the teachings of Black Elk, a Sioux holy man, who explains the importance of the circle in Indian spirituality:

> You have noticed that everything an Indian does is in a circle, and that is because the Power of the World always works in circles. . . . The sky is round, and I have heard that the earth is round like a ball, and so are all the stars. The wind in its greatest power whirls. Birds make their nests in circles, for theirs is the same religion as ours. The sun comes forth and goes down again in a circle. The moon does the same, and both are round. Even the seasons form a great circle in their changing and always come back again to where they were. The life of a man is a circle from childhood to childhood, and so it is in everything where power moves. (Neihardt, 1961, pp. 198–200)

The fundamental feature of a circle is preservation of all its parts. From the centre the circle is created by the flinging out of all its parts and by the holding to itself of those same parts.

The Circular and Linear Model for Political Action in History

One of the cohesive traditions that has kept the prairie a unique type of place to live has been the unifying power of protest, protest that got its muscle from the social gospel. Although the social gospel had roots in various parts of Canada, it was on the Prairies that it became militant. Protest at political decisions made outside the power of regional control; protest at railways holding western settlers captive with high freight rates and a land-locked staples economy dependent on international trade; protest at land speculators; protest at economic markets subject to price fluctuations from commodity groups and high-cost machinery; and protest at banks with heartless abandon foreclosing on debt-ridden farmers. The church leaders who led the movement were politically active in the farm or labour movements. But they also had a model in the Bible. To understand this, consider the prairie hinterland and its parallels to the birthplace of Jesus. Like Palestine during the time of Jesus, the Prairies are located off the main routes of travel. Consequently, the question often asked is, "Can anything important come from the Prairies?" In Jesus' time the question asked was, "Can anything good come out of Nazareth?" (John 1:46).

In the days of Jesus, Nazareth was a secluded village in Galilee, the centre of anti-Roman feeling and messianic expectations. Biblical scholar Joachim Jeremias (1969, p. 73) explains that "Pilate's [punitive] measures in the Holy Place against the Galilean Passover pilgrims were scarcely taken without good reason." Pilate knew that the pilgrims from Galilee could use the occasion to hatch plots against Rome: "There were some present at that very time who told him of the Galileans whose blood Pilate had mingled with their sacrifices" (Luke 13:1).

While Nazareth was an insignificant town in an occupied region of Galilee in the divided land of Palestine, it was a highly volatile area of the Roman empire. Similarly, the prairie hinterland, although insignificant and powerless in relation to the metropol, was a highly volatile area of Canada. The protest that developed out of the social gospel was motivated by the belief in the coming of God to a marginalized people. Central to social gospel belief is the conviction that it is impossible to love God and neighbour without developing a theology of hope. That meant becoming immersed in political structures; it meant "building the New Jerusalem" on the streets of every city and hamlet on the Prairies. The protest parties that grew out of the social gospel were instrumental in developing hospital insurance, medicare, rural electrification, good roads, generalized public and high-school educational opportunities, dental plans, and old age pensions. The social gospel got the group involved in protest because it was important to build the "realm of God"[2] in everyday events. It suggests moving ahead and progress, which has been the catchword for theologies that take political action. How often we hear of "progressive" parties talk about "progress." It seems to be the catchword of getting ahead, and every political movement wants to get ahead. But in their haste to be involved in building a just society, they have often distorted the record of their own achievements and gradually become inured to criticism. This produces smugness.

But I have included also the aboriginal model for political action based on the circle. No one knows better than indigenous people in Canada the power of the metropol in their lives because they have been marginalized to a geographical hinterland. Their struggle for justice has been harder than it would have been if they had resided in a metropol like Ottawa, Toronto, Montreal, Vancouver, or any of the large industrial centres of Canada.

The circle has one great advantage in building unity in organization: it suggests solidarity. You have to be patient to bring the whole group along. But the circle can also become introverted. The same issues can be debated endlessly. Talk can become a substitute for action.

In the final analysis, it is impossible to get the right model for political action. God has a way of using all our attempts at building a just society in history with a certain scepticism.

My vision of the heart rejects both the linear view of history of the social gospel movement and the circular identity of aboriginal spirituality. Both have drawbacks. They lack a critique of their good causes. The essential failing of political movements is that they are very prone to self-righteousness. The German theologian Karl Barth was very aware of the inadequacy of liberal cultural theology in dealing with the oppressive forces he faced with the rise of Hitler in Germany. He suggested that liberal social gospel theology is too accommodating to culture, which stems from over-confidence in the endowments of human endeavour. It has no doctrine of sin. By stressing the importance of what human beings can do to change the world, liberal theology doesn't allow for the pretensions of our good causes. I am reminded of a famous statement of Reinhold Niebuhr (1946, p. 1238), who said "every shepherd king of history is more king and less shepherd than he pretends."

GENERAL DIFFICULTIES IN CROSS-CULTURAL RESEARCH

My vision of the heart is aware. As the apostle Paul pointed out: "I know nothing against myself, but I am not thereby acquitted, it is God who judges me" (1 Cor. 4:4). God has a way of using our critics to give us the message all white people should hear. The uncomfortable reality for those of us born into a life of relative privilege is in having people who are oppressed by their identity telling us how it is for them. I was startled when the United Church of Canada made an apology to Native people at the general council of the United Church in 1986.

The Apology of the United Church

Long before our people journeyed to this land your people were here, and you received from your elders an understanding of creation, and of the Mystery that surrounds us all that was deep, and rich and to be treasured.

We did not hear you when you shared your vision. In our zeal to tell you of the good news of Jesus Christ we were closed to the value of your spirituality.

We confused western ways and culture with the depth and breadth and length and height of the gospel of Christ.

We imposed our civilisation as a condition of accepting the gospel.

We tried to make you be like us and in so doing we helped to destroy the vision that made you what you were. As a result you, and we, are poorer and the image of the Creator in us is twisted, blurred and we are not what we are meant by God to be.

We ask you to forgive us and to walk together with us in the spirit of Christ so that our people may be blessed and God's creation healed. (United Church, 1986, p. 85)

Native Peoples' Response to the Apology

The apology appears to be a sincere confession of the church's mistreatment of Native people. In August 1994, the Reverend Stan McKay, a Cree Indian, secretary of Native ministries in the United Church (since moderator of the United Church, 1992–1994), offered a preliminary response on behalf of the Native people. This was made concrete by the 35th general council of the United Church, held in August 1994 at Fergus, Ontario. It established a "healing fund" of $1 000 000 to be raised by voluntary subscription of United churches, to be raised over five years (1995–99).

The fund is to be made available to Native groups throughout the land in such a way as to promote healing by those scarred by the residential school experience.

The fund is to be vested in the All-Native Circle Conference and the Division of Native Ministries of British Columbia Conference, and is to be distributed through a technical implementation group. The United Church has also called on sister churches to set up a similar fund, and on the federal government to address their responsibility for harm done by the residential school system.[3]

Although the intent of the United Church's apology is better than no apology at all, and the tangible action makes the apology more than empty words, I see a cross-cultural difficulty with the class division between aboriginal people, who are at the bottom of the economic ladder, and white people, who have the privileges. For example, to say that we all suffer from the sin of avarice seems obvious. But greed in people living on a Native reserve does not have the power to harm the environment in the same way as the greed of shareholders in Quebec Hydro, who stall on paying land claims and go ahead with hydro projects because they have to appease international investors. If everyone should confess the sin of greed, then we all have to repent of the same wrongdoing. Expecting our neighbour to confess the same sin is to assume that there is an equality of power between people who are at different places on the economic ladder. It is too easy to ignore class bias in the liberal church.

The following story is one example of the reality that Native people live every day of their lives. Wolfgang Stegemann, a German biblical scholar, is one theologian who criticizes bourgeois churches for not recognizing economic disparities among their parishioners. He makes his point with the parable of the Pharisee and the tax collector (Luke 18:10–14):

> The parable needs only to be altered slightly, namely, in good Lutheran- [or any Protestant- or Roman Catholic-] Pauline tradition, it would have to tell of a wealthy Christian who no longer points with pride to his or her religious "achievements," but confesses their sinfulness before God. Of course, one would immediately include the [paupers] beside oneself in the confession of guilt and accuse [them] of being [sinners] also. The master accuses the servant of a similar abstract sinfulness instead of repenting of his own sin and refraining from sinning in the future by directly or indirectly participating in the pauperisation of his servant. This treatment of rich and poor, master and slave, as equal in relation to sin, is itself sin "before God," since "before the world" it is paralleled by an often cruel reality of nonequality. (Stegemenn, 1984, pp. 60–61)

But we know that Native people, aware that they are oppressed, see serious flaws in their struggle, but they use a non-judgemental approach without an emphasis on sin. They see the need for judgement on their pretensions, but they refuse to drag down their own people in public. Rev. Janet Silman, a graduate of the Toronto School of Theology with a Th.D. in social ethics, is a Cree-Scottish Métis who teaches biblical studies at the Dr. Jesse Saulteaux Centre in Beausejour, Manitoba. She describes a scene where she and a number of aboriginal women were listening to two male leaders in the church arguing about family values. The Native church leader was being almost as sexist as the white man, but the women kept silent because they were not going to expose their Native leader to ridicule before a mixed audience. Janet took the different approach of Native women, which preserves their own identity. In teaching aboriginal women, she describes scenes from the Bible where women see their main responsibility as being to preserve life and not to confront. For example, Moses was hidden in the bulrushes in Exodus 2 and preserved from the cruelty of the killing off of infant male babies by order of the pharaoh. Pharaoh's daughter took him into her home and preserved his life from the cruel edict.[4]

The mindset of our dominant group in their political action as a cultural approach is to identify the bad guys and to be militantly political and confrontational, but it is not the style of aboriginal women. The approach they adopt in bringing political change is very effective. Silman describes how the Tobique women from New Brunswick, through community organizing, brought about changes that ended over a hundred years of legislated sexual discrimination against Native women.

In the mid-1970s, Tobique women decided they were no longer going to accept their situation without a struggle. Over the years, more and more women were being thrown out of their homes by husbands. While the men then moved their girlfriends — often white — into the family home, the Indian women and children had to move in to condemned homes or in with relatives who were already overcrowded. Since the Indian Act gave men sole ownership of property *through certificate of possession*, women had no housing rights or recourse to help through the law. Finally, in 1977, when yet another woman was evicted from her home, two women, Eva Saulis and Glenna Parley, started to gather women together to protest against the situation. Their actions included a sit-in in the band council office for four months because they had got no satisfaction from their Native leaders. Nor did they get help from the bureaucrats in Indian Affairs. But at each stage of political action the women grew stronger and stronger. As Janet Silman explains:

> The injustice was obvious. Under the Indian Act a person's case was determined by a patrilineal system, that is by a person's relationship to "a male person who is a direct descendent in the male line of a male person. . . . " When she married a non-status man, an Indian woman born with status lost it, unable to regain it even if she subsequently was divorced or widowed. Along with her status the woman lost her band membership, and with it her property, inheritance residency, burial, medical, educational and voting rights on the reserve. In direct contrast an Indian man bestowed his status upon his white wife and their children. Consequently every Indian woman was dependent on an Indian man for her identity and rights under the Indian Act. (Silman, 1987, p. 16)

To raise the awareness of the Canadian public regarding Native women's problems, the Tobique women of New Brunswick decided to take the issue of Canada's violation of human rights to the United Nations. At the same time, the women organized a 100-mile march on Ottawa. In 1981 the United Nations ruled in favour of the women who had brought the case. It so embarrassed the Canadian government internationally that the Indian Act was changed in 1985 to ensure the marital status and property rights of Native women in the Canadian Parliament. Janet Silman says the Tobique women of New Brunswick

> do not share their testimony without risk, because they have been candid about a sometimes bitter struggle in their own community. However, telling their story is worth the risk involved — not to settle any old scores, but to show people what life is like for Indian women in Canada, and to demonstrate how a group of women can work together to create a better future for themselves and their children. (Silman, 1987, p. 15)

There is a fascinating way of doing history in Janet Silman's methodology. She preserves the cultural oral tradition of the Native women. She lets the drama of their own lives tell the story in all its fascinating eloquence. What starts as a complaint about inadequate housing on a remote reserve finishes before the United Nations and the Parliament of Canada before justice is done.

PROBLEMS WITH STUDYING
DEPENDENT POPULATIONS

Aboriginal people see collusion between missionaries and the Department of Indian Affairs when they receive "expert advice" on how they should act. They see great progress in the struggle for land claims and honouring historic treaty rights, which they have won for themselves without the help of missionaries or any white group. But Native people are uneasy with the decisions made by their own leadership, when self-government is used as the right to run casinos on reserves. The quick-fix solution of bringing money into the impoverished band council coffers is always a temptation for dependent economies. Recently, the Meadow Lake tribal council, which represents nine Indian communities in northern Saskatchewan, has been looking at the possibility of profiting from the disposal of nuclear waste in the Canadian shield. Although the plan is opposed by anti-nuclear activists, Atomic Energy of Canada says waste can be safely stored. The pro argument is that if there is a benefit to putting radioactive waste back in the ground it was taken from, why shouldn't the Cree and Dene profit from it? The matter will have to be put to a referendum of 7000 Indians on the nine reserves (Ulbrich, 1995, p. A1).

But a more insidious temptation is the proliferation of casinos on reserves, where Native self-government is used as the right of Native people to run their own casinos.

The temptation to store nuclear waste is not very likely to prevail, because it has been already pointed out that Native spirituality constantly reiterates harmony of all creation, and doing anything to the ground with a toxic waste mortgages future generations of life with a ticking time bomb.

But the temptation to build casinos and the hope of a "lucky break" is more than a temptation. It is becoming a social disease. Martin Wolcott, in an article in the *Manchester Guardian*, looks at gambling as a pervasive force in all modern societies (Wolcott, 1994, p. 12). He compares gambling with the sale of indulgences in the Middle Ages as an offer of salvation with a cash transaction. In 1517 Tetzel, a Dominican monk, made a name for himself in insuring freedom from the torments of hell and winning salvation through the sale of indulgences. It was a case of drawing on the good works of the saints who had built a credit balance of good works. By the intercession of the saints, you could receive pardon by the payment of cash. Tetzel, travelling around Europe, assured the buyer of an indulgence "as soon as the money fell into the coffer a soul was released from purgatory to heaven" (Latourette, 1953, pp. 707–8). The indulgences were justified as money for a good cause — namely, building St. Peter's cathedral in Rome. The modern assurance of happiness, says Wolcott, is the lottery and the casino; it reinforces the same outlook of buying happiness and salvation. But it is not just an issue of people buying nirvana with the occasional flutter. It is built into the warp and woof of our capitalist society. Stock exchanges are gamblers with paper money with no productive labour behind them.

The term "casino capitalism" is used by Eric Kierans the economist and Walter Stewart the journalist to describe the nature of modern "venture capital." Like a casino operation, there are huge profits to be made with little risk and nothing of value produced. They explain:

> Casino capitalists shift their capital around. Firms which are productive but have large inventories are vulnerable to take-over. The casino capitalists buy them out by appealing to absentee shareholders who, with no loyalty to the firm, see a chance to make a profit and enhance their portfolio. The conglomerates who buy out their weaker neighbours this way make up for the inflated costs of this kind of buy-out by laying off employees and "streamlining" the operation. This does not make them more productive and efficient, however; it makes the bought-out company a prize for looting. (Kierans and Stewart, 1988, p. 34)

There are outcries from some liberal academics who would ask, why lay a trip of global political analysis on Native people when they enjoy gambling, which is a relief from the terrible boredom of life on a reserve or in an urban area of poor housing and the endless visits to the food bank? Why be a killjoy? The answer is that virulent capitalism is everywhere, particularly in an economically dependent satellite like Canada. Canadian historical economist Harold Innis reviews Canada's economic history, when it gradually separated colonial ties from Britain. It became economically independent, particularly after the World War II, and then became a "hewer of wood and drawer of water" to the United States as the country moved from "colony to nation to colony" (Innis, 1956; 1973, p. 405).

One could argue that dependency occurs where people find themselves at the bottom of the economic ladder. Many Canadians, although living in a dependent hinterland to the United States, have done very well by working for international U.S. companies and selling off Canadian ownership. Brian Mulroney is the epitome of the American broker selling off Canadian-owned assets. Because of this dependency, aboriginal people find their representatives in the federal government making the excuse that they have no money and that their just claims are pre-empted by what Wall Street decides. So the Canadian social safety net is in jeopardy because of the international money market, and the thumbscrews applied by the United States, which has always bolstered its own economy by beggaring its neighbour, affects Canada's obligation to fulfil its responsibility to its Native people.

This self-inflicted impotence of Canadian political leaders is a common sight on the international scene. The Canadian Catholic economist Romeo Mahone (1995) describes the world economy, where indentured labour has been replaced by indentured governments. But the last election showed that Canada has an angry electorate, and anger might succeed if it becomes focussed and persists in reaching for a vision of justice.

To kindle hope for a better future is what I consider my primary task as a hinterland theologian. The best way to kindle that hope is to know what is going on, because the first step to hope is knowledge, and ignorance and cynicism lead to paralysis and despair. Rev. Deborah Laing, a perceptive United Church minister whose parish was in a poverty-stricken area of the eastern townships of Quebec, describes three generations of total unemployment in that area. She asked leading dignitaries of the three towns in her parish if they could see signs of hope; they saw no hope. To combat the cynicism, she organized a group of women in the area, and in a bible study they got insights from the biblical scholar Walter Bruegermann (1987, pp. 80–89, cited in Laing, 1995, pp. 12–13). He shows that the biblical prophets teach that people do not move from a condition of despair to a psychological euphoria of hope; it is not a journey from darkness to light. The normal habitat of hope emerges among those who publicly articulate and process their grief over their suffering. To publicly name the despair is not natural; we would rather cover up the shame, particularly those people who have no sense of self-worth. But we have seen from our examples that when oppression comes out in the open and is publicly proclaimed, it gives power, because in a hinterland you know that a lot of other people suffer with you. So people move from dependence to interdependence. The political awakening comes after we develop eyes to see that we can organize against "the Beast" of metropol oppression, and those with power are very vulnerable to the glare of national publicity.

Fortunately, aboriginal people are getting more militant as they see allies join their cause as injustices are exposed. The fact is that it is impossible to avoid the publicity, and politicians hate the glare of publicity. Interdependence of the First Nations' tribal councils brings astuteness in the area of politics. Court challenges and parliamentary lobbies are taking the place of the Oka rifle.

THE DILEMMA CONFRONTED IN THE INNER WORKINGS OF SOCIETIES BASED ON ORAL TRADITIONS

The great advantage of oral traditions in developing a vision of the heart is that it is bound to be personal. The written word is detached and abstract. But there is a whole philosophical school of modern thought that emphasizes the existential, where "existence precedes essence." Existentialism concentrates on plays and short stories that capture the reader in the drama. The purpose of the drama in most existential plays is to involve the person, whether he is in the audience or on stage. Its main purpose is to bring about political change by confronting people with their own lives.

My daughter Ruth Smillie, who is artistic director of Catalyst Theatre in Edmonton, started using the medium of oral speech to bring out the drama in the aboriginal youth of Saskatoon at the Native Survival School. She found she did not have to write a gripping plot for the actors or audience. The drama was in the lives of these young people who wanted to act. They had gone through more exciting experiences in their short lifespan than middle-class kids whose lives were quite conventional. She also found that drama brought out their own identities as they told their own stories.

One of the students gives this testimony:

> Everybody has a very important experience in his/her life. Today I would like to tell you about my exciting experience. It all started out when I registered at the Native Survival School (now called the Joe Duquette High School). . . . Drama taught me a lot. It taught me not to be shy, it also taught me to laugh, to work with all sorts of people. It gave me strength. Strength I never dreamed I would have. Drama also gave me courage. It made me understand people. Having a lot of courage means a lot to me. I never dreamt I had that much courage. Cheryl McDonald 1985. (Smillie and Murphy, 1986, p. 98)

THE PROBLEM WHEN THE ORAL TRADITION DIES OUT

This is a problematic question because most oral traditions do not die out, they continue in mantras, often calling to remembrance the myths of joy and sorrow that sustain the nation. The oral tradition of the Bible did not die out. One might say it was recaptured in written word in the 66 books of the Bible. Protestants became the fanatics of the written word, with Pilgrim pioneers founding Ivy League universities in the United States. The Bible was given impetus through the sons and daughters of large families who needed an education. It became a sort of reading primer. In New France this was not the case. The settlers in New France, living along the St. Lawrence, had amazing homogeneity in the Roman Catholic sacraments. The Mass could become the basis for communicating the word of God through the five senses of touch, taste, smell, sound, and sight. The Roman Catholic church did not need an intellectual literate elite to keep the tradition going.

This is comforting for me to realize as the son of educational missionaries, because one thing that has happened over the space of my life is that the church has lost its imperial power. It no longer sets the agenda that everyone follows. It has had to take a humble role, partly because Native people have developed an autonomy on what they choose to appropriate. So it is not a case of trying to redress wrongs with a new solution, but of taking the role of sharing the lament for the past and praying for a new day of peace in the future.

I see the missionary now as taking the role of the "kneeling woman" (see Smith, 1995, p. 131). I adopt the metaphor of the kneeling woman because this is suggested by the Rev. Bob Smith, a United Church minister, who was moderator of the United Church when it made its apology to Native people in 1986. He now heads the committee to make financial restitution to Native people to bring healing for the harm done to Indian people in residential schools.

His prognosis is that the church is dying and the role of its ministry is to do what it is doing, constantly ministering to the aged to help them prepare for death. The closing doors of churches, which are crumbling with the increasing secularization of society, leaves the minister of the church in the role of a "knee woman." Smith takes the metaphor from that person in an Irish village whose task it is to be on her knees at the bedside of a person dying, and also at the bedside of a mother giving birth. She uses her skills to bring new life into the world. The church, which has lost its imperial power, can recite the lament and intercession for the nation. It can also proclaim the promise of new birth.

In 587–86 Before the Common Era (B.C.E.), the Babylonian king laid siege to the city of Jerusalem. Those who were not killed on the streets were starved out or succumbed to disease. The city was ransacked by the invading army and from all outward signs the situation seemed hopeless. The eerie aftermath of the destruction is described in the book of Lamentations. The author is asking God to remember the people's plight, just as the kneeling woman brings sorrow and comfort. Rev. Deborah Laing, who as I have said, ministers in the poor area of the eastern townships of Quebec, brings a modern lament describing the relentless poverty of her parish but also the poverty that is common to all poor people who live in a neglected hinterland:

> Our children are taken and sold at the bars for the price of a case of beer.
> Our young women escape trouble at home through pregnancy, and the government cheques that support them.
> Our women are paid to bear children to increase Quebec's declining birthrate. The desperately poor have many.
> Our parents suffer from grave alcohol and drug addictions. They lose themselves to the substances and are robbed of the ability to feed or clothe or raise their children.
> Our youth leave school and wander the streets unwilling to go home, looking for meaning and escape.
> Our cocaine dealers sell death on the streets and collect money with torture and intimidation.
> Our old women are afraid to go out at night; the screaming of neighbours and women keep them in.
> Men violate women they have promised to love; parents violate children they have brought into the world.
> Men who raped children walk free in our streets nervously watching, watching.
> Our elderly do not rest easy in their homes for fear of theft. Our dead do not know respect in their graves for vandalism.

Our law courts mete out justice sparingly.
There is no trust. Our people sue one another for the hope of gain.
People move from bed to bed looking for safety and love, refusing to be tested for sexually transmitted diseases.
AIDS has come to kill in our midst, but its victims remain silent, afraid of the violent response of ignorance.
How long O God must we live in such shame? How long before we are totally broken? Where is the life that you have promised? (Laing, 1995, p. 11)

The promise of Isaiah of the peaceable realm remains the hope I have as I live in sorrow over death but also with hope of new beginnings:

The wolf shall live with the lamb,
the leopard shall lie down with the kid,
the calf and the fatling together,
and a little child shall lead them. . . .
They will not hurt or destroy in all my holy mountain;
for the earth will be full of the knowledge of God
as the waters cover the sea. (Isa. 11:6–9)

NOTES

1. My theological orientation is most clearly outlined in Smillie (1991). See the annotation in Further Readings.

2. I am using the "realm of God" rather than the familiar phrase "kingdom of God" because "realm" is more inclusive and is used by feminist biblical scholars.

3. Resolution of the 35th General Council, Fergus, Ontario, August 1994, quoted from the docket of the General Council, distributed to all delegates.

4. Telephone interview with Janet Silman in Winnipeg, January 26, 1995.

DISCUSSION QUESTIONS

1. In *Visions of the Heart*, there is a temptation for writers and readers of personal histories to react with personal feelings. There is a danger of "looking down into the well of history, only to see the reflection of your own face." "The Missionary Vision of the Heart" is really a confession of complicity in the zeal of missionaries, which became a cover-up for racism. Can you list the positive and negative effects of the missionary experience, trying not to let your prejudices influence your judgement?

2. This chapter looks at the wider perspective of the oppressive effects of a global economy, with transnational companies engaged in non-productive "casino capitalism." The chapter also accuses liberal academics of ignoring the economic issue of class. Should advocacy work for aboriginal people bring economics to the fore? Should aboriginal people become immersed in the political structures of economic power when they fight for land claims and aboriginal self-government?

3. Taking the circle as a model for Native and religious identity, suggest ways we can enhance Native solidarity without producing a docile acceptance of everything as inevitable.

4. Kindling hope in the hinterland includes naming publicly the powers that oppress. What religious and cultural stories of hope give you power to face the daily oppression of being Native in a racist society?

5. With regard to the white middle-class male who reads this book, suggest some practical steps we can take that will use the influence we have from birth to bring change, so that we can look down the well of history and see someone reflected in the water who has a wiser, gentler, more incisive image than what we inherit from our missionary past.

FURTHER READINGS

Grant, John Webster. 1984. *Moon of Wintertime*. Toronto: University of Toronto Press. This is a scholarly, well-researched book on missionary work among the Indians of Canada over a span of 450 years, from 1534, when Jacques Cartier first erected a cross before Indians of the Gaspé, to the present. Grant examines both the aims and activities of missionaries of all denominations, and the varying responses of Indians at different times and under different circumstances.

Kierans, Eric and Walter Stewart. 1988. *Wrong End of the Rainbow: The Collapse of Free Enterprise in Canada*. Toronto: Collins. This is a good exposé of large multinationals and how they plunder small productive companies, relying on takeovers and tax holidays to amass wealth while laying off organized workers who have full-time jobs.

Ladd, George Van Der Goes. 1986. *Shall We Gather at the River?* Toronto: Canec. A small book by a United Church minister who served on the Peguis Reserve in Manitoba. He exposes how well-intentioned missionaries became agents of government land grabs.

Miller, J.R. 1994. "Native Residential Schools in Historical Context." Paper presented at the annual meeting of the Canadian Catholic Historical Association, University of Calgary (June 14). Professor Miller teaches history at the University of Saskatchewan. This excellent unpublished paper may be quoted with permission. J.R. Miller, History Department, University of Saskatchewan, Saskatoon S7N 0W0.

Neihardt, John G. *Black Elk Speaks: Being the Life Story of a Holy Man of the Oglala Sioux*. Lincoln: University of Nebraska. Neihardt recorded a series of interviews with Black Elk in May 1931.

Silman, Janet. 1987. *Enough Is Enough: Aboriginal Women Speak Out*. Toronto: Women's Press. Janet Silman gives a graphic portrayal through interviews with women from the Tobique Indian band of how they struggled, including taking their case to the United Nations, to end 100 years of sexual discrimination against Native Indian women. The passing of Bill C-31 in the Canadian Parliament in June 1985 officially legislated an end to sexual discrimination under the Indian Act.

Smillie, Benjamin G. 1991. *Beyond the Social Gospel: Church Protest on the Prairies*. Toronto and Saskatoon: United Church Publishing House and Fifth House Publishers. This book most clearly outlines "hinterland theology" as my theological orientation in addressing the Canadian reality. With the second largest landmass in the world, Canada is a nation defined by geography. The hinterland is of paramount importance in addressing the context of oppressed people in Canada because they have no access to cheap transportation and they remain prisoners of their location. Hinterland theology builds on the theology of the social gospel, which was instrumental in producing the protest of the agrarian revolt and the labour movements in the first two decades of this century in Canada. Hinterland theology includes the insights of liberation theology in doing class analyses and bringing judgement on the sinful social structures of capitalism. It includes the orientation of feminist theology in dealing with the sexism in patriarchical interpretations of the Bible, which reinforce the oppression of women, where the Bible is used as an instrument for canonizing the power of men in society. It honours the emphasis of Native spirituality in its concern for all creation. Native spirituality stands as a corrective to the Judeo-Christian tradition, which has used the creation story in Genesis 1 to legitimize the plundering of nature. Hinterland theology criticizes from the underside of powerlessness, from geographically obscure places like "Nazareth": "Can any good thing come out of Nazareth?" No one knows better than indigenous people in Canada the power of the metropol in their lives because they have been marginalized to a geographical hinterland. Their struggle for justice has been harder than it would have been if they had resided in a metropol like Ottawa, Toronto, Montreal, Vancouver, or any of the large industrial centres of Canada. International and Canadian capital exercises its power from the central location of the metropol. Banks, insurance companies, the headquarters of multinationals — all issue their directives on layoffs, "rationalization," and plant closures from the metropol.

REFERENCES

Bruegermann, Walter. 1987. *Hope Within History*. Atlanta: John Knox Press.

Drache, Daniel. 1978. "Rediscovering Canadian Political Economy." Pp. 28–32 in *A Practical Guide to Canadian Political Economy*, ed. Wallace Clement and Daniel Drache. Toronto: James Lorimer.

Grant, John Webster. 1984. *Moon of Wintertime*. Toronto: University of Toronto Press.

Innis, Harold. 1956; 1973. *Essays in Canadian Economic History*, ed. Mary Q. Innis. Toronto: University of Toronto Press.

Jeremias, Joachim. 1969. *Jerusalem in the Times of Jesus*. London: SCM Press.

Kierans, Eric and Walter Stewart. 1988. *Wrong End of the Rainbow: The Collapse of Free Enterprise in Canada*. Toronto: Collins.

Ladd, George Van Der Goes. 1986. *Shall We Gather at the River?* Toronto: Canec.

Laing, Deborah. 1995. "Living with Trouble, Looking for Hope." In *Hinterland Theology in an Ecumenical Context: Essays in Honour of Benjamin G. Smillie and Charles F. Johnston*. Saskatoon: St. Andrew's College.

Latourette, Kenneth Scott. 1953. *A History of Christianity*. New York: Harper.

Mahone, Romeo. 1995. "Understanding the Global Economy." *Prairie Messenger* (February 20). (Box 190, Munster, Saskatchewan S0K 2Y0.)

Miller, J.R. 1994. "Native Residential Schools in Historical Context." Paper presented at the annual meeting of the Canadian Catholic Historical Association, University of Calgary (June 14). (Unpublished.)

Neihardt, John G. 1961. *Black Elk Speaks: Being the Life Story of a Holy Man of the Oglala Sioux*. Lincoln: University of Nebraska Press.

Niebuhr, Reinhold. 1946. *Discerning the Signs of the Times: Sermons for Today and Tomorrow*. London: SCM Press.

Silman, Janet. 1987. *Enough Is Enough: Aboriginal Women Speak Out*. Toronto: Women's Press.

Smillie, Benjamin G. 1991. *Beyond the Social Gospel: Church Protest on the Prairies*. Toronto and Saskatoon: United Church Publishing House and Fifth House Publishers.

Smillie, Ruth and Kelly Murphy. 1986. *Story Circle*. Saskatoon: Education Library, University of Saskatchewan.

Smith, Robert F. 1995. "The Knee Woman." In *Hinterland Theology in an Ecumenical Context: Essays in Honour of Benjamin G. Smillie and Charles F. Johnston*. Saskatoon: St. Andrew's College.

Stegemann, Wolfgang. 1984. *The Gospel and the Poor*. Philadelphia: Fortress Press.

Taylor, J.T. 1916. *In the Heart of India: The Work of the Canadian Presbyterian Mission*. Toronto: Board of Foreign Missions of the Presbyterian Church of Canada.

Ulbrich, Jeffrey. 1995. "A Home for Nuclear Waste? Meadow Lake Tribal Council Expresses Interest." *Saskatoon Star Phoenix* (February 24): p. A1.

United Church of Canada. 1986. *31st General Council Record of Proceedings*, Sudbury (August 13–22).

Wolcott, Martin. 1994. "Punters Seek Security in the Lottery of Life." *Manchester Guardian* (September 16).

CHAPTER 3

The Role of Native Elders:
Emergent Issues

Joseph E. Couture[1]

Shorn of the various surface features from different cultures, Coyote and his kin represent the sheerly spontaneous in life, the pure creative spark that is our birthright as human beings and that defies fixed roles or behavior. He not only represents some primordial creativity from our earlier days, but he reminds us that such celebration of life goes on today, and he calls us to join him in the frenzy. In an ordered world of objects and labels, he represents the potency of nothingness of chaos, of freedom — a nothingness that makes something of itself (Erdoes and Ortiz, 1984, p. 39).

In discussing the relationship of humankind to the Earth, we must understand the basic difference between the Navajo view of Mother Earth, and what the Western European or contemporary American mind means when it tosses around poetic metaphors like "mother nature," or "mother earth."
    The contemporary American means that the earth and all of nature is like his natural mother. But the Navajo (and other American Indians) means that his natural mother is the closest thing he will ever know that is like his real mother — The Earth. (Begay, 1979, p. 28)

There are those who say that the Native Way holds a key, if not *the* key, to the future survival of mankind. They say that it is in the nature of the Native's relationship to the cosmos, the land, to all life-forms, to himself, manifest in ritual and ceremony. They say that to learn the "how and why" of the traditional Native stance is to find the key, to discover a "saving grace" of insights and a creative power beyond any rationality, all crucial to human continuance (see Berry; Brumble, 1980; Steinmetz, 1984). If that is so, as I know it to be, then, central to this discovery, and primary to the Native existential positioning, is the presence and function of Elders. This chapter is dedicated as a tribute to their contemporary emergence.

To that end, comments to situate somewhat my experience with Elders and some of the difficulties in writing about them are presented, some events are highlighted and interpreted, the importance of a number of Elder teachings are underscored, and the relevance of Elder inner and outer behaviours is set forth. A discussion of several other Elder-related issues leads to a conclusion to this chapter.

INTRODUCTORY REMARKS

I agree with Brumble (1980, p. 34) who says that Elders have become the focus of a "cultural dialectic." Involved are Elders in treaty and non-treaty communities, as well as Natives and non-Natives. Included are social scientists of all stripes pushing to observe and analyze, striving for their syntheses, as well as increasing numbers of Natives engaged in a return to their roots. Both tend to look indiscriminately to Elders, wherever they can be found, for insights and guidance (see Brown, 1982, p. 119, for similar views). Both experience difficulties in this endeavour, the former hardly aware that what they expect to observe is restricted by the conditions necessary for their presence as observers (Carter in Rothman, 1987, p. 71) and the latter confused by the rarity of top or true Elders and by the relative immaturity and unsteadiness of younger spiritual teachers and ceremonialists.

It is true, in my view, that Elders themselves, of whatever type and development, form an unusual phenomenon. Like all other Natives, they too have been influenced by the forces and consequences of "Contact." Early on, they were, so to speak, hammered back into the woodwork. Long proscribed and banned by governments and churches, now barely emerged from decades of withdrawn, underground activity, they are perceived, not as harbingers of a lost Eden, but as the oral historians, guardians of the Secrets, as interpreters of the Life of the People, as unusual teachers and way showers to the People.

In the late 1960s, triggered by a sudden, strong wave of seekers, Elders, although flattered and grateful, were initially flustered and were forced initially to rethink and redefine themselves and their roles. They were faced with dire and unsettling questions about identity and survival, and with the basic paradoxes regarding the nature of the Native world and the fundamental issues about the world in which humans live.

My views on Elders derive in general from experiences with a number of true Elders over the years since 1971, and particularly from apprenticeship with several Medicine Elders initiated that same year.

Use of the term "Native" herein connotes inclusivity. It refers to all Original Peoples in Canada. In the context of this kind of discussion, by choice I favour this broad connotation since Elders themselves of all Tribes stress Native identity as being a state of mind, as it were, centred in the heart. The late Abe Burnstick's frequent reply to "Who is an Indian?" was to exclaim, with finger stabbing his heart area, "An Indeeyin is Indeeyin rawt heah!"[2]

A difficulty confronting Native writers is to write for print-literate read-ers, especially of social science and professional education perspectives, as though these readers will somehow respond as to an oral literature.

To so write, for one thing, requires keeping in hand an immense oral "reference bibliography," i.e., the stories, legends, prophecies, cere-monies, songs, dance, language, and customs of the People. To so write also requires that the qualitative dimensions of these sources be expressed and conveyed with integrity, e.g., the non-verbal of the story-teller and the ceremonialist — and that is virtually impossible. And, although Elders have declared that the " . . . time has come to share the secrets . . . " its achievement remains most awkward, if not painful.

Nonetheless, in my view and that of Brumble, the task of written shar-ing and communication, at this time in our history, however, must reso-lutely begin (Brumble, 1980, p. 42; see also Buller, 1980; Gould, 1988; Lincoln, 1980). There is a need in the contemporary Native world to artic-ulate traditional views, and to transmit with discernment and discretion to the extent possible, something of the fullness of the Traditional Experi-ence and Story — as embodied in the highest, most evolved Elders — in its intricacies, beauties, and ineffabilities. Further, in the view of Berry and others, there is a worldwide human need to survive to which Native North Americans have something significant to contribute (see Fox, 1972, 1983; Hansman, 1986; Steinmetz, 1984).

There is therefore a challenge, and the tentative solution followed here is to write as a storyteller as much as possible, from a general, social sci-ence perspective. In others words, as I now proceed, the best I can, with the expression and sharing of my thoughts and feelings regarding my experience with Elders, my endeavour attempts to circumscribe that expe-rience and amplify it to some extent by deliberate association with west-ern social science and education constructs.[3]

In so doing, the hope is to avoid what someone has called the "bar-barism of reflection," i.e., the over-refinement which is unable to sustain the poetic wisdom and imagination that establishes and sustains true Elders, and better yet, to suggest something of how normal and natural it is for Elders to think and behave a certain way.

My proposition assumes that traditional values are dynamic,[4] and can be and are being re-expressed in new forms, and that such, as it so behooves, is being brought about by Elders now at grips with an ever-increasing flow of Natives and non-Natives seeking advice and counsel, healing and inspiration, interpretation of the past and present, in their apprehension and concern over future survival.

SOME HISTORY

The late 1960s and early 1970s witnessed the political emergence of Native organizations in Alberta. The opening round of activity by both political and service leaders and organizers, initially enthusiastic, climaxed in early 1969 in much discouragement and deep, angry frustration. Both deliberate and unwitting obstacles to program development were formidable. In negotiations, mutual distrust predominated. Confrontation was required and frequently resorted to, and conflict became a working condition in the drive to break open bureaucratic and political doors. It was a time also when programs were exceedingly difficult to start and maintain, largely for lack of adequate core and development monies, and partly for lack of skill and insight on both sides. In the midst of this period of dismaying hurt and resentment, a major shift in consciousness, nonetheless, slowly dawned. It started that same year with Native leaders seeking out Elders, and continued subsequently when others also began the trek back to the Elders of their Tribes.

Amazingly, and concurrently, and virtually everywhere in North America, signs of revitalization appeared. However, because past and current efforts to resolve the enormous cultural, socio-economic, and political difficulties were stark, they were unsettling failures.

So began a period of intense introspection, induced by a sharp perception of disheartening results, and encouraged by an intuitive sense that Natives, through a return to cultural origins, might allay their profound consternation and anger, and find answers to the basic question of "How can we change the direction of the destructive currents? The white man hasn't got any answers. What can we do for our children and our children's children? Maybe, if we talked to some old people. . . . " That incipient awareness became the theme of the beginning struggles, a theme soon variously played across the country.

A second event, paralleled also subsequently in other areas of the continent, such as the Smallboy and Mackinaw camps in the Alberta Rockies, the Rolling Thunder camp in Nevada, etc., occurred in the fall of 1972. It is most noteworthy for it presents clear, milestone evidence of ominous stirrings within Native consciousness.

Elders from six different tribes in Alberta gathered for twelve days on the West Coast of Vancouver Island under the leadership of the Indian Association of Alberta. After two days of discussion on education-related issues, in substance, the following was declared:

> In order to survive in the 20th century, we must really come to grips with the White man's culture and with White ways. We must stop lamenting the past. The White man has many good things. Borrow. Master and use his technology. Discover and define the harmonies between the two general Cultures, between the basic values of the Indian Way and those of Western civilization — and thereby forge a new and stronger sense of identity. For, to be fully Indian today, we must become bilingual and bicultural. We have never had to do this before. In so doing we will survive as Indians, true to our past. We have always survived. Our history tells us so.[5]

In discussion of that statement, the following comment was made by an Elder:

On a given day, if you ask me where you might go to find a moose, I will say "if you go that way you won't find a moose. But, if you go that way, you will." So now, you younger ones, think about all that. Come back once in a while and show us what you've got. And, we'll tell you if what you think you have found is a moose.[6]

Because of its obvious, singular importance, one particular event has been underscored. However, and once again, that one incident is to be understood within a continental context of similar contemporaneous events throughout "Indian Country." Since that era, and understandably, attention to Elders continues to accrue, especially to both their role and function, and to the relevance of their teachings to contemporary Native identity and survival.

SOME TEACHINGS

A few recurring sayings reveal characteristic simplicity, range, and richness. For example:

"Don't worry. Take it easy. Do your best. It will all work out. Respect life. Respect your Elders. It's up to you. You have all the answers within you."

"Listen to what Mother Earth tells you. Speak with her. She will speak to you."

"What is Life but a journey into the Light? At the centre of Life is the Light."

"Soon I will cross the River, go up the Mountain, into the Light."

These typical sentences set forth a deep, strong, moral, and spiritual vision and understanding. These interrelated principles are corollaries or facets of a unitary, primary traditional insight that is variously stated. For example:

The centred and quartered Circle is the sign of wholeness, of inclusiveness of all reality, of life, of balance and harmony between man and culture. (Traditional saying)

There are only two things you have to know about being Indian. One is that everything is alive, and two is that we're all related. (Anonymous Indian)

COMMENT

One sees here the classical themes of holism and personalism, of relationality, of an environment and cosmos which are alive. A broad characteristic goal of traditional education has always been that the whole person in the whole of his/her life be addressed. In the traditional setting, one effectively learns how to become and be a unique expression of human potential. These same traditional processes, in the context of extended family and community Elders, describe a strong sense of responsibility both toward self and toward the community.

Such statements also, in my view, provide reference points to the seeker in his/her journey "back," and suggest something of the richness of the spirit of Tradition, and provide as well "memory-bank data," as it were, for Elder reinterpretations, of which the 1972 Declaration is a prime example.

The 1972 statement is several-fold in its importance. For example, for the first time since the signing of the western treaties, top Elders responded in assembly as the historians of their tribes, as philosophers and teachers of Tradition. They expressed anew for the people the meaning of their history, in light of present conditions, and pointed out a saving and safe direction to pursue so that the People's History be sustained and forwarded.

Crucial also is that to describe the behaviour needed, Elders focussed on needed connections between the two general cultures, urging discerning openness and selectivity over distrusting and closed defensiveness. A further declaration emphasis is the redefinition of Native identity — a landmark moment — for, to become bicultural is designated as being a positive, warranted, existential act. At that meeting, it was clearly understood that to be bilingual would always be "better" and "richer," but what the Elders affirmed is that bilingualism is not essential for a core-sense of self as Native, keeping open thereby the possibility of authentic Nativeness to those large numbers of Natives who, for whatever reason, do not speak a Native language.

Thus, criteria were defined whereby the survival movement could judge whether or not it has found a "moose." That day Elder mediation, empowered, sanctioned, and formalized, redirected the struggling emergence of the People.

Grown men cried that day. . . .

Traditional Native holism and personalism as a culturally shaped human process of being/becoming, is rooted in a relationship with Father Sky, the cosmos, and with Mother Earth, the land — a characteristic which has lead comparative religionists to rank Native American religion as a fifth classical world religion. These experts point to the centrality of land in Native spiritual and religious experience as its distinctive dimension (see Hultkranz in Capps, 1976, pp. 86–106; see also Berry; Fox, 1972, 1983). This relationship with the land/cosmos is personalized and personal, and marked by a trust and a respect which stems from a direct and sustained experience of the oneness of all reality, of the livingness of the land.

The richness of this holism and personalism extends further. When one looks beyond or behind the externals of local and regional custom, language and history, more of the core dynamic of the Native Way of life is revealed. In the west, classical existentialism stresses the utter validity of subjectivity, i.e., of the feeling, reflective subject who has the freedom to make choices, and to determine thus his/her life. Therefore, what one does is of keystone importance. The doing that characterizes the Native Way is a doing that concerns itself with being and becoming a unique person, one fully responsible for one's own life and actions within family and community. Finding one's path and following it is a characteristic Native enterprise which leads to or makes for the attainment of inner and outer balance. This is in marked contrast with general western doing, which tends and strains toward having, objectifying, manipulating, "thingifying" every one and every thing it touches (see Couture, 1987, pp. 180–82).

BEHAVIOURAL FEATURES

The exemplars of such a way of living, relating, and perceiving, of course, are the most evolved, or "true" Elders. The preceding references to typical sayings may now be usefully supplemented by a description of a number of Elders' behaviours.

It is no simple matter to describe Elder behaviour, because of the deep interconnectedness of all facets of their behaviour. The observations which follow are not rigorously organized in pyramidal fashion, but rather as one link leading to the next, in cyclical fashion up and around a same conceptual axis — Elders.

COMMENT

I am of the opinion that true Elders are superb embodiments of highly developed human potential. They exemplify the kind of person which a traditional, culturally based learning environment can and does form and mould. Elders also are evidence that Natives know a way to high human development, to a degree greater than generally suspected. Their qualities of mind (intuition, intellect, memory, imagination) and emotion, their profound and refined moral sense manifest in an exquisite sense of humour, in a sense of caring and communication finesse in teaching and counselling, together with a high level of spiritual and psychic attainment, are perceived as clear behavioural indicators, deserving careful attention, if not compelling emulation.

To relate to Elders, to observe and listen carefully, and to come to understand the what, why, and how of such behaviours, grounds, or enroots one, so to speak, in the living earth of Native Tradition.

It is not possible to study and examine Elders in the conventional sense simply because that is not the "way." One learns about Elders by learning from them over a long period of time, by becoming comfortable with a learning-by-doing model. Their counselling and teaching focus on learning from one's experience. Thus, through respectful and patient observation, evidence of remarkable, incisive intellect, of tested wisdom, of sharp and comprehensive ability, allied with excellent memory recall, and of well-developed discursive ability, is eventually perceived.

Further signs of Elderhood are found in their level of trust of both life itself and of their own experiences, by being into true feelings (i.e., into the spiritual side of feelings, without sentimentality), by the art of being still, quiet, unafraid of darkness and nothingness, by the ability to laugh at one another, as well as at self. All that is so because they are trained in the lessons of how the very nature of our being is in at-one-ment with the cosmo-genesis. And so, they hold to the land, ceremony, medicine, linked to the past, in Spirit (see Cordova, 1938, pp. 23–24; Buller, 1980, p. 166).

What is the "secret," if any, behind those admirable multibehaviours? My experience suggests that it is their knowledge of and skill in "primordial experience."[7] Primal experience for true Elders, in my view, is centred in the pervasive, encompassing reality of the Life-Force, manifest in "laws" — the Laws of Nature, the Laws of Energy, or the Laws of Light (Couture, 1989, pp. 22–23). In other words, true Elders are familiar with Energy on a vast scale, in multiple modes, e.g., energy as healing, creative, lifegiving, sustaining. Both the experience and perception of such manifestations, the manifestations themselves, reveal that all is one, is natural, and is the realm of creative Spirit — the mysterious "Life-Force" (the Wakan-Tanka of the Sioux). There is no "between," between the God-Creator, Source and Sustainer-of-life, and the Cosmos, the environment, all life forms, and Native soul (see Couture, 1989).

Such outstanding qualities, levels of insight and skill, testify to an inner and personal, fundamental, consistent, and unchanging process, to a capacity to respond to life as its conditions invariably change. "We have always survived. Our history tells us so."

Elders are an invitation to taste existence within the functioning of the natural world, to experience the mystique of the land. They are, Berry says, in " . . . fascination with the grandeur of the North American continent . . . " (Berry, 1987a, p. 185). They acquire knowledge and insight into the nature of the universe. For centuries, they have wondered over the revelation of the universe. . . .

It strikes me that their "wisdom" is rooted in Immanence and Transcendence, i.e., this wisdom is attuned to the Immanent in time and space, in the dimensions and seasonal rhythm of the universe, and to the Transcendent, the Above of the confines of historical space and time. This timeless positioning makes for the Story, as carried down through the ages to it being retold and reshaped presently, leading to the discovery of new forms needed to transform current conditions of Native individuals and groups, and thereby of humankind.

Elders hold the secrets of the dynamics of the New Vision. They are propelled by the past, are drawn absolutely to the future. Theirs is a bio-concentric Vision, i.e., a vision of earth and community — an ecological vision of an enduring Mother Earth and the People, a relationship intertwined in a single destiny. In other words, Elders hold a depth insight into the structure and functioning, and manifestation of the entire ecological process (Berry, 1987a, p. 185).

The powerful and awesome beauty of Elder vision and experience includes the contemporary state of the ecology — a deep point of agony for the state of Mother Earth and Father Sky is in a worldwide, unprecedented state of ecological devastation and disintegration.[8]

Elders have, what Berry calls, "an earth response to an earth problem" (Berry, 1987a, p. 186). "We need only to listen to what Mother Earth is telling us," the Elders repeatedly utter. Their "earth response" is the Story that has never ceased, that carries the dream of the earth as our way into the future. In a sense, this Story holds the "genetic and psychic encoding" needed by humankind for survival.[9] Their "earth response" is processive through and through, and the only immutable reality is the Life-Force itself.

True Elders are so, and do what they do because they have shamanic personalities, that is they have a non-romantic, brilliant sensitivity to the dimensions and patterns of manifestations of the natural world, in its most challenging demands and delights. As humans, as one of the earth's life-forms, they are capable of relations so that all others can equally flourish. Their power and personality hold the ability to shake us and lead us out of the current global cultural pathology, and bring us along into and through a healing and restructuring at a most basic level. They facilitate healing because they have sensitivity to the larger patterns of nature, in its harsh and deadly aspects as well as in its life-giving powers, always in balance with all life-forms.[10]

More can be said about Elder perception. Once again, their perceived world is radically, entirely relational, that is, all realities are constituents of that perception. These are what Fontinell (1988, p. 138) calls "fields" of being and what Fox refers to as "isness."[11] Therefore their "faith," if that is an appropriate term, or their "knowledge" and their "wisdom," is of these "fields." Theirs is a "faith" founded in what they experience. Characteristically, their "faith" is a fundamental mode of experience, rather than an intellectual grasp and understanding of concepts. It is also perforcedly a "knowing" which is ongoing, an open-ended task because, for one grounded in Nature, there can be no once and for all determination of just what is authentic (as opposed to that which is apparent, absolute revelation).

Elders should not be considered as concerned, therefore, with a western sense of "belief," i.e., a going beyond that for which there is evidence at the present moment, but as having "faith," i.e., experiential knowing, an integrating experience ". . . whereby all modes of experience are brought together in a relatively cohesive whole which is expressed in the life of the person, thus rendering human life meaningful" (Fontinell, 1988, p. 140).

I suspect that the traditional Elder capacity to accommodate change, upon contact with western Christianity forms, readily led them to become Christian, but in a way that allowed not only transformation of perception, but sustained a full continuity with the faith of the People.[12] My hypothesis is that conversion was a simple instance of new growing out of the old, forming a new syncretism congruent with their "faith."

SUMMARY

I concur with Gravely who says that a true Elder is not classifiable as a " . . . passive informant on the traditional past . . . ," but as " . . . a creative theologian, open to the possibilities of his situation, to new ideas and symbols, and to a dialogue between the traditions" (Gravely, 1987, p. 11). Elders manifest consistency in the life process and in relationship to several worlds, moving in and out as shamans are wont to do, with seriousness and humour, with persistent attention and awareness.

Elders possess keys to a classical journey of human and earth ecological transformation. In this era, they are being called upon to reinterpret and to apply the Tradition, the Story, in a new way. There is urgency to this for Mother Earth is no longer looking after herself naturally, but is an earth looked after, and badly, by man. Elders are now so engaged.

SOME ISSUES

Every turn in this chapter raises questions, or issues, which deserve more extensive exploration, but which an overview description such as this precludes. Nonetheless, in this last section, aspects of either a practical or academic concern are reviewed.

The rapid decrease in numbers of true Elder's is most alarming. Who is to replace them? For some decades now, significant numbers of communities across Canada have lost all traditional Elders. Many individuals, forced to seek out Elders in other tribal traditions, initially encounter some difficulty because of differences in ways. This is a two-way pressure on both Elder and seeker.

The range of kinds of Elders also is bothersome. An Elders' prediction states that these times of emergence are to be marked by chaos and confusion before changing into a time of light and peace. Certainly a significant part of this difficult phase is attributable to "instant" Elders, overnight wonders who, with limited ceremonies and an abundance of clichés, confuse and stall many in their personal journey. The mantle will fall to those spiritual people, less evolved, of less ability and knowledge. "True" Elders are those who have gone through painful encounter with spiritual realities, and who become thereby, in the perception of the People, intermediary between their respective cultural communities and the spiritual forces of the universe, and defenders of the community's psychic integrity. They are those who have enacted and sustained a personal relationship with Nature.

Elders are a national issue because of their qualities and rarity (see Phillips, Troff, and Whitecalf, 1976; Phillips and Troff, 1977). The needs of the People require guiding wisdom as assurance of a continuing, living Native presence in Canada, and for during the time needed to acquire a "faith" about the real possibility of survival.

The practical requirements of establishing and maintaining a relationship with Elders are not readily perceived. First of all, at the level of individual need and change, much time and patience are required. There are no shortcuts to attitudinal and spiritual change, no possible end-runs around phases of inner change. A complete and enduring commitment is required. Secondly, the "return" is not only to "primal roots," to the living core of the Tradition itself, but is conditional on personal achievement, so as to arrive at presenting to the world an authentic mode of living (see Berry in Hausman, 1986, p. 7). And, that is not an easy matter.

The "knowing" of Elders is problematic to those who, for a range of reasons, were not schooled in oral tradition. Elders as "knowers" know intimately, directly, and are non-dualistic in their perceptions and understandings. Western-trained people are inherently scholastic and dualistic in perception and thinking. True, the sense of identity of Elders is marked by an ordered consciousness. However, at the same time, it is unbounded by space and time, all the while remaining in direct consideration of both dimensions of historical time and space. Again, attainment to that state of development is a basic challenge.

Problematic also, and for that same kind of mind, is that Elders have consistency, continuity, and clarity of insight and skill regarding paradigmatic alteration (i.e., reinterpreting the Story) which, in my view, as Grim declares " . . . germinates understanding of the creative role of imagination and intuition in human history" (Grim, 1987, p. 235). Elders are positioned, I would suggest, to contribute to facilitating to what Wilson (1985, p. 55) calls "quantum leaps" in developing new models of thought.

It would seem that presently there are growing numbers of western academic approaches hinting at hitherto unknown possible amenability with Native mind. Keutzer, commenting on the work of such physicists as Bohm, Einstein, Capra, etc., suggests that such physicists are becoming students of consciousness itself (see Keutzer, 1984). Their concepts of "flow" and "hologram," for example, and statements that "everything is alive," are very suggestive. To Keutzer's list, I would add the names of such theologians and historians as Fox and Berry, and of the physicist-philosopher Swimme.

A corollary to the issue of "knowing" is that of mysticism (currently a much abused and misapplied concept, in my view). From a Native spiritual standpoint, as I see it, mysticism is a question of becoming/being rooted or grounded in relationships with all constituents or dimensions of reality. I like Fox's description of mysticism because it is congruent with my understanding of Native spiritual experience. He holds that " . . . the essence of the mystical experience is the way we are altered to see everything from its life-filled axis, to feel the mysteries of life as they are present within and around us" (Fox, 1972, p. 77). That's Indian!

To arrive at a direct experiential understanding of that definition is a primary learning task. To discover how ceremonies, for example, mediate helping energy and teaching takes some doing. Prayer, ritual, and ceremony ground one in life for "It's all deah, in de sereemonees!"[13]

To acquire an awareness of all earth forms as having a life of their own, to become aware of all as Spirit-bearing, as Spirit-expressing, takes some doing. To become steeped in, adept in Native mysticism is to enter into the beautiful, the truth, the Oneness, in balance against all negativity and absence. It is to activate and sustain personal discovery which leads to a true sense of self-understanding, to a sense of future time through awareness of the past — which leads to learning how to intuit the close relationship between one's culture and one's genetic impulses.

Elders have teaching challenges to deal with. One is with regard to non-Natives. They are aware of the currently unfolding prophecy that "The White brother will come to the Red brother for teaching." There is acceptance of the non-Natives who come to them. However, they find themselves struggling with a different mind-set and affectivity, as well as with language barriers. Also, because of the knowledge level of both Native and non-Native seekers, so many are not grounded in a sense of the real but mysterious power of nature in mountains, rivers and lakes, rocks, lifeforms, all as enmeshed in the web of the universe. So, the legends and stories require pedagogical adaptation. The stories have to be retold, reshaped, and refitted to meet contemporary seekers' changed and changing needs.

Such encounters are but necessary moments in the retelling and reshaping of the Story, as in the case of the 1972 Declaration above. New legends as well as forthcoming across the continent, sparked by medicine Elders' dreams and visions. Tradition through Elders is converged on the present, revealing forgotten depths of perception and understanding.

Present Elder endeavour is in a tensional context. They are aware of the tensional exchange between the Story of the People and the need for a new direction, as we have seen. They are aware of the tensional exchange between immanent direction within living matter itself and the transcendent source of the creative impulse. They are aware of the tensional character of awakening, of the inner dynamics of spiritual and socio-political life.

CONCLUSION

We look to Elders for the way words are used, for the structural devices they employ, for the teaching and counselling approaches they utilize, for the philosophical and spiritual perspectives of the world, experienced and envisioned. We look to them to show us the " . . . the archetypal essences appearing in animal forms . . . " as Brown says (1983, p. 7). In other words, to show us the Way.

We look to them to tell us about the "Moose."

Daniel Deschinney, a Navajo Blessingway singer, explains how a Navajo experiences the sacred mountains' inner forms, and says:

When a Navajo experiences the sacred mountains' inner forms kindling new strength within himself, he says "I am invincible. I am beautified." To be invincible is masculine. To be beautified is feminine. These two concepts together are a powerful entity. There is no strength from only one. Power comes from the interaction between them. When you have strength, you recognize your opportunity, you know what you must do, and you have the grace to do it. (Quoted by Johnson, 1988, p. 47)

NOTES

1. The author is an Alberta Métis of Cree ancestry. His Ph.D. training and experience are in the areas of Native development, psychology, and education at all levels. His work experience includes teaching, addictions counselling, community development, and research. He has been apprenticed to elders since 1971.

2. The late Elder Abe Burnstick, Stoney Nation, Paul's Band, Duffield, Alberta, was pre-eminent as an orator and teacher.

3. This position I take regarding the difficult issue of oral-literate mind versus print-literate mind finds support in the views of Geertz and Jules-Rosette, for example. Geertz holds that the main task in interpreting cultures is one of "explicating explications" (Geertz, 1973, p. 18). In other words, it is imperative to acquire the feel for the "homely in homely context," for to fail to do so is a failure to place common-sense thought within context of its use. The development of the "thickest descriptions" possible becomes therefore both an ideal and necessary objective.

   It also means, as Jules-Rosette points out, dealing frontally with the problems of subjective interpretation (1978, p. 563). The "veil of objectivity" masks an inability to grasp another interpretive system, or style of perception. Objectivity has "totally falsified our concept of truth" (Polanyi in Jules-Rosette, 1978, p. 289) — the "veil of objectivity" is as a protective shield of one's own oracular structure. It covers what G. Wilson calls "profound parasitic lay assumptions" (1987, p. 118). This difficulty is illustrated by the case of Casteneda. His construct of reality was so impenetrable that drugs were needed to forcefully assault it to allow him to receive spiritual insight.

4. For more detail about the creative capacity of Native culture see Couture (1987, pp. 180–84).

5. Declaration rendered by Elder Louis Crier, Cree Nation, Ermineskin Band, Hobbema, Alberta.

6. Observation made by the late Elder Charlie Blackman, Chipewyan Nation, Cold Lake Band, Cold Lake, Alberta.

7. Huston (1953, p. 276) claims that " . . . there is, first, a Reality that is everywhere and always the same; and second, that human beings always and everywhere have access to it."

8. See Akwasasne Notes. This internationally established Iroquois journal of social comment, over two decades now, has reported on ecological deterioration abundantly and consistently. With special attention to aboriginal regions worldwide, its regular columns, in cause–effect terms, describe the autistic relationship between the ecological vision and the industrial vision.

9. See Berry (1987b) for a provocative, insightful discussion of this concept.

10. See Berry (1987b, pp. 211–12) and Kelsey (1978) for more detail on shamanic personality and qualities.

11. "Isness" as term is frequent in all of Fox's writings.

12. See Gravely (1987) for discussion of the adaptability of Black Elk.

13. Elder Abe Burnstick.

DISCUSSION QUESTIONS

1. Why were elders so important to Native communities in the past, and what contributed to the waning of their roles?

2. How would you explain the re-emergence of different types of elders within and outside Native communities?

3. In what respects have elders become the focus of a cultural dialectic? What difficulties do you think this might pose for elders and the communities in which they live?

4. Do you know someone who is a true elder? If you do, how is this person similar to and different from the ideal, true elder outlined in this chapter?

5. In what respects might the bio-centric vision of elders benefit humanity in the future? Can you think of other ways of thinking and doing that could hinder the continued re-emergence of elders?

FURTHER READINGS

Bouchard, Dave (text) and Roy Henry Vickers (images). 1990. *The Elders Are Watching*. Vancouver: Raincoast Books. Combined images and texts that convey lessons from Native elders past and present. A call to reflect and dream, to imagine and envision the meaning and hope that can be drawn from the wisdom of all of our elders.

Brown, Joseph Epes. 1964. *The Spiritual Legacy of the American Indian*. Wallington, Pa.: Pendle Hill Publications. Brown asserts that ignoring or denying the spiritual legacy offered by Native Americans contributes to the impoverishment of all peoples. He invites readers to appreciate the ways in which the living religions of Native Americans can inform and enrich our everyday lives, our cultural sensibilities, and our social, economic, legal, and political structures.

Cardinal, Douglas and Jeanette Armstrong. 1991. *The Native Creative Process*. Penticton, B.C.: Theytus Books. Douglas Cardinal and Jeanette Armstrong share their understanding and vision of "our Native way" by blending conversational commentary with striking images.

Patt, Neal, ed. 1991. *Place Where the Spirit Lives: Stories from the Archaeology and History of Manitoba*. Winnipeg: Pemmican Publications. Seven stories of Native people in Manitoba based on the writings of archaeologists are combined with seven teachings from Native elders and teachers. An example of the way in which legend and science can complement and enrich one another.

Wolfe, Alexander. 1989. *Earth Elder Stories: The Pinayzitt Path*. Saskatoon: Fifth House. Stories belonging to the descendants of Pinayzitt that tell of how Earth Elder and his people survived sickness, participated in treaty-signing, obtained the grass dance, and lived in relation to Indian agents and other non-Native people. Invites the reader into a mystical encounter with history and a historical encounter with mysticism.

REFERENCES

Begay, I. 1979. "The Relationship Between the People and the Land." *Akwesasne Notes* (Summer): pp. 28–30.

Berry, T. 1987a. "Creative Energy." *Cross Currents* (Summer/Fall): pp. 179–86.

———. 1987b. "The Dream of the Earth: Our Way into the Future." *Cross Currents* (Summer/Fall): pp. 200–15.

———. 1987c. "The New Story: Comment on the Origin, Identification and Transmission of Values." *Cross Currents* (Summer/Fall): pp. 187–99.

———. 1987d. "Twelve Principles for Reflecting on the Universe." *Cross Currents* (Summer/Fall): pp. 216–17.

Brown, J.E. 1982. *The Spiritual Legacy of the American Indian*. New York: Crossroad.

———. 1982. "The Bison and the Moth: Lakota Correspondences." *Parabola* 8(2): pp. 6–13.

Brumble, D. 1980. "Anthropologists, Novelists and Indian Sacred Material." *Can Ev. Amer. St.* 11 (Spring): pp. 31–48.

Buller, G. 1980. "New Interpretations of Native American Literature: A Survival Technique." *American Indian Cultural Research Journal* 4(1 and 2): pp. 165–77.

Capps, W., ed. 1976. Seeing with a Native Eye. New York: Harper and Row.

Cordova, Viola. 1938. *Philosophy and the Native American: The People Before Columbus*. Albuquerque: Southwest Indian Student Coalition, University of New Mexico.

Couture, J. 1987. "What Is Fundamental to Native Education? Some Thoughts on the Relationship Between Thinking, Feeling, and Learning." Pp. 178–91 in *Contemporary Educational Issues: The Canadian Mosaic*, ed. L. Stewin and S. McCann. Toronto: Copp Clark Pitman.

———. 1989. "Native and Non-Native Encounter: A Personal Experience." Pp. 123–54 in *Challenging the Conventional: Essays in Honor of Ed Newsberry*, ed. W. Cragg. Burlington: Trinity Press.

Erdoes, R. and A. Ortiz, eds. 1984. *American Indian Myths and Legends*. New York: Pantheon Books.

Fontinell, E. 1988. "Faith and Metaphysics Revisited." *Cross Currents* (Summer): pp. 129–45.

Fox, M. 1972. *On Becoming a Musical, Mystical Bear: Spirituality American Style*. New York: Paulist Press.

———. 1983. *Meditation with Meister Eckhart*. Sante Fe: Bear and Co.

Fox, M. and B. Swimme. 1982. *Manifesto for a Global Civilization*. Santa Fe: Bear and Co.

Geertz, C. 1973. *The Interpretation of Cultures: Selected Essays*. New York: Basic Books.

Gould, Janice. 1988. "A review of Louise Erdrich's 'Jacklight.'" Pp. 11–14 in *The People Before Columbus*. Albuquerque: Southwest Indian Coalition, University of New Mexico.

Gravely, W. 1987. "New Perspectives on Nicholas Black Elk, Oglala Sioux Holy Man." *The Illif Review* 44 (Winter): pp. 1–19.

Grim, J. 1987. "Time, History, Historians in Thomas Berry's Vision." *Cross Currents* (Summer/Fall): pp. 225–39.

Hausman, G. 1986. *Meditation with Animals*. Albuquerque: Bear and Co.

Huston, S. 1953. "Philosophy, Theology, and the Primordial Claim." *Cross Currents* 28(3): pp. 276–88.

Johnson, T. 1988. "The Four Sacred Mountains of the Navajos." *Parabola* (Winter): pp. 40–47.

Jules-Rosette, Benetta. 1978. "The Veil of Objectivity: Prophecy, Divination, and Social Inquiry." *American Anthropology* 80 (September): pp. 549–70.

Kelsey, M. 1978. "The Modern Shaman and Christian Belief." *Transcend* 22: pp. 1–6.

Keutzer, C. 1984. "The Power of Meaning: From Quantum Mechanics to Synchronicity." *Journal of Human Psychology* 24 (Winter): pp. 80–94.

Lincoln, K. 1980. "Trans — to the Other Side of, Over, Across." *American Indian Cultural and Research Journal* 4(1 and 2): pp. 1–17.

Philips, Donna and R. Troff, eds. 1977. *Enewuk*. Saskatoon: Saskatchewan Indian Cultural College.

Philips, Donna, R. Troff, and H. Whitecalf, eds. 1976. *Kataayuk: Saskatchewan Indian Elders*. Saskatoon: Saskatchewan Indian Cultural College.

Rothman, T. 1987. "A What You See Is What You Beget Theory." *Discovery* (May): pp. 90–96, 98–99.

Steinmetz, P. 1984. *Meditation with Native Americans: Lakota Spirituality*. Santa Fe: Bear and Co.

Swimme, B. 1987. "Berry's Cosmology." *Cross Currents* (Summer/Fall): pp. 218–24.

Wilson, G. 1987. "What Is Effective Intercultural Communication?" *Canadian Ethnic Studies* 18(1): pp. 118–23.

Wilson, R.A. 1985. "Quantum Leaps." *New Age* (June): pp. 52–55, 80.

CHAPTER 4

The Framing of Aboriginal Art

Rita L. Irwin and Ruby Farrell

INTRODUCTION

Visual and performing modes of expression have been important within aboriginal[1] and non-aboriginal communities throughout time. In most aboriginal cultures, life is expressed through richly integrative symbol systems and lifestyles that often appear to others from Eurocentric cultures as artistic (or dramatic or musical) forms of activity. Yet what does "throughout time" really mean? Using a Eurocentric conception of linear time, one would conceive of a history of ideas as a sequence of events and evolution of topics. However, an aboriginal conception of time is often much different from this. Often, time is not linear but circular or simultaneous in which all things are happening right now. Therefore, as we endeavour to discuss conceptions of visual art from a socio-historical perspective, we feel compelled to begin by questioning some of the assumptions that often permeate such discussions. In addition, we hope you consider or reconsider shifting your understanding of the world to include a discussion of the points and scenarios we raise in this chapter. It is not our attempt to convince you of any right answers, but rather to question what is often presented as fact, and therefore to realize that there is always more than one way of understanding the world.

Over the last few years, we have both been involved with aboriginal groups, particularly in the field of education with a special interest in art education. This interest has prompted us to take a hard look at educational practices and theories. As you will learn later, our educational research interests endeavour to start from the aboriginal perspective, something that has only recently become accepted in academic circles. Being influenced by many aboriginal people, their ideas and philosophies, their beliefs and values, has encouraged us to "frame" this chapter in a certain way. We say this because before European contact with Canadian First Nations peoples, aboriginal communities did not practise art per se. Rather, life was viewed as an integrated activity and much of that activity accessed skill, beauty, form, and function. It was not important to separate out and describe or interpret these characteristics from daily life activities. In essence, life was a harmonious whole. Yet there are many Eurocentric accounts that in fact do categorize the life of these early peoples to include art, even after they recognize that the communities could not (Anderson, 1990). Theoretically, this does not necessarily mean that these cultures did not practise art, but rather that their conception of the world and of visual forms of expression was fundamentally different from others. One could say that Eurocentric academics have "framed" art in a particular way after studying the lives of these peoples.

Probably one of the biggest influences we have both experienced in our research communities has been the incongruity of understanding time, not in the stereotypical differences between cultures, but in the actual conception of history. In working with community-based research assistants who in turn interviewed community members, we found that it was incredibly difficult to ask about "traditional" art forms, because "what is traditional?" Again, we were faced with Eurocentric categories. Our efforts were meant to try and tease out oral histories of the times before white settlement, but what we uncovered was the artificiality of the question. It is true that much of that oral history has been lost, but it is also true that much of it remains and therefore cannot be limited to a certain time period. A similar misconception could easily be found with the working artists of today, who simultaneously employ characteristics of other contemporary artists yet carry with them the enduring beliefs of their cultures. To provide an account of First Nations art and craft in Canada through a linear perspective detailing dates and places would be to perpetuate a certain kind of "framing" of aboriginal art. We have decided not to continue with this frame and would prefer to invite you into the discussion of reframing, or perhaps even unframing, the socio-historical field of aboriginal art.

As educators teaching in arts-related fields, we have become concerned with tensions often found between Euro-western views of art and craft and aboriginal views of art and craft. The purposes of this chapter are twofold.[2] First, we want to examine several controversies involving Eurocentric discipline-based approaches guiding the artistic community and educational community with an aboriginal approach in a context-centred framework. Briefly, a discipline-based approach to visual arts and visual arts education is derived from and organized around the four parent disciplines of studio production, criticism, history, and aesthetics. These disciplines and their structures influence societal perceptions and expectations of the arts. A context- or community-centred approach integrates visual forms of expression with the daily activities and spiritual life of the community. This is not necessarily unique to aboriginal communities, but it is most appropriate. Second, we want to provide an inside look into one Native community in northern Ontario.[3] By providing an in-depth look into visual forms of expression of the people, we hope to offer you an opportunity to gain greater understanding of one aboriginal culture and the variety, depth, and power of its forms of visual expression.

The significance of portraying these two purposes to you rests in the underlying issue of how each and everyone of us "frames" our views toward aspects of life. In this chapter we are exploring how different cultures essentially perceive, respond to, and find significance in visual symbols. Each of us frames our understanding of visual symbols according to cultural or societal beliefs. Unfortunately, dominant cultures often ignore alternative views, and thus, historically, a multiplicity of frames have been suppressed in favour of Eurocentric-based universal frames toward visual expression. One might say that aboriginal art has been confined, defined, and restrained through the physical and spiritual limitations of *framing art*. Others might say that a natural evolution of cultures is exemplified in breaking new ground for young contemporary First Nations artists as they frame their visual forms of expressions in new ways. Revealing these frames offers us "rich insights into the dilemmas our society faces" (Bellah, 1985, p. vii). A picture may be worth a thousand words, but whose thousand words and what perspective those words come from are quite another issue. The rich dilemmas our society faces may be cast as controversies for First Nations peoples and artists to consider.

CONTROVERSIES IN FIRST NATIONS ART

Controversies that surround First Nations art are often embedded in the disjunctures or tensions that exist between and among Eurocentric and aboriginal conceptions of art, craft, and culture. Keeping in mind that there will always be a "lack of fit" against a predetermined criterion that does not "fit" another culture's expression, it is interesting to consider the extent to which controversies affect each of us. Within each of the controversies explored here exist elements of the parent disciplines defined earlier as studio production, criticism, history, and aesthetics. These disciplines are strong forces in the dominant culture of Canadian and American art education and in the contemporary art world. Although these disciplines will not be detailed here, the following discussion will inevitably reveal features of these disciplines as they are found within each of the examined controversies.

Jamake Highwater (1986) writes extensively about the art of First Nations peoples. He discusses six controversies in Native American art, which will provide stepping stones for us as we study controversies embedded within First Nations art in Canada. These controversies deal with personal and cultural identity, imagery, history, individuality, modernism, and success and recognition. Others that we will add deal with museums, aesthetics, and art education. We will also combine the controversies of personal and cultural identity with that of individuality, since these overlap significantly. It is important to reflect upon each of these sites of controversy in turn. From a linear perspective, it is tempting to study these controversies as they are played out within certain periods of time. However, in keeping with the findings of our research, we prefer to treat these controversies as containing elements that have existed across time and particularly since white settlement. Perhaps the single greatest change since white settlement has been the commodification of visual expression in aboriginal communities: that is, "art" for the tourist trade in addition to or instead of "art" as an active agent of the cultural fabric of the community. Although this may seem straightforward, there is still sufficient overlap among ideas before and after white settlement to warrant caution about overcategorizing the life and times of the peoples.

Suffice it to say that it is also important to reflect upon how specific controversies exist within broad controversies. Each of the broad controversies discussed here is briefly examined in such a way as to encourage you to think about underlying tensions in varying belief systems. If you choose to explore these controversies in greater detail on your own or through directed study, you will inevitably discover that further, and perhaps more specific, controversies exist within these brief reviews of controversies. What is most important for you to realize is that varying frames or conceptions of understanding are brought to the areas of art and art education. As many of these conceptions as possible need to be recognized and considered when any form of decision-making occurs. Let's begin with one controversy that subsumes many of the subsequent controversies.

Personal and Cultural Identity

Juane Quick-to-See Smith, a Flathead painter and curator, says that aboriginal peoples, despite attempts to assimilate them, have continued to make art. "Art was never a separate endeavour in any tribe. In fact, there is no word for art in any of our 3000 languages. Art and identity are linked in the process of living. Art is a celebration of life and a reaffirmation of identity" (College of Webster Art Museum, 1992, p. 12). Art is not separate from everything else (see also Zastrow, 1977, whose informer considers songs to be art). Pakes (1987) explains that "at best we may say that Indian art reflects a certain system of thought which enables it to be identified as such [Indian art]. . . . The concept of art as we know it does not really exist either" (p. 3). Pakes goes on to say that "Alexander (1953) noted that [an Indian] has no understanding of art, only understanding in art" (p. 3).

These comments point out the pervasiveness of visual expression in aboriginal communities without succumbing to categorization. As we will show, our research site in northern Ontario has yielded us valuable insights into the beliefs of the community. It is particularly interesting to consider here that our participants consider art to be everything that is created from the heart, mind, and spirit. It is a genuine experience that cannot be artificial or contrived, all the while keeping in mind that "art" as a word or concept did not and does not actually exist in the indigenous language. Yet there are experiences that the community members who understand the ways of the past and the present can talk about as representing a view of art.

Jamake Highwater (1986) suggests that there have been many examples of Indian and non-Indian artistic pursuits that have met with positive reconciliation rather than perpetual stalemates between such issues as the definition of art, particularly as we are now beginning to anthropologize the west. However, the greatest tension exists between the experience of Native people and non-Native expectations or ideals. When conflicts have arisen, First Nations artists have had to make some strong personal and cultural stands.

Probably the greatest single question is "what imagery is *really* Indian?" (Highwater, 1986, p. 223). Aboriginal peoples before white settlement actively engaged in visual forms of expression in their daily lives. As white settlers encroached upon their lands and beliefs, a tourist trade emerged that gradually eroded the dynamic character of their lives and created a tourist industry. Obviously, the control of their imagery changed dramatically according to the purpose of the creation. Tourist items were created according to what would sell, thereby often trivializing the imagery of the community. Contemporary Native artists wish to control the imagery of their own art rather than allowing non-Native peoples to define the nature and role of art. This domination is readily apparent in the power structures of art galleries and museums, and in the consumer world. Although it would be easy to suggest that the search for artistic identity is a result of Native peoples on one side and non-Native peoples on the other side, it would not be true. Some First Nations artists are concerned with traditional images and media while other artists "are fighting for the freedom of their imaginations against conservative Indians and non-Indians who attempt to promote a form of Native imagery that is both questionable in its historical basis and outmoded in its aesthetic conviction" (Highwater, 1986, p. 223). The reality of today is that contemporary First Nations artists are becoming more individualistic, rather than tribal, in their artistic achievements.

As our participants remind us, there is an unspoken obligation among First Nations artists to find their own style (not to copy others) while learning techniques through observation of others working through the process. The harmonious coming together of heart, mind, and spirit of the creator ensures a personal style that is nurtured in the aboriginal context. This is consistent with Highwater's (1980) belief that what makes an Indian painting "Indian" is not the choice of subject matter — that is, Indian scenes — but rather the mentality that is used in the process of creation. That mentality may choose conventional or traditional techniques, styles, etc., just as easily as choosing a more contemporary approach without losing the "Indianness" of the painting. The artist transforms the world through the acts of seeing and creating. The mysterious way this transformation occurs accounts for the inseparability of visual expression from spiritual beliefs in most tribal cultures. "Art is one of the central ways by which mankind ritualizes experience and gains access to the ineffable — the 'unspeakable' through images and metaphors" (Highwater, 1980, p. 19). Every aspect of daily life, activity, thought, and feeling permeates the artist's vision of the world. In this way, the outward artistic expression is very much a reflection of life, activity, thought, belief, and feeling.

In recent years, concern has been raised regarding a form of cultural plagiarism or appropriation of images when one culture's images influence another. For instance, some critics say that some Native artists were influenced by cubism, while some Native people would say that cubists were influenced by tribal art. Still others believe that these borrowed influences are acceptable as long as the influences that are borrowed are transformed by the mentality of the people or individual into their own *experience*. The issue of appropriation continues to be debated.

In traditional or prewhite settlement times, it was heresy among many tribal groups for an individual to question or depart from tribal ways or communal mentality. Harmony within the group was valued above all else. In fact, the highly individualized Eurocentric notion of artist and the artist's efforts to be original, assertive, and innovative were virtually unheard of in pre-1960s First Nations peoples. It was an offence to the community to "act out of personal conviction" (Highwater, 1980, p. 17). Concurrently, some non-aboriginal artists have rebelled against notions of individualism in their own artistic production, suggesting possible cross-cultural influences.

Over the last three to four decades, several groups of rebellious artists have defied tribal rules. A group of Woodland artists from northern Ontario are one such group. This group has focussed on the oral traditions of the Ojibwa–Odawa–Cree peoples and the visual representation of legends of their region. Ojibwa artist Norval Morriseau brought this imagery into the modern art world by defying the rules of the community (McLuhan and Hill, 1984). His influence has been felt on such other artists as Daphne Odjig (Odawa), Samuel Ash (Ojibwa), and brothers Goyce and Joshim Kakegamic (Cree). Although Morriseau went against tribal rules, he still presented himself as an Ojibwa individual. Many objected to his use and public display of images that were once held sacred and holy, highly spiritual, and powerful: it may have been perceived as sacrilegious to display the work in this way. For him, however, his images were sanctioned by the creator to be seen by a wider audience (see Hill, 1994).

Native artists often repeat artistic symbols. Dimondstein (1992) states that "inherent in such traditional forms are symbols that embody the memory of a specific people" (p. 50). Pakes (1987) also supports the notion that " . . . it is important to realize that despite the differences in materials — say acrylic and oil paints versus Native dyes and paints — underlying concepts from the old days continue unbroken into the present. There are ties with the past in the work of the present" (p. 1). "Culture is dynamic, ever changing, and there is no black and white division between traditional and contemporary. . . . It is almost a state of mind. Tradition cannot be measured, it simply exists within everything; it is an essence that tells us who we are" (Coe, 1976, p. 46). "Time is ignored in favor of continuity. It is not intellect, but heart" (Pakes, 1987, p. 2). "Art and belief for any true artist are inseparable and coterminous" (Pakes, 1987, p. 3).

A self orientation is commonly found among westernized countries and cultures. In this system, individuals are expected to pursue private interests without concern for the group or community. On the other hand, a collectivity orientation, often found in First Nations groups, expects individuals to consider the welfare of the group first (Warner, 1986). Cultures change and it is true that no culture fits perfectly into either orientation, but there are strong tendencies toward one or the other.

Coe (1976) states that there has been a "sense of continuity" within Native art objects despite many cultural changes over the years. "It is partly because their scale is psychic, not material, so they relate to one another under the encompassing umbrella of the sacred circle" (p. 19). As long as this state of mutual strength and understanding exists, the art will survive. This would seem plausible if artists expressed themselves in terms defined by their cultural beliefs and values. Despite the seeming cultural cohesion, there is a distinct individualism that one artist cannot duplicate the other. Therefore, one artist's work is quite distinct from the others. Hill (1972) explains that an artist "must express feelings and emotions he knows; only someone who has lived and shared the life of an Indian community, as have Allan Sapp or Daphne Odjig, can gain the insight necessary to recreate that life in their art" (p. 2).

Many First Nations artists must deal with the issue of personal and cultural identity, or individuality and collective identity. As Houle (Saulteaux artist and curator) suggests, "individuality operates in the language of paradox, irony, and ambivalence" (cited in Watson, 1993, p. 37). Watson extends this by saying, however, that "a collective sense of identity requires a unifying language of spirituality" (p. 37). First Nations artists attempt to combine these identities in their lives and works of art. Other cultural groups may also exhibit a similar sense of collective identity in their visual production.

Imagery

There is a "common belief that traditional art has the power to preserve a threatened culture" (Highwater, 1986, p. 225) through the heart, mind, and soul of the people. Highwater criticizes this view, saying that painting and sculpture created in the first half of the twentieth century were based on stereotypical views of what it meant to be Indian and also what the appropriate media were for Indian artists to use. Typically, these views were not grounded in distant history. For instance, buttons now on button blankets (Haida) were introduced by Europeans. Historically, these blankets were made with shells. Numerous other examples also exist, such as the introduction of silver, seed beads, and print-making. Each of these introduced materials became integrated into the work of First Nations artists and craftspeople.

While on reservations, Native artists produced art for members of society, often for white Canadians. These products were not considered art by their creators, since what they created could not be separated from daily life. In order to secure the economic well-being of the community, goods were produced that in turn were sold to white people. The creations were tradition-oriented but with a mixture of outside expectations in order to ensure sales. Thus, the commodification of expression began.

It is important to remember that cultures are dynamic rather than static. Thus, it is unwarranted to debate what materials are appropriate to First Nations cultures and to prescribe that imagery remain pure to a traditional ideal. What is more important is to consider what images and attitudes are appropriate in First Nations art. Artists respond to their thoughts and feelings. If these thoughts and feelings correspond with materials and styles that are conventional in nature, the artist will choose conventional materials and styles. However, if the artist has ideas and emotions that are far removed from his or her cultural roots, the individual may be inclined to use new materials and styles to express a personal individualism. Highwater suggests that "the images and feeling of any kind of art are the sole province of the artist, and no ethnic or nationalist mandate should be allowed to divert painters or sculptors from whatever they determine to be the vision inherent in their work" (1986, p. 226).

This brings us to the issue of who has the right to define First Nations art. Historically, Native peoples have been segregated in various ways by the dominant culture — for instance, on reservations and in residential schools. One could also argue that experts in the field of art working in art galleries and museums (and other aspects of society) who insist on speaking for First Nations peoples are actually continuing to segregate Native peoples by doing so. Unfortunately, there also remain factions within Canadian First Nations communities that do not allow for widespread consensual support of First Nations leadership.

Townsend-Gault (1991) states that Native art really is not a category, "but a sociopolitical situation, constituted by a devastating history, by tribal and local Canadian politics, by the shifting demographics of the non-Native in a pluralistic society like Canada, by the worldwide ethnic revival" (p. 67). Art, therefore, is inseparable from cultural identity. And if we can call it Native art, one must also remember that it has many diverse voices.

History

The individual First Nations artist as historian — that is, as a witness to historical events — has been neglected in many accounts of history. Highwater (1980; 1983; 1986) details accounts of Native artists who recorded events as far back as the beginning of the nineteenth century. The unfortunate controversy surrounding these artifacts exists because many institutions and individuals do not recognize or accept the possibility that these are factual documents. For instance, rock pictographs record the appearance of the first ships to arrive in Canada. The Micmac oral tradition describes these images as floating islands with the sailors and rigging as bears in trees (MacDonald, 1993). Although these interpretations may not match many others, they form a particular perspective from that time period. This form of alternative history has gone virtually unrecognized in the compiled records of Canadian history.

Another area of controversy exists in the domain of history. The discipline of art history as commonly understood in Eurocentric philosophy subscribes to eight key concepts (Calvert, 1988): landmark works, style categorization or style development, attribution or authentication, iconography, function, restoration, socio-cultural interpretation, and provenance.[4] In the study of First Nations forms of visual expression from the past, certain problems arise from the lack of "fit" with these concepts. It may be wise to look at each of them in turn, keeping in mind that the following descriptions are brief and presented from a purely formalist point of view in common practice. In fact, not all historians, nor all cultural-historians, would necessarily subscribe to these views. In recent years, other forms of art history have become prominent in the field (see, for example, Fitzpatrick, 1992, and Addiss and Erickson, 1993). One of the fathers of twentieth-century art history, Erwin Panofsky, would caution us in the following three levels of analysis: "the first requires practical experience from the viewer; the second demands knowledge of the cultural sources, themes, and concepts; and the last calls for synthetic intuition, an understanding of the human spirit" (Addiss and Erickson, 1993, p. 50). Ideally, these levels should be handled not separately but simultaneously. Unfortunately, Panofsky's notion of understanding cultural influences of the work before interpreting the work was often misunderstood or ignored, as expert and lay historians, until very recently, more often than not neglected to consider contextual meaning in a significant way. Therefore, try to consider the following points as they have been commonly played out in the public domain of art history, keeping in mind that the discipline of art history is constantly changing.

First, we are probably all familiar with well-known artists such as Picasso whose art is considered exemplary. Landmark works are seen as exemplary works of a particular style or period. The view that certain works require our attention points to an underlying assumption that change is an improvement and the unique is better than the traditional. This view is contrary to the views of traditional societies that sought continuity in cultural beliefs and used replicated motifs in their imagery.

Style categorization or style development is a concept that assumes that the artist is first and foremost an individual seeking to discover his or her individuality. Granted, styles are also situated within cultures and thus can be categorized and identified, but, again, the emphasis is upon change and explaining change as a result of other individual artists. For some First Nations artists, style analyses may not be appropriate. Often, visual expressions are governed by tradition and continuity rather than the promotion of change.

Attribution or authentication is concerned with who made the object. The value of an object is directly connected with the name of the particular artist. Prior to the modern Indian art movement, First Nations artists and craftspeople were seldom identified with objects. Again, the individual is not promoted, and the collective sense of the community and the culture is a characteristic of many First Nations cultures.

Iconography is concerned with the meaning of visual symbols. In Eurocentric art history, this has commonly come to mean in practice that works of art have their own detached and objective meanings, separate from daily life. Therefore, art is separate from everyday life (although Panofsky would disagree with this interpretation, it unfortunately holds even today for many people). For most Native art forms, the meaning is assumed to be embedded in the symbolic and metaphorical attributes of the purposes and materials in the piece. Sometimes the meanings are hidden from view by shamans who purposely did not disclose the ritual meanings of objects.

The functions of objects are another area of controversy. In Eurocentric thought, art objects are typically not functional, yet in First Nations groups, the functions of objects, are essential to understanding the meanings and values of the objects to the community. Objects have power through the ceremonies and beliefs of the culture.

The concepts of restoration and preservation are uniquely valued by Eurocentric thought. Original objects, or objects as close to this state as possible, are viewed as evidence of earlier times. The value of an object increases with age and rarity, and thus great efforts are made to restore and preserve objects. The assumption underlying the concepts of restoration and preservation is that linear time exists. For many cultures, time is not linear but rather experienced simultaneously in unity with nature. The present moment is the important moment, not the past or the future. Thus, objects were made as needed and according to specific purposes. These cultures would prefer to use and replace objects as they became worn out. Many First Nations cultures did not seek to acquire objects as possessions.

Socio-cultural interpretations of objects are necessary in considering the influences of the society and immediate culture on the creation of works (Phillips, 1993). Although this is often a separate category in the description of art within formalist art history, it is absolutely critical and central to Native art history. A socio-cultural understanding is needed of the integrated nature of First Nations cultures that leads up to the creation of the work.

Finally, the concept of provenance seeks to situate the history of the work itself. Until the arrival of the Europeans, understanding the provenance of a work was not important. In fact, many questions surrounding Native-made artifacts simply cannot be answered. Calvert (1988) tells of the curator for the Glenbow Museum (Calgary) exhibition "The Spirit Sings" who found a beaded and embroidered Micmac tea cozy in a European museum that had been labelled "Micmac chief's headdress" (Harrison, 1987, p. 15). Interpretations may be misinterpretations, but nevertheless become points for discussion among Native and non-Native groups regarding Native art history.

The discipline of art history has been dominated by western thought but is being challenged by other ways of framing and understanding the world. The conflicts embedded in the central concepts of western art history point to controversies that art historians and consumers of art should address. The conflicts also help us to appreciate that no culture is static and that First Nations cultures must be allowed to evolve like any other culture (Young Man, 1992). Investigations into Native art history should portray these changes. It is very exciting that First Nations peoples are helping to redefine art history in the postmodern era.

Modernism

As soon as Europeans landed in North America, trading began. Artistic creations soon became defined through a tourist mentality (see, for example, Feest, 1992). In order to trade artifacts that Europeans would buy or trade goods for, First Nations craftspeople and artists altered the size, styles, and materials used in their goods. The selling of these goods would support their local economies.

Art is not created in an isolated context, but rather in a complex social, cultural, and economic context. Modernism in art was originally a European trend that drew upon the subjects, forms, and styles found in France, Germany, Italy, England, and Scandinavian countries. It was characterized by three attributes: questioning the portrayal of reality as purely objective and, in turn, the subject's right to measure reality; placing the role of the artist in the middle of the conflict between subject and object, the individual and society, the conscious and unconscious, thus creating great conflict for artists and often alienation; and the creation of new art forms as a way of dealing with these conflicts and in particular as a way of developing a kind of spiritual or psychic awareness (Hoffman, 1993b). Four modern styles or methods (Hoffman, 1986) deeply influenced Native art: the decorative style, used by Gauguin and Matisse; cubism, used by Picasso; abstraction, employed by such artists as Kandinsky; and the magical dimension of the thing or idea, influenced by Kandinsky yet developed by Native artists themselves. Native artists used decoration for an expressive portrayal for their belief in an all-pervasive spiritual context similar to the beliefs held by western decorative artists. Native artists often combined cubism with the decorative aspects of line, colour, and shape to form a unified expression. In fact, many artists combined decoration, cubism, and abstraction into a unified form of expression. Daphne Odjig and Norval Morriseau viewed their art in this way. Still other artists discovered that the silent life of objects possessed certain mysteries or magic that had been lost in contemporary life but were honoured in traditional rituals such as dancing. They sought to revitalize these feelings and experiences. Again, Morriseau and Odjig used these dimensions in their work as they sought to portray the mythical yet magical dimensions of their cultural legends (Hoffman, 1993a, 1993c) (see also such artists as Edward Poitras, Métis, and Joanne Cardinal-Schubert, Blood).

Houle argues that "modernism in art was not derived solely from European sources" (cited in Watson, 1993, p. 37). Kwagiulth art inspired Barnett Newman, and Navajo sand paintings influenced Jackson Pollock's drip paintings. Alex Janvier (Dene) is sometimes referred to as the first Canadian Native modernist. Unlike the Woodlands school, which consciously uses traditional sources for imagery, Janvier's vision is highly subjective and characterizes his personal spiritual quest. Much of his early work signifies personal and cultural conflict, as symbolized by his signing his works with his treaty number, 287, rather than his name.

Although these artists may have been influenced by European artists, they were not led by the same ideological conceptions. Modernism in the western world pointed to a crisis of the times, whereas the visual expressions in Native modern art represented a real alternative understanding of spirituality for specific fourth-world cultures (Graburn, 1993; Hoffman, 1986), thereby diluting or cancelling the tensions that defined western modern art. In western terms, some artists continually searched for the spiritual element that was absent in society. In Native art, however, spirituality is communally defined and oriented toward non-crisis. The controversy then becomes a debate that posits a modern or postmodern perspective of the art world against an interpretation of *ethnic art*. Unfortunately, it was modernism and postmodernism that labelled First Nations art as *primitive art*, then *primal art* and, more recently, *ethnic art* (see, for example, Vogel, 1994 and Hoffman, 1986). These euphemisms paved the way for misunderstanding. In fact, much of the *traditional* aboriginal art has not been written about as art but as artifact, as static primitive phenomena within unchanging cultures. Holding this premise, any changes denote inauthenticity, a criticism that is simply illogical. All cultures change and should be allowed to change.

In postmodernism, modernist thought is in crisis. With postmodernism comes anti-modernism. Modernism had its roots in exclusion, hierarchy, and colonization. Postmodernism has eroded divisions between high and mass culture in favour of an eclectic culture. Postmodernism is also associated with a "global village" rather than nationalism, and with that comes an influence of cultures across the world (Todd, 1992). Consequently, there exists much debate about what may be considered an influence or actual appropriation. Many aboriginal people believe that most

> Canadians do not understand the concept of cultural property, of family or cultural copyright (the history of inherited privileges passed down through public mechanisms such as the potlatch), and as such they are unprepared to deal with appropriation. Much of the discussion about appropriation and the First Nations seems to wage around two quite different interpretations of the same term to denote a contemporary or Postmodern mode of production. Artists of First Nations, however, often use the term and its implied practice as a site of cultural and political struggle. (Houle and Podedworny, 1994b, p. 75)

Pluralism is the mark of postmodernism, and with it comes an emphasis upon the uncertain and unconnected, the superficial and fictional. As personal and cultural identity issues surface in this debate, new understandings and issues will emerge.

Walking Stick (1992) proclaims that all exhibitions and panels should have minority artists rather than be multicultural art exhibitions that further segregate peoples. Many artists dealing with postmodernism are facing the issue of representation within the art establishment. However, they are also dealing with the issue of personal and cultural representation through postmodernist imagery. As such, they are addressing issues of prostitution, identity, environmental destruction, and land claims as potent subject matter for their art (see, for example, Gray, 1993 and Ryan, 1992). In so doing, they challenge viewers to reconsider taken-for-granted images of Native peoples and to reconsider the socio-political forces affecting the lives of First Nations peoples (see work by such artists as Bill Powless and Shelly Niro, Mohawk; Carl Beam and Ron Noganosh, Ojibwa; Jane Ash Poitras, Cree; Lawrence Paul Yuxweluptun, Coast Salish/Okanagan; and Bob Boyer, Métis).

For First Nations artists, postmodernism points to an emphasis upon pluralism, exploring questions of difference and similarity, and breaking down the canons of institutional art worlds. With this comes greater opportunities for expression, success, and recognition.

Success and Recognition

Highwater (1986) discusses the controversy around the success and recognition of First Nations artists. In Canada, the Thunder Bay Art Gallery sponsored *Mandate Study 1990–1993: An Investigation of Issues Surrounding the Exhibition, Collection and Interpretation of Contemporary Art by First Nations Artists* (Houle and Podedworny, 1994a). Highwater and Houle and Podedworny express many similar concerns and issues. In the 1990s, there is an underlying concern among Native artists about the labelling of their art as Native art or art created by persons of Native ancestry. This distinction may seem insignificant, but in the contemporary art world, "Indian art" is still considered a long way from ready international recognition. Many Native artists who prefer to pursue their art with little emphasis upon their ethnicity have been accepted in the international art scene. This tension is further supported by the reluctance of some art critics to give serious attention to the work of Native artists.

It took until 1992 for the National Gallery of Canada in Ottawa and the Canadian Museum of Civilization in Hull to organize and mount international art exhibitions dedicated solely to the work of First Nations artists. "Land, Spirit, Power" (Nemiroff, Houle, and Townsend-Gault, 1992) and "Indigena: Contemporary Native Perspectives" (McMaster and Martin, 1992a and 1992b) represented major exhibitions for contemporary Native artists in Canada. In western time, 1992 marked the 500th anniversary of Columbus's arrival in the Americas (at Turtle Island). "Land, Spirit, Power" brought together 53 works by 18 artists from Canada and the United States in an effort to show that Native artists are connected to the land spiritually and politically. "Indigena" re-examined "the barbarous history and bitter legacy of colonization, from the early extinction of the Taino people of the Caribbean to contemporary culture, marked by land claims and [unallayed] demands for aboriginal autonomy" (Rushing, 1993, p. 14). The two institutions created a moment in revisionist history when Native voices, Native representation, and Native communities could celebrate success and recognition. This celebration is indicative of cultural change, because in prewhite settlement Native cultures, individuals and individual achievement were not celebrated (though they were recognized) within most aboriginal communities. Ironically, not one major American institution organized an exhibition of contemporary Native American art in 1992.

The controversy of success and recognition is directly linked to another site of controversy: museums. Museums and galleries, which have different mandates in Canada, are both dealing with issues related to Native voice, Native representation, and Native community support.

Museums

Museums have traditionally collected cultural artifacts as a way of recording vanishing cultures (McMaster, 1993). Today the First Nations cultural objects collected and displayed in museums in Canada and other countries are often unrecognizable to Native families, or even worse, are stolen belongings of deceased family members. Incredibly, some people sold their belongings because they believed they would never be allowed to show them in public (Webster, 1992). Conversely, to non-Native peoples, these collections of objects are often stereotypical representations of First Nations peoples from decades or centuries ago. In recent years, though, changes have been occurring and plans are being made to stop defining the museum as an institution of cultural elitism (Menezes, 1989; Townsend-Gault, 1992), a place that honours the theft of cultural property, in favour of forging new definitions of what museums could become.

From a western perspective, objects themselves possess meaning, and therefore museums are charged with protecting objects from extinction. In that context, objects are allowed to speak aesthetically on their own without formal interpretation (Townsend-Gault, 1993). For Native people, objects represent meaning and that meaning can be clearly understood only in the culture that produced the objects. However, if you were not from that culture, the meaning may not be readily apparent. To understand the meaning, one needs to be enlightened by individuals within that cultural group. Unfortunately, curators and museologists often ask aesthetic, historical, and anthropological questions of artifacts without knowing their inherent, sacred meaning. Curators also market objects without regard for sacred meaning.

These actions have given rise to a debate regarding the return of cultural properties to the owners (Gathercole, 1986), and prompted museum personnel to reflect upon the appropriate goals of museums in a postmodern era. Many museums are calling upon First Nations people to become personally involved in museum life. This may mean sitting on museum boards, teaching curators about artifacts, or collaborating in other meaningful ways (Lynch, 1993). With land claim settlements comes the question of repatriation of cultural objects. These issues are integrated for First Nations peoples. Native peoples of today see some museums as "sites of struggle," and the struggle is just beginning.

Perhaps the most noteworthy struggle was against the 1988 Olympic organizing committee and the Glenbow Museum in Calgary for their failure to involve aboriginal peoples in the planning process for the exhibition "The Spirit Sings: Artistic Traditions of Canada's First Peoples" (Hill, 1994). The international boycott by the Lubicon Cree of northern Alberta provided the impetus to bring aboriginal peoples and museums together:

> Intending to embarrass the Canadian government at an international event, the Lubicon Cree and their supporters argued that it was hypocritical to mount a Canadian exhibition that celebrates traditional cultures when governments were still dealing unjustly with First Peoples. Caught in this whirlwind of controversy were the patrons of the exhibition, particularly, the Shell Oil Company. The Lubicon Cree took exception to Shell Oil, which owned the exploration oil leases on what the Lubicon Cree claimed to be their land. (Hill, 1994, p. 40)

The Lubicon sought to persuade museums to refrain from loaning their objects to the exhibition committee. Because of this confrontation and controversy, there has been much more dialogue between aboriginal peoples and museums, with the result being "(1) increased involvement of aboriginal peoples in the interpretation of their culture and history by cultural institutions; (2) improved access to museum collections by aboriginal peoples; and (3) the repatriation of artifacts and human remains" (Hill, 1994, p. 41).

Aesthetics

The concept of aesthetics is derived from European traditions, and although there has been a strong tendency to construct universal systems of aesthetics, recent scholarship views aesthetic feelings, thoughts, even systems as varying from culture to culture and group to group. Aesthetics at its most basic level is concerned with questions of value, beauty, truth, and goodness. What is beautiful or valuable to one group of people may not be beautiful or valuable to another. Often, it takes time and immersion in different cultural traditions to appreciate the experience and reasoning behind certain perceptions, values, and beliefs. For those of us raised in the dominant culture and its versions of reality, this shift of understanding may be difficult, but it is necessary. "No system of aesthetics applies to all art" (Haberland, 1986, p. 109).

Few First Nations languages have words that mean art or artist, and when they do, the reference is usually to "talents involving skill and craftsmanship" (Maurer, 1986, p. 144). Modernist thought tells us to look at aesthetics apart from qualities of skill and craftsmanship. This prompts a further separation of art from life in the dominant culture. In First Nations traditions, visual expression was a part of everyday life. Each individual contributed to the social well-being of the group by creating harmonious objects uniting beauty and function. These objects in turn represented the sacred nature of people's lives in harmony with the earth. "The aesthetic and technical quality of the object was a visual metaphor for a spiritual attitude, a mental state of being; consequently, even functional objects, such as spoons, bowls, robes, or moccasins, could be regarded as symbols of spiritual power or personal feeling" (Maurer, 1986, p. 144).

In the past, aestheticians and historians have assumed that because tribal cultures did not value visual expression in the same way as the Europeans, tribal cultures did not create fine art. To some, functional Native objects might be better labelled as forms of craft. Needless to say, this is an area of controversy in itself. How should art or craft be defined? Heath (1992), who has studied Native cultures and art forms, suggests that art is "a total human activity rather than a specialized ocular and aesthetic experience" (p. 29). If art must be defined, perhaps it should be considered as "the giving of form to thought" (p. 29). Using this definition, there is no need for the word "craft." Visual expression begins with thought and the meaning of life. From creative thought, form is created.

Vastokas (1992) describes the disjuncture between Eurocentric and aboriginal views toward art and aesthetics in a similar way. She believes that Eurocentric thought concentrates on art as an object, as a work unto itself with all of the apparent concrete restrictions and limitations. In this sense, art is only what goes on inside the frame. However, from an aboriginal perspective, "we are still leaving out of consideration the most vital aspect of our total experiences of these works. We leave them out because they are intangible, invisible . . . it is the intangibles which have primacy in

Native world view. The material world is simultaneously spiritual and that spirituality is manifested in the material" (pp. 29–30). Thus, Native dancers wearing masks are subject to the effects of the context, the environment, and the ceremony in which the dance takes place. Vastokas suggests that "Native art as performance" (p. 40) is perhaps the best definition of art in that it shows that the viewer must be actively participating with the work, just as the creator of the work has been actively involved. If this definition is taken seriously, all other concerns and issues in the world of aboriginal art change.

Given the conflicting views of what art may or may not be, one is left to reconsider personal and cultural forms of expression. One is also left to consider how these issues should be presented in art education classrooms.

Art Education

The curriculum for art education should respond to the controversies listed and discussed above through an approach that gives voice to a variety of cultural perspectives. In particular, Native art history, aesthetics, imagery, and response must involve First Nations peoples and non-First Nations peoples. Ideally, each of the controversies should be thoroughly studied and considered within any visual arts education setting, whether with young children or with adults in post-secondary education programs. The difficulty facing art educators becomes one of degree and depth. Living in a postmodern world indicates that many cultures and their voices need to be heard. Therefore, whose perspectives should be taught, and how much should one learn of other cultural points of view? With so many varying perspectives or frames of reference, how can educators and the public determine a sense of continuity and standards within the curriculum? These qualities may be diminishing in importance, but if they are, what qualities should educators seek for a postmodern curriculum?

Art education is one area of study in which people come together to learn about, and from, one another. Whatever philosophical view determines your perspective or frame, keep in mind that there are many other valid frames to consider as well. It is better to raise questions in an effort to begin the process of understanding than it is to remain naïve about the questions. It may also be better to spend time learning about the daily activities, thoughts, feelings, and beliefs of a particular community as a way of learning about the art or visual expression of the culture. The curriculum for art education should be based in the context of the community. Aboriginal communities may also decide to have an art(s) curriculum that is intimately situated in the life of the community, thus offering a way of learning and teaching that is situated, relevant, personal, and political. In this way, aboriginal communities would endeavour to provide a contextually based rather than a discipline-based curriculum, or, if that were not possible, to provide more emphasis upon the community than is currently the case.

The first half of this chapter has been concerned with presenting a variety of issues and controversies facing First Nations artists and their communities as they come together with other cultural views. Conflicts and tensions emerge and vie for attention and resolution. Cultures evolve and change, and with this process of evolution comes the constant search for greater understanding of the past and the constantly changing future. In presenting the following narrative summary of one community in northern Ontario, we hope to bring you to a greater appreciation of one cultural group.

A NARRATIVE SUMMARY OF ONE ABORIGINAL COMMUNITY

The following description is taken from preliminary results of a study currently in progress that examines the effects of white settlement on the art and craft of two aboriginal communities in Canada. One site is in the Pottawatomi, Odawa, and Ojibwa community of Wikwemikong Unceded Indian Reserve #26,[5] on Manitoulin Island in Ontario, and the other is at the Sechelt Nation of Sechelt, British Columbia. The purpose of our study is to collect oral histories from elders and other community members about how their artists and craftspeople assimilated, adapted, or rejected European art and craft traditions.

Research Methodology

It has been the experience of many First Nations communities across Canada that researchers have gone into Native communities to conduct research, only to depart without leaving something of benefit with the community. With this in mind, we have tried to be as unintrusive as possible, and sensitive and receptive to community involvement. Every effort has been made to fully involve the communities at each stage of the study in order to ensure that the outcomes reflect the interests and perceptions of those involved (Clifford, 1988). An archival collection of transcribed taped interviews benefits the historical society within the community.

The project is a historical (MacMillan and Schumacher, 1989; Shumway and Hartley, 1973) and ethnographic study (Clifford, 1988; Hammersley and Atkinson, 1983), using conventional historical approaches with some adaptations. Oral history techniques are essential to the study and necessary to establish a commonality of knowledge about the past and to widen understanding of a particular culture. Some participant observation has been employed to view art and artifacts as elders or community members share the oral history surrounding the creation of the objects. It is apparent that interviewees readily discuss ideas that have been passed down for two or three generations. Little knowledge remains from the era prior to white contact.

The first stage of the project involved workshops to train community members on conducting taped interviews, on the nature of questions to be asked, and appropriate techniques for eliciting valid oral history data. Any translations of interviews conducted in the Native language were also done by the community interviewers to ensure correct translations into the English language. Although one of us speaks fluent Ojibwa, there are instances where one unfamiliar word in a different dialect will completely change the meaning of a statement. The non-verbal communication that accompanies a conversation may also be "out of sync" with the non-verbal meaning attributed to a given gesture in that culture (Farrell, 1993). Therefore, it is important to have community people involved in the translation of interview transcripts.

Several community member interviewers selected people to be interviewed who were known in the community as sources of valuable information. Through mutual agreement with the interviewee, they determined the time and location of the interview. Cultural protocol that accompanies such requests is determined and followed by the community interviewers. Ongoing analysis has occurred through a discovery of themes arising from the data or transcribed interviews (Spradley, 1980; 1979).

The benefits to the community include the collection of oral history interviews, which will be stored as an archival resource within the community for curriculum development or whatever further use the community determines. The community will also benefit from the research through an improved understanding of the effects of white settlement on their art and craft forms. Monetary compensation was provided for all participants and interviewers, along with all necessary equipment required to conduct the research. Copies of all taped interviews and typed transcripts remain with the community.

The following narrative summary focusses on the transcripts collected at the Manitoulin Island site. Wikwemikong is officially recognized as an unceded Indian reserve, the only reserve on Manitoulin Island that did not sign a treaty. It is the home of the Three Fires Confederacy of the Odawa, Ojibwa, and the Pottawatomi. It is a community rich with culture and history. Its members comprise artists, actors, and authors with a wide array of talents in traditional and contemporary forms. The oral history project in Wikwemikong is a study that collects the oral history of the Anishinawbe culture while paying particular attention to the maintenance of, or changes that have affected, the arts and crafts of the community.

Interviewers were given considerable autonomy in designing openended interviews. In collaboration with several of the interviewers involved in the process, we designed an interview guide with thematic headings and suggested questions to elicit comments. The interview guide consisted of the following headings: Anishinawbe art[6] forms, pictographs, changes in art and craft as a result of white settlement, experience of arts and crafts in school, suggestions on how Anishinawbe arts and crafts should be taught in schools today, creativity and/or talent, community use of research material, and additional comments. The study is still in progress and therefore the following discussion is limited to the information gained from interviews collected to date. Nevertheless, much can be learned from these oral testimonies.

It is very important to note that at the initial discussion with the community research site interviewers, the question arose as to how "arts" or "crafts" could possibly be translated into the Native language. Since there are no words for these, the group resorted to a long descriptive sentence in the Native language. Interviewers also had great difficulty in understanding the importance of "precontact" and "postcontact" periods of times or concepts. Through lengthy discussions, we came to understand that it was our Eurocentric academic stance that wanted to categorize their experiences and beliefs — something that they had great difficulty in providing. In the end, we came to appreciate their point of view and declined to categorize their experiences as precontact or postcontact. After all, for them, the experience was continuous. One way of life did not abruptly end and another begin. Rather, there were threads of meaning running through the experience of life. This conception of time and experience has greatly influenced our thinking as is probably evident in the preceding pages of this chapter.

To set the stage for the preliminary findings of our study, the following information offers a glimpse of community life from the memories of the first- and second-generation interviewees. In earlier times, a sleigh road provided the only land access to the village and the people make reference to the fact that it was quite a rough ride. The horse-drawn sleighs or wagons being pulled over deep ruts and muddy holes are still remembered today by the people who endured the teeth-rattling ride. They lived in square timber houses, log cabins, or cottages. Most of the people also had farms and gardens. Others mention livestock and orchards, along with the traditional activity of obtaining food from hunting and fishing and collecting wild fruit and vegetables. They would tend their gardens between picking seasons of the herbs, wild fruits, and vegetables like wild rice, maple sugar, berries, and so on.

In the winter, dog teams and sleighs were still used for transportation during hunting and fishing activities. Rabbits and partridge were a daily source of food and one person remembered "baked rabbits with brown gravy and mashed potatoes" (J:31,8).[7] The traditional method of catching rabbits involved a wooden trap. The inner bark fibre of a tree was soaked in very salty water and it was strong enough to hold the weight of a log. The salt attracted a rabbit who would begin to chew on the fibre. When it chewed through the bark fibre, the log would fall on it (W:6,2). Later, snare wire was available for those who could afford to buy it.

There is also a description of dances and dinners, at the end of which was a game where biscuits, one with a marker baked inside, were passed around. The person who got the marked biscuit would have to host the next dinner the following week (J:30,8). There is no mention whether this was done only at certain times of the year or not.

Four thanksgiving ceremonies, including the hunting ceremony and the berry-picking ceremony, were held each year. In all aspects, the animals would not be forgotten, for they provided the food all year round. In every ceremony, a bit of the food expected to be eaten would be included, to show gratitude to the spirits of the animals (L:11,6).

One person mentioned how fishing was done before commercial fishnets came into use. A bait in the form of a four-inch fish carved out of cedar was jigged in a hole chopped in the ice. A spear with a rope attached would be used to spear the fish when it grabbed the bait (P:63,11). Later, the people made their own fishnets. One person who still makes fishnets learned how to make them from his father (A:22,4). The nets were not sold but used only by this family to catch fish for food.

Anishinawbe Art Forms

To begin discussion of ideas related to visual expression, some people stated that "anything that is made by hand and made out of natural materials" was Native arts and crafts, thereby signifying its authenticity (W:14,5). Another person said, "Nishnawbe art is anything that is made using natural materials and fibres" (R:19,4). As you will notice in the following descriptions, this includes a great deal of handmade materials used in the everyday life of the community.

Not everything that was made was necessarily regarded as craft work. It was a necessary item for day-to-day living (L:5,2). There was an embedded spiritual aspect for every creation. Non-Native people saw the designs as decorations when they were actually there for spiritual reasons, "to keep the spirit together, to ward off the negative," and to keep "the spirit happy" (L:6,3). There were many designs and each design carried a significant spiritual meaning. Many of the designs were also changed or hidden to accommodate the church influence.

During feasts, reed mats ten to twelve feet long were used primarily to keep a person dry while sitting on the ground, but they also had designs that were meant to keep "a person's spirit intact" (L:5,2). The reeds for the mats were collected along the shoreline, dried and dampened to make them supple, and dyed with roots and berries. The trimmings on some mats were made with pine roots. These roots, 50 to 60 feet long, were interwoven with the reeds for added stability. Sweetgrass was also woven into the centre of the mats (L:11,6). There was a meaning behind each step of the process and there were teachings that went with the creation of each mat and for its purpose (L:5,3). Every aspect of the mats — their placement, the direction they faced, how they were hung, the certain time of day they were hung (a child could not run underneath one), and the number of them — had a significant meaning (L:10,5).

Creativity and Talent

Everyone is capable of being creative and has talents and gifts that can be nurtured with a little encouragement, praise, and self-esteem[8] (R:32,7). Therefore, out of necessity, any items required could be made by anyone (J:19,5). Every Anishinawbe was very good at making everything (J:34,9). In most circumstances, there was no one to buy the supplies from or money available to purchase necessary items. At that time, everything that was made was for their own use (A:22,4). Items mentioned in the transcripts include quilts, fishnets, buckets, baskets, plates, bowls, spoons, ladles, snowshoes, axe handles, and clothes made from moose or deer hides.

One artist stated, when asked about a design, "it is all in your head. . . . You already picture which one you like . . . what's going to be the colour of it and what's going to be the meaning of it" (P:22,4). Everything he creates holds special meaning. He stated, "I put lots of memory in that . . . what it's going to be . . . sometimes in the dream, they're alive, things that you want to carve there. Seems to be pushing you to make that totem pole" (P:27,6). He mentioned that although he had never been to the area, he went straight to the cedar that he needed; "right away I see what I am going to make" (P:27,6). Another reference to images and dreams appears in one oral history account, where an artist dreams of a recurring thing as guidance to an artistic expression (H:67, 33).

Artistic Expressions

Quilts

Quilts were made from new and old things. Double-knitted dresses that are no longer in style are very strong, and warm blankets can be made by using up old woollen skirts. Everything was put to good use and nothing was wasted. There were no garbage dumps back then (R:31,6).

Carved Kitchen Utensils

There were people who made wooden spoons and they would go around to other members, selling spoons of all sizes (J:32,9). Birch was usually used for spoons because it is a soft wood. White ash and maple are much harder, but they can split if they're dried too quickly (J:33,9). The spoons made from maple were very well made, sandpapered and smooth, and they'd last a long time. Another person knew of a person in the community who made utensils like plates, bowls, spoons, and ladles from yellow birch (W:7,2).

Axe Handles

Another item that required a specialized skill was axe handles. There were different handles for different types of axe. Two kinds of ash are generally used. One is black ash that has a darker wood, but the grain is the same.

Birch could also be used as a substitute if the white ash was not available (J:34,9). This person expressed an intimate knowledge of trees as indicated in the following statement: "It is difficult to find the right white ash as they all behave differently. You have to select a tree depending on the branches" (J:35,10). One recent addition to the process is the use of the mill to make boards ready for axe handles. The choice of wood is ironwood. Then the boards are carefully selected for suitability.

Snowshoes and Leatherwork

Another person used black ash for making snowshoes. It is a very pliable wood and easy to bend to shape. In this area, deer hide was used for the webbing. The leather strips would be cut an inch and a half wide and stretched until they were only half an inch wide. It would take about two deer hides to make a pair of snowshoes (A:14,2). Other uses of deer hide include insoles for shoes, socks, dog harnesses, and the collars for dog harnesses. There were also deer-hide jackets and shirts, which kept in the heat in winter and kept you cool in summer. There were also leather coats with rabbit skin on top, and fox-fur underwear (L:13,8). One person makes jackets and dresses, beaded or braided, and laced together, creating her patterns as the market demands today (Pt:35,19). The list of creations for this person includes fans made of spread partridge tailfeathers, leather bags, jackets, sweetgrass fans, model moccasins, beadwork, vests, and skirts (Pt:47,22). In earlier times, goods were traded among tribes before currency became available.

Violins

An unusual talent is that of the violin maker. He stated, "I found some wood in the bush, curly maple" (A:24,5). Spruce is used for the top and maple for the bottom, sides, and neck. There are two pieces of wood, from the top piece, inside the violin. The black fingerboard comes from France and the violin strings come from the United States. He laments the loss of the violin players of days gone by (A:30,4). The hardest things to make, it seems, are the violin screws, which require a lot of time and patience (A:42,6).

Totem Poles

With the influx of tourists, 5- to 24-inch totem poles brought in about $300 or $400 a week in one household. Many hours were spent cutting them out, carving, and painting them. The people had been making them for at least two generations. The designs include bear faces, beaver, kingfisher, owl, eagle, woodpecker, and anything else in the area (P:22,4).

Birch Bark

There are many references to the process of removing birch bark from the tree. The following are some examples depending on the purpose, the size, and time of year. The family would head for the woods in the horse and wagon. It was a hard rough ride. The trees had to be selected with care. This would be around late June or early July. As one person said, "You could tell by the texture of the birch tree if the bark was good and firm" (R:3,1). Some people used ladders to go higher to cut the bark off. Then the sheets of bark would be left under the shade of a tree to dry out, or at times they would be wiped off with a cloth. When it was time to leave, they would be tied together with strips of inner bark or with roots. Bark scraps were wrapped on the outside to protect the good ones in the middle. "It was very heavy and hard to load into the wagon. Then you store it in a good place in the cellar for the winter" (R:4,2). Another person talked about stripping bark in the bush, where it would lay in heaps and piles. Then they were tied up until they were ready for use (A:20,3). The birch bark would be used mainly in winter when there was more time.

Birchbark Canoes

Small 14-inch birchbark canoes were made for sale. The inner bark of a bass tree was used for tying and sewing the small canoes. Children would collect the fresh roots. The smaller saplings about one or two inches wide were the best kind for the strongest root (W:10,4). The roots were only used for the bigger canoes. The root would be picked early in the spring, in May or June. It can be kept throughout the winter (A:20,3). The bass tree itself is grey on the outside but the inner bark is white in colour and it is very strong (W:11,4). Later, they dyed the roots with powder from the store (W:12,4). No one seems to remember what the price was for the canoes, but they were made in various sizes. In this family, sometimes two sacks of them would be taken to town to sell (W:14,5).

One family made a miniature canoe pattern out of cardboard and traced it on to the sheets of birchbark and cut it out to make little birchbark canoes. Little dry cedar sticks were used on the larger canoes to sew on the edges of the canoe to prevent the tearing of the bark (R:6,2). Porcupine quills had to be put on the pattern first before it was sewn together (R:13,3). Sweetgrass was also used for the little canoes, and this was picked in the middle of summer. It was picked from the roots and the brown dried parts cleaned off. The nice green ones were tied together and later thrown into boiling water to burn off insects, then they were hung to dry in the shade. Again, these were traded for food or clothing. They were also shaped a bit differently from how they were long ago (R:15,4). Fake sinew is now used, and some have tried using paint on the canoes instead of quills, but they were not accepted. The tourist market demanded the canoes be made the way they always were (R:17,4).

Birchbark Buckets

Birch bark was also used for maple syrup. Birch bark buckets were made to catch the sap. These buckets would last two to three years, if they didn't blow away (A:55,8). Some of the syrup would be sold and the rest kept for the summer. Sugar candies were also made from the syrup.

Pelt Tanning

The dogwood tree was used to dye the pelts during tanning. The tree is an orange colour. When it is used, the colour is a deep yellow, depending on how much wood or bark is used for the desired colour (J:20,6). The wood is chopped in lengths and boiled. The pelt is immersed when the fluid has cooled. This is also what was used for dying shoepacks, which are like mukluks. Although waterproof, they apparently get very slippery on the outside when wet (J:21,6).

Skin Tanning

The preparation of animal hide takes about two weeks. Each method depends on the kind of animal hide, time of year, and available natural resources. One method is described as follows. The fat is scraped from the hide, then the skin is soaked for about three to four days, and ash from the fire is added to the water. The skin is then stretched and a very sharp bone is used to scrape off the hair. It is then put back into the water and left to soak in ash, cedar, and bark from an ironwood tree. Two days later, the skin is stretched and wrung dry by putting it around a tree and winding it around a turn stick. It is then pulled and pulled until it begins to dry under the friction. By then it is soft and dry. Then the edges are sewn together to form a sack, and it is then suspended over a smoking pot. The smoking pot consists of dry brown rotted maple sticks to create smoke. The desired shade of the skin depends on the length of time it is smoked. Clothes made from this process are washable and they dry without hardening (L:11,8).

Quill Boxes

Quill boxes were originally used before the white man came for giving special gifts or asking for a special favour. Tobacco would be put in these boxes. That is why we still know them today as tobacco boxes. They are still very prized by people who buy the boxes (W:14,5).

Glue

Glue was made from the backbone of a sturgeon. The backbone is soft gristle and it boils down to a cement consistency. It was used for sealing and patching canoes, along with spruce gum (P:23,18).

Games and Toys

One person made a little cart to pull around, with wheels made from a poplar tree sawed into disks. The children played with these and loved them (J:26,7). There were horses that pulled various things, like stoneboats for hauling water or wood. Stoneboats are a flat platform sled that rocks could be rolled on to in order to clear the fields. They were also used for hauling water. Another wagon was used for hauling wood. The children saw these and copied them to make toys (J:27,7). There were also sleighs that the children made themselves. "Over the next field was a better hill that we cleared for sliding" (J:30,8). There were no store-bought toys. There were also balls. One person mentioned a ball made out of cloth with a little stone at the core. There was also hockey. They made their own hockey sticks, and played on a pond (J:28,7). As he said, "sometimes at night too with a lantern hanging. We were never lonesome or bored. We would make a fire, or we would go sliding" (J:29,7). They would also climb on the rail fences for fun. There were also skin dolls made out of tanned hide. It was skin wrapped to form the head and the rest of the hide would fall into a shawl (L:23,13).

Blueberry Harvest

Blueberries only grew on the mainland. There were none on the island and so boats were required to reach the mainland. All of the sailboats were made by the people. The mast was made out of spruce. The bigger the boat, the higher the mast. At the end of the day, the berries would be sold at one dollar a basket (now they are about fourteen dollars or more for a basket). Cranberries were also picked from the marsh which could be sold for groceries (A:69,10). To show the interconnectedness of art as the process of living, the closeness to the earth manifests itself in various forms, whether in harvesting natural fibres for the creation of objects, gathering herbs for medicinal use, or in celebrating the other bounties of the earth by picking the herbs, berries, and vegetables of the land.

There are many references to people picking blueberries to sell (J:3,1; 4,2), but also for their enjoyment. "There was a red, flat dumpling made when the berries were made into a jam. There was this dumpling with it and everyone had a good feed" (J:5,2). One person states that her grandmother told her that if she went out to pick blueberries every summer, she would have great strength and magic in her life, that she would be close to nature and never forget where she came from. So every summer, she picks blueberries to remind her that she is very close to the earth (L:23,13).

Medicinal Plants

There was one reference to a grandmother who knew which herbs to pick to heal a sick child but that the parents did not (W:2–5, 1–2). This was in direct reference to the residential school system. Another individual referred to a grandmother picking the herbs while the grandfather ground them with pestle and mortar. The herbs would be picked at certain times of the year, usually in the summer, and these would be dried for winter use (L:16,9; W:2–5,1–2). A particular mortar was used for the medicinal herbs only. One person stated that in an emergency, a person's understanding and closeness with nature would sustain him or her in the bush. Nature was there to look after you and not to be afraid of. There is comfort in the oneness with self, and the ability to know what to do through the art of healing. "Everything has a purpose, everything has a reason" (L:29,16).

Garden Vegetables

Ground corn was used for corn soup and corn bread. Hominy corn was made by soaking the corn in ashes and boiling it. There were many kinds of vegetables grown: beans, carrots, turnips, cucumbers, pumpkins, and even watermelons, but "nobody grows watermelon now" (W:9,3). There were also potatoes, peas, and barley. There are stories of returning home after picking berries to get the vegetables that had ripened (J:3,1). A big root house was used for vegetable storage over the winter months. The vegetables were not grown for sale (A:46,6–7). Yellow birch had many uses in the kitchen as a material for utensils, and pestles made from yellow birch were used to grind the corn in the mortar (W:8,3).

The Views of Contemporary Artists

Although the few contemporary artists whom we interviewed are familiar with the above oral histories of their community, they are also intensely aware of the artistic community as defined by the dominant society. They recognize that "we still have the colonial type of economic system playing here" (LB:12,16–18). Implicit within that system is the continuing concern for the tentative economic well-being of artists and craftspersons creating Native art in the community. The contemporary artists often have agents who promote their work outside the reserve. If they do not have agents, they find ways to become their own promoters, either by starting their own businesses or by opening their own galleries on the reserve. Off the reserve, agents take a share of the profits that the aboriginal artists believe should be returned to the community whenever possible. They hope to bring much of the market to them, even though they will still promote their work outside the community. The contemporary artists also recognize the inequity between the market value of their paintings and prints and that of the more traditional forms of art and craft (for instance, quill baskets). One artist in particular tried to assist basket makers in selling their art for a price that recognized the time and effort involved, but admits consumers are not inclined to pay those prices. On the other hand, his paintings sell for hundreds or thousands of dollars.

Although not all of the artists agreed on some things, there was a consensus that Native art is created from the integration of heart, mind, and soul in concert with using natural resources. Native art cannot be made without feeling. Native art cannot be authentically made with machines that reduce or cancel the feeling behind the original reason to create the image. "You have to love what you are doing with all of your heart" (JS:3,1). Art creation is an attempt to understand the world, to find the truth of your own world (JS:7,9; LB:5,10–13). There was great concern for the appropriation of Native imagery by other countries that could reproduce aboriginal objects for less cost through either cheap labour or technological means. The concern was not only for the lack of economic returns to the community but also for the inauthenticity of the creations, which are divorced of meaning and feeling.

These beliefs are also intimately tied to an understanding of creativity. Although the artists could discuss creativity as a process of doing and thinking, they are also quick to point out that creativity and art are again artificial distinctions that the dominant society wishes to see (GT:14,4–7). In Ojibwa, there are no words that delineate art and creativity. The artists would agree, however, that we are all creative, and through our efforts and perhaps discipline (JS:4,20–21) we can discover how best to be creative in order to express our feelings and heart's desire.

Suggestions for Teaching Children

Many of the interviewees had attended residential schools and this experience had severed the knowledge base to the activities and creations of their parents and grandparents.

For one person, animals were used often in storytelling to provide examples of moral values. One animal would be used to teach about stealing, another about patience and strength, another about speed, and another about the magic of expectation. You don't forget anything when it is taught to you through descriptive and contextual parables (L:20,11). The little stories heard from the grandmother were so real "I could identify with them in everyday life" (L:22,12). The time for learning about things that will protect you, help you grow, and heal you is at a very young age. "I think it's a beautiful time for a child to learn these things because your mind is so open . . . when you're a child, you're so close to the spiritual world" (L:21,12).

Storytelling was often used to provide real-life examples or analogies for individuals to take what they needed to learn at the time. This learning strategy was often discussed by community members as a typically Native teaching tool. Another idea that was also expressed was apprenticeships: spending time with individuals who were good at what you were interested in learning how to do. That way, you would learn by doing. You would also be learning the Native culture through your active involvement with it. It was very important that individuals learn about the culture of the community in the community rather than through formal schooling.

Many of the interviewees expressed some level of frustration, stating that children do not listen anymore and that they do not know anything. One person said of the teachings he received from the elders, "I have all of these things in my memory" (W:15,5; 18,6). The people seemed distressed by what they saw on television and its possible effects on the children (J:25,6; R:38,8; L:31,16; and W:18,6). One suggested that we should teach our children what good values are and why they are important (R:36,8; 38,9).

When asked about educating young people, one person suggested that children should be taken into the bush by an elder to look at the trees, being careful not to destroy other plants, thus teaching them about "good environmental living," and that children should understand and appreciate the hard work involved in each creation (R:26,5). Again, learning about the culture through cultural ways was a theme often expressed by elders and others in the community.

Conclusion

It is clear that any item made of natural material must be appreciated not only for the aesthetic effect but also the hours of work that went into its construction. The natural materials themselves have to be discussed and knowledge obtained about the process of their preparation for use.

The designs on these creations also held a spiritual significance, which was stated as "to keep the spirit together, to ward off the negative . . . to keep the spirit happy" (L:6,3). That significance is also referred to in Pakes (1987), who says "an artistic motivation was nearly always present with an intention to make the work beautiful or good or good spirit, but at the same time it was always an expression of belief; art and belief for any true artist are inseparable and coterminous" (p. 3).

Within Native communities, all forms of daily activities can be an expression of lived experience shared within the culture. Sewing, painting, writing, carving, and so on sprang from the same artistic and creative source within each individual. When a basket is examined, it is important to tell where all the materials came from, as well as how, where, and when they were picked. Every piece of material that goes into making a new whole came from another whole that needs acknowledgement to truly understand the new creation from the "mix" of others. An example of this is birchbark baskets. Students studying about the baskets would research all they could about the birch tree. They would learn at which time of the year the sap runs and the time of year the bark is easy to peel. They would also go in search of information on the pine trees whose roots were used for sewing. Depending on the area, the types of materials used would vary. This variance would be a great educational source of information on the adaptations necessary for people living in one area.

An array of arts and crafts from the same period, or from one location, would provide information about the geographical location of its makers, the land, animals, and the climate in that region. A study of moose or other animals would lead to information of its habitat, hunting methods both historical and present, leather preparation and use, hair, and everything that would be used from the animal. This would involve the complete listing of the use of every part of the animal and a description of the process of preparing the animal parts for each use.

Zastrow (1977) quotes a New Mexico potter as saying, "I believe that the children should be aware of the work that goes into it and the time that you spend making pottery; and those are the things that are of value to me, as an artist. The time and effort I put into my work" (p. 28). This statement also holds true for the people in this community. To get a "feel" for the value of something, you have to understand how and why each of the materials came to be where they are used, and in so doing you come to truly appreciate the work that went into the creation of the object.

Within the community, there are frequent references by artists to seeing images in their minds prior to the actual artistic creation. They see the finished object in their minds, or dream these objects or figures beforehand; then they introduce and shape the idea or image to the receiving media.

In McLaws (1993), Daphne Odjig commented, "There's nothing else that I like to do more than creating something out of my mind and heart, nothing else. I live it, I eat it, I breathe it" (p. 1). In one transcript from the research site (JS:5), the interviewee stated that the picture was already in his head, and he knew what colour it was to be and what the meaning was going to be. He further stated that the objects he was to carve were very much alive in the dream, and although he had never been in the area before, he knew exactly where to go for the material necessary for the carving. This is an example of the imagery or visionary source of inspiration often mentioned by Native artists.

Although this research is currently in progress and we are still working together on learning how aboriginal art has been framed, the findings to date may help to reframe the art of the people. We hope that you take the controversies and ideas away with you to reflect upon, question, and consider and reconsider often in your professional practice. Educators and members of communities need to examine "taken-for-granted" beliefs and assumptions. In so doing, we can all come to better understandings of each other's cultural beliefs and personal identities.

NOTES

1. A variety of terms denoting aboriginal peoples are used in this chapter: First Nations, Anishinawbe, Indian, Native, Métis. None of these terms should be considered offensive but rather as recognition of a multiplicity of voices.

2. An earlier version of this chapter was presented as a paper at the Canadian Society for the Study of Education conference, June 15–18, 1994 at the University of Calgary.

3. The authors gratefully acknowledge the Social Sciences and Humanities Research Council of Canada for research funding support for oral history projects currently under way with an Ojibwa, Odawa, and Pottawatomi community in northern Ontario and a Coastal Salish community in Sechelt, British

Columbia. Rita Irwin would also like to thank the Centre for Curriculum and Instruction, Faculty of Education, at the University of British Columbia, for research support.

4. The following discussion is based on Calvert's (1988) description of concepts. For a more thorough discussion of historical matters, art history students should seek many other sources that may disagree with some of the ideas presented here.

5. We would like to take this opportunity to thank all those in Wikwemikong who participated in this research and particularly Honorine Wright, Al Shawana, and Phyllis Williams, who carried out the on-site interviews. Special thanks are given to Honorine Wright, who co-ordinated the effort through her role as president of the historical society.

6. The term "Anishinawbe" is used to describe all forms of visual expression prior to, during, and after white invasion. As researchers, we first thought we could discuss "traditional art forms," but for the community interviewers this phrase posed a problem. What was traditional and what was not? In the end, we agreed to avoid using the term "traditional" in favour of "Anishinawbe."

7. References are to individuals from the community who were interviewed. A letter is attributed to each individual; the first number refers to the paragraph on the page, and the second number refers to the page of the transcript.

8. Additional insights may be gained from Irwin and Reynolds (1995) for perceptions of creativity in Ojibwa communities.

DISCUSSION QUESTIONS

1. What makes "Indian art" different from other styles and forms of art?

2. What is the role of the individual as an artist within specific First Nations cultures?

3. Who were some of the modern First Nations artists who changed the relationship of the individual to the tribe and thus the expression of personal and cultural ideas from a sacred domain to the public domain? What significance did their work have for other First Nations artists?

4. Can a non-Native person create Native art and craft? Can an Ojibwa artist create Haida art and craft? When is art appropriated and when is imagery personally created and meaningful?

5. Since there is no word for art in traditional aboriginal cultures, describe how one might interpret "art" of a traditional culture to a non-Native person without using the word art.

6. How does First Nations art benefit or suffer from a special status in the art world?

7. What objects can you identify that were made for the tourist trade?

8. Try to recall stories, values, or beliefs that may be attributed to an object. What meanings are associated with the object? Would these meanings be readily apparent?

FURTHER READINGS

Canadian Museum of Civilization. 1993. *In the Shadow of the Sun: Perspectives on Contemporary Native Art*. Hull, Que.: Canadian Museum of Civilization. This is an exhibition catalogue of the first major retrospective of contemporary Canadian Native art. The edited book combines the views of twenty artists, curators, and scholars regarding the development of contemporary Canadian Native art.

Highwater, Jamake. 1980. *The Sweet Grass Lives On: Fifty Years of Contemporary North American Indian Artists*. New York: Lippincott & Crowell Publishers. A very readable text that describes the development of contemporary Indian art in the United States and Canada. The author highlights a group of significant First Nations artists.

Lippard, Lucy. 1990. *Mixed Blessings*. New York: Pantheon Books. This book examines issues facing contemporary artists in multicultural America. Ethnicity and gender are studied in detail according to issues, themes, and influences.

McMaster, Gerald and Lee-Ann Martin, eds. 1992. *Indigena: Contemporary Native Perspectives*. Hull, Que.: Canadian Museum of Civilization. A scholarly exhibition catalogue of one of the most significant all-Native art exhibitions in Canada, held in commemoration of 500 years of colonization.

Nemiroff, Diana, Robert Houle, and Charlotte Townsend-Gault. 1992. *Land, Spirit, Power: First Nations of the National Gallery of Canada*. Ottawa: National Gallery of Canada. An exhibition catalogue that accompanied the National Gallery's first major First Nations art exhibition. Each artist is portrayed individually and within the context of the artistic community.

Wade, Edwin L., ed. 1986. *The Arts of North America Indians: Native Traditions in Evolution*. New York: Hudson Hills Press. An excellent text that raises a variety of issues and debates facing Indian artists in the postmodern era.

REFERENCES

Addiss, Stephen and Mary Erickson. 1993. *Art History and Education*. Urbana, Ill.: University of Illinois Press.

Anderson, Richard L. 1990. *Calliope's Sisters: A Comparative Study of Philosophies of Art.* Englewood Cliffs, N.J.: Prentice-Hall.

Bellah, Robert N. 1985. *Habits of the Heart: Individualism and Commitment in American Life.* New York: Harper & Row.

Calvert, Ann E. 1988. "Native Art History and DBAE: An Analysis of Key Concepts." *Journal of Multicultural and Cross-Cultural Research in Art Education* 6(1): pp. 112–22.

Canadian Museum of Civilization. 1993. *In the Shadow of the Sun: Perspectives on Contemporary Native Art.* Hull, Que.: Canadian Museum of Civilization.

Cinader, Bernhard. 1976. "Woodland Indian Art." Pp. 153–54 in *A Heritage of Canadian Art: The McMichael Collection,* ed. McMichael Canadian Collection and Paul Duval. Toronto: Clarke, Irwin & Company Limited.

Coe, Ralph T. 1976. *Sacred Circles: Two Thousand Years of North American Indian Art.* London: Hayward Gallery, The Arts Council of Great Britain.

College of Webster Art Museum. 1992. *We, the Human Beings: 27 Contemporary Native American Artists.* Wooster: College of Webster Art Museum.

Dimondstein, Geraldine. 1992. "Mythology Is not a Child's Fairytale; It's a True Inner Meaning of an Event: Discovering Cultural Kinship Through Metaphoric Connections." *Art Education* 45(3): pp. 48–53.

Farrell, Ruby. 1993. "Native Teaching Methods: An Exploration of the Use of Traditional Practical Knowledge in the Classroom." Master's thesis, Lakehead University.

Feest, Christian F. 1992. *Native Arts of North America.* London: Thames and Hudson.

Fitzpatrick, Virginia L. 1992. *Art History: A Contextual Inquiry Course.* Reston, Va.: National Art Education Association.

Gathercole, Peter. 1986. "Recording Ethnographic Collections: The Debate on the Return of Cultural Property." *Museum International No. 151* 38(3): pp. 187–92.

Graburn, Nelson H.H. 1993. "The Fourth World and Fourth World Art." Pp. 1–26 in *In the Shadow of the Sun: Perspectives on Contemporary Native Art,* ed. Canadian Museum of Civilization. Hull, Que.: Canadian Museum of Civilization.

Gray, Viviane. 1993. "Indian Artists' Statements Through Time." Pp. 137–63 in *In the Shadow of the Sun: Perspectives on Contemporary Native Art,* ed. Canadian Museum of Civilization. Hull, Que.: Canadian Museum of Civilization.

Haberland, Wolfgang. 1986. "Aesthetics in Native American Art." Pp. 107–31 in *The Arts of North America Indian: Native Traditions in Evolution,* ed. Edwin L. Wade. New York: Hudson Hills Press.

Harrison, Julia D. 1987. "Introduction." Pp. 10–16 in *The Spirit Sings: Artistic Traditions of Canada's First Peoples,* ed. Glenbow-Alberta Institute. Toronto: McClelland & Stewart.

Heath, Terrence. 1992. "Warm Art." Pp. 21–28 in *Keynote Addresses: Proceedings to the National Art Education Association Conference: The Land, the People, the Ecology of Art Education,* ed. Ronald N. MacGregor. Phoenix, Arizona, May 1–5.

Highwater, Jamake. 1980. *The Sweet Grass Lives On: Fifty Years of Contemporary North American Indian Artists.* New York: Lippincott & Crowell Publishers.

————. 1983. "North American Indian Art: A Special Way of Seeing." *Artswest* 8(5): pp. 13–17.

————. 1986. "Controversy in Native American Art." Pp. 223–42 in *The Arts of North America Indian: Native Traditions in Evolution*, ed. Edwin L. Wade. New York: Hudson Hills Press.

Hill, Tom. 1992. "Introduction." In *Indian Arts in Canada*, ed. Olive Patricia Dickason. Ottawa: Indian and Northern Affairs Canada.

————. 1994. "Between Two Potentially Strong Allies." Pp. 40–44 in *Mandate Study 1990–1993: An Investigation of Issues Surrounding the Exhibition, Collection and Interpretation of Contemporary Art by First Nations Artists*, ed. Robert Houle and Carol Podedworny. Thunder Bay, Ont.: Thunder Bay Art Gallery.

Hoffman, Gerhard. 1986. "Frames of Reference: Native American Art in the Context of Modern and Postmodern Art." Pp. 257–82 in *The Arts of North America Indian: Native Traditions in Evolution*, ed. Edwin L. Wade. New York: Hudson Hills Press.

————. 1993a. "The Aesthetics of Inuit Art: Decoration, Symbolism and Myth in Inuit Graphics; Material, Form, and Space in Inuit Sculpture; the Context of Modernism and Postmodernism." Pp. 383–423 in *In the Shadow of the Sun: Perspectives on Contemporary Native Art*, ed. Canadian Museum of Civilization. Hull, Que.: Canadian Museum of Civilization.

————. 1993b. "The Art of Canada's Indians and the Modern Aesthetic." Pp. 165–96 in *In the Shadow of the Sun: Perspectives on Contemporary Native Art*, ed. Canadian Museum of Civilization. Hull, Que.: Canadian Museum of Civilization.

————. 1993c. "Postmodern Culture and Indian Art." Pp. 257–301 in *In the Shadow of the Sun: Perspectives on Contemporary Native Art*, ed. Canadian Museum of Civilization. Hull, Que.: Canadian Museum of Civilization.

Houle, Robert and Carol Podedworny, eds. 1994a. *Mandate Study 1990–1993: An Investigation of Issues Surrounding the Exhibition, Collection and Interpretation of Contemporary Art by First Nations Artists*. Thunder Bay, Ont.: Thunder Bay Art Gallery.

————. 1994b. "Thunder Bay Art Gallery Mandate Study: Analysis of the Survery." Pp. 69–75 in *Mandate Study 1990–1993: An Investigation of Issues Surrounding the Exhibition, Collection and Interpretation of Contemporary Art by First Nations Artists*, ed. Robert Houle and Carol Podedworny. Thunder Bay, Ont.: Thunder Bay Art Gallery.

Irwin, Rita L. and J. Karen Reynolds. 1992. "Creativity in a Cultural Context." *Canadian Journal of Native Education* 19(1): pp. 90–95.

————. 1995. "Ojibwa Perceptions of Creativity." *Journal of Multicultural and Cross-Cultural Research in Art Education*.

Lynch, Bernadette. 1993. "The Broken Pipe: Non-Native Museums and Native Culture: A Personal Perspective." *MUSE* 9(3): pp. 51–54.

MacDonald, Joanne. 1993. "'The Whites Are Thick as Flies in Summertime': Indian/White Relations in the Nineteenth Century." Pp. 27–46 in *In the Shadow of the Sun: Perspectives on Contemporary Native Art*, ed. Canadian Museum of Civilization. Hull, Que.: Canadian Museum of Civilization.

Maurer, Eva M. 1986. "Determining Quality in Native American Art." Pp. 143–55 in *The Arts of North America Indian: Native Traditions in Evolution*, ed. Edwin L. Wade. New York: Hudson Hills Press.

McLaws, Miranda. 1993. "Daphne Odjig — Artist, with Paintbrush in Hand." *K'noowenchoot Aboriginal Adult Education Newsletter* 3(1): p. 1.

McLuhan, Elizabeth and Tom Hill. 1984. "The Image Makers: An Examination of the Woodland School." *Artswest* 9(4): p. 19.

McMaster, Gerald. 1993a. "Object (to) Sanctity: The Politics of the Object." *MUSE* 9(3): pp. 24–25.

McMaster, Gerald and Lee-Ann Martin, eds. 1992a. *Indigena: Contemporary Native Perspectives*. Hull, Que.: Canadian Museum of Civilization.

———. 1992b. "Indigena: Perspectives of Indigenous Peoples on Five Hundred Years." *American Indian Art Magazine* 17(4): pp. 66–77.

McMichael Canadian Collection and Paul Duval, eds. 1976. *A Heritage of Canadian Art: The McMichael Collection*. Toronto: Clarke, Irwin & Company Limited.

Menezes, Claudia. 1989. "Museum of the Indian: New Perspectives for Student and Indigenous Population Participation," *Museum International No. 161* 41(1): pp. 37–41.

Nemiroff, Diana, Robert Houle, and Charlotte Townsend-Gault. 1992. *Land, Spirit, Power: First Nations of the National Gallery of Canada*. Ottawa: National Gallery of Canada.

Pakes, Fraser. 1987. "Traditional Plains Indian Art and the Contemporary Indian Student." *Canadian Journal of Native Education* 14(1): pp. 1–14.

Phillips, Ruth B. 1993. "'Messages From the Past': Oral Traditions and Contemporary Woodlands Art." Pp. 233–55 in *In the Shadow of the Sun: Perspectives on Contemporary Native Art*, ed. Canadian Museum of Civilization. Hull, Que.: Canadian Museum of Civilization.

Rushing, W. Jackson. 1993. "Contingent Histories, Aesthetic Politics." *New Art Examiner* 20 (March): pp. 14–20.

Ryan, Allan J. 1992. "Postmodern Parody: A Political Strategy in Contemporary Canadian Native Art." *Art Journal* 51(3): pp. 59–65.

Todd, Loretta. 1992. "What More Do They Want?" Pp. 71–79 in *Indigena: Contemporary Native Perspectives*, ed. Gerald McMaster and Lee-Ann Martin. Hull, Que.: Canadian Museum of Civilization.

Townsend-Gault, Charlotte. 1991. "Having Voices and Using Them: First Nations Artists and 'Native Art.'" *Arts Magazine* 65(6): pp. 65–70.

———. 1992. "Ritualizing Ritual's Rituals." *Art Journal* 51(3): pp. 51–58.

———. 1993. "News From the Northwest." *Canadian Art* 10(2): pp. 46–51.

Vastokas, Joan M. 1992. *Beyond the Artifact: Native Art as Performance*. North York, Ont.: Robarts Centre for Canadian Studies, York University.

Vogel, M.L. Vanessa. 1994. "More Totems and Taboos: Cultivating Alternative Approaches to First Nations Art and Artists." Pp. 45–67 in *Mandate Study 1990–1993: An Investigation of Issues Surrounding the Exhibition, Collection and Interpretation of Contemporary Art by First Nations Artists*, ed. Robert Houle and Carol Podedworny. Thunder Bay, Ont.: Thunder Bay Art Gallery.

Wade, Edwin L., ed. 1986. *The Arts of North America Indian: Native Traditions in Evolution*. New York: Hudson Hills Press.

Walking Stick, Kay. 1992. "Native American Art in the Postmodern era." *Art Journal* 51(3): pp. 15–17.

Warner, John A. 1986. "The Individual in Native American Art: A Sociological View."
Pp. 171–202 in *The Arts of North America Indian: Native Traditions in Evolution*,
ed. Edwin L. Wade. New York: Hudson Hills Press.

Watson, Scott. 1993. "Whose Nation?" *Canadian Art* 10(1): pp. 34–43.

Webster, Gloria C. 1992. "From Colonization to Repatriation." Pp. 25–37 in *Indigena: Contemporary Native Perspectives*, ed. Gerald McMaster and Lee-Ann
Martin. Hull, Que.: Canadian Museum of Civilization.

Young Man, Alfred. 1992. "The Metaphysics of North American Indian Art." Pp.
81–99 in *Indigena: Contemporary Native Perspectives*, ed. Gerald McMaster
and Lee-Ann Martin. Hull, Que.: Canadian Museum of Civilization.

Zastrow, Leona M. 1977. "Two Native Americans Speak on Art Values and the Value
of Arts." *Journal of American Indian Education* 16(3): pp. 25–30.

CHAPTER 5

Contemporary Indian Women

Cora J. Voyageur

INTRODUCTION

> Indian people must wake up! They are asleep! . . . We were in touch but
> now we are not. Part of this waking up means replacing women to their
> rightful place in society. It's been less than one hundred years that men lost
> touch with reality. There's no power or medicine that has all force unless it's
> balanced. The woman must be there also, but she has been left out! When
> we still had our culture, we had the balance. The women made ceremonies,
> and she was recognized as being united with the moon, the earth and all
> the forces on it. Men have taken over. Most feel threatened by holy women.
> They must stop and remember, remember the loving power of their grand-
> mothers and mothers![1] (Rose Auger, Cree elder, Alberta)

Wake up! This statement has been repeated by First Nations women
across Canada for the past 25 years. They have been trying to get the
attention of Indian men, Indian chiefs and band councillors, the Federal
government, and mainstream society. They want to create awareness of,
and subsequently change, the circumstances of Indian women in Canada.
According to a Department of Indian Affairs demographic profile, Indian
women rank among the most severely disadvantaged groups in Canadian
society. They are worse off economically than both non-Indians and
Indian men (Indian and Northern Affairs Canada, 1979, p. 31).

Change for Indian people began after World War II. They had fought for
Canada, but when they returned they were relegated to their subordinate
position in Canadian society.

In 1969, the Liberal government's *White Paper on Indian Policy* united
Indian people in solidarity. The government was attempting to renege on
its treaty obligations and dissolve the reserve system, a move that drew a
storm of Indian protests from across the nation. The white paper was subsequently withdrawn but not before it served as a catalyst for Indian political organization.

Women organized lobby groups such as Indian Rights for Indian Women and the Tobique Indian Women's Group and forced women's issues and concerns back on the agendas of tribal administration and the government. Women had grown increasingly frustrated with their economic, social, and political situations within their communities. They had decided that they must attempt to equalize the gender biases prevalent in their communities and in Canadian law.

The gender bias in the Indian community and in Canadian legislation has a long history. Since contact with Europeans, First Nations women have been placed in a precarious situation by governments, both foreign and domestic. In the 500 years since the Indians "discovered" Columbus, the traditional role and status of First Nations women has changed dramatically.

In many communities, they were removed from their roles as advisers and respected community members by adopted foreign ideologies. Native academic Paula Gunn Allen states that Indian women and their egalitarian system were replaced by a male-dominated, hierarchical system at the behest of Jesuit missionaries (Gunn Allen, 1992, pp. 40–41). In return, Indian men were given authority and social standing. Patricia Albers, editor of *The Hidden Half: Studies of Plains Indian Women*, states that Indian women are ancillary to the male-dominated universe of Native diplomacy, warfare, and hunting featured in books, scholarly articles, and movies (Albers and Medicine, 1983, p. 2).

Women were also subjugated in the spirit world. Gunn Allen further states that female deities were systematically replaced by male deities in tribes after European contact. For example, the Hopi goddess Spider Woman was replaced by Tawa; the Cherokee goddess River Foam was replaced by Thunder; and the Iroquois divinity Sky Woman now gets her ideas and power from her dead father (Gunn Allen, 1992, p. 41).

Despite all the changes endured by indigenous peoples, many aspects of the traditional Native woman's role have remained constant. Indian women are still responsible for maintaining culture, stabilizing the community, and caring for future generations. They still play an influential yet unrecognized and unappreciated role in the community.

Contemporary Indian women share many of the concerns of women in general — for example, children, family, economics, employment, and political rights. In addition, Indian women find themselves in a unique political and social situation. In a submission to the Royal Commission on Aboriginal Peoples, the Manitoba Indigenous Women's Collective wrote:

> As Aboriginal women, we face discrimination and racism because we are Aboriginal and because we are women. We lack access to jobs, to support, to training programs, and to positions of influence and authority. (Green, 1993, p. 111)

Indian women are in a worse economic situation than non-Indian women and Indian men. They generally hold fewer jobs and have a lower life expectancy. An Indian and Northern Affairs study (1979) showed that Indian women constituted 26 percent of the Indian labour force compared with 43 percent for non-Indian women (Indian and Northern Affairs Canada, 1979, p. 20). This same study showed that a 50-year-old Indian woman's life expectancy was two years less than that of non-Indian women (Indian and Northern Affairs Canada, 1979, p. 20).

Indian women have a much tougher battle to fight in their pursuit of social and political recognition and equality. Indian women have many adversaries: government, mainstream society, and, at times, their own people. Sociologist Linda Gerber calls the situation of contemporary Indian women a "multiple jeopardy" (Gerber, 1990, p. 69). She states:

> native females suffer multiple jeopardy on the basis of a number of objective indicators of social and economic well being. The fact that Indians as a group are disadvantaged and Indian females in particular suffer the greatest disadvantage suggests that Indian status, with its historical trappings of colonial dependency does indeed create additional barriers to economic and social health. The position of Indian women with respect to labour force participation and income, suggests that they are the most severely handicapped in their exchange relations with employers. (Gerber, 1990, p. 72)

This chapter examines the roles and concerns of Indian women in contemporary Canadian society. It argues that specific events such as the creation of the Indian Act in 1869 and the passing of Bill C-31 in 1985 have had a great impact on Indian women.[2] To fully understand the present social, political, and economic position of Indian women in Canada, one must first look at Indian women in a historical context. It is certain that past events laid the foundation for the current situation.

Since the early 1970s, Indian women had organized and found their own political voice. Indian women had had their voices appropriated by others and thus were essentially silenced. Métis academic Emma LaRocque, in the preface to *Writing the Circle: Native Women of Western Canada*, states that Native women were "wordless," that their words were literally and politically negated (LaRocque, 1990, p. xv). Their concerns and needs were determined and articulated by their husbands and fathers, missionaries, and government agents. This has changed; Indian women are no longer relying on the government or male-dominated Native political organizations to determine their fate. They are speaking for themselves collectively for the first time since European contact. Kenneth Lincoln, author of *Native American Renaissance*, refers to this articulation as a "rebirth" (Tsosie, 1988, p. 2).

The tenacity and relentless efforts of Indian women such as Sandra Lovelace, Yvonne Bedard, and the late Jenny Margetts have won them recognition as worthy adversaries. However, this political activity also brought them scorn and resentment. Nellie Carlson, an activist with Indian Rights for Indian Women, states:

Indian women worked so hard to have [Bill C-31] passed. We had no
money; our lives were threatened, we were followed everywhere we went,
our phones were tapped — that's how Indian women were treated for
speaking out.[3]

She further stated that Indian Rights for Indian Women fought for 16
years to regain status for Indian women. Their hard work brought some
victories, such as the passing of Bill C-31 in 1985. Bill C-31 attempted to
eliminate the sex discrimination in the Indian Act by reinstating Indian
status to women who married non-Indian men and others who lost their
status for a variety of reasons.

It has been a long struggle for Indian women to tell their own story.
Women have emerged from the purely domestic roles to share in the
rebuilding of their communities. Their concern for community improvement has made them tireless workers and enduring advocates. However,
Indian women still encounter many obstacles in their pursuit for a better
community.

Indian women must contend with many archaic notions that date as
far back as contact with Europeans. Racism and the stereotyping of
Indian women illustrate this. American Indian lawyer and scholar
Rebecca Tsosie speaks of the myth of Indian women in the bifurcated role
of either "Pocahontas" or the "squaw," as illustrated in a series of Holly-
wood movies (Tsosie, 1988, p. 2). Although some of these situations have
faded over time, the legacy of past attitudes is still being felt by Indian
women today.

FACTORS LEADING TO THE PRESENT SITUATION

Many factors have led to the lower social, economic, and political situation
experienced by most Indian women. These factors include the European
hegemonic view of the New World; the historical unimportance of women
in European society; the subjugation of Indian people; ethnographic practices that misinterpreted or ignored women's issues; and the adoption of
European values and governing systems by Indian men in the community.

European Hegemony

European expansion marked the transition to modern times (Clough and
Rapp, 1975, p. 139). With colonization, the Europeans brought a self-
imposed burden of "civilizing the barbarians" (Clough and Rapp, 1975,
p. 125).

Upon contact, Europeans had established opinions of cultural, intellectual, and structural[4] supremacy over those encountered in the new land.
European ideology stated that their civilization was superior to all others;[5]
Indians were savages; women were socially and politically invisible; individualism and patriarchy[6] prevailed. These attitudes caused the Europeans

to "fix" unacceptable social conditions. They also affected the recording and writing of history dominated by men. Europeans viewed men, the holders of power and privilege, as the creators of civilization: analytical, logical, and inherently superior to women (Chalus, 1990, p. 32).

The Historical Unimportance of Women

History was, and some may argue still is, a man's world. With the exception of the likes of Cleopatra, Joan of Arc, Queen Elizabeth I or Queen Victoria, few women have been viewed as significant to the course of history. In public affairs, women have been invisible, viewed as chattels owned by men. They were not given political or social rights. Thus, European women had little or no political or economic power.

European men set standards for woman's decorum, which stated how a cultured woman should conduct herself. Restraint, modesty, submission, compliance, and piety all combined in the creation of a gender role for women (Chalus, 1990, p. 38). Women were seen as being psychologically unstable, physically fragile, and morally susceptible. It is not surprising that these attitudes and standards were transported to the New World and imposed upon Native women by European men.

Prior to colonization, women were a strong force in many Indian societies.[7] Legal scholar Robert Williams states that in a number of North American Indian tribes, women traditionally selected male chiefs as political leaders and could also remove them (1990, p. 1034). Also, in many tribes, women owned substantial property interests, including the marital home, and exercised exclusive dominion over the means of production and the products of major subsistence activities such as farming (Williams, 1990, p. 1034). Women in many tribes held the power to initiate or call off war.

The Iroquois confederacy operated on a matriarchal system prior to the arrival of the Europeans (Native Women's Association of Canada, 1992, p. 2). This system was based on the concepts of equality between the genders. Iroquois women played a profound role in the political and economic life of the community. They traditionally played important roles in their communities as nurturers, educators, and providers.

Ethnocentric Historical Records

Since the written word is considered the "true medium" of historical accuracy, history was left to the discretion of the literate. Those with the ability and opportunity to write had their own agendas to promote. Early accounts of the position of Indian women in their cultures were written by male European fur traders and missionaries. These early accounts tell us as much about the ideological perspectives of the authors as they do about the subject at hand. Explorers and traders were part of the patriarchal and hierarchical structure that dominated women. As a result, they did not acknowledge the contributions made by Indian women to everyday life. Patricia Albers writes that journalistic accounts ignore or trivialize women's activities and experiences by dealing with and writing about Indian men (Albers and Medicine, 1983, p. 3). Much of the early literature on Indian women contradicted what was to come later. The early ethnographic record supplies ample evidence of a variety of roles for Indian females. For example, anthropologist Judith Brown states that older women in the Wabanaki, Algonquin, Delaware, Powhatan, and Iroquois tribes had authority over kinsmen and had the right to exert power over them and extract labour (Brown, 1982, p. 144). Females in the Wabanaki tribe achieved positions of leadership in both religious and political spheres when they reached middle age (Ezzo, 1988, p. 141).

Despite evidence from some early descriptions of women's authority, it is clear that reporting of Indian activities has often been based on purely ethnocentric interpretations.

Anthropologist Alice Kehoe states that at the turn of the century, ethnographers were frustrated in their quest for data by the traditions of their discipline (1983, p. 53). However, because they viewed Indians as a "dying breed," it became important that details of Indian life be collected for posterity. As a result, there was a big push for ethnographic information related to Indians.

Encounters between recorder and subject were limited in duration and frequency. The resulting data were sometimes inaccurate and contained both gender and ethnocentric biases. One example of misinterpretation is the explanation why a woman walks behind her husband. The assumption of the female's inferior status clouds the real reason the Indian man walks in front of his wife: it is the man's responsibility to protect his wife because she is the giver of life and more powerful than he.

Data collection was guided by conventions that did not allow for accurate depictions of either the roles or the contributions of Native women. Ingrained biases were prevalent in all aspects of information gathering. One reason is that anthropologists were predominantly male. Their scholarly custom was to speak exclusively to male subjects (Kehoe, 1983, p. 54). Common practice dictated that the ethnographer and his male assistant interview a limited number of middle-aged and elderly Indian men about life in the community (Kehoe, 1983, p. 54). If and when Indian women were interviewed, the situation was uncomfortable for the women, who were accustomed to being insulted by European men (Kehoe, 1983, p. 54). In addition, it was culturally inappropriate for Indian women to discuss "women's roles and practices" with males (Kehoe, 1983, p. 54).

The hegemonic ideals of European traders and missionaries supplanted the indigenous perspective on Indian women. In contrast to what was written about Indian women, indigenous customs held women in high regard; they were powerful within their communities.

Subjugation of Indian People

One of the primary reasons for the situation of Indian women today is that Indians, in general, were subjugated by the immigrant European society. The subjugation was based on the myth of the savage Indian, who could not own land. Europeans viewed the land as vacant and therefore free for the taking (Cumming and Mickenberg, 1972, p. 18).

Missionary and government ideology held that the only way for Indians to survive was to give up everything that defined them as a people: religion, language, lifestyle, and identity. For example, residential schools were created to convert Indian children from "savages" to "civilized" citizens for the betterment of the Indian and society as a whole (Voyageur, 1993, p. 2).

Duncan Campbell Scott, assistant deputy superintendent of Indian Affairs, implemented an assimilation policy to rid Canadians and the government of the "Indian problem" (McDonald, 1987, p. 30). The Parliamentary Subcommittee on Indian Women and the Indian Act (1982) noted:

> Between 1913 and 1930 the administration of Indian Affairs followed a rigid policy of forced assimilation. Traditional practises such as the Sundance and the Potlatch were prohibited and traditional languages were suppressed. Duncan Campbell Scott in explaining the rationale for changes to the legislation in 1920, said "Our object is to continue until there is not a single Indian in Canada that has not been absorbed into the body politic. This is the whole object of this Bill. (McDonald, 1987, p. 30)

The elimination of the Indian would occur through education and religious training in European customs and values. Separate legal Indian status was conceived as a stopgap measure by white legislators, who expected that Indians would gradually abandon their Native identity in order to enjoy the privilege of full Canadian citizenship — a state to which all would and should aspire (Francis, 1993, p. 201).

When Indians met the minimal requirements for citizenship — literacy, education, and "acceptable" moral character — they were allowed the rights of full citizenship through voluntary enfranchisement.[8] They would be allowed to vote, purchase alcohol, and obtain land under the homestead system, and would no longer have to live under the aegis of the repressive Indian Act. It is ironic that enfranchisement, the right of full citizenship, was used as both a reward and a punishment for Indians. It was a reward if you obtained a university degree, joined the military, or became a minister. But enfranchisement was a punishment if you were caught in possession of alcohol or raised the ire of the Indian agent who had the discretion to delete anybody from the band list.

The Indian Act

The British North American Act of 1867 gave the power of legislative control over Indians and their lands to the federal government. Thus empowered, the Canadian Parliament began drafting provisions for what was to become the Indian Act. The Indian Act was, and perhaps still is, the most oppressive legislation in Canadian history. Prior to the Indian Act, the statutory definition of Indians was all persons of Indian blood, their spouses, and descendants. This definition was to be applied when determining the rights to possess or occupy lands. However, in 1869,[9] the government passed an act aimed at the gradual enfranchisement of Indians. The act determined the scope of government responsibilities with those who entered into treaties.

The first Indian Act to bear the official title the Indian Act was passed in 1876. This act redefined Indian as:

> Firstly: any male person of Indian blood reputed to belong to a particular band;
> Secondly: any child of such person;
> Thirdly: any women who is or was lawfully married to such a person. (Paul, 1993, p. 19)

The Indian Act encompassed virtually every aspect of Indian life. It was primarily social legislation, but it had a broad scope with provisions for liquor control, agriculture, education, bylaws, mining, Indian lands, and band membership (Paul, 1993, p. 13).

Impact of the Indian Act on Indian Women

The Indian Act of 1876 consolidated legislation already in place. The measure depriving an Indian woman of her status when she married a non-Indian was first legislated in the 1869 Indian Act (Jamieson, 1978, p. 72). This act was also the first legislation that *officially* discriminated against Indian women by assigning them fewer fundamental rights than Indian men. Gender-based, discriminatory provisions within the Indian Act limited Indian women's social and political rights.

The enactment of discriminatory legislation aimed at Indian women through the Indian Act placed women in a subordinate position to men. This contributed to cultural changes in many Indian tribes that had previously acknowledged the political power of women. For example, the treaty process required that "official" representatives be elected. This practice eliminated women from local and national politics. Men were legally given more political power than they possessed under traditional politics.

Until 1951, the Indian Act denied Indian women the right to vote in band elections, to hold elected office, and to participate in public meetings that decided band business (Fiske, 1990, p. 122). The few administrative and political decisions allowed to Indians by the Indian Act were to be made by Indian men. Thus, Indian women's traditional social and political powers were legislated to Indian men.

The 1869 Indian Act determined legal status by patrilineal affiliation. Indian women were not legal entities and had virtually no rights. The political status accorded them was that of chattel of their husbands, much like the political status accorded to European women in their patriarchal society. If an Indian man were enfranchised, his wife and minor children were automatically enfranchised. At the time, it was thought by Euro-Canadians that enfranchisement as Canadian citizens was the most desirable goal for Indians to attain.

If an Indian woman married an Indian man from another reserve, she then became a member of her husband's band. The act stated that an Indian woman must follow her husband. If her husband were to die or she were to divorce her husband, she could not return to her reserve.

There were provisions stating that upon the death of an Indian man, his estate passed to his children, not to his wife.

The most troublesome portion of the 1869 Indian Act for women was section 12(1)(b). This section further illustrates the male bias in the Indian Act. It pertained specifically to Indian women losing their status by marrying non-Indian men. It stated:

> 12.(1) The following persons are not entitled to be registered, namely . . .
>> (b) a woman who married a person who is not an Indian, unless that women is subsequently the wife or widow of a person described in Section 11.[10] (Jamieson, 1978, p. 8)

If an Indian woman married a non-Indian man, she then became a non-Indian in the eyes of the government: she became one with her husband, who became in effect her owner under the patriarchal legislation. She was stripped of her Indian identity and not able to live on the reserve with her extended family. Many Indian women who married out had no idea that they had lost their Indian status until they attempted to return to their reserves following the breakup of their marriages.

What made this section so discriminatory was that if an Indian man married a non-Indian woman, he did not lose his status. Yet a non-Indian woman who married an Indian man became an Indian in the eyes of the law and was given band membership. The new-found Indian status was not stripped from non-Indian women if or when they were divorced or widowed. These non-Indian women and their children maintained band membership.

Indian women were adversely affected by the male bias in the Indian Act. They were not independent. They were adjuncts to their fathers or husbands and were not legal entities unto themselves. They had no legal recourse.

THE BEGINNING OF CHANGE

Legislative Changes

The 1960s brought a number of legislative changes that greatly affected the political position of Indian people. As Indian organizations formed, they fought for and achieved many changes. As demands for aboriginal and treaty rights grew, so too did demands for equality by Indian women.

The discriminatory treatment of Indian women was chipped away by a number of legislative changes. The most significant were the Bill of Rights, 1960; the Charter of Rights and Freedoms, 1982; and Bill C-31, 1985.

The Bill of Rights

The Bill of Rights was enacted by the federal government in 1960. Unlike the United States, which had a bill of rights added almost immediately to their constitution, the Bill of Rights was omitted from the Constitution Act, 1867 in Canada. It was not until after World War II that Canada, like most developed countries, saw the need to protect civil liberties (Hogg, 1992, p. 779). Section 2 of the Bill of Rights provided that any federal statutes or regulations that infringed any of the rights listed in the bill would be brought to Parliament's attention. However, there was a legal debate about the effect of this provision: did section 2 render the infringing laws null and void, or was it merely to be used as a guide? This was not settled until the *Drybones* case. Section 1 of the Bill of Rights guaranteed equality to all under the law regardless of race or sex.

Court challenges, dealing with a variety of issues, contributed to amendments to the Indian Act. For example, the *Drybones* case dealt with Indians being treated differently from non-Indians, while the *Lavell*, *Bedard*, and *Lovelace* cases dealt with gender discrimination under the Indian Act.

The first important Indian case to challenge the Bill of Rights was the *Drybones* case in 1969. Drybones was an Indian man charged with possession of alcohol. The Indian Act discriminated on the basis of race because an Indian was not permitted to possess alcohol off a reserve. The basis for the legal argument was that since this was not true for non-Indians, the law discriminated against Indians. The *Drybones* case successfully argued that Indians and non-Indians were not treated equally under the law. This case also saw the Supreme Court of Canada decide the effect of section 2 of the Bill of Rights. It held that any federal law that infringed the Bill of Rights would be inoperative. Thus, section 2 was more than a guide.

Other Bill of Rights cases that dealt more specifically with Indian women were the *Lavell* and *Bedard* cases. These were the first cases to attempt to gain Indian women recognition as "full persons" with the same rights and status as Indian men (Atcheson, 1984, p. 12). They challenged section 12(1)(b) of the Indian Act as being discriminatory against Indian women and sought to have the section declared inoperative.

Jeanette Corbiere Lavell was an Ojibwa woman who lost her status after marrying a non-Indian man. She challenged the band administration's decision to strike her name from the band list (Atcheson, 1984, p. 12).

Yvonne Bedard, a Six Nations women, tried to return to her reserve to live in a house that was left to her in her mother's will. Because she had married a non-Indian, her name was taken off the band list. Since she was not considered a band member, she and her children were ordered to leave the reserve (Atcheson, 1984, p. 12).

Lavell and Bedard argued that they were discriminated against on the basis of sex, which contravened the Canadian Bill of Rights. The two cases were heard together before the Supreme Court of Canada. The Supreme Court affirmed a lower court's decision upholding the validity of section 12(1)(b), which deprived Lavell and Bedard of their Indian status. The decision stated that the Canadian Bill of Rights meant equality only in the administration and enforcement of the law. The actual substance of the law could discriminate between men and women as long as the law was applied by its administrator in an even-handed way (Atcheson, 1984, p. 12). Thus, the Supreme Court of Canada backtracked from the *Drybones* case by refusing to declare a federal discriminatory section of the Indian Act inoperative.

Another important case to challenge section 12(1)(b) of the Indian Act was the *Lovelace* case of 1981. Sandra Lovelace, a Maliseet women, lost her status and band membership when she married a non-Indian man. She took the Canadian government to an international court, the United Nations Committee on Human Rights, because her rights as an Indian women were denied by section 12(1)(b), which the Supreme Court of Canada had upheld as valid legislation (Stacey-Moore, 1993, p. 22). She won her case and brought international shame to the Canadian government. The Human Rights Committee found the government of Canada in breach of the International Covenant on Civil and Political Rights to freedom from sexual discrimination (Silman, 1987, p. 251). However, the government of Canada delayed four years before amending this discriminatory legislation. Meanwhile, other Indian women's groups were lobbying the government, national Native organizations, and local band administrations to deal with their concerns. For example, the Tobique women marched from their New Brunswick reserve to Ottawa to protest housing conditions. This action saw 200 women and children make the seven-day trek (Silman, 1987, p. 149).

The Bill of Rights lost most of its significance with the adoption of the Charter of Rights and Freedoms in 1982.

The Charter of Rights and Freedoms

In 1982, the Canadian Constitution Act terminated the United Kingdom's imperial authority over Canada and the Charter of Rights and Freedoms was adopted. The Charter protects certain fundamental rights and freedoms, one which is equality before the law. Indian rights had to be entrenched in the Constitution for the paternalistic attitude of the Canadian government to end. Indian organizations had to do some effective lobbying in Canadian Parliament to get aboriginal and treaty rights entrenched.

Section 15(1) of the Charter states:

> Every individual is equal before and under the law and has the right to the equal protection and equal benefit of the law without discrimination and, in particular, without discrimination based on race or sex.

In addition, section 28 states:

> Notwithstanding anything in this Charter, the rights and freedoms referred to in it are guaranteed equally to male and female persons.

Although both sections stated that discrimination on the basis of sex and race would contravene the Charter of Rights and Freedoms, the Indian Act continued to do exactly that. It was not until three years later that the discriminatory provisions of the Indian Act were amended.

Although section 35 of the Charter of Rights guarantees aboriginal and treaty rights to Indian people and section 27 states that rights apply equally to men and women, Native women were not assured by governments or Native leaders that they could speak to their concerns. The Native Women's Association of Canada wrote the following about the process of entrenching aboriginal rights into the Constitution: "These arrangements are required to provide an arrangement that gives Native women and their children a destiny that they can participate in full and direct themselves" (Stacey-Moore, 1993, 21).

The entrenchment of the Charter of Rights was a major step toward ensuring the rights of Native women and would assist in fighting discrimination based on gender.

Bill C-31

Bill C-31 came into effect on April 17, 1985. This bill was meant to rectify the infamous section 12(1)(b) of the Indian Act. Bill C-31 was also meant to restore Indian status to people who had been enfranchised. Some have argued that Bill C-31 is an Indian issue rather than solely an Indian women's issue, since enfranchisement occurred for a number of reasons: obtaining a university degree, joining the military or the clergy, or voluntary enfranchisement (Sanders, 1984, p. 38). However, it should be seen primarily as a women's issue because women were affected the most by involuntarily losing their status for marrying a non-Indian man. Joan Holmes, researcher for the Canadian Advisory Council on the Status of Women, states that 12 305 of 16 980 losses of status, or 72.5 percent, were to women because of marriage to non-Indians (1987, p. 9). A United Nations Human Rights Committee report states that in Canada for the period 1965 to 1978, there were 510 marriages between Indian women and non-Indian men, while there were 448 marriages between Indian men and non-Indian women (McDonald, 1987, p. 28).

The Indian Act requires that Indians be registered on a central registry and that applicants apply for Indian status to the registrar (Paul, 1993, p. 6). Bill C-31 states that those eligible to be registered as status Indians include:

1. women who lost status as result of marriage to non-status men;

2. individuals who lost status or were denied status under other discriminatory provisions of the Indian Act;

3. individuals who lost status through enfranchisement, a process under the old act whereby persons could voluntarily give up status; and

4. children of persons in any of the above categories (Paul, 1993, p. 6).

In addition, Bill C-31 gave individual bands the authority to determine their own band membership. In other words, only Indian Nations should be able to decide who their members are, and what their rights and responsibilities are to those members. This is where much of the present-day contention lies.

Although the principle of the Bill C-31 was to rectify the past injustices of the Indian Act, it appears to have created new problems. For example, Bill C-31 allows for a separation of status[11] and band membership.[12] The band determines membership while the federal government determines status. Band councils made up primarily of men determine whether Indian women who married out can become band members again.

Therefore, Bill C-31 has created new problems by stratifying Indian status: status Indian, band member, and combined status and band membership.

CONTEMPORARY INDIAN WOMEN'S CONCERNS

Anthropologist Joanne Fiske studied the link between political and social life on a British Columbia Indian reserve. She writes that Indian women's domestic responsibilities are undifferentiated from community obligations (Fiske, 1991, p. 127). Women are expected to share their surplus food, to assist young people, and to intervene in domestic disputes in an effort to restore harmony. She concluded that the Indian women could not fulfil their domestic goals without political action (Fiske, 1991, p. 136).

The Indian world is a political world; there is no getting around it. As Karen Illnik states, "If you don't want to get involved, you really have to work at it" (1990, p. 37).

Women of the New Brunswick Tobique Reserve took some radical steps to improve their economic and political situation. Women were desperate for housing. Many women found themselves and their children out on the street with no place to go. Some women were kicked out of their houses by their husbands.[13] Since the Indian Act gave men sole ownership of the family houses through certificates of possession, their wives had no housing rights and no legal recourse (Silman, 1987, p. 11). They took action by marching on Ottawa to protest their situation.

Indian women found themselves at the mercy of their husbands, the Chief and Council, and the federal government. This situation of male domination in the Indian community[14] was brought about by many factors.

Adoption of European Values

One of the major problems faced by contemporary Indian women is male domination. There is a discrepancy between the traditional respect accorded to Indian women and the reality of gender tensions generated within the community (Fiske, 1991, p. 130).

In a submission to the First Nations Circles on the Constitution, Mary Stanaicia addresses the adoption of non-traditional leadership principles by Indians. She writes:

> The Indian Act imposed upon us a patriarchal system and laws which favoured men. By 1971, this patriarchal system was so ingrained the "patriarchy" was seen as a "traditional trait." Even the memory of our matriarchal forms of government and descent was forgotten or unacknowledged. How can our Aboriginal leaders argue a case for traditional laws and customs when they continue to exclude women? Recognizing the inherent right to self-government does not mean recognizing and blessing the patriarchy created in our communities by foreign governments. (FNCC, 1992, p. 34)

It appears that Indian men have adopted the attitude that Indian women are dispensable. This has likely resulted from their indoctrination in residential schools, the practices legislated by the Indian Act, and through Euro-Canadian control of the socialization process of society in general. A submission to the First Nations Circles on the Constitution echoes the impact of the Indian Act on Indian government. It states:

> Contrary to our traditional systems, the Indian Act system provides a political voice only to elected chiefs and councillors, normally residents on reserve and usually male. The Indian Act silences the voice of the Elders, women, and youth. We believe that true Aboriginal government must reflect the values which our traditional governments were based. (FNCC, 1992, p. 34)

Indian leaders — that is, Indian men — must loosen their grasp on the power given to them by the government. They must remember that they are there to serve the people. Men must be re-educated about the nature of their responsibilities in our efforts to abolish the experience of subjugation of women in our communities (Monture-Okanee, 1992, p. 260). Indian women have suffered from the lack of respect and validity shown to them by those who were traditionally their protectors — Indian men.

Community Conflict over Legislative Change

Another reason for the contemporary situation is the conflict raised in the communities over the legislative changes described above. Challenges by Native women to the non-status issue were attacked by male-dominated Indian organizations, the largest being the National Indian Brotherhood (which later became the Assembly of First Nations, or AFN). They feared that if the Indian Act could be struck down on the basis of discrimination, Indian people generally might lose certain special rights under the Indian Act. They also felt that the Indian Act should be kept intact for use as a bargaining tool with the federal government (Paul, 1993, p. 31). The National Indian Brotherhood and other organizations lobbied the government to allow bands to deny women their full status. They wanted to be able to determine band membership. Noel Starblanket, president of the National Indian Brotherhood, stated:

> The Canadian Government cannot change one section of the Indian Act without looking at the effect those changes will have on the Indian people of our communities. We feel the wrong being done to Indian women and their offspring cannot be undone by imposing further hardship on the rest of Indian people. (Paul, 1993, p. 31)

There was a general fear that the success of any equality argument would undermine the Indian Act's special protections, and the white paper's policy could succeed through court decisions, even though it had been defeated politically. Chiefs and councillors are primarily concerned about the long-range cultural and economic impact in their community (Opekokiw, 1986, p. 16).

There has been much conflict between Bill C-31 Indians (those recognized under Bill C-31) and band members over the distribution of already scarce resources. Housing has been the source of one such conflict (Silman, 1987, p. 11). Reserves usually have a long waiting list for housing. Reserve people already on the waiting list for housing grew resentful of the perceived "special status" given to new Indians who desired to move back to the reserve (Paul, 1993, p. 68). There was a belief that Bill C-31 Indians did not have to wait as long for houses or were placed at the front of the waiting list.

Some bands have not given band membership to people given status by the federal government because they do not have the resources or the land base. Most reserves are already overcrowded. Many feel that conditions will worsen if there is a rush of reinstated Indians wanting to return to the reserve. Pamela Paul, in her study of the impact of Bill C-31 on First Nations people, states that many reinstated people say that they are not interested in returning to the reserve because they are established off the reserve and that the reserve has nothing to offer them as far as housing or employment is concerned. They say that they are more interested in health and education benefits (Paul, 1993, p. 108).

This has created a great deal of tension and conflict between reinstated members and band councils. In some cases, such as the Sawridge Band in Alberta, there has been a continuance of discriminatory practices. The band has developed a rigorous and prying membership code so that few, if any, can qualify for membership. Indian women have not been welcomed back with open arms and warm hearts, which is the normal Native custom. Patriarchy cannot be solely blamed for this situation. It can be viewed more as an economic guarding of scarce resources by the band. However, continued discrimination by band administrations has left many Indian women sceptical about whether male-dominated organizations and band councils will ensure their political rights.

Reinstated Indians are referred to as "C-31s" and sometimes scornfully called "paper Indians" or "new Indians" (Paul, 1993, p. 94). Bill C-31 has further divided the Indian community, and given rise to negative attitudes on the reserves toward reinstated Indians. It seems that C-31s are being blamed for creating or exacerbating social problems occurring on the reserves. One band administrator stated that the influx of C-31 people is bringing a change in the culture, a change in ideas into the community. He also blames them for increased drug, alcohol, and child abuse problems. He even blames them for a decrease in church attendance[15] (Paul, 1993, p. 97). But this band administrator ignores the fact that Indian culture is not retained when non-Indian women become mothers of their children. In fact, according to Kathleen Jamieson, a researcher for the Advisory Council on the Status of Women/Indian Rights for Indian Women, during the period from 1965 to 1976, the ratio of Indian men marrying non-Indian women to Indian women marrying non-Indian men was 0.8:1 (1978, p. 66). These data show a constant increase in the number of Indian men marrying non-Indian women — from 258 in 1965 to 611 in 1976. These men did not lose their status for marrying out as Indian women did. It is sad that Indian men feel obliged to protect their non-Indian wives' newly found Indian status at the expense of the status of their own mothers, sisters, and aunts.

The fear of the influx of reinstated Indians to reserves has been unfounded to date. Gail Stacey-Moore, spokesperson for the Native Women's Association of Canada, states that of the 70 000 reinstated Indians, only 1400 (2 percent) have moved back to the reserve (1993, p. 22).

Political Inequality

A third factor of concern to Indian women is political inequality. Most of the elected leaders in the Indian community are male. Although traditionally many leaders in the Indian community were male, women's input was sought in decision-making. This practice stopped when Indian agents and other Indian Affairs officials chose to deal exclusively with Indian men. Locally elected Indians have been placed in the position of intermediary between the Department of Indian Affairs and the people. It is a state-

bound authority. The department makes all important and fiscal decisions. Sometimes the band in question is informed and consulted and
sometimes it is not. The band administration simply carries out instructions given by the department.

The chief and council are the allocators of the scarce resources to band
members. Joanne Fiske calls them "power brokers" (1990, p. 123). They
determine which band members receive limited band employment opportunities, education funding, occupational training, housing allocation,
housing repairs, and other band-administered services. This power, however limited, has a great impact on the day-to-day lives of band members.
In some respects, the chief and council have taken over the role of Indian
agent as intermediary and allocator of resources. It is in the best interest
of the band members to stay in the favour of the allocators.

Although women make up about 50 percent of the population, they do
not make up 50 percent of the leadership. There are only a handful of
women chiefs.[16] There is no guarantee that the concerns of women, such
as child care, housing, education, family violence, and social programs,
will be heard and acted upon. A very high percentage of Indian women are
single parents and this may lessen their influence with the male-dominated council. Single mothers may have less political influence in the
community or less time to deal with community issues. The inability to
muster political power can cause a person to be disregarded.

Women hold many of the administrative positions[17] but few of the decision-making positions. They do the preparatory work and must receive
approval from a superior, usually a male. However, this situation may
change over time because more women than men are receiving post-secondary education.

Women remain in good standing with the reserve administration. If
they speak out against inequality and injustices, they are labelled as "trouble makers." This can set up barriers for them in subsequent encounters
with the band. Glenna Perley summed up the political climate when she
stated, "the chief treated us like we were invisible," after she and other
women exposed the treatment they had received at the hands of the chief
and council to the media (Silman, 1987, p. 124).

SPEAKING WITH OUR OWN VOICES

Indian women have taken the initiative to protect their own rights and
interests. The past has shown that Indian men have not always acted in
the best interest of Indian women. Bold moves on the part of Indian
women have ruffled a few feathers in the Indian community. For example,
the Native Women's Association of Canada attempted to block the national
referendum on the Constitution because they were excluded from constitutional negotiations. They charged that the consultation process used by
male Indian leaders infringed upon their right to freedom of expression

(Stacey-Moore, 1993, p. 21). Indian women demanded a seat at the constitutional table to ensure that women's issues would be addressed, and demanded a portion of the funding given to male-dominated political organizations.

This action caused a stir in the Indian community. It pitted males against females. The Native Women's Association of Canada was accused of placing individual rights over the rights of the collective. They were accused of going against tradition. It is ironic that these same males live under the untraditional Indian Act. Women were also pitted against women because NWAC was seen as dividing the Indian community and wiping out the image of a "united front" under the Assembly of First Nations.

By speaking on their own behalf, Indian women can pursue their own priorities and concerns. For example, family violence is of great concern to Indian women. It is thought that since women and children are usually the victims and men are the usually perpetrators, women are concerned that male-dominated organizations and band councils will not give this issue priority. It is seen as a woman's problem and not a general societal problem. If the Indian communities cannot address Indian women's concerns, then women must advocate on their own behalf.

CONCLUSION

It appears that the tension between Indian women and male-dominated organizations began when Indian women decided that they would stand up for their rights as individuals.

Women have reached a point in their political and individual growth where they will not be denied. They will not sit helplessly by while others negotiate their future, because this has not worked for them in the past. They have gained their own voice and can now articulate their own needs and concerns. They must work against adversity because some leaders are not prepared to relinquish power.

Women are moving ahead. Women as the workers and care-givers feel a responsibility to the children and grandchildren in the community. They initiate and sustain many community programs and services. They are prepared to deal with societal problems such as family violence, child abuse, unemployment, and alcohol abuse. They do not want these issues to be swept under the rug. Elder Joyce Leask states:

> There are lots of times that people have things to say that hurt us, but that's what life is all about: a lot of frank statements that must be made. We must be strong enough to be honest. (FNCC, 1992, p. 56)

Indian women are playing a greater part in the education of their children and in promoting health, training, and recreational programs in the communities.[18] They are concerned by the loss of cultural identity and the decrease in language retention in the youth because of pressures from the dominant society.

Indian women were able to bring about social, educational, and economic change through their relentless efforts and unwavering commitment to their community. Indian women were in desperate situations and felt they had nothing to lose because their children's welfare and their cultural identity as Indian women were at stake.

In many respects, Indian women still play the traditional role they played before European contact; they are still the care-givers, the transmitters of culture, and the nurturers, and they are ultimately responsible for the future of the community; only time and the conditions have changed. Although they are no longer the social and political equals of Indian men that they once were, Indian women be will not be given the respect and recognition they deserve until Indian men heed their call. Wake up!

NOTES

1. Excerpt from Rose Auger's chapter in Meili (1991), p. 25.

2. The perspectives put forth in this chapter are based on the author's personal experiences as a Native woman, conversations with other Native women, and a survey of existing literature.

3. Personal interview with Nellie Carlson, activist and founding member of Indian Rights for Indian Women in Edmonton, April 4, 1993.

4. Structural supremacy means the hierarchical structure of European society at the time of contact.

5. This ethnocentric view may be shared by all people, but we are dealing specifically with the European view of Indian people and the results of that view.

6. According to *Webster's Ninth New Collegiate Dictionary*, patriarchy is a social system marked by the supremacy of the father and the legal dependence of wives and children, and the reckoning of descent and inheritance in the male line.

7. It must be understood that there is no "pan-Indian" form of social structure or hierarchy with regard to the treatment of women. Tribes were individual in their customs and values and must not be viewed as a homogeneous group. The practice of viewing all Indians in the same light is one that exists to this day and that must be resisted.

8. There is a distinction between voluntary enfranchisement, which a person could apply for and be granted, and involuntary enfranchisement, which occurred when an Indian person lost his status through offences such as possession of alcohol.

9. The Gradual Enfranchisement Act of 1869 was the first legislation to deal with Indians after Confederation, but there had been earlier acts. The Act for the Gradual Civilization of the Indian Tribes of Canada was passed in 1857.

10. Section 11 states:
    11(1) Subject to Section 12, a person is entitled to be registered if that person
        (a) on the 26th day of May 1874 was, for the purposes of An Act providing for the organization of the Department of the Secretary of State of Canada,

and for the management of Indian and Ordinance Lands, being chapter 42 of the Statutes of Canada, 1868 as amended by section 6 of chapter 6 of the Statutes of Canada, 1869, and section 8 of chapter 21 of the Statutes of Canada, 1874, considered to be entitled to hold, use or enjoy the lands and other immovable property belonging to or appropriated to the use of the various bands or bodies of Indians in Canada;

(b) is a member of a band
   (i) for whose use and benefit, in common, lands have been set apart or since the 26th of May 1874 have been agreed by treaty to be set apart, or
   (ii) that has been declared by the Governor in Council to be a band for the purpose of the Act;

(c) is a male person who is a direct descendent in the male line of the male person described in paragraph (a) or (b);

(d) is the legitimate child of
   (i) a male person described in paragraph (a) or (b), or
   (ii) a person described in paragraph (c);

(e) is the illegitimate child of a female person described in paragraph (a), (b) or (c);

(f) is the wife or widow of a person who is entitled to be registered by virtue of paragraph (a), (b), (c), (d) or (e).

11. Status means registration on the Main or Central Indian Registry in Ottawa.

12. Band membership means that the band accepts and recognizes a person as a member.

13. On the Tobique reserve, some men kicked their wives and children out of their homes and moved their girlfriends in. Women had no place to live and resorted to living in abandoned shacks or tents.

14. Community means the reserve and the urban area.

15. It is interesting that church attendance is viewed as a measure of tradition in a community, especially since traditional religious rituals do not occur in a church.

16. Currently in Alberta, two of 44 Indian chiefs are female. There may be a number of reasons for this situation. Females running for chief may not have the sufficient community support to attain the office. In addition, women may choose not to venture into the primarily male domain until there are more females holding the post.

17. Administration means secretarial and support staff.

18. The author drew this conclusion after attending a number of conferences dealing with Native women's issues.

DISCUSSION QUESTIONS

1. How did European society subjugate its women?
2. How was the Canadian government responsible for the current situation of Indian women?
3. What was the impetus for Indian women to organize?
4. Why is it in Indian men's best interest to maintain the status quo?

5. What are some of the benefits and some of the drawbacks of Bill C-31 status?
6. Will Indian women's social, economic, and political position ever equal Indian men's?

FURTHER READINGS

Green, Joyce. 1993. "Constitutionalizing the Patriarchy: Aboriginal Women and Aboriginal Government." *Constitutional Forum* 4(4): pp. 110–119. This article details the political jockeying between the Native Women's Association of Canada (NWAC) and male-dominated political organizations during the constitutional negotiations in 1992. It explains NWAC's position.

Holmes, Joan. 1987. *Bill C-31 Equality or Disparity: The Effects of the New Indian Act on Native Women*. Ottawa: Canadian Advisory Council on the Status of Women. This background paper was commissioned by the Canadian Advisory Council on the Status of Women to gauge the impact of Bill C-31 on Indian women. It clearly explains sections of the Indian Act that discriminated against Indian women.

Jamieson, Kathleen. 1978. *Indian Women and the Law in Canada: Citizens Minus*. Ottawa: Minister of Supply and Services Canada. This classic was commissioned by the Canadian Advisory Council on the Status of Women and Indian Rights for Indian Women. It laid the foundation for social and political arguments that are still cited almost 20 years later.

Paul, Pamela Marie. 1993. *The Trojan Horse: An Analysis of the Social, Economic and Political Reaction of First Nations People as a Result of Bill C-31*. Master's Thesis, University of New Brunswick. This thesis analyzes the social, economic, political, and cultural complexities as viewed by the people affected by Bill C-31. It is a candid review of the internal and external conflicts caused by this policy, which was to correct past wrongs.

Silman, Janet. 1987. *Enough Is Enough: Aboriginal Women Speak Out*. Toronto: Women's Press. This book details the struggles of the Tobique women of New Brunswick in their fight for political and social rights and their part in the implementation of Bill C-31. It contains memoirs of the women involved in their ongoing struggles with fellow reserve members, band administrators, and government officials who helped.

Stacey-Moore, Gail. 1993. "In Our Own Voice." *Herizons: Women's News and Feminist Views* 6(4): pp. 21–23. Gail Stacey-Moore speaks to the recent reclaiming of Indian women's social and political voice. Indian women have begun to articulate their own issues and concerns and have confronted male-dominated Indian organizations with those same issues.

REFERENCES

Albers, Patricia and Beatrice Medicine, eds. 1983. *The Hidden Half: Studies of Plains Indian Women*. New York: University Press of America.

Atcheson, M. Elizabeth. 1984. *Women and Legal Action: Precedents, Resources and Strategies for the Future*. Ottawa: Canadian Advisory Council on the Status of Women.

Brown, Judith. 1982. "Cross Cultural Perspectives on Middle-Aged Women." *Current Anthropology* 23: pp. 143–53.

Canada (FNCC). 1992. *First Nations Circle on the Constitution*. Ottawa: First Nations Circle on the Constitution.

Chalus, Elaine H. 1990. *Gender and Social Change in the Fur Trade: The Hargrave Correspondence, 1823–1850*. Master's Thesis, University of Alberta.

Clough, Shepard and Richard T. Rapp. 1975. *European Economic History: The Economic Development of Western Civilization*. New York: McGraw-Hill Book Company.

Cumming, Peter A. and Neil H. Mickenberg. 1972. *Native Rights in Canada*. Toronto: Indian-Eskimo Association of Canada and General Publishing Co.

Ezzo, David A. 1988. "Female Status and the Life Cycle: A Cross Cultural Perspective from Native North America." Pp. 137–44 in *Papers of the Nineteenth Algonquian Conference*. Ottawa: Carleton University.

Fiske, Joanne. 1990. "Native Women in Reserve Politics: Strategies and Struggles." *Journal of Legal Pluralism* 30: pp. 121–37.

Francis, Daniel. 1993. *The Imaginary Indian*. Vancouver: Arsenal Pulp Press.

Gerber, Linda M. 1990. "Multiple Jeopardy: A Socio-Economic Comparison of Men and Women Among the Indian, Métis and Inuit Peoples of Canada." *Canadian Ethnic Studies* 22: pp. 69–80.

Green, Joyce. 1985. "Sexual Equality and Indian Government: An Analysis of Bill C-31 Amendments to the Indian Act." *Native Studies Review* 1(2): pp. 81–95.

———. 1993. "Constitutionalizing the Patriarchy: Aboriginal Women and Aboriginal Government." *Constitutional Forum* 4(4): pp. 110–19.

Gunn Allen, Paula. 1992. *The Sacred Hoop: Recovering the Feminine in American Indian Traditions*. Boston: Beacon Press.

Hogg, Peter W. 1992. *Constitutional Law of Canada*. Scarborough: Carswell Thomson Professional Publishing.

Holmes, Joan. 1987. *Bill C-31 Equality or Disparity: The Effects of the New Indian Act on Native Women*. Ottawa: Canadian Advisory Council on the Status of Women.

Illnik, Karen. 1990. "Breaking Trail." *Arctic Circle* 1(3): pp. 36–41.

Indian and Northern Affairs Canada. 1979. *A Demographic Profile of Registered Indian Women*. Ottawa: The Branch.

Jamieson, Kathleen. 1978. *Indian Women and the Law in Canada: Citizens Minus*. Ottawa: Minister of Supply and Services Canada.

Kehoe, Alice. 1983. "The Shackles of Tradition." Pp. 53–76 in *The Hidden Half: Studies of Plains Indian Women*, ed. Patricia Albers and Beatrice Medicine. New York: University Press of America.

LaRocque, Emma. 1990. "Here Are Our Voices — Who Will Hear?" Pp. xv–xxix in *Writing the Circle: Native Women of Western Canada*, ed. Jeanne Perreault and Sylvia Vance. Edmonton: NeWest Publishers.

McDonald, Michael. 1987. "Indian Status: Colonialism or Sexism?" *Canadian Community Law Journal* 9: pp. 23–48.

Meili, Diane. 1991. *Those Who Know: Profiles of Alberta's Native Elders*. Edmonton: NeWest Publishers.

Monture-Okanee, Patricia A. 1992. "The Roles and Responsibilities of Aboriginal Women: Reclaiming Justice." *Saskatchewan Law Review* 56: pp. 237–66.

Native Women's Association of Canada. 1992. *Native Women and the Charter: A Discussion Paper*. Ottawa: Native Women's Association of Canada.

Opekokiw, Delia. 1986. "Self Identification and Cultural Preservations: A Commentary on Recent Indian Act Amendments." *Canadian Native Law Reporter* 2: pp. 1–25.

Paul, Pamela Marie. 1993. *The Trojan Horse: An Analysis of the Social, Economic and Political Reaction of First Nations People as a Result of Bill C-31*. Master's Thesis, University of New Brunswick.

Silman, Janet. 1987. *Enough Is Enough: Aboriginal Women Speak Out*. Toronto: Women's Press.

Stacey-Moore, Gail. 1993. "In Our Own Voice." *Herizons: Women's News and Feminist Views* 6(4): pp. 21–23.

Tsosie, Rebecca. 1988. "Changing Women: The Cross Currents of American Indian Feminine Identity." *American Indian Culture and Research Journal* 12(1): pp. 1–31.

Voyageur, Cora J. 1993. "An Analysis of the University of Alberta's Transition Year Program, 1985–1992." Master's thesis, University of Alberta.

Williams, Robert. 1990. "Gendered Checks and Balances: Understanding the Legacy of White Patriarchy in an American Indian Cultural Context." *Georgia Law Review* 24: pp. 1019–44.

CHAPTER 6

Aboriginal Leadership

Peter McFarlane

A t the time of contact with Europeans, the First Nations of Canada
had developed finely tuned political institutions that were remarkably successful in keeping order, respecting individuals, and promoting
social harmony. As in all other aspects of Native cultural, economic, and
political life, however, Native political institutions were as varied as the 50
or so peoples who make up the First Nations.

The semi-settled Iroquois differed significantly from woodland peoples, who in turn were very different from the Plains Indians and the fisher
peoples of the West Coast. Each group — indeed, each nation — had
developed its own distinct institutions to serve its specific needs.

The arrival of the Europeans posed an unprecedented challenge to
Native societies and, by extension, to Native leadership. As European
power began to gain greater control over larger and larger areas of North
America, Native societies were subjected to — in a relatively short time —
the aggressive evangelism of the Christian churches, successive plagues
of deadly new diseases, and the gradually engulfing wave of European
settlement. From contact to the arrival of the settlers, Native leaders were
faced with the challenge of trying to prevent, or at least to slow, the European onslaught. After traditional Indian lands were settled and the colonial powers were exerting effective control over First Nations territory, the
challenge became one of preserving First Nations sovereignty and seeking redress on the land question. That struggle continues today.

In this chapter, we will look at how individual Indian leaders, from traditional leaders like Big Bear to modern organizers like George Manuel,
fought first to hold onto their peoples' sovereignty and later struggled to
win it back from a Canadian state that was determined to undermine their
efforts with an array of political, legislative, and, in some cases, military
manoeuvres.

TRADITIONAL NATIVE LEADERSHIP

Although the differences among Native societies at contact were consider-able, there were a number of broad similarities in both the style and the role of Native leadership within their communities. Most cultures, for example, had some system of hereditary or life-chiefs, with built-in checks and balances to ensure that the successor represented the interests of the people and that the serving chief did not abuse his powers.

Part of the success of the hereditary chief system can be attributed to the fact that the next in line for the position generally was trained in his role from a very early age by the elders in the community.[1] In the case of the Plains Cree, for example, the young hereditary chief was examined closely in his youth to make sure that he displayed the qualities of indus-triousness, courage, and self-control needed to carry out his future responsibilities (Mandelbaum, 1979, p. 106).

Like other Native political institutions, the process for anointing lead-ers drew much of its strength from its flexibility. If the youth showed that he did not have the mettle for the job, he could be passed over and someone else would be found to fill the role. Similarly, in most societies, if a hereditary or any chief showed incompetence, lack of self-control, or anti-social behaviour, or if he pursued policies that a significant number of people in the community opposed, the dissidents could simply drift away and informally coalesce around someone they thought a more worthy leader.

In some cultures, this practice occasionally led to a band's having two or more chiefs, who were recognized as such, serving with a minimum of friction between them (Mandelbaum, 1979, p. 108). At other times, a serv-ing chief would step aside and make room for the more successful rival. Clinging to power was extremely difficult, if not impossible, since the peo-ple could refuse to co-operate, even with a hereditary or life-chief.

The fact that the people could withdraw their support from a leader at any time made it essential that the chief not only serve the people's will, but also try to ensure that rifts did not develop in the community on important issues. Consensus politics was not merely a shared value but an integral part of the Native political system.

A successful chief would have to master the art of building a consensus not only among his immediate followers, but also within the community as a whole. Along with earning the respect of the people, the chief had to retain the support of various other individuals representing separate cen-tres of influence. In woodland hunting societies, these centres of influ-ence tended to be unofficial. For example, certain individuals would be recognized as spiritual leaders and their counsel, as well as that of the elders, would be weighed along with the chief's. The most successful hunters would also be recognized as community leaders, and together the elders, spiritual leaders, and leading hunters would be given favoured places around the council fire and their words special consideration.

In semi-settled and plains hunting societies, the chief's power was more formally diluted by the separate centres of power that controlled policing, war-making, hunting strategies, and religious observances. These institutions often included a young men's or warrior's society and a women's society, as well as recognized community officials like a village crier and messenger, a religious leader, an elder who led the marches to and from the seasonal camping areas, and a war chief who generally assumed complete control of the band during times of crisis. The head of each institution was accorded his or her measure of respect while performing well-defined roles in the life of the community.

In both the wandering and semi-settled societies, this often meant that the chief's main responsibilities were guiding meetings toward consensus, managing trade, negotiating treaties with the leaders of neighbouring nations, preserving group harmony, sponsoring ceremonies, and ensuring that the basic economic needs of the people were being met.

It was in this latter role of ensuring the distribution of wealth within a society that chiefs were often judged by their own people (Manuel and Posluns, 1974, p. 95). If a family was hungry, it was primarily the chief's responsibility to ensure that they were fed. When guests visited the community, the chief was expected to feed and house them. During ceremonies, he was expected to contribute more than anyone to the communal feast. In some societies, when there was a dispute between two members of the band, the chief would sometimes be compelled to settle it by paying restitution to the injured party from his own goods in order to preserve group harmony (Mandelbaum, 1979, p. 107).

This exceptional material generosity expected of the chief extended also to the spirit. In some groups, like those of the Plains Indians, even if one of the chief's relatives were murdered, the chief was expected to forgo the blood vengeance that would be the right, or in some cases even the duty, of one of his fellow band members.

The local chief's need to promote harmony and political consensus was also felt at the tribal or national level. On issues like treaties with other First Nations, which required the agreement of the national council, the ranking chief faced the same constraints as the local chiefs. Important decisions could be taken only after a consensus had been reached — often after days of discussion. As Bruce Trigger pointed out in his study of the Huron people, "not even the smallest units were required to surrender any of their rights. No headman could rely on officially sanctioned power to see that his decisions were enforced" (Trigger, 1987, p. 54). At the national as well as the local level, the chief's influence on any issue rested on the personal trust he had earned over time and on his ability to marshal convincing arguments for or against an issue at council meetings. Even when the council came to a decision, there was no formal way to compel a dissenting band or community chief to join in the agreement.

Once a consensus had been reached, it was the ranking chief's role to sit down with his counterpart to discuss the treaty terms and to strike a final deal, which would be followed by ceremonial gift-giving and community celebrations. The gift-giving and celebrations were an essential part of the process, since most treaties were less business arrangements than genuine testaments of friendship between peoples, which the parties were assumed to have entered into in a spirit of mutual generosity.

Among the First Nations in Canada, as in the rest of North America, the natural function and style of leadership was interrupted by the arrival of the Europeans. During the period of the explorers and traders, however, those challenges often came in the form of new economic opportunities. Most Native societies already had long-standing trade relations with neighbouring peoples, so the arrival of European traders simply offered them new partners with new products to exchange. The roles of Native leaders in both inter-First Nations and European trade were also similar. They tried to maximize the economic benefits for their people by playing local suppliers off against each other, or by making an exclusive arrangement with one supplier in exchange for special price considerations.

Although the early trade between the First Nations and the Europeans tended to be beneficial to all parties, including the Native societies that acted as middlemen in the trade between the Europeans and their neighbours, the arrival of the Christian missionaries was more problematic. The conversion of part of a band or nation was a strain on the harmony of the group that was aggravated by the missionaries' systematic attacks on Native culture.

Still, it was by the arrival of the European settlers and their governments, with their vast claims on First Nations territory, that traditional Native societies were most seriously undermined. In trying to settle the European land claims, the leaders of the First Nations faced a technologically powerful force operating on a set of unfamiliar values that viewed Native societies as either opportunities to be exploited or obstacles to be shoved aside.

EUROPEAN APPROACH TO NATIVE LEADERSHIP

The British system for transferring the ownership of much of the North American continent to European hands was a deceptively simple one. After the Royal Proclamation of 1763 acknowledged the existence of aboriginal title (Smith, 1975, pp. 2–3), the British set out to extinguish it, piece by piece, by signing formal treaties with the First Nations. Native leaders were thus an essential element in the whole process, since it was their signatures on the documents that conferred legitimacy on the territorial annexations.

In general, treaties were not initiated by the British until they required a specific piece of land for settlement. Only then would a government agent be sent out to arrange a meeting with the Native group in the area. The agent generally was someone, like a missionary or a former trader, whom the local chiefs knew personally, and his job was to announce the date and the place of the treaty talks.

Although some of the trappings remained, like the exchange of gifts, the whole tenor of the treaty process changed when the chiefs were confronted by the representatives of the European settlers. Unlike disputes between rival First Nations, which could involve conflict over a particular hunting ground or the need to secure safe passage through territories, the settlers' representatives would arrive demanding that the First Nations cede virtually all of their national territory to the colonizing power.

The difficulties in addressing such drastic demands were greatly increased by the fact that most chiefs were asked to sign treaties that had been unilaterally drawn up by a group of legislators and bureaucrats operating out of a far-off capital, long before the emissary arrived for the negotiations. The Native leaders would rarely be given a chance to discuss the terms with the actual framers of the treaties in London or Ottawa, and the government agent, even when he was sympathetic to the Native position, would have little leeway in renegotiating them.

More often than not, while the treaty talks were being undertaken, the colonial government was already operating a series of fortified military posts in the region and parts of the land under question were already being cleared and settled.

If Native leaders resisted signing the treaty, it would generally be made clear during the negotiations that, whether they signed or not, settlers would come and the First Nations would be left with no guarantee of having any payment or any land reserved for them in the future. In the end, most Native leaders signed the British and later Canadian treaties with a greater or lesser degree of reluctance, while they continued to protest the terms of the treaty and seek renegotiation.

This British pattern was followed most faithfully in Upper Canada between 1764 and 1854. The results were the so-called lettered treaties with the Mississaugas, Chippewas, and Mohawks.[2] These pre-Confederation treaties involved an initial gift or cash payment and small annuities to the members of the tribe or band (GBC, 1913, pp. 472–74).

When the Dominion government formally took over from the British in 1867, it continued the well-established British practice with its so-called numbered treaties. In the early years of Confederation, the priority was western expansion, so the focus of treaty numbers 1–8 was to gain control of First Nations lands on the prairies. This meant expropriating both Indian and Métis lands and subjugating their peoples to the power of the Dominion.

In negotiating the numbered treaties, Ottawa had a significant liability: the prairie Indians were aware that the signing of the British treaties contributed to certain social problems for Indians living in Ontario. This liability would be offset in the west, however, by the very real fears of the Plains peoples in the 1870s that the rapidly disappearing buffalo could leave them facing starvation.

The extinction of the buffalo was a determining factor in Canada's successful push into the region. The massive herds had been the heart and soul of the Plains Indians' economy. The buffalo was their main food source and its hides provided not only clothing and shelter, but also their primary source of income in the buffalo hide trade. By the 1870s, an estimated 160 000 Canadian buffalo a year were being slaughtered by American hide hunters moving up from the south and by the large, well-organized Métis hunting parties moving west from Manitoba and Saskatchewan. The Chippewa and Plains Cree, and later the Blackfoot people, watched with alarm as the foundation of their way of life, their culture, and their very existence was being destroyed.

It was at the moment when the Plains Indians were staring into the face of hunger that the Canadian government agents arrived on the scene with their treaty proposals. In dealing with the Dominion government, Native leaders were faced with three unacceptable alternatives. They could submit to the unilaterally drawn-up treaty terms. They could refuse to sign and try to pursue their traditional life with the knowledge that their lifeblood, the buffalo, was disappearing and that the settlers would continue arriving. Or they could stand and fight and risk the destruction of their people at the hands of the superior military force the settlers had at their disposal. As we will see in the rest of this chapter, during the settlement and development of Canada, and up to the present day, Native leaders have at various times exercised all three options.

In Manitoba and parts of Saskatchewan, where settlement was most concentrated and where the buffalo were the first to disappear, the local Cree and Chippewa accepted the treaty terms. Treaty Number 1 was signed at Stony Fort in Manitoba in 1871 and gave the First Nations small reserves, agricultural implements, and an annuity of three dollars per head in exchange for an enormous tract of land in southern Manitoba (GBC, 1913, p. 474). During the next five years, the Canadian state followed the disappearing buffalo westward with treaty numbers 2–5.

If all of the leaders of the Plains Indians had faced the collapse of the herd in the same way — by submitting to the government's treaty terms — we might conclude that Ottawa was simply a hard, if rather heartless, bargainer with the First Nations. But when it came time to sign Treaty Number 6, the government ran into a stone wall in the form of a short, wily, single-minded Plains Cree leader called Big Bear, who refused to sign a unilaterally determined treaty that would surrender title to traditional Cree lands and lead to the destruction of his people's way of life.

The resistance of Chief Big Bear, and later of his war chief Wandering Spirit, not only brought to light the extreme pressures the Native leaders in Canada were operating under during the early years of Confederation, but also showed how determined the settlers' government was to crush all resistance. In the short and medium terms, the failure of Big Bear's resistance validated the decision of the Indian leaders who signed the treaties and accepted the allotted reserve lands — if only to ward off military conflict or starvation. But in the longer term, Big Bear's actions have lived on as a symbol of First Nations resistance to the unjust terms of the treaties and as an inspiration to generations of Native leaders who followed.

BIG BEAR, WANDERING SPIRIT, AND THE PATH OF RESISTANCE

The first official Canadian government contact with the Plains Cree chief Big Bear came in 1875, when Ottawa sent a number of agents to the west to prepare for treaty meetings at Fort Pitt and Carlton House for the following August.

George McDougall, a Protestant missionary who had some experience with the Plains Indians, had been sent to Big Bear's camp bearing the usual gifts — knives, ammunition, tea, sugar, and tobacco — to announce the meetings.

At the time, the situation was becoming increasingly difficult for Big Bear and his people. By 1875, only remnants of the once great buffalo herds could be found on the plains, and each year the numbers continued to decline. New settlers were continuing to arrive on Cree lands that were ceded under treaty numbers 1–5 and the North West Mounted Police were installing themselves in a series of forts across the vast section of the prairie that still belonged to Big Bear's people.

As the alarm grew among the interior Plains Cree, more and more Cree were turning to Big Bear for spiritual as well as political leadership. Among his people, Big Bear's medicine bundle was said to give him the power to become invisible, and he had demonstrated in his youth a certain ability to see into the future when he had a vision of "the coming of the white man, his purchase of the land," and the gradual weakening of the Cree people (Dempsey, 1984, p. 17).

As a leader, Big Bear dedicated his life to trying to ensure that his vision would not be fulfilled, and by 1875 Big Bear's direct following had swelled into the hundreds as the Cree of the central plain looked to him to him to preserve their freedom.

It was not surprising, then, that when George McDougall arrived to speak about Treaty Number 6, he was given a chilly reception. In fact, Big Bear even refused his gifts.

"We want none of the Queen's presents," he told the government agent. "When we set a fox trap we scatter pieces of meat all around but when the fox gets into the trap we knock him on the head. We want no baits! Let your Chiefs come and talk like men with us" (Dempsey, 1984, p. 63).

His last statement, "Let your Chiefs come," was a call Big Bear would make at numerous times, to numerous interlocutors, in the continuing hope that, if he could negotiate chief to chief with the head of the white government, he could strike a deal that he and his people could live with.

But Big Bear's call to meet with the non-Native leaders would remain unanswered. Canada had already incorporated the lands of the Plains Indians into its maps and it was not about to recognize what it saw as a competing claim to Dominion sovereignty. Big Bear would be given ample opportunity to talk to government agents, but they would be people who had no authority to negotiate any of the fundamentals of the treaties (Dempsey, 1984, p. 63).

The Dominion's attitude toward the Cree leader was reflected in McDougall's report of their initial meeting. Rather than advising Ottawa to try to work to win Big Bear's support for the treaty, McDougall suggested it simply bypass his objections. The reason was that Big Bear was half Ojibwa. As McDougall put it, Big Bear was "a Soto [Ojibwa] trying to take the lead in their Council." Big Bear, he added, "for years has been regarded as a troublesome fellow. These Sotos are mischief makers through all this Western country and some of them are shrewd men" (Dempsey, 1984, p. 63).

Big Bear showed how troublesome he could be by spending the next year meeting with other Cree chiefs and trying to build a common front against the treaty. His biographer, Hugh Dempsey, estimates that by the summer of 1876, Big Bear had won support for his stand against the treaty from the majority of the chiefs of the central plain.

In response, the government sought to isolate him and his followers by making separate deals with the more co-operative leaders in the region. When the Carlton House and Fort Pitt meetings were set to take place in August 1876, government emissaries ensured that only the more accommodating chiefs — particularly the Christian chiefs who were being strongly urged by the missionaries to accept the government's offer — were present.

When the provisions of Treaty Number 6 were announced to the assembled chiefs that summer, they were similar to the previous five treaties, but with a slight increase in the cash settlement. In exchange for the Plains Cree ceding to the Dominion 120 000 square miles of Cree land, or more than twice the combined area of the three Maritime provinces, the government was offering $12 per person as a signing bonus, an annuity of $5 per head, and a promise to help the Cree get started in agriculture (GBC, 1913, pp. 473–74).

Word travelled quickly on the Prairies, however, and the assembled chiefs knew from the example of the more eastern Cree that what was being offered amounted to a very bleak future for their people. But with the devastation of the buffalo herd, they also knew that the decision was between accepting the thin gruel of the government treaty and having their people face widespread famine with the disappearing buffalo.[5]

After two days of painful discussions and vain attempts to have the terms of the treaty improved, the assembled Cree leaders resigned themselves to their fate and signed.

Big Bear had heard about the meeting while he was out on the plains with his followers and he rushed to Fort Pitt to try to take part in the negotiations, but he arrived too late — the signatures were already on the document. When some of the chiefs tried to convince him to add his signature to theirs, Big Bear reacted angrily. "Stop, stop, my friends. I have never seen the Government before; I have seen [the government agent] many times. I heard the Government was to come and I said I shall see him. When I see him, I will make a request that he will save me from what I most dread; that is, the rope to be about my neck" (Dempsey, 1984, p. 74).

Big Bear continued to insist that Indian land "isn't a piece of pemmican that can be cut off and given back to us," and he set out to win support for his position from Indians across the prairie (Manuel, 1972). He was, however, acutely aware that he was walking a fine line in refusing to bend to Canadian power. His refusal to sign, he knew, would not make the whites go away, and he was concerned that it might cause the Canadian government to dispense with the discussions altogether and send the military after his people. The fear was expressed in a vision Big Bear had after the Fort Pitt meeting.

"I saw a spring shooting up out of the ground," he recounted, "I covered it with my hand, trying to smother it, but it spurted up between my fingers and ran over the back to my hand. It was a spring of blood" (Dempsey, 1984, p. 45). With the vision, Big Bear feared — as it turned out correctly — that continued agitation would lead to war.

Despite these concerns, Big Bear could not bring himself to surrender his people to the constrictive terms of Treaty Number 6. So he began an eight-year odyssey of almost Homeric proportions, leading his people across the plains searching for the rapidly disappearing buffalo and trying to find a way to preserve Cree independence from the encroaching Canadian state.

By the late 1870s, the thunderous herds of buffalo of only two decades earlier had been reduced to a few small, isolated groups. By the early 1880s, starvation began to stalk the very old and very young of Big Bear's band. Several times during this period, Big Bear approached government forts to ask for emergency rations for his people, but he was essentially told: sign or starve.

Under such extreme pressure, the consensus that Big Bear had built among his followers against signing the treaty document began to slip away. Facing what appeared to be the starvation of their children, small groups began to break away from Big Bear's band and head to the Canadian forts in search of food. Under the authority of the Canadian state, the local official would acknowledge one of the band members as chief and, in exchange for regular rations, the newly appointed chief would offer his signature to Treaty Number 6. The band would be allotted reserve lands and the cash payment called for under the treaty and the newly created chief would renounce his people's right to the traditional Cree homeland.

By 1882, even members of Big Bear's family were beginning to abandon him. So he led his bedraggled band to Fort Walsh, where the local
Indian agent was doling out treaty moneys. The sight of Big Bear and his
hungry people was a surprise to the agent, but he was even more surprised when the by-then famous hold-out chief said he would sign Treaty
Number 6 in exchange for food.

Big Bear's apparent capitulation was front-page news throughout
Canada. But if the Indian Affairs officials thought this was the end of Big
Bear's resistance, they were mistaken. Big Bear delayed his people's departure to their reserve as long as he could while they fed on Canadian rations.
When he finally set out, he did not go to the appointed lands. He began
wandering again, while he carried on a drawn-out, long-distance negotiation with the authorities on the location and size of his people's reserve. As
it turned out, he would never lead his people onto that or any reserve.

In 1884, Big Bear made a final attempt to have the treaty provisions
overturned. He called a mass meeting of all of the Plains chiefs on Chief
Poundmaker's reserve in Alberta in the hope that, if they stood together,
the Plains Indians could negotiate a new deal with the government.

The turnout of disaffected treaty Indians was remarkable, with thousands of Prairie Indians gathering together to discuss how they might
work together to have the treaties renegotiated. The meeting started with
the Plains chiefs appointing Big Bear as their spokesman. The plan was to
have Big Bear travel to Ottawa and try to find someone who would not
only listen, but who had the power to make changes to the treaties they
had signed under duress.

It was a crucial moment in Canadian history. Despite all of the forces
ranged against them, the Prairie Indians had managed to make a last
stand around a leader who had the strength, the vision, and the oratorical
skills to make their case to the foreign powers. There is no way of knowing whether or not Big Bear's journey to Ottawa would have slowed the
Canadian move onto Indian land, but there is no doubt that Big Bear's
arrival in Ottawa at that crucial moment in time would have offered the
Plains Indians a historic opportunity to state their case to the country at
large. At the very least, such an intercession by Big Bear could have
avoided the bloodshed that was to follow.

Big Bear, however, would not get his chance to confront the law-mak-
ers in the Canadian government. After the meetings on Poundmaker's
reserve were over, the chiefs and thousands of Plains Indians held a traditional thirst dance. While the ceremony was taking place, a scuffle broke
out between a Cree man and a non-Native shopkeeper in the nearby village. A contingent of North West Mounted Police officers, which had been
strategically stationed in the vicinity, quickly moved in to make an arrest.
What followed was an indication of just how explosive things were becoming on the prairie.

As soon as the Cree warriors saw the red coats moving in, they took to
their mounts and began to circle the police, challenging them to fire the

first shot. Greatly outnumbered, the police held their fire, but from the moment the warriors went into action, Big Bear was no longer in control of the camp. According to the Cree tradition, when hostilities were imminent, the war chief, in this case Wandering Spirit, assumed full authority.

Wandering Spirit remained in command of Big Bear's band after the camp broke and the other Cree returned to their reserves. But after the terrible suffering of his people during the previous eight years, Wandering Spirit was no longer trying to avoid confrontation, he was seeking it. And he found it the following year when Louis Riel electrified the plains with his Métis uprising.

Wandering Spirit was one of the few Cree leaders to openly align himself with the Métis forces. As soon as he heard that the Métis had taken up arms, he led his warriors into the settlement of Frog Lake and took the local whites hostage. The situation escalated dramatically when the local Indian agent, Thomas Quinn, refused Wandering Spirit's order to accompany him to the Cree camp. In a fit of rage, Wandering Spirit raised his rifle and shot Quinn in the head. A killing spree followed; minutes later, nine whites were dead.

The massacre at Frog Lake and the eventual crushing of the second Riel Rebellion was the end of any hope Big Bear had of negotiating with the Dominion government. Canadian troops, bolstered by volunteers from the east, swept onto the plains and seized military control of the territory.

Big Bear's band was hunted down along with the Métis rebels. Wandering Spirit and seven of his Cree followers were sent to the gallows for the Frog Lake killings. Big Bear was spared that fate when the white witnesses to the massacre testified that he had tried vainly to get his war chief and warriors to stop the killing. But on his arrest, Big Bear, along with other leaders involved even obliquely in the rebellion, was stripped of his hereditary chief's position by the governor of Indian Affairs. Big Bear was released after three years in custody, but by then he was a tired, sick old man and he died shortly after. The remainder of his band was scattered throughout Cree communities on the prairie, never to be reunited.

Henceforth, the prairie would be under Canadian control. Native leaders would no longer face the challenge of negotiating a fair deal with the settler government, but rather the more difficult task of freeing themselves from the sophisticated system of social and political control that the Canadian state gradually brought into force. Isolating, and then undercutting, the Native leadership would become a key element of Ottawa's strategy of overcoming Native resistance.

DESKAHEH AND THE IROQUOIS RESURGENCE

As a traditional leader operating outside the Canadian-backed band council system, Big Bear was part of a disappearing breed. In fact, even while Big Bear was being approached by McDougall in 1875, Ottawa was moving quickly to put Native leaders under the direct control of the Department of Indian Affairs.

At Confederation, the Dominion government had awarded itself all powers "over Indians and Lands reserved for the Indians" in section 24 of the British North America Act. A year later, in 1868, the government gave itself the power to decide who and who would not be recognized as chief. According to the 1868 legislation, the governor of the Indian Affairs branch could move into any band, remove the chief, and order government-sponsored elections to take place to decide on a candidate who passed the government's criteria for honesty, temperance, morality, and, later, the catch-all category of "competency."

Along with giving the governor of the Department of Indian Affairs (DIA) the right to depose serving chiefs, the Indian Act defined the chiefs' role in a way that eviscerated their powers. Under the act, the chief was given the authority only over regulations pertaining to public health, the observance of "order and decorum" at meetings, the repression of intemperance and profligacy, and the maintenance of roads and public buildings.

This reduction of the chief's areas of influence continued in 1880 when measures were introduced to suppress the potlatch, traditional dance ceremonies, and other important Native religious practices. As a result, the chiefs who played a central role in these cultural events lost even more of their influence in the community.

Over the next 25 years, Ottawa also saw that most of the remaining traditional chiefs were replaced by the government-controlled band council chiefs who served under Ottawa's direction. By the World War I, most chiefs were elected under the DIA system and there was no doubt about whose interests they were expected to serve. As the last numbered treaty, Treaty Number 11, put it, chiefs were to be "responsible to His Majesty for the faithful performance by their respective bands" (Smith, 1975, p. 208). From representing largely self-governing bands within independent Native nations, the Indian leaders had been reduced, in legal terms, to servants of His Majesty.

It is not surprising, then, that the two most prominent Native leaders during the first half of the twentieth century, Deskaheh and Andy Paull, were not band chiefs elected under the government-controlled system.

Andy Paull rose to national prominence through the newly formed, and generally regionally based, Indian organizations that began to take shape before the World War I and grew significantly during the 1920s.

Deskaheh, on the other hand, was a traditional chief from the Iroquois Longhouse who was able to use the unique historic position of his people — as allies of the British during the French and American wars — to push his case for international recognition of the Iroquois nation.

The upsurge in Iroquois resistance in the 1920s was linked to the fact that the Iroquois had preserved a large measure of their traditional political structures, their constitution (the Great Law of Peace), and the superstructure of the Iroquois Confederacy. Iroquois history was also recorded on the wampum belts, and this allowed successive generations of Iroquois people to keep traditional values alive.

Deskaheh was the strongest leader who emerged to challenge the Dominion government during the period. Born on the Six Nations reserve in 1873, Deskaheh (whose Christian name was Levi General) had been brought up within the Longhouse. As a relatively young man, his leadership skills were recognized when he was given the important post of Longhouse speaker.

Initially, Deskaheh's main concerns were cultural. He was determined that his people would not lose their language and traditions under the unrelenting Anglo-American cultural onslaught. But during the World War I, Deskaheh began to move into the political arena. The issue that led him there was conscription. When Ottawa announced that members of the First Nations would be drafted to serve in the Canadian military, Deskaheh and a group of his supporters immediately went to Ottawa to argue that the Canadian government had no jurisdiction over their people.

Eventually, the Dominion government acknowledged that, since Native people were not technically citizens of Canada (they lacked the right to vote or serve in professions), they should be exempt from the draft.

The admission was seen as a significant victory by the First Nations in gaining acknowledgement of their separate status from other Canadians. In 1921, Deskaheh tried to expand on that wartime victory by travelling to London to lobby the Colonial Office for recognition of the Iroquois claim to independence. Deskaheh travelled on his own Iroquois passport and tried to impress upon the British that the treaties recognizing Iroquois sovereignty that his people had signed with the representatives of George III must be recognized by the current monarch, George V.

The British were dismissive. They told Deskaheh they had already turned the whole Indian question over to the Dominion government, so he should go back home and address his plea to Ottawa. In 1922, the Dominion government responded to the Iroquois petition by agreeing to set up a three-person arbitration panel to decide on the question of Iroquois sovereignty (Six Nations, 1976, pp. 7–8).

The initial hopes of the Iroquois were dampened when it became known that Ottawa wanted the panel members to be drawn from the Supreme Court of Ontario — part of the very group of Canadians responsible for administering the laws underpinning the territorial and jurisdictional claims of the settler society. When the Iroquois asked that the panel be made up instead of international jurists, the Dominion government refused, offering as a concession only that one member of the panel could be selected by the Iroquois, but that he or she had to be a "British subject."

What Ottawa was offering, the Mohawks suspected, was a bit of political theatre, where Mohawks would be invited to speak their minds, their words would be duly recorded, and then the government-appointed panel would summarily dismiss their case.

Deskaheh, therefore, decided to seek a higher authority to hear the Iroquois plea: the League of Nations. The league had made the protection of small nations from the aggression of the bigger powers one of its cornerstones. In 1923, Deskaheh, still travelling on his Iroquois passport, headed off to Geneva to put his case directly to the nations of the world. After months of diligent lobbying, Deskaheh managed to have four members of the league — Ireland, Panama, Persia, and Estonia — agree to jointly put the case for Iroquois sovereignty on the international order paper. As a preliminary step, the League of Nations invited both the Iroquois nation and Canada to submit their case to a special hearing.

The Dominion government reacted with a mixture of surprise and alarm at the news from Geneva. Duncan Campbell Scott, deputy minister of Indian Affairs, indicated in a private letter that the Dominion government would not stand idly by while the Iroquois went abroad to campaign for sovereignty. As he put it, "The Indians concerned are taking this course at their own risk and with the full knowledge of the facts and I fear must suffer the consequences" (Six Nations, 1976, p. 4).

Ottawa's first move was to undermine Deskaheh diplomatically by asking for British help in scuttling the hearings. All the British could do was to get a delay, but, as it turned out, that was all that the Dominion government needed. While Deskaheh was continuing to win support for the Iroquois cause (Norway, the Netherlands, and Albania joined the original four states backing it), Ottawa moved against his Longhouse supporters in Canada by force.

Using the powers the government had given itself in the 1880 amendment to the Indian Act, the minister responsible for Indian Affairs dissolved the Longhouse government and ordered DIA-sponsored elections be held in the Six Nations community. Immediately after the announcement, RCMP officers were sent onto the reserve to confiscate the Iroquois papers and symbolic articles, like the historic wampum belts.

The move against the Longhouse in Canada was used by Ottawa to isolate Deskaheh abroad. While the Iroquois leader was still trying to drum up support in Geneva, Canadian and British delegates were informing the international community that Deskaheh was no longer the legal representative of his people. With his political base effectively cut out from underneath him, Deskaheh was forced to leave Europe in defeat.

Deskaheh went into exile in the United States where he continued to agitate for Iroquois sovereignty. In 1925, he made a radio broadcast from Rochester, New York in which he accused the Canadian government of genocide against his people. Ottawa, he said, was trying "to punish us for trying to preserve our rights. The Canadian Government has now pretended to abolish our government by Royal Proclamation, and has pretended to set up a Canadian-made government over us, composed of the few traitors among us who are willing to accept pay from Ottawa and do its bidding" (Six Nations, 1976, p. 16).

Deskaheh died later that same year. But the Longhouse and Mohawk traditions have proven remarkably resilient. Even today, many decades after the DIA-backed band chiefs were installed in all Mohawk communities, a sizable portion of the people in each community continue to reject Canadian citizenship, with the leadership insisting their people are part of the independent Iroquois nation that Deskaheh fought for.

The persistence of the Longhouse went a long way in preserving at least part of the traditional Iroquois polity, but in other areas of the country, the Canadian drive to replace the traditional Native leadership with the band council system was more complete. The Department of Indian Affairs' control of the councils, however, only led to the emergence of new Indian organizations and what might be called independent "Indian populists," in an attempt to find new mechanisms to put First Nations grievances forward.

ALLIED TRIBES AND ANDY PAULL

While many Iroquois, particularly Mohawks, continued to look to the by-then largely underground Longhouse for leadership, Native activists in other parts of Canada were busy building Indian organizations that would allow them to take their case to Ottawa, outside the controls of the Department of Indian Affairs' band council system.

Most of those organizations were regional in nature and they were founded by local activists who travelled from reserve to reserve to build new local alliances. This type of organizing was greatly hampered by the fact that, in some parts of the country, Indians were required to get permission from the Indian agents even to leave their communities. Organizing often had to be carried out in semi-secrecy and the only funding was passing the hat at community meetings.

One of the largest and most important of the new regional organizations was the Allied Tribes of British Columbia. The Allied Tribes had been founded in 1916 at a meeting of 16 B.C. chiefs at Spences Bridge sponsored by James Teit, a sympathetic anthropologist. What made it such a significant concern to Ottawa was that its main focus was the so-called B.C. land question, which stemmed from the fact that most B.C. natives had never signed a treaty ceding their lands to British or Canadian authorities.[4]

This was due not so much to resistance on their part as to the fact that the governors of British Columbia had never bothered to negotiate treaties with the First Nations of most of the colony. After the province entered Confederation in 1871, the matter of treaties was simply brushed aside and forgotten.

The Allied Tribes' main strategy was to put together a legal case to take to the Privy Council in Britain to argue for their unextinguished aboriginal title to the land. At the same time, the organization was also active at the community level with organizers travelling to Indian communities across the province to win support for its goals and to urge people on to acts of resistance in their daily lives.

In 1926, the Allied Tribes sent a delegation to London to look into the possibility of Privy Council hearings on the B.C. land question. The leadership stated its case frankly in a petition to the king that read in part: "We Indians want our Native titles to our Native lands, and all our land contains as we are the original people of Canada. We Indians want our consent before laws are made upon our possessions."[5]

The British gave the Allied Tribes delegation the same response they had given Deskaheh five years earlier: they told it to go home and take the matter up with the Dominion government. And once again, Ottawa agreed to hold a special hearing on the issue. But, as was the case with the Mohawks five years earlier, Ottawa was not about to have its control of aboriginal lands seriously questioned.

In the government's view, such recognition would mean that not only B.C. Natives, but also First Nations in Quebec, northern Ontario, and the Yukon and Northwest Territories would have similar rights, since few treaties had been signed in those areas either. As the deputy minister of Indian Affairs, Duncan Campbell Scott, put it, recognition of the B.C. land claim would "smash confederation" (Canada, 1961, p. 583).

When the Allied Tribes leaders assembled in Ottawa for the March 27, 1927 hearing, the deck had already been stacked against them. The committee was made up largely of B.C. senators and M.P.s who were not prepared to give an inch of their province's territory to the First Nations. The only concession the politicians would make was to give B.C. Indians $100 000 a year in compensation for the fact that they were not receiving treaty money. (On a per-person basis, this amounted to roughly the same five-dollar annuity the signatories of Treaty Number 6 had received 50 years earlier.)

While the government was rushing to close the door on the B.C. claim, and on the claims of aboriginal title to the other unceded parts of the country, it was also working on a more ambitious plan to shut down the young Indian organizations. Three days before the Allied Tribes hearings began, the federal government passed legislation making it illegal for anyone to collect money from Indian band members for the purpose of pursuing a land claim.

The new clause was inserted into the Indian Act under section 149a, which stated that "every person who solicits or requests from any Indian any payment or contribution or promise of any payment or contribution for the purpose of raising a fund for the prosecution of any claim" would be liable to fines or imprisonment (Manuel and Posluns, 1974, p. 95).

As a justification, the Department of Indian Affairs argued that the measure would protect First Nations people against unscrupulous lawyers. To the leaders of the Allied Tribes and other organizations, however, the legislation appeared to be directed at their attempts to contest their claims of aboriginal title in the courts. The 1927 legislation was so broadly written that it could also be interpreted to make groups like the Allied Tribes — which focussed on the land issue and were funded directly by Indian people — illegal.

Indian leaders have referred to section 149a as "the darkest hour in the history of the Parliament of Canada" (Manuel and Posluns, 1974, p. 95). In retrospect, the draconian measure shows not only the lengths that the Dominion government would go to in trying to subvert First Nations claims to their homelands, but also how nervous the government was about its own legal title to the land.[6]

While the 1927 proscriptions were an immediate and serious blow to the Indian movement, they did not completely crush First Nations resistance. In the short term, they sank organizations like the Allied Tribes, but similar Indian organizations survived by shifting their focus away from the question of aboriginal title toward more local concerns.

This period also saw the rise of what can be termed "Indian populists" — individual activists who emerged to fill the gap left by the more aggressive land claim organizations like the Allied Tribes. Probably the most influential of these populists was the B.C. Squamish leader Andy Paull.

Andy Paull had, in fact, been one of the leaders of the Allied Tribes. He attended the organization's first meeting at Spences Bridge in 1916 and he had travelled to Ottawa five times as an Allied Tribes spokesman to promote the B.C. Indians' claims. After the collapse of the Allied Tribes, Paull continued to pursue the issue with his informal network of contacts. In a sense, he served as a living link to the small isolated Indian organizations across the country. When Paull took the train to Ottawa, he would get off at numerous places along the way to visit local Indian communities and meet with activists. On his way back, he would stop again to report on how his meetings had gone and on his future plans. For the scattered Native organizations and community-based activists, Andy Paull became the personification of the wider struggle.

During the late 1920s and through the 1930s, Andy Paull also served as a much-needed beacon of hope. With the Depression, most bands were once again finding themselves stalked by hunger. The government refused to give the people the same amount of relief it gave to whites, under the pretext that Indians could get most of their food from hunting and fishing. At the same time, a web of legislation had been enacted restricting Indian fishing and hunting rights and the ability of farm-based Native economies to sell their produce in the open market.

While the economic situation deteriorated, the physical health of the people began to fail. A new scourge, tuberculosis, was moving through the reserves, claiming hundreds and even thousands of lives each year — with the annual body count perfunctorily listed in Parliament during the Department of Indian Affairs budget debates.

Politically, the communities were more tightly controlled during this period than they had ever been before or since. The local Indian agents, who were often retired military men, held sway over everything, from the number of days a band member could hunt and fish to when and how long individuals could leave the reserve, and even how many hours a day a band member could spend in a pool hall.

In those difficult days, it was individual leaders like Andy Paull who demonstrated that resistance was still possible. In Paull's case, he would suddenly arrive in a community in worn-out country clothes and urge the people to stand up to the local Indian agent and the priests who ran the residential schools, and demand their right to fair treatment and Depression-era financial assistance. As he told his followers: "White people have not yet paid for this country. They must treat us in decent way, not wield dictatorial powers over us" (Paull, 1951, p. 14).

Andy Paull also continued to use every opportunity to travel to Ottawa to press the Native case. Part of his effectiveness in dealing with the parliamentarians came from the legal training he had received in a Vancouver law office. As a young man, he had served as a legal assistant for four years and had acquired enough experience to be called to the bar. But Paull was ineligible because status Indians were considered minors before the law (Dunlop, 1989, p. 40).

Virtually all professions during this period were closed to status Indians. The only way they could be admitted was to renounce their Indianness and became "enfranchised" as full Canadians. It was a route that a small number took, but Paull refused. Instead, he became known by the then-oxymoron of an "Indian lawyer."

When he was in Ottawa, Andy Paull changed his country clothes for some of the flashiest suits in the capital and went toe to toe with the M.P.s and bureaucrats in debate. As a leader, he was particularly effective in shaming the government into honouring its meagre treaty commitments and in giving emergency aid to communities that required it.

In the 1940s, World War II opened up new avenues for furthering the Native cause. The conscription issue again offered both a threat and an opportunity for reaffirming First Nations sovereignty. Like Deskaheh before him, Paull fought hard against the threatened Native draft, and once again Ottawa backed down. But Paull was never satisfied with small victories. As the war drew to its obvious conclusion, he began arguing that the First Nations of Canada should be given a separate place at the peace negotiating table with the other self-governing members of the empire like Australia and New Zealand.

Paull's radical-sounding demand for self-governing status surprised even many of his fellow Indian leaders. As might have been expected, Ottawa ignored the request, but the postwar period did offer the Native movement a considerable opening. Partly as a result of the surge in postwar liberalism, Ottawa pledged to undertake a major revision of the Indian Act in 1949–50, which led to the lifting of the restrictions on Indian organizing.

By then, Andy Paull was building a new and much more ambitious organization: the North American Indian Brotherhood. With this vehicle, Paull was aiming at nothing less than organizing all of the First Nations peoples on the continent for redress of historic grievances.

His plan was probably too ambitious, at least for the times. As one Mohawk activist put it, "the train can't run until the track has been laid,"[7] and in the 1940s, the track that would allow the First Nations to build a national organization was still decades from being laid.

Still, Andy Paull was able to elucidate a vision that those who followed could put into practice. George Manuel, one of Paull's protégés, described Andy Paull as the last of the "one-man shows," but he was also "the inspiration and the spark" that ignited the modern Indian movement.

In his face-to-face lobbying of parliamentarians, Andy Paull was also fulfilling the goal Big Bear had set for himself half a century earlier: getting an opportunity to stand before the people who held the power to put forward the First Nations case.

Big Bear had hoped that if he explained the position of the Cree nation, he could convince the settlers' government to respect the Cree's way of life, their aboriginal title to the land, and their right to govern themselves. By Andy Paull's time, it was clear that simply stating the First Nations case would not be enough. It would take not only the efforts of many other far-seeing leaders like Big Bear, Deskaheh, and Andy Paull, but also the efforts of hundreds, even thousands, of activists working to build a movement that was strong enough to force Ottawa to respond to the First Nations' historical demands.

THE NEW GENERATION: GEORGE MANUEL AND THE NATIONAL INDIAN MOVEMENT

Building the national Indian movement was a long and arduous task that involved Native leaders from across the country slowly building up local and regional organizations.

The first boost to the effort came when the proscriptions on Indian organizing were lifted in the 1951 revision of the Indian Act (see Smith, 1975, pp. 154–96). But the movement was also aided by the postwar economic boom, which offered employment opportunities for the members of many bands. It was a time when more Native families were able to afford a car, and this fact was not inconsiderable in allowing Indian activists to travel easily to surrounding communities, and across their provinces, to carry out organizing activities.

There was also a general improvement in the health in the communities. Although First Nations people continued to lag far behind other Canadians in health (as in wealth, employment, etc.), the plague of tuberculosis, which killed thousands of Native people a year in the 1930s and 1940s, was subsiding in most Native communities.[8]

The small-scale but persistent organizing efforts of the previous generation were also beginning to pay off. Natives in the prairie provinces, in particular, had managed to create increasingly effective provincial organizations that, by the end of the 1960s, were led by a trio of strong and very politically adept leaders — Harold Cardinal in Alberta, Walter Deiter in Saskatchewan, and Dave Courchene in Manitoba — each of whom played a key role in launching the first national status Indian organization.

The final organizing drive was inadvertently spurred on by the Department of Indian Affairs itself, when measures were introduced to devolve certain additional powers to the band chiefs to make them something like village reeves rather than mere departmental factotums.[9]

The small but real increase in powers for the chiefs helped raise their status in the community, where in some places their subservient position to the Indian agents had made them objects of ridicule. As the chiefs and their band councils gradually assumed more power, the office began to attract men and women who saw the position as a way to challenge Ottawa on an array of local issues.

The same sort of unintended effect occurred from 1965 to 1968 when the Department of Indian Affairs brought together representatives of the various Indian organizations into the National Indian Advisory Board, which was given the mandate of reviewing the Indian Act.

On the face of it, it looked like a progressive move by the department. But the Indian "advisers" soon discovered that what the department was looking for from the board was a stamp of approval for its plan to abolish not only the Indian Act, but also virtually all First Nations rights, including their rights to their reserve lands.

The department's plans would be made public in the summer of 1969 in the Indian policy statement, known as the white paper, presented by the minister of Indian Affairs, Jean Chrétien. But in the late 1960s, the National Indian Advisory Board itself was used by the Native leaders as an important organizing tool. The official meetings, under the co-chairmanship of the Department of Indian Affairs deputy minister, Robert Battle, and the Shuswap Indian leader, George Manuel, were characterized by push-and-pull debates between department officials and Native representatives. But as George Manuel and the other Native leaders saw it, the real meetings took place in the hotel rooms afterward, where Native leaders, who had been brought together from across the country, quietly planned the founding of a national Indian organization.

That organization, the National Indian Brotherhood (NIB), was launched in December 1968 under the provisional leadership of Walter Deiter of Saskatchewan. The NIB was a major breakthrough in Indian politics. It gave a single voice to status Indians across the country with a membership in the hundreds of thousands, rather than the mere hundreds of people represented by most band chiefs. George Manuel replaced Dieter as the president of the National Indian Brotherhood a short time later, and went on to dominate Native politics in Canada for the next decade.

George Manuel had grown up on the Neskonlith reserve in the interior of British Columbia and came from a family active in the First Nations struggle. His true mentor, however, was Andy Paull. Manuel's first contact with Paull came in his youth when Paull visited Neskonlith on his frequent trips through the B.C. interior. As a young boom man on the South Thompson River, Manuel became directly involved with Paull when he was fighting a ruling that required gainfully employed Indians to pay their own medical costs. Manuel had contacted Paull about the issue, and soon after George Manuel became a local organizer for Andy Paull in the B.C. interior. On Paull's death in 1959, George Manuel emerged as the most prominent Indian leader in British Columbia, and then in the entire country.

George Manuel was elected president of the newly formed National Indian Brotherhood in 1970. At the time, the NIB was largely a paper organization without an office, funding, or a clear political direction. During his six years of leadership, Manuel transformed it into the largest lobbying organization in Ottawa with a mandate to pursue self-government for all of the 50-some First Nations in Canada. Under George Manuel's leadership, the rather bureaucratic structure required to run an organization like the National Indian Brotherhood was set within the larger framework of Native consensus politics. He insisted, for example, that anyone working in the Native movement should always "consult the people, politicize the people and never get too far ahead of them, because when all is said and done, they are your masters" (cited in McFarlane, 1993, p. 226).

It was also during George Manuel's tenure that the modern ideology of the movement began to take shape. In the early 1970s, the NIB was caught up in the general swirl of extra-parliamentary opposition activities that shaped the period. The Native movement was influenced by the Black Power movement in the United States and by the Third World anti-colonialist ideology that had developed during the African wars of liberation. Young Indian activists began to speak of "Red Power" and incorporate a certain Marxist perspective into their world view.

After George Manuel set up the National Indian Brotherhood headquarters in Ottawa, he used his first year in the capital to acquaint himself with the local power structure and to meet with representatives of the generally leftist Third World countries of Africa. His contacts with the Tanzania High Commission led him to tour the African country at the end of 1971, where he met and became friends with one of the architects of African liberation, Julius Nyerere.

From Deskaheh's time to Manuel's, looking beyond Canada's borders for allies in the First Nations drive toward self-government had become, if not commonplace, at least a frequent tactic used by First Nations leaders. George Manuel took it further and launched the U.N.-affiliated World Council of Indigenous Peoples in 1975 at a Port Alberni, British Columbia, conference that included indigenous peoples from North, Central, and South America, Eurasia, and the Arctic — and even a delegation of Sami reindeer herders from northern Scandinavia.

Within Canada, George Manuel had the task of directing a movement and an organization that were peopled by strong regional figures. He could call on the political expertise of the prairie leaders who had help put him in power, as well as people like the Mohawk chief Andrew Delisle, a strong force in Quebec, and Phillip Paul, a close Manuel ally from British Columbia. Most of these leaders had decades of experience in Native politics and they had built and run organizations of their own.

One area of political development where George Manuel played a significant role was in making room for more women in the mainstream of the movement. As an organizer in the B.C. interior, one of his strongest allies had been Genevieve Mussel, who at the time was one of the few female band chiefs in Canada. During the 1950s, most Native women political activists were sequestered off in the Homemaker's Association and played primarily a supporting role to the largely male-staffed organizations. When George Manuel took over as president of the NIB, he hired Marie Smallface Marule, a Blackfoot Indian who had spent three years working in Africa, as his executive director. Marie Marule was given almost complete power over the organization when George Manuel was absent, and he relied on her as a primary source of political advice. With Marie Marule in charge, a number of other very talented Native women were attracted to the organization and filled many of its most important posts.

During the early 1970s, however, the number of powerful regional figures in the Native movement and their often conflicting interests made the National Indian Brotherhood a difficult horse to ride. Within the provincial organizations, rivalries and suspicions still existed between different tribal groups, and nationally, the treaty and non-treaty Indians often saw issues differently. A nationwide consensus on any issue was always a challenge, and generally at least a few bands would withdraw their support from a national initiative they could not agree with.

Yet, given the broad historical and cultural differences among the First Nations, a surprising degree of unity was attained in a relatively short time. Much of the NIB's early success can be attributed to the sheer force of Manuel's personality, which combined Andy Paull-type charisma with the organizational skills needed to build a national movement. At the core of Manuel's leadership style was his traditional background. He had been raised in the B.C. interior by his grandfather, who had grown up before widespread settlement in the area, and George Manuel had inherited much of his grandfather's traditional world view and an understanding of the special relationship between the Native community and its leaders.

For Manuel, this understanding translated into a step-by-step approach to leadership. In the early 1970s, he worked on specific issues that could mobilize and radicalize the people in the communities. He first drew the battle lines over Indian control of education. His immediate goal was to have the right to educate Indian children returned to Indian communities. But in the longer view, he was trying to use the schools issue as a model for similar battles — over control of economic development, Native justice, and culture — that the movement would undertake in the future.

Another of the ramparts Manuel frequently attacked was the Department of Indian Affairs itself. Instead of a frontal assault, however, he used a tactic that department had so often used against Native leadership in the past — by trying to isolate it with a view of undercutting its influence.

In this case, Manuel successfully lobbied the Prime Minister's Office for the creation of a joint NIB–cabinet committee. The first meeting in 1972 was a historic one, as George Manuel managed to sit down with what Big Bear personified as "the Government" to make the First Nations case for self-government and justice on the land question. By the early 1970s, the Native movement had clearly set out on the road to regaining lost lands and liberty, but reaching its destination would require a long and difficult struggle.

In the short term, the joint NIB–cabinet committee allowed Indian leaders to circumvent to some degree the Department of Indian Affairs bureaucracy and speak directly to the various ministers. For example, the NIB was able to address the minister responsible for housing about the need for better housing on reserves, or the health minister about the need for more clinics in isolated communities. In this way, the stranglehold the Department of Indian Affairs had held over the First Nations was loosened and the national Native leadership was able to play one department off another to get the best deal possible for their people.

The activists in Ottawa were also greatly aided by a new restiveness in Native communities that was causing concern in Ottawa, where fears were being expressed that the Canadian Indians might take the militant path of the Black Panthers in the United States. To be fair, under the Liberal regimes of Lester B. Pearson and Pierre Trudeau, there was also a new willingness in Ottawa to at least address Native concerns. Taken together, the surge in activism from below and a new willingness to listen in Ottawa presented George Manuel and his team of activists with a number of important opportunities for furthering the First Nations cause.

While George Manuel made significant progress on most fronts during his six years in Ottawa, the one area where he and his organization ran into a stone wall was the recognition of their people's aboriginal right to the land. The bitterest defeat came with the signing of the James Bay agreement between Quebec and the Cree and Inuit in the province in 1975.

The James Bay agreement was described as the first "modern" treaty; but the final result and the process leading up to it were remarkably similar to the unilateralism of the numbered treaties of the nineteenth century. Quebec waited until it was already moving bulldozers onto Cree territory before it entered into negotiations with the Cree leaders; and throughout the discussions, officials from the Quebec government and the James Bay Corporation let it be known that if the Crees refused to sign, the hydroelectric project would be built anyway. "Sign or starve" had been replaced by "sign or you get nothing."

George Manuel's term as NIB president ended in 1976, but instead of retiring, he returned to British Columbia to launch and lead what he described as his "peoples' movement." Manuel later explained that his experience in Ottawa, and especially during the "gun-to-the-head" negotiations leading up to the James Bay agreement, had taught him that governments and their agencies respond only to shows of power.

Since the indigenous peoples in North America were small minorities in their homelands, Manuel believed that the ballot box was insufficient to give them power over their lives. What he proposed was an Indian movement that would not only lobby the government through organizations like the NIB, but also have at its base a strong activist grass-roots organization that could back up the self-government demands by the other means available in a democratic society, including public protests, direct action, and civil disobedience.

George Manuel spent the next three years building such a movement in British Columbia. In 1980, he had an opportunity to put it to work on the national stage. And the issue was one that would dominate the Native movement, and the political life of the whole country, for much of the next decade: the Constitution.

When Prime Minister Trudeau introduced his constitutional repatriation package in 1978, George Manuel and other Native leaders realized that some of its provisions, especially the Charter of Rights and Freedoms, could override protections of First Nations hunting and fishing rights and their right to collectively possess their reserve lands. For Indian leaders, the constitutional battles ahead would be important in their own right, but they would also serve as important symbolic issues to be used to radicalize people in the communities and to win acceptance of broader First Nations powers within Canada from the public at large.

From his B.C. base, George Manuel launched a court case to block the Trudeau package and mobilized his peoples movement in a so-called constitutional express of a thousand activists who travelled to Ottawa by train to protest against any constitutional changes at the expense of First Nations rights.

Manuel led the Native protesters to the steps of Parliament and managed to win public sympathy for the Native cause, while sending fears of a widespread Indian insurrection through the government. Largely as a result of his efforts, the formal recognition of aboriginal rights was inserted into the Constitution, with a mandated set of negotiations between the federal and provincial governments and the Native organizations over the exact content of those rights.

George Manuel would not be part of those negotiations. While in Ottawa fighting on the Constitution issue, he suffered the first of a series of debilitating heart attacks, and he was forced to withdraw from most of his political activities. The breach would be filled by a new generation of leaders who would draw their inspiration from men like Big Bear, Deskaheh, Andy Paull, and George Manuel while they searched for new ways to carry the struggle forward.

NATIVE LEADERSHIP TODAY

When George Manuel stepped down as the head of the National Indian Brotherhood and returned to British Columbia in 1976, he was replaced by a Saskatchewan Cree, Noel Starblanket, who served only two years and was followed by Del Riley. In 1982, the NIB changed its structure and its name to the Assembly of First Nations (AFN). Instead of being based on provincial organizations, the new Assembly of First Nations would be made up directly of the bands. This solved some of the tensions that had grown up within the provincial organizations, which in places like British Columbia often forced the organization to speak with one voice for radically different groups like the coastal and interior Indians. Henceforth, the national organization's membership would be composed of the 600 or so band chiefs, each of whom would have an equal voice in the assembly.

The change from the provincially based NIB to the constituent assembly model of the AFN was completed under the leadership of the Saskatchewan Cree leader David Ahenikew. But it was the young Dene leader George Erasmus, who took over as national chief in 1984, who represented the status Indians during the negotiations with the federal and provincial governments on the nature of the treaty and aboriginal rights that were to be included in the Constitution. Erasmus remained the national chief for six years and proved to be the most effective leader since George Manuel in promoting unity in the First Nations movement. Erasmus was able to use the ongoing constitutional negotiations with the federal and provincial governments as a focal point for discussion and planning on self-government issues.

The constitutional negotiations ultimately broke down, but the 1980s saw significant gains for the movement as Native leaders were able to use the national profile of the negotiations to win broad (although not necessarily deep) support from the Canadian people for their self-government demands. During the negotiation of the Charlottetown accord in the early 1990s, the growing public support was reflected in the fact that the new leader of the Assembly of First Nations, Ovide Mercredi, as well as the leaders of the non-status Indian and Inuit organizations were invited to the table with the prime minister and premiers to discuss Canada's constitutional future.

In the end, the Charlottetown accord was defeated in a national referendum, but the federal and provincial governments had acknowledged that the First Nations of Canada had an "inherent right" to govern themselves.

If such an acknowledgement had come a century or so earlier, it would have gone a long way to addressing the concerns of Native leaders like Big Bear. But by the 1990s, it was seen as just another small step on a very long road. The Native leaders of today have set themselves the task not only of winning constitutional recognition of their status as nations, but also of rebuilding those nations in the modern world. That task will not be an easy one.

Many decades of assimilationist policies, like the residential school system, have taken their toll on Native cultures and languages. The challenge will not be simply restoring lost political rights, but reviving Native cultures and economies. Although the national leadership has tended to focus on the political battles, there are perhaps even more far-ranging changes going on at the local level, where activists have been trying to envision and, to a certain extent, put in place the form of self-government that would best serve the interest of their individual nations. And just as the movement saw a rapid growth in provincial organizations in the 1960s as a prelude to building the national organization, the 1980s saw the growth of so-called tribal councils as the beginning of new Indian governments.

It was a natural evolution. Native leaders were basing their right to govern themselves on the fact that their people, whether Cree, Shuswap, or Haida, had been governing themselves for thousands of years. In the hunting societies, the people had spent much of the year in relatively small bands, but generally they had come together at least twice a year, in the fall and the spring, to hold religious festivals, arrange marriages, and convene national councils where treaty-making and other tribal issues would be discussed. Today, the tribal councils are the forum where the individual First Nations work to preserve and promote their culture, language, and historic values, and where the drive for sovereignty is often most strongly expressed. The challenge for the national leader of the Assembly of First Nations, by both necessity and tradition, has become very much a matter of building a broad consensus within the constituent First Nations for any national initiatives he or she might want to take.

In this sense, the rise of the tribal councils has made the task of the national leadership more difficult, as power and influence in the movement becomes more dispersed across the country. A powerful Cree leader, Matthew Coon Come in Quebec, for example, often eclipses his AFN counterpart, Ovide Mercredi, on the national and even international stage. The national leader has to win not only the consensus of 600 or so isolated band chiefs, but also the support of the new and often powerful tribal leaders. In the need for consensus-building among strong and largely independent groups, it seems that the future will call for more, not less, of the traditional style of leadership.

As in the past, the basis of unity will likely be found in the fact that the ultimate goals that Native leaders across Canada have pursued have changed little since the days Big Bear was roaming the prairie. Big Bear's demand to speak to "the Government" is little different from today's demands for nation-to-nation negotiations between the leaders of the First Nations and the Canadian state. Then, as now, Native leaders have been preoccupied with obtaining a new deal on the ownership and use of their traditional lands and with gaining recognition, in fact and in law, of the First Nations right to govern themselves.

NOTES

1. "He" is used in this instance because women were not traditionally chiefs, although in a number of societies, like the Iroquois, heredity passed from mother to child, and women, specifically the clan mothers, were given the job of choosing chiefs.

2. They were called "lettered treaties" because the British referred to the treaties simply as A, B, C, etc. After Confederation, the Dominion government listed the treaties by number: Treaty Number 1, Treaty Number 2, etc.

3. As Dempsey (1984) points out, a number of Cree spokespeople at the meeting made a direct connection between signing the document and receiving emergency rations from the government in times of mass starvation.

4. The idea of "aboriginal title" has long existed in the British tradition. By definition, indigenous peoples can be said to have aboriginal title to an area if they can show long-term, continuous use of that area before the Europeans arrived, as long as that title has not been extinguished by a treaty. Most courts, however, have suggested that, at most, aboriginal title confers on the First Nations the right to carry on traditional hunting and fishing activities in the area. Native leaders, on the other hand, assert that aboriginal title confers at least as much ownership right as the Europeans acquired by simply arriving on the shores of North America, planting their flag, and claiming the territory as part of their own national territory.

5. The petition is in the Shuswap Nation Archives, Kamloops, British Columbia.

6. At the time, Ottawa had some basis for its concern about the Allied Tribes attempt to take the case of the B.C. Indians to the Privy Council in London. In 1921, the Privy Council had ruled that the indigenous peoples of Nigeria still held aboriginal title to their land because the colonial authorities had never "extinguished" that title through the treaty process.

7. Bill Badcock interview.

8. The exceptions were in the isolated communities of the far north, where tuberculosis continued to take a deadly toll for decades.

9. One of the main reasons behind the devolution of powers during the period was to prepare for the DIA's plan to remove special status from Indian lands. The reserves, as part of the national territory of the First Nations, would cease to exist and Indian communities would be transformed into simple municipalities under the control of the provinces.

DISCUSSION QUESTIONS

1. Virtually all of modern Canada was part of the territory of one of the First Nations. What was the main Native nation in your region?

2. How did the colonial authorities address the question of aboriginal title for that nation? Were treaties signed? If so, what were the terms? If not, why not?

3. What was the role of Native leaders in the treaty process during the time of the numbered treaties?

4. What was the main role of Native leaders after the last numbered treaty was signed in 1921?

5. What are the main challenges that Native leaders face today?

FURTHER READINGS

Churchill, Ward. 1993. *Struggle for the Land*. Monroe, ME: Common Courage Press. Individual lands claims are looked at in the perspective of the overall struggle for Native rights in North America.

Manuel, George and Michael Posluns. 1974. *The Fourth World: An Indian Reality*. Toronto: Collier Macmillan. Covers George Manuel's life before his election as the president of the National Indian Brotherhood.

McFarlane, Peter. 1993. *From Brotherhood to Nationhood: George Manuel and the Modern Indian Movement*. Toronto: Between the Lines. Covers George Manuel's role in building the modern Indian movement from the 1950s to the 1980s.

McGhee, Robert. 1941. *Ancient Canada*. Ottawa: Canadian Museum of Civilization. Archaeologist McGhee reconstructs selected scenes from Canadian precontact history, and in the process examines some unsolved mysteries. Why, for example, was an adolescent buried with great ceremony on the Labrador coast 7000 years ago? And what is the explanation for those hilltop fortresses in British Columbia? Answers are still being sought.

REFERENCES

Canada. 1961. *Proceedings of the Joint Senate–House of Commons Committee on Indian Affairs*. May 25. Ottawa: Supply and Services.

Dempsey, Hugh A. 1984. *Big Bear: End of Freedom*. Vancouver: Douglas & McIntyre.

Dunlop, Herbert Francis. 1989. *Andy Paull: As I Knew Him*. Vancouver: Standard Press.

Geographic Board, Canada (GBC). 1913. *Handbook of Indians of Canada*. Ottawa: GBC.

Mandelbaum, David G. 1979. *The Plains Cree: An Ethnographic History and Comparative Study*. Regina: Canadian Plains Research Centre, University of Regina.

Manuel, George. 1972. Speech to the UBCIC annual meeting. November.

Manuel, George and Michael Posluns. 1974. *The Fourth World: An Indian Reality.* Toronto: Collier Macmillan.

McFarlane, Peter. 1993. *Brotherhood to Nationhood: George Manuel and the Modern Indian Movement.* Toronto: Between the Lines.

Paull, Andy. 1951. "Article." *The Native Voice* (October): p. 14.

Six Nations Museum Series. 1976. "Deskaheh: Iroquois Statesman and Patriot." *Akwesasne Notes.*

Smith, Derek G., ed. 1975. *Canadian Indians and the Law: Selected Documents 1663–1972.* Toronto: McClelland and Stewart.

Trigger, Bruce G. 1987. *The Children of Aataentsic: A History of the Huron People to 1660.* Montreal: McGill-Queen's University Press.

CHAPTER 7

The Politics of Jurisdiction: Indigenizing Aboriginal–State Relations

Augie Fleras

.

INTRODUCTION: RESETTING THE AGENDA

In the colonialist context that historically shaped settler discourse, indigenous populations were routinely defined as a "problem people" in need of control or solution by way of government intervention. A precondition of such internal colonialism was the establishment of state bureaucratic structures for the administration of government aboriginal policy (Blauner, 1972). Ostensibly directed toward the well-being of indigenous populations, these "total institutions" (see Goffman, 1963) were more aptly concerned with national "interests" related to society-building than with aboriginal well-being. But colonialist structures are no longer defensible, with aboriginal peoples everywhere locked in struggles to sever the bonds of dependency and underdevelopment.

Both government policy and state bureaucracies have evolved in response to increasingly assertive demands for the restoration of aboriginal rights (Fleras and Elliott, 1992; also Eckholm, 1994). Central to this reconstruction are proposals to "indigenize" the interactional grounds of aboriginal–state relations. But ambiguities continue to pervade the restructuring process despite the removal of structures that dominate or control. Hidden policy agendas and multiple administrative mandates remain a factor in defining who gets what (see Weaver, 1981). Evidence, in other words, confirms the notion of aboriginal–state relations as a "contested domain" involving a protracted struggle between opposing ideologies for control over jurisdiction.

A parallel situation exists in Canada, where a federal bureaucracy has long presided over aboriginal policy and its administration by various Indian Affairs departments (Ponting and Gibbins, 1980). Historically, aboriginal concerns were routinely compromised by restrictions within the Indian Act or constrained by the organizational imperatives of an expanding bureaucracy. But aboriginal peoples have long struggled to disengage from the bureaucratic clutches of the Department of Indian Affairs. A rational control model that once secured aboriginal compliance with the state is being challenged by "indigenous" models for revitalizing the aboriginal agenda. Although fiercely contested, a new administrative paradigm is widely heralded as a driving force for restoring aboriginal control over unceded jurisdictions.

Yet reaction remains mixed to the presence of an Indian Affairs bureaucracy — even one in the throes of debureaucratizing. The resulting debate over retention or reform has sharpened many of the contradictions intrinsic to aboriginal–state rebuilding. This controversy has also reinforced a perception of the Department of Indian Affairs and Northern Development (DIAND) as a "paradox" between overlapping interests and divided loyalties, against a backdrop of "national interests" (Boldt, 1993). More important, the crisis serves to remind us that the plight of the First Nations is "by far the most serious human rights problem in Canada, and that failure to achieve a more global solution can only continue to tarnish Canada's reputation and accomplishments" (Canadian Human Rights Commission, 1994, 20).

Objectives and Content

This chapter examines the largely ambivalent role of the Indian Affairs Department in reshaping the contours of aboriginal–state relations. The chapter argues that jurisdictional wrangles over a proposed realignment of powers strike at the "heart" of different "visions" for Canadian society. Efforts to "debureaucratize" the aboriginal agenda are widely anticipated as necessary and overdue; nevertheless, proposals for "indigenizing" this relationship along postcolonialist lines must contend with political and bureaucratic interests, both of which resist fundamental change for fear of destabilizing state functions. The fallout from such disarray is shown to have transformed aboriginal–state relations into a "contested site," with a variety of intersecting perspectives over who controls what, and why. The chapter concludes by unmasking hidden agendas in the restructuring process, in effect exposing how the "logic" of bureaucracy may prove to be an impenetrable barrier to the indigenizing of aboriginal–state relations.

Two points of contention predominate. First, the current crisis in aboriginal–state relations is not about inherent self-government per se, nor is it about land claims or treaty rights. Rather, the fundamental dynamic that animates this struggle for control is centred on questions about "power" with respect to land, government, and treaty rights. Second, any satisfactory resolution to the problem of jurisdiction must confront the bureaucratic "logic" that has infused aboriginal–state relations at policy and administrative levels. An unshakable commitment to "rational control" appears to disqualify DIAND from an active role in indigenizing the aboriginal agenda. Yet the combination of aboriginal resistance and administrative renewal should prove to be formidable adversaries in the struggle for jurisdictions.

Caveats: "Bureaucratization" and "Indigenization"

Some terms require clarification before proceeding. The concept of "bureaucratization" can be defined as a style of interaction pervaded by the "logic" of rational control (Hummel, 1987). It consists of actions whose calculated efficiency is endorsed as legitimate and self-sufficient in its own right, without need of justification or explanation, even if such actions deny, exclude, or disempower clients (Nelson and Fleras, 1994). This pursuit of control for control's sake is not necessarily deliberate or spiteful, but *systemic* and inadvertent, often reflecting the unintended consequences of standard procedures or even well-meaning acts (Elliott and Fleras, 1991). A similar line of reasoning can be applied to the dynamics that historically have driven aboriginal–state interaction. Patterns of routine, hierarchy, and standardization have reinforced the bureaucratic "logic" underpinning DIAND's regulatory actions with aboriginal "clients." Recent efforts to superimpose aboriginal agendas have encountered difficulties, however, primarily because of systemic biases that distort the department's responsibilities under existing legislation (Deputies Council for Change, 1991; also Little Bear et al., 1984). In short, the "logic" of rational control permeates the interactional basis of all aboriginal–state relations, and moves to modify this bureaucratization have proven to be illusory.

In contrast, the term "indigenization" can be interpreted as the antithesis of bureaucratization. If bureaucracy connotes a zeal for control and order, the concept of indigenization implies open-endedness, a bilateral commitment to negotiations and nuances, and a willingness to explore specifics over cookie-cutter conformity. Indigenization refers to the infusion of aboriginal perspectives and realities at all levels of decision-making and power-sharing. The concept can also invoke additional referents depending on the circumstances, including:

1. The elimination of the Indian Act mentality, followed by replacement with structures and values more consistent with aboriginal concerns and aspirations.

2. A willingness on the part of the state to acknowledge "aboriginality" and aboriginal rights to inherent self-government as a basis for realigning powers and national status.

3. The acknowledgement of self-government as a transfer of jurisdictions from federal authorities to aboriginal governments, along with a reallocation of resources to secure this shift in powers.

4. The restoration of aboriginal control over the design and delivery of local services and programs.

5. A revised social contract between the state and aboriginal peoples, with the principles of aboriginality as a basis for sorting out who controls what.

In short, indigenization can encompass a variety of meanings, ranging in scope from a repositioning of aboriginal peoples within an existing framework to directly challenging the legitimacy of the state over aboriginal jurisdictions (see Tanner, 1993). Between these poles lies the notion of exclusive or shared control over aboriginal domains once monopolized by central authorities. Aboriginal claims for the reinstatement of jurisdiction are not without precedent, nor are they technically about grievances related to governance, identity, or culture — at least, no more so than provocations between Quebec and Ottawa are about language, but rather a jockeying for position in federal–provincial relations. It is impossible to predict outcomes at this point; nevertheless, these jurisdictional tussles could well transform Canada into a "nesting box" of concentric and overlapping sovereignties, with radically different styles of citizenship and belonging (Kaplan, 1993).

Finally, a word on the scope of this chapter. Because of the emphasis on bureaucracy and federal policy, this chapter is concerned primarily with status Indians and band governments rather than aboriginal peoples in general (including urban aboriginals, or Métis, non-status, and Inuit). Data for the chapter are based essentially on secondary analyses of published material. However, the chapter is informed by nearly four years of ethnographical field research at policy and administrative levels with the *tangata whenua o Aotearoa* (the Maori of New Zealand). The pitfalls of any gratuitous comparison between different circumstances have been well documented (Weaver, 1984). Still, a cross-cultural appreciation can be gained by comparing and contrasting trends in aboriginal–state relations, partly because of structural similarities inherent within white settler colonies (Fleras and Elliott, 1992).

ABORIGINALITY, THE STATE, AND SITES OF CONTEST

State initiatives for managing aboriginality are integral to society-building in Canada. The construction of aboriginal–state relations is conducted through official policy and administration, yet secured at the level of tacit assumptions and reinforced through patterns of entitlements, symbols, and discourses. For central authorities, the onus rests on their taking control of policy environments that are difficult to subdue without a loss of legitimacy. Nowhere are these concerns more contentious than at the level of aboriginal policy. The proposed reconstruction of aboriginal–state relations on a government-to-government basis has set in motion a political process, as contested as it is unprecedented (Deloria Jr. and Lytle, 1984; Fleras and Elliott, 1992). No assurances exist as to when state initiatives for managing aboriginality will take hold in any substantial sense.

Much ultimately depends on how adroitly "national interests" can absorb a paradigm shift of such magnitude.

The structure of the relationship between First Nations and the Canadian state is manifest in the machinery of government policy and its administration by federal departments of state (Hawkes and Devine, 1991). Obviously, neither the construction of aboriginal policy nor its implementation by DIAND exists in a political vacuum. Both must be situated instead within a broader context of history and economy as it applies to the struggles of society-building. Debates about accommodating aboriginality invariably raise questions about the role of the state in contemporary contexts (Fleras, 1992). The state in advanced capitalist societies is often engaged in three analytically distinct, but mutually related, activities: accumulation, legitimation, and sovereignty (Resnick, 1990; McBride and Shields, 1993). These functions not only furnish the rationale for competing models in state management of aboriginal relations (see Pal, 1993; Simmons and Keohane, 1992); they also frame responses to ethnically based political claims when the legitimacy of the sovereign state is directly challenged (Connor, 1973; Levin, 1993a).

Managing Diversity

A neo-Marxist analysis situates the state within the framework of a capitalist economy (Panitch, 1977). Capitalist systems are driven to fulfil two basic if somewhat contradictory functions (Offe, 1984). First, they must create conditions (transport infrastructures, etc.) necessary for capital formation. Second, they must secure a social climate conducive to accumulation, in part by assuming responsibility for ameliorating the social costs of private production, and in part by pre-empting potential subversion. In consolidating the realities of the marketplace through persuasion or force, the state can hardly be indifferent to contradictions within the capitalist system, but must suppress or appease resistance based on class, gender, race, or aboriginality (Gupta, 1994). State policies for "managing diversity" (for example, multiculturalism) are driven by the logic of control and co-optation rather than justice or fair play (see Lewycky, 1993). In short, the state is obligated to protect class interests and private property, yet sustain the illusion of neutrality or common good. For neo-Marxists, then, the reconstruction of aboriginal–state relations is properly couched within the framework of political economy, with its dual emphasis on capitalist patterns and aboriginal resistance (Wotherspoon and Satzewich, 1993).

A second interpretation is more consistent with Weberian analysis. This perspective acknowledges that power and status are no less salient than wealth in the shaping of state management of social relations. The state exists as a relatively independent force, with considerable scope for pursuing goals, at times seemingly contrary to class interests (Miliband, 1973; Poulantzas, 1975). Through symbols, discourses, and practices, the state actively confronts the minority-relations policy field in the teeth of opposition, diversity, or change (Simmons and Keohane, 1992). The quest for legitimacy transforms the diversity agenda into a struggle between unequally endowed and diverse sectors. The restructuring process itself is complex, subject to conflicting ideologies and interests, and vulnerable to outside forces, including various forms of local resistance and community renewal (Wotherspoon and Satzewich, 1993). Inasmuch as this is possible in democratic societies, the state is expected to defuse these challenges to its authority by silencing opposition, undercutting credibility, deflecting criticism, discrediting options, advocating modest concessions, and nullifying the threat of confrontation — inasmuch as this is possible (Habermas, 1976; Fleras and Elliott, 1991). This Weberian perspective does not necessarily discount or discredit the economics of policy or administration. It merely acknowledges the interplay of competing forces, in addition to material conditions, as a basis for decision-making or power-sharing.

The Politics of Aboriginality

The restructuring of aboriginal–state relations has not proceeded smoothly in the past. State initiatives are rarely cohesive or fully rational. Nor is there reason to see improvements in the immediate future. At the core of this impasse is a failure to appreciate the implications of aboriginality as a politicized ideology for radical change. Aboriginality is political in that choices about who gets what are out in public and subject to debate. These debates are concerned with "distributive ideals" in the allocation of powers and resources (Sharp, 1990). The discourse is political because aboriginal claims constitute grievances against the state, as well as the institutional correlates of that domination — namely, policy and administration. Initiatives that once focussed on understanding and compassion are now channelled into struggles for control over jurisdiction as a "nation within" (Levin, 1993b; Mercredi, June 15, 1994 AFN leadership conference). There is another sense in which aboriginality is political. Recognition of aboriginality not only legitimizes aboriginal participation in the political (or constitutional) process; it also bolsters aboriginal claims for "nationhood" status (Levin, 1993c).

Even the tabling of aboriginal demands is inherently political. Political parties became entangled in controversies dealing with aboriginal issues, and the state itself is implicated when its legitimacy as a sovereign state is directly challenged. This political aspect is embedded not only in the partisan sense of political parties and party agendas. It is also manifest in the broader sense of value judgements about the preferred vision of society. More important, the politicization of aboriginality strikes at the very core of the governing process: it draws the state into the most contentious of all relations — namely, the relationship between co-equals in the political arena, with each claiming intrinsic authority and separate jurisdiction over powers, resources, and status (Sharp, 1990).

Canadian State versus Aboriginality

Central authorities in Canada have stumbled in responding to aboriginal demands for indigenizing aboriginal–state relations. The promises of lofty rhetoric notwithstanding, there remains a noticeable lack of political will to implement much of this rhetoric (Weaver, 1993; Macklem, 1993). A willingness to acknowledge aboriginality as a negotiating principle is counterbalanced by fears of unhinging Canadian society (Levin, 1993a; Webber, 1994). Government officials prefer to endorse aboriginal self-government as a political concession, both contingent and delegated on a band-to-band basis, with accountability to Parliament and the Constitution, rather than as an inherent right derived from natural or spiritual law (Tennant, 1985). Federal initiatives do not necessarily spring from a sense of outrage or injustice, but from a self-serving need to offload departmental functions under the guise of aboriginal empowerment (AFN, 1992; Seguin, 1994).

Policy officials are understandably wary about dissolving once habitual patterns of domination in the uncharted waters of nationhood or sovereignty (Levin, 1993a). Many are reluctant to reopen debates over jurisdictions for fear of compromising the national interests of Canada (Boldt, 1993). Consider only the implications of establishing a third order of government in Canada (Raphals, 1991; Clark, 1990). Aboriginal governments would possess primary authority over jurisdictional matters, neither subordinate to nor derivative of federal or provincial powers, but sovereign within their sphere (Webber, 1994; also *New York Times*, May 22, 1994). Provincial and federal authorities could no more encroach upon aboriginal jurisdictions than on each other's (speech, Mercredi, 1994).

For central authorities, the very concept of ethnonationalism poses a paradox (Levin, 1993a). On the one hand, state suppression of racial, ethnic, or aboriginal nationalism can culminate in the outbreak of intergroup strife; on the other, official endorsement of diversity can unintentionally intensify ethnic cleavages and territorial dismemberment. Strategies for compromise have varied in the past, but most call for the placement of racial and ethnic minorities into a settled hierarchy, with all sectors sharing in a common goal as well as an agreed-upon set of rules (Sharp, 1990). Since the late 1960s, minority–majority relations have been constructed around the principle of minority co-optation through involvement and consensus, without the taint of heavy-handed state intervention or loss of control over the national agenda (Fleras and Elliott, 1992; Fleras, 1994; Gupta, 1994). Canada's multiculturalism strategy is premised on precisely such principles (Fleras and Elliott, 1991).

In the case of aboriginal peoples, however, the ground rules are shifting and openly contested (Weaver, 1990; 1991). Aboriginal claims against the state are articulated by those who assert an intrinsic authority, not as subjects or as citizens, but as co-equals with inherent rights to construct or to improvise as circumstances dictate (RCAP, 1992). Radical assertions for "nations within" status are profoundly disturbing to orthodox state structures. Central authorities must not only reconsider the first principles underlying settler colony governance. They must also grasp the thrust of aboriginality as nothing less than a discourse about jurisdiction and powers, albeit within the framework of Canadian society (Asch, 1993). Clearly, then, aboriginal resistance has jumped from a focus on cultural survival and formal equality to a demand for radical renewal and power-sharing reform. This clash of competing paradigms — nationhood versus statehood — will continue to resonate throughout the policy and administrative fields as long as formal initiatives tinker with symbols rather than substance.

Gridlock or Growing Pains?

In the face of growing competition and conflict, the state has moved to repair its relationship with aboriginal peoples. This reconstruction process is motivated by uncertainties in divvying up jurisdictions. The state may be powerful because of its capacity to set agendas and fix outer limits of debate, yet its hegemony is never secure in defending its "turf" against intruders. Even with power and resources at its disposal, the state is constantly on guard against any potential threat to its legitimate authority (Habermas, 1976). Interests groups are willing and able to confront the state. In recent years, they have openly contested even the legitimacy of the state as a ploy to secure benefits or extract concessions. Not unexpectedly, what passes for a state policy position is often a balancing act of last resort, demanding a workable accommodation through negotiation and compromise.

Economics has also proven a major stumbling block. Aboriginal policy at present is defined by a fiscally restrained policy-making context (Morse, 1989; Angus, 1990). Downsizing the public sector in general, and aboriginal services in particular, has coincided with a political resolve to curb escalating expenditures (Pratt, 1989). The government is anxious to reduce "unnecessary" expenditures, arguing that only about 25 percent of current funding in Native Affairs is necessary to meet legal obligations (Angus, 1990). The remainder is discretionary, and theoretically, at any rate, subject to negotiation and discard. Outright curtailment of federal expenses represents another option. The government has proposed the removal of the Indian Affairs Department, with current programs and responsibilities transferred to existing line departments (Angus, 1990). It also has attempted to (1) roll back federal programs, (2) transfer service responsibility to local communities, (3) disengage from active involvement, and (4) delegate authority to the provinces, which technically may bypass legal, constitutional, or treaty agreements (see Bull, 1994; Pratt, 1989). Such moves are consistent with wider developments elsewhere for "downsizing" federal fiduciary obligations to purely legal requirements. Evidence, in other words, points to a conflict of interest between aboriginal aspirations and political concessions. Substantial changes will not come easily. More time will pass before federal authorities abandon their "trench warfare mentality" (Harold Cardinal, in Comeau and Sandin, 1990, p. 20) for one based on partnership and power-sharing. It may take even longer to put empowering principles into practice in the light of vested interests and competing loyalties.

This chapter argues, as have Simmons and Keohane (1992) elsewhere, that the pursuit of legitimacy and control are integral to state efforts to manage "aboriginality." The state confronts a notoriously daunting challenge in its quest for legitimacy, especially since proposals for aboriginal restructuring imply a redivision of powers so fundamental as to threaten the fabric of society (Macklem, 1993). The imperative for survival propels the state into a series of proactive measures as one way of deflecting potential criticism away from itself. It also engages the state in a series of rearguard actions for shoring up strengths by camouflaging weaknesses. This is especially true of Canada where a series of botched constitutional reforms has left the state especially vulnerable to second-guessing or blackmail. In the wake of these potentially damaging events, state concessions to aboriginal nations (as well as the Quebecois and multicultural minorities) must be interpreted within the extenuating circumstances of a country in constitutional disarray (Simmons and Keohane, 1992; also Webber, 1994). In the case of aboriginal–state relations, the inclination to build bridges with "troublesome constituents" is preferred over brooking further opposition or outright confrontations. The question for this chapter is whether existing bridges — namely, the Indian Affairs Department — are sufficient to meet the challenge.

FROM BUREAUCRACY TO DEVELOPMENT

[T]he whole idea of the federal stewardship over aboriginal peoples — and its manifestation in the Indian Act and a Department of Indian and Northern Affairs — has been an attempt to rationalize and legitimize the relationship between colonizers and colonized. (Canadian Human Rights Commission, 1994, p. 24)

The various departments comprising Indian Affairs have long exerted a powerful influence on aboriginal communities. These departments originated within the context of the Indian Act, and continue to draw their mandate from its Victorian-era provisions. The content, objectives, and style of Indian Affairs departments, not to mention the magnitude of its influence, have evolved over time. Current developments suggest a fundamental restructuring of aboriginal–state relations along partnership lines (Fleras and Elliott, 1992; DIAND, 1993b). Appearances, however, can be deceiving, and a brief overview of Indian Affairs history provides a different perspective on contemporary changes.

The Mandate: The Indian Act

Aboriginal relations with the Canadian state are mediated by a series of legislative initiatives known as the Indian Act. With passage of the Indian Act in 1876, the Department of Indian Affairs was given sweeping power to invade, control, and regulate the minutest aspects of reserve life, even to the point of curbing constitutional and citizenship rights (Morse, 1989). Aboriginal languages, cultures, and identity were suppressed, and band communities were locked into patterns of dependency and despondency with little opportunity for escape (AFN, 1992).

This legitimizing document sought to standardize and regulate ("bureaucratize") federal interaction with status Indians. As part of this bureaucratization process, the Indian Act defined who came under its provisions, what each status Indian was entitled to under the government's fiduciary obligations, who could qualify for disenfranchisement, what could be done with reserve lands and resources, and how local communities were to be ruled. Traditional leadership was replaced with elected band councils, most of whom were perceived as extensions of central authority, with limited powers subject to prior approval or to Ottawa's arbitrary whims (Webber, 1994). Even economic opportunities were curtailed. Under the Indian Act, aboriginal people could not possess direct title to land or private property, nor could they generate revenue from the sale or lease of band property. Punitive restrictions not only foreclosed aboriginal property improvements, but also precluded the accumulation of economic development capital for investment or growth (Eckholm, 1994). Historically, then, bands have had difficulty in financing commercial endeavours on reserves because aboriginal land held in Crown trust was immune to mortgage, collateral, or legal seizure (McMillan, 1988).

That the spirit of the Indian Act survives into the present is a commentary on the powers of inertia. The Indian Act persists as an essentially repressive instrument of containment that subverts aboriginal control over jurisdictions of local concern. Even more remarkable is the degree of bureaucratization that pervades aboriginal–state relations as a result of the Indian Act. Program design and funding continue to be controlled by Ottawa, thus hampering community endeavors, and federal authorities routinely reject band council bylaws on the grounds that they violate Indian Act provisions (Platiel, 1994b). Aboriginal men and women have soundly repudiated the act as inflexible and restrictive, and at odds with even limited aboriginal aspirations (AFN, 1992). Yet others acknowledge its usefulness in affording legal protection from outside interests (see RCAP, 1993). Federal authorities have been no less vociferous in rebuking the Indian Act as patronizing or regressive (DIAND, 1993b). Evidence suggests the days of the Indian Act are numbered, although no one is willing to predict "how" or "when," and with what effect.

Indian Affairs in Historical Perspective

State complicity in the control and dispossession of aboriginal peoples has been well documented; by now, little can be learned from a rehashing of the negative consequences of even well-intentioned actions by Indian Affairs officials, who were often more interested in careerism and empire-building than in aboriginal empowerment (Ponting and Gibbins, 1980; Ponting, 1986; also Shkilnyk, 1985). Nevertheless, the Department of Indian Affairs has undergone a change of "heart," with significant repercussions all around. For convenience, the history of the Indian Affairs can be partitioned into three stages: *control, devolution,* and *empowerment.* As an "ideal type" in the Weberian sense, this division is heuristic rather than accurate to the last detail. Nor can these stages be considered mutually exclusive and self-contained, except for analytical purposes. Finally, this threefold typology conforms more or less with commonly accepted divisions within the aboriginal policy field (see Tobias, 1976).

Control (1868–1965)

In 1867, the federal government assumed jurisdiction over aboriginal affairs with the establishment of an Indian affairs branch under the secretary of state (Ponting and Gibbins, 1980). Prior to this, the British Colonial Office had relied on the military for the control of aboriginal affairs and the recruitment of allies against the French and later the Americans (Boldt, 1993). By the 1830s, priorities had shifted to land and settlement; Indian affairs and responsibility for controlling and civilizing the indigenous peoples were subsequently transferred to civilian authorities, but continued to be staffed by military officers (Platiel, 1994b). Subsequent passage of the 1876 Indian Act created the legal framework for the administration of aboriginal affairs under federal jurisdiction as stipulated in the British North America Act of 1867.

The Indian Affairs portfolio has been shuffled from one federal agency to another, depending on the needs and perceptions of central authorities (Wotherspoon and Satzewich, 1993). A separate Indian Affairs department was established in 1880, although the minister of the interior served as the superintendent-general of Indian Affairs. In 1936, the department was brought under Mines and Natural Resources; in 1945, it was transferred to Citizenship and Immigration, where it remained until 1965, when it came under Northern Affairs and Natural Resources. It was not until October 1966 that a free-standing Department of Indian Affairs and Northern Development was instituted by an act of parliament with a minister responsible for the Indian and Inuit Affairs Program.

Early department activities were consistent with the mandate and provisions of the Indian Act. Ostensibly, the department was responsible for implementation of the Indian Act, with its numerous trust obligations pertaining to land claims. As a total institution, however, Indian Affairs established dictatorial reign that intruded into all aspects of community life. The Indian agent — a political appointee — on each reserve yielded powers equivalent to the colonial governor (Platiel, 1994b). Its colonialist/paternalistic character reflected a perception of aboriginal peoples as childlike wards of the state in need of superior guidance and protection. Through a combination of incentives and sanctions, Indian Affairs sought to destroy the cultural basis of aboriginal society; transform aboriginal peoples through exposure to Christianity and arts of civilization; and assimilate (absorb) them into society as self-reliant and productive citizens. The success and failure of departmental policy was evaluated by the numbers of enfranchised Natives — that is, those who formally renounced Indian status for the trappings of Canadian citizenship (Ponting and Gibbins, 1980). It was also measured by how effectively the aboriginal population was kept out of sight and under control (Frideres, 1993).

Devolution (1966–1990)

Until the late 1950s, the Indian Affairs Department directly delivered virtually all programs and services to the First Nations. Such a mindset reflected a bureaucratized view of aboriginal peoples as a "problem" whose cultural and social idiosyncrasies precluded a smooth absorption into society. Shortly after World War II, political vision of the solution to the "Indian problem" switched from cultural assimilation to modernization through eradication of poverty at local levels, coupled with a commitment to formal equality and integration (Shkilnyk, 1985). From the government's point of view, the Indian problem resided in the communal (read "communistic") aspects of tribal life. Salvation lay either in urban migration or in reserve improvement through government expenditures and state-supported programs related to job creation, infrastructure, and economic self-sufficiency. The role of DIAND was critical in this restructuring, given its mandate to "administer the affairs of the Indians of Canada in a manner that will enable them to make the necessary adjustments to become fully participating and self-supporting members of the communities in which they live" (DCI, 1958). The provision of social services and physical improvements on the reserve in concert with increased local responsibility for community-based initiatives were touted as critical in accelerating this transition from "pathology" to "progress."

By the mid-1960s, the control-and-deliver mentality began to subside. Federal efforts to reorganize service delivery through direct band involvement had commenced in 1956 with the funding of several local education committees. The rationale for this restructuring drew strength from three assumptions: first, the necessity to establish aboriginal rather than federal control over community affairs; second, a perception that properly resourced communities were better equipped to solve local problems; and third, a suspicion that centralized structures were ineffective for problem-solving when dealing with a geographically dispersed and culturally diverse people. In short, the shift toward devolution and decentralization bolstered the move toward community-based control over local jurisdictions. It also conceded the importance of softening the harshly bureaucratic image of the department.

This commitment to devolution culminated in the late 1970s with establishment of detailed provisions for aboriginal administration of departmental programs, coupled with funding in support of basic local government programs (DIAND, 1993b). Such a shift was consistent with political moves toward fiscal restraint, curtailment of direct federal services, political rationality, and a downsizing of the social policy agenda (see Prince, 1987). In 1986, federal authorities announced a policy of community self-government negotiations as part of the reform package — for the most part consistent with cabinet-approved guidelines for community self-sufficiency, but outside any federally imposed blueprint. Passage of the Indian Self-Government Community Negotiations Act was viewed as a means of experimenting with different approaches to self-government on a band-by-band basis (Hawkes and Devine, 1991). The act was also heralded as a practical albeit interim alternative, to be pursued in conjunction with ongoing negotiations for constitutional entrenchment of inherent self-governance.

A revised social-political contract based on enlarging aboriginal jurisdiction over local affairs has achieved moderate success. Service delivery on a program-by-program basis has moved over for more flexible funding arrangements in terms of decentralized administration, local decision-making, and mutual accountability (DIAND, 1993b). Government funding is increasingly "unconditional," as had been recommended in the Penner report of 1983, thus allowing for greater discretion (within limits) in the allocation of funds. Alternative funding arrangements ("comprehensive funding agreements") have proven attractive since they allow priorities and programs to be established along aboriginal lines. Responsibilities for delivery and effectiveness of local programs are localized, with band members increasingly accountable for the management of resources, services, and programs. In this sense, DIAND has repositioned itself as a developmental agency for the transfer of federal funds to self-government structures in the same way that provinces receive federal block funding for programs and services

Empowerment (1990–Present)

Current government objectives are geared to preserve "the special place of our first citizens in the country" within the constitutional framework of Canadian society. These initiatives rest on the four policy pillars: accelerate land claims settlement; improve socio-economic status on reserves; rebuild aboriginal–state relations; and address aboriginal concerns as announced by the prime minister in September 1990. On paper, the government has shifted its policy operations toward limited acceptance of aboriginal peoples as a "distinct" society with certain rights to self-government. In the words of Minister of Indian Affairs Ronald Irwin, "The federal government is committed to building a new partnership with Aboriginal people, a partnership based on mutual respect and trust. Working steadily towards the implementation of *the inherent right of self-government is the cornerstone of that relation*" (Canada, 1994, emphasis added). Many applaud Liberal claims to recognize inherent self-government arrangements as an existing treaty right, with or without constitutional backing. These promises, however, are vague and unenforceable, as are the terms of reference and means of implementation, thus allowing the government to wriggle out of commitments if realities outstrip expectations (*Wataway News*, April 7, 1994). Moreover, conferral of inherency can also be manipulated to amplify the role of aboriginal peoples as pawns in a constitutional cat-and-mouse game between Quebec and Ottawa.

Arguably, Canada's First Nations constitute domestic dependent nations comparable in status and stature with aboriginal tribes in the United States. The right to self-government on unceded lands is derived from guarantees with the British crown, and this sovereignty by virtue of original and continuous occupancy has been upheld by Canada's top courts. A distinct level of polity alongside the provincial and federal level is inherent within and derived from aboriginal people rather than delegated from legal authority. Elijah Harper (RCAP, 1992, p. 19) expressed it succinctly when he said: "Self-government is not [something] that can be given away by any government, but rather . . . flows from Creator. Self-government . . . is taking control and managing our own affairs, being able to determine our own future and destiny. . . . It has never been up to the governments to give self-government. It has never been theirs to give." In recent years, the concept of aboriginal self-government has been linked with moves to indigenize the interactional basis of aboriginal–state relations. Discourse over jurisdiction — who gets what — is no less central to this restructuring. Negotiations over jurisdictions extend to an array of topics related to procedures of government, legal status, membership, land and resource management, financial arrangements, service delivery, and social assistance.

To date, several viable community self-government enterprises in line with block funding arrangements have been negotiated pursuant to self-governing legislation (DIAND, 1993b). A growing number of bands now exert limited control over finances, and several, including the Sechelt of British Columbia, have negotiated self-governing arrangements beyond the confines of the Indian Act. Implementation of self-governing apparatus has taken place among Cree-Naskapi of James Bay in 1984 and the Sechelt in British Columbia in 1986, with negotiations currently under way elsewhere (see Taylor and Paget, 1989). But progress has been made at a glacial pace, according to an auditor's report in 1993 (York, 1994). Seven years after the passage of federal enabling legislation in 1986, only one additional self-governing arrangement (with the tiny Sawridge band in Alberta) had been negotiated, but at a cost of $50 million, with several others nearing completion. Even the number of discussions with aboriginal bands had dwindled to 15 from about 400, many of which had cited breakdowns in communications because of excessive bureaucracy.

Indigenizing the Bureaucracy

DIAND is best described as a geographically decentralized federal bureaucracy, located in eleven regions across Canada. It is responsible for the well-being of aboriginal and non-aboriginal peoples in the Northwest Territories and Yukon through a combination of direct program expenditures and transfer payments — not altogether different from what happens in other government departments (Deputies Council for Change, 1991). The objective of the Inuit and Indian Affairs Program, according to Part II of the *Main Estimates*, 1992–93, is to "support Indians and Inuit in achieving their self-government, economic, industrial, cultural, social, and community development needs and aspirations." Firmly rooted in the antiquated 1876/1951 Indian Act, the Indian Affairs division evolved into a largely custodial/regulatory agency whose primary role as a "money-moving" agency was to allocate funds on the basis of compliance with organizational directives (Ponting, 1986; Weaver, 1990; Frideres, 1990). The department drew its clout from control over funding and allocation. In the deft phrasing of Juanita Perley, "Indian Affairs is holding you with a noose around your neck — they've got you with just your toes on the ground — dangling that money over you" (from Silman, 1987, p. 223).

In recent years, DIAND has undergone a major shift in content, organization, and style. A partnership commitment in support of community-based self-government has displaced the concept of direct service delivery. In its role as a smaller, more responsive agency, DIAND has endorsed a developmental and advisory orientation, with a responsibility to advance First Nations concerns; to enhance autonomy and self-reliance; to mediate relations with central authorities; and to service negotiated agreements (Weaver, 1991; Boldt, 1993; DIAND, 1993b). Indian Affairs has also sought to simplify funding relationships with First Nations through increased flexibility and community-based discretion (Frideres, 1993). With a broad spectrum of comprehensive funding arrangements at their disposal, in other words, each First Nations government is now expected to assume ownership over program delivery at a pace tailored to meet specific community interests; ensure greater local control and accountability; and enhance service delivery capacities.

The Cost of Administration

As stipulated by the Indian Act, the department retains a comprehensive range of obligations and services toward aboriginal peoples. The department has primary responsibility not only to fulfil the federal government's obligations to "Indians and Lands reserved for Indians," but also to administer the Indian Act through the delivery of select programs and services (DIAND, 1993b). In some instances, these programs embrace obligations specified in existing treaties. In others, the diversity of programs is comparable with those delivered to other Canadians by provincial and municipal governments. Federal programs for Indian reserve communities include services in health, education, social assistance, housing, community infrastructure, justice, culture, and economic growth. Funding and responsibility for meeting First Nations needs is not limited to DIAND. Health and Welfare Canada is responsible for health services, and territorial governments and provinces such as Newfoundland have assumed responsibilities for service delivery under a cost-sharing agreement with federal authorities (DIAND, 1993b). In addition, the department has a number of important legal responsibilities related to Indian estates, the resolution of outstanding comprehensive land claims, and continuing fulfilment of Canada's constitutional obligations and statutory responsibilities.

Administering aboriginal affairs has not come cheaply. Several government departments are responsible for the $5.041 billion spent on aboriginal affairs based on 1992–93 estimates, with DIAND at 72.3 percent, Health and Welfare Canada at 11.4 percent, Canadian Mortgage and Housing at 5.4 percent, and Employment and Immigration at 4 percent (DIAND, 1993a). DIAND's estimates for expenditure in 1992–1993 stood at $3.646 billion, with the bulk directed at education — from primary to university ($903.3 million), social development ($816.3 million), capital facilities and community services ($665.1 million), and northern affairs ($572 million). Additional expenditures have focussed on various programs for enhancing economic self-sufficiency and development on reserves under the department's Economic Development Sector and the Canadian Economic Development Strategy. Although some caution must be exercised in interpreting these data, the government will spend about $12 412 for each status Indian living on reserve or on crown land (DIAND, 1993a).

Funding for the First Nations has grown steadily since 1975–76, when it stood at $703 million, or 2.11 percent of federal expenditures (excluding debt), to a current figure of 4.22 percent of the government's budgetary expenditures (excluding debt). Increases in funding of aboriginal affairs since 1975 may reflect enhanced services as part of a federal commitment to observe trust obligations. These increases may also be more apparent than real because of rapid population growth (including reinstatement following Bill C-31) and inflationary effects, suggesting that per capita spending may have declined (Hawkes and Devine, 1991).

Even more significant is growing First Nations control over departmental funding. By 1992–93, 77.3 percent of DIAND's budget was being administered by First Nations bands through various funding arrangements, up from 41 percent in 1984 (DIAND, 1993a). Only 11 percent was applied directly by DIAND for direct service delivery, with 12 percent paid out against funding arrangements with the provinces. Funds are allocated to the First Nations on the basis of resourcing formulas (reflecting demographic information); they also reflect a system of prioritization anchored on the definition of need. Finally, the number of persons employed by DIAND has continued to decline, dropping from a high of 8000 in 1975–76 to fewer than 4000 in 1992–93. At the same time, the indigenization of departmental staff continues. The number of aboriginal officials within DIAND has increased by 19 percent in that same period, although systemic biases toward pale male models of management and service delivery remain in force, in effect precluding much movement into the higher echelons (Deputies Council for Change, 1991). Finally, the percentage of DIAND's budget for administrative overhead has declined to about 3.4 percent of the total budget from 6.0 percent in 1986–87 (DIAND, 1993a).

Fiscal Politics

A fresh approach to aboriginal–state relations is symbolized by more generous funding arrangements. In the past, DIAND had assumed all responsibility for centrally controlled and direct service delivery to aboriginal communities. DIAND funds were limited and conditional, subject to extensive legal and administrative barriers (Wotherspoon and Satzewich, 1993). The department was accountable to Parliament for program success, yet financial risks could be diminished through the monitoring of reserve activities by a dispersed field staff.

Ottawa has loosened the financial noose in recent years in response to aboriginal demands for control over jurisdiction. Funding that tolerates some degree of discretion in spending, leeway in priority-setting, and local accountability is now available to bands. Yet appearances can be deceiving: band budgets continue to be established by the Treasury Board, and Ottawa remains the only source of revenue for many band governments. Ottawa may decide on appropriate levels of expenditures, then transfer responsibilities to an elected band council whose essential duties include disbursement of funds according to predetermined formulas in health, housing, sanitation, and education (Comeau and Sandin, 1990). Band governments must answer to federal authorities rather than the local community; they also must operate within the agreed-upon funding ceiling over the multiple-year terms of agreement. Nor can bands request additional funding during the life of the agreement (Hawkes and Devine, 1991). In short, the shift from bureaucracy to indigenization as reflected in discretionary spending patterns may be more apparent than real. Still, the process and goal of indigenization represents an improvement over the bureaucracy of the past.

Multiple Mandates, Competing Agendas

The Department of Indian Affairs remains a convenient target for criticism (AFN, 1992; RCAP, 1993). To one side, there are calls for its outright abolition, followed by a transfer of functions and funding to government agencies or aboriginal bands. Since coming to power in 1993, the Liberal government has proposed to scrap DIAND by transferring responsibility for services in health or policing away from federal authorities to aboriginal jurisdictions — with a ground-breaking agreement with Manitoba chiefs singled out as a test case for future developments (Platiel, 1994a). To the other side, there are appeals for the retention of DIAND, albeit in a modified form, as a buffer in shielding aboriginal ambitions from predatory interests.

Hostilities continue to mount, both internally and externally, despite initiatives to debureaucratize and indigenize the aboriginal agenda (in 1991 the Treasury Department voted DIAND the best-run federal department (Boldt, 1993)). In the words of Phil Fontaine, grand chief of the Assembly of Manitoba Chiefs, "There is nothing more fundamental to our well-being at this time than getting rid of the Indian Affairs department" (quoted in Nagle, 1994, p. F-10). Such an observation is hardly surprising in view of DIAND's reputation as an instrument of colonial domination and administrative control (Ponting, 1986). DIAND has been taken to task for doing "too much" for aboriginal peoples, thus robbing them of initiative while deterring self-reliance though excessive red tape, top-heavy administration, and welfare dependency. It has also been scrutinized for doing "too little" in pursuit of aboriginal needs and aspirations. Criticism is fuelled by the impossibly wide mandate of DIAND — namely, to administer the provisions of the Indian Act, to provide a broad range of services and programs to status Indians, and to advance the cause of aboriginal self-sufficiency and community self-government. Nor can DIAND ignore the northern development component of its mandate, which in effect complicates its relations with the First Nations because of conflicting interests with resource-driven multinationals (Wotherspoon and Satzewich, 1993). Charges also stem from the department's central function as a regulatory agency with responsibilities for allocating funds to aboriginal groups and organizations — a situation conducive to allegations of abuse, favouritism, and paternalism. Finally, DIAND's low-priority status within the government decision-making caucus — a small, wobbly Indian wheel in the federal machinery as stated by Menno Boldt (1993, p. 109) — has also hindered its effectiveness as a forum for aboriginal grievances.

DIAND as Rational Control

How accurate are these attacks? Is it a case of criticism for the sake of criticism, or can these charges be empirically substantiated? Much of the criticism fails to acknowledge the difficult circumstances in which the bureaucracy finds itself. On the one hand, the department is required by an act of Parliament to labour under dated legislation in a society that is altogether different from the one that drafted the Indian acts (Deputies

Council for Change, 1991). On the other, many shortcomings reflect DIAND's status as a bureaucracy in charge of a culturally diverse and geographically dispersed peoples. The "logic" behind departmental decisions is no different from that of other bureaucracies — namely, the pursuit of "rational control" by (1) reinforcing rules ("go by the book"), (2) proper communication and standardized procedures ("get it in writing"), (3) primacy of conformity ("don't make waves"), and (4) pervasive hierarchy ("up through the channels") (see Weber, 1947; Hummel, 1987). The potential for meaningful interaction diminishes when relationships are sorted into patterns of impersonal and hierarchical authority, formal rules, standardized procedures, and a complex division of labour. Under these circumstances, administrative decisions conform with bureaucratic dictates rather than aboriginal sensibilities (Miller, 1989; Deputies Council for Change, 1991).

DIAND's status as a state bureaucracy is further problematic. All government departments possess two main functions vis-à-vis their clients: one is to represent client interests at national decision-making circles; the other is to serve as agents of social control (Wotherspoon and Satzewich, 1993). This dual mandate is inimical to positive aboriginal–state relations. As an agency of the state, DIAND's functions cannot be separated from state functions in a capitalist society, including the needs to legitimize the distribution of wealth and power in society and to reproduce the social order (Panitch, 1977). That being the case, the primary (if latent) function of DIAND continues to be the containment and control of aboriginal peoples, in large part by steering aboriginal aspirations into politically acceptable channels. In other words, neither maliciousness nor conspiracy can account for the strain in aboriginal–state relations. Rather, as Menno Boldt (1993) points out, blame rests with the state's unwillingness to accommodate aboriginal needs, however inadvertently, when these diverge from "national interests."

In short, the department finds itself in the paradoxical position of mediating the tension between statehood and nation-seeking aboriginal peoples. In such a compromising role, DIAND must fulfil its obligations to the government and state, yet be responsive and answerable to aboriginal peoples, without much support from either sector (Deputies Council for Change, 1991). Efforts to restructure DIAND's relationship with aboriginal nations are subject to contradiction because of this systemic bias. Even more transparent are those moves to indigenize the interactional basis of aboriginal–DIAND relations. Instead of power-sharing, the devolutionary process is perceived as pawning off federal responsibility for the delivery of programs and services. But responsibility without power is tokenism. Not only does this disempowerment reinforce the system of control; it also ensures that many aboriginal people remain trapped within structures of domination, both removed and remote. These conflicts of interest have subjected the department to aboriginal anger and frustration over hidden agendas.

The long-term status of DIAND is open to conjecture. Conventional wisdom dictates the eventual demise of the department as a federal bureaucracy (Platiel, 1994a). Its elimination is perceived by many as inevitable and necessary for indigenizing aboriginal–state relations along the lines of the "nations within" (Fleras and Elliott, 1992). Yet there is no guarantee that deleting the department will automatically transfer state authority into aboriginal empowerment. Moreover, the formidable presence of DIAND will not yield readily to demands for repeal or reform (Boldt, 1993). Not only is the department a conduit of considerable depth and breadth, but it also houses a daunting array of senior officials who exercise authority over a broad range of programs across 40 district offices. Such tenacity and scope underscores the ambivalent status of Indian Affairs. Neither a monolithic fortress impervious to change nor a wind tunnel subject to the slightest external pressure, DIAND is essentially a "contested site" in which opposing groups compete for jurisdiction in an unremitting struggle to establish who controls what.

DISCUSSION: "OVERLAPPING SOVEREIGNTIES"

Aboriginal people are usually defined as the living descendants of what commonly are thought to be the original inhabitants of a territory (Burger, 1987). In structural terms, they now occupy an encapsulated status as subordinate subjects of a larger political entity (Stea and Wisner, 1984). Historically, aboriginal–state relations in settler colonies fall into a set pattern: destruction of aboriginal culture and society; transformation of aboriginal peoples into models of self-sufficiency and progress; outward compliance with dominant values; and absorption into the mainstream for national interests and capitalist growth. Yet these assimilative pressures did not dissuade aboriginal peoples from continuing to identify with a cultural lifestyle at odds with "conventional" assumptions. Nor have they blunted aboriginal aspirations for jurisdictional control over a range of political, social, economic, and cultural domains.

The concept of aboriginal "nationhood" is critical to the restructuring process. Unlike refugee or immigrant groups who are looking to "put down roots" or "remove discriminatory barriers," aboriginal peoples assume the politically self-conscious stance of a "nation" when they go beyond cultural concerns and physical survival (Fleras and Elliott, 1992). The additional step consists of the assertion that they possess a special relationship with the state, along with a corresponding set of collective entitlements that flow from inherency and first principles. The distributive ideals associated with "aboriginality" are varied, but typically involve demands for aboriginal sovereignty over land, resources, culture, and identity.

Aboriginal peoples in Canada also have taken the initiative to sever the bonds of colonialist dependency and underdevelopment (Bienvenue, 1985). In the space of just over two decades, aboriginal peoples have recoiled from the brink of social extinction to occupy a pivotal status in the reconstruction of Canadian society. Such a reversal originated and gained legitimacy when the "costs" of excluding aboriginal peoples from the national agenda proved to be unacceptably high in social, political, and economic terms (Fleras and Krahn, 1992). But the politics of restructuring often conceal hidden agendas and contested realities. The fundamental objective of various Indian Affairs departments — to eliminate the aboriginal "problem" through local self-sufficiency — has not wavered over the years (Ponting and Gibbins, 1986). Only the means have altered, with crude assimilationist strategies giving way to more sophisticated channels that co-opt aspects of aboriginal discourse for self-serving purposes (see Bull, 1994). The establishment of a "community negotiation process" and modified block funding arrangements may bolster DIAND's commitment to reduce band dependency, broaden reserve decision-making powers, improve effectiveness, and enhance mutual accountability (DIAND, 1993b). It may also have the effect — however inadvertent — of advancing the assimilationist agenda.

Calls to improve aboriginal–state relations through devolution and decentralization are strewn with administrative landmines. At the crux of this perilous process are the politics of jurisdiction. In the final analysis, aboriginal demands for self-determination are inseparable from concerns over "who controls what" with respect to wealth, power, and status. Yet central authorities are reluctant to relinquish jurisdiction unless such concessions are consistent with "national" or "sectarian" interests (Boldt, 1993; see Wotherspoon and Satzewich, 1993). They are even more hesitant to assert aboriginality as a basis for redrawing powers for fear of destabilizing Canada's legitimacy as a sovereign state. In contrast, First Nations prefer to maximize jurisdiction and powers as a means of reclaiming control over their lives and life chances. The interplay of these contested positions shapes the dynamics at the "heart" of aboriginal–state restructuring.

Patterns and Themes

This chapter has argued that the politics of jurisdiction are central to any understanding of the current crisis in aboriginal–state relations. Several key themes are apparent in the restructuring of aboriginal–state jurisdictions at the level of policy and administration.

1. The dynamics of aboriginal–state relations are inherently bureaucratic in style, scope, and outcome. This *bureaucratization* of the aboriginal agenda arose from a need to control the First Nations; it was legitimized by regulations within the Indian Act, expressed in the logic of departmental actions, and imposed on the lives and life chances of aboriginal communities. Recent efforts to *debureaucratize* this relationship are aimed at *indigenizing* the interactional basis of aboriginal–state relations. Central to the indigenizing process are

debates over *jurisdiction* — that is, who controls what with respect to resources, power, and status. Only a fundamental redivision of powers between First Nations and central authorities holds out hope for renewal and healing.

2. Government departments are ostensibly in charge of aboriginal protection and well-being. Yet they are poorly positioned to address issues of empowerment in a manner consistent with aboriginal aspirations (Fleras, 1989). The "rational control" ethic at the core of bureaucracy not only regulates through standardizations; it also inhibits the sharing of jurisdictions with respect to gaming, education, policing, and health. Likewise, this rational control mentality can subvert the dreams of those whose priorities are culturally sensitive and community-based rather than impersonal and calculated. With pressures to debureaucratize on all sides, the future of DIAND is open to conjecture (but see Boldt, 1993): conservative forces are anxious to retain as much of the status quo as possible; reform forces are willing to modify DIAND without relinquishing absolute control; and activists prefer to scuttle the department in exchange for control over jurisdiction.

3. Aboriginal policy and administration encompass a variety of agendas, both overt and hidden. But the one constant underlying all aboriginal initiatives is a concern with *self-sufficiency* at individual and community levels. The means to achieve this goal have varied over time, with an emphasis on individual assimilation evolving into community-based development as the preferred option. Still, perceptions of self-sufficiency are subject to dispute. On the one side, central authorities view self-sufficiency as a means of securing aboriginal compliance while reducing costs in the process. Federal concessions often entail little more than fobbing off administrative responsibilities for local service delivery. On the other side, First Nations see self-sufficiency as more than an offloading of departmental functions. Self-sufficiency is embraced as conditional on aboriginal control over economic, cultural, political, and social fronts.

4. Wide disparities continue to disrupt consensus over goals and means, as well as underlying rationales, behind the reconstruction process. State initiatives to restructure aboriginal–state relations are not necessarily motivated by compassion, but by calculation to eliminate the aboriginal problem as expeditiously as possible. Similarly, proposals to dismantle DIAND and repeal the Indian Act have more to do with "national interests" than with aboriginal empowerment. This suggests that care must be exercised in distinguishing between rhetoric and reality, between manifest goals (explicit statements of formal goals that often legitimate the department's existence) (Perrow, 1980) and latent functions that may contradict explicit goals or conceal hidden agendas (Boldt, 1993).

5. Politicians and First Nations often employ similar words but still speak a different language. Terms such as self-government and sovereignty are essentially Anglo-Saxon terms that rarely reflect the experiences of aboriginal realities. Consider the concept of autonomy. For many, autonomy conjures up images of secession and dismemberment; for aboriginal peoples, autonomy resides in the restructuring of their relationship with Canada to secure control over (a) self-government; (b) treaties; (c) land claims; (d) economic development; (e) service delivery; and (f) culture, language, and identity (RCAP, 1993). Not surprisingly, central authorities perceive autonomy in terms of municipal-level, self-governing, administrative structures under provincial jurisdiction. In contrast, aboriginal views of self-government and autonomy are defended on grounds other than crown authority, as self-contained and inherent, not delegated (Cassidy, 1994). This inherent right provides aboriginal communities with the legitimacy to exercise jurisdiction over areas once under state monopoly.

6. The politics of jurisdiction are a driving force behind aboriginal–state reconstruction. Controversies over "who controls what, and how" are focussed primarily on the benefits and entitlements that flow from inherency and special status. Policy outcomes with respect to jurisdiction cannot be viewed as final or authoritative, any more than they can be preoccupied with "taking" or "finalizing," but must be situated in the context of "sharing" and "extending" — in effect, allowing wisdom and justice to precede power (Cassidy, 1994). Doubts remain about whether such a process can be achieved without a complete overhaul of aboriginal–state relations at policy and administrative levels.

CONCLUSION: "PARADIGM MUDDLES"

Before we had to play a sort of poker. But the civil servants dealt us our cards face up, kept theirs close to the chest and asked us how much we wanted to bet. But we Natives don't have to play poker any more because we've learned how to play bridge. (Gene Rheaume, commenting on the Mohawk blockade of the Mercier Bridge in Montreal during the Oka crisis, quoted by Viola Robinson in National Proceedings, 1993, p. 38.)

As Canada lurches into the 21st century, it may well be perched on the threshold of an aboriginal paradigm shift. The rhetoric of revolution is compelling but premature, despite an atrophying of colonialist structures. Aboriginal efforts to redefine their relationship with the state in Canada (as well as in Australia, the United States, and New Zealand) are fraught with ambiguity and deception in the light of competing paradigms and entrenched interests (Fleras and Elliott, 1992). Governments have endorsed the idea that aboriginal peoples (1) are a distinct society, (2) possess a threatened culture and society, (3) depend on government trust responsibilities for survival, (4) desire more control in line with local priorities, and (5) prefer to achieve their goals in partnership with central authorities (Government of Canada, 1994).

Yet, understandably, many are opposed to the creation of fundamentally separate structures with a distinctive power base and parallel institutions. As principle or practice, aboriginality poses an unprecedented challenge to the balancing act in any society constructed around a series of compromises. Central authorities prefer instead a benign neocolonialist arrangement that compartmentalizes the aboriginal platform into packages of institutional flexibility and delegated responsibility. Nor are they particularly enthusiastic about the prospect of reconciling aboriginal nationhood with the realities of Canadian society-building. Barriers must be removed and innovative arrangements implemented under an evolving set of rules. Inasmuch as the intent is simply to rearrange the furniture without altering the floor plan, the government's aboriginal agenda is more likely to focus on appearance than substance.

Aboriginal–state relations in Canada are currently under assessment at policy and administration levels. A proposed paradigm shift is gathering momentum — partly in response to escalating aboriginal pressure and prolonged public criticism, and partly to deflect a growing crisis in state legitimacy. But the widely heralded realignment of jurisdictions is riddled with inconsistencies and contradictions as competing interests "lock horns" over a new aboriginal agenda. To one side, the bureaucratic paradigm rooted in the pursuit of "law," "formality," and "control" (Weaver, 1990, p. 15) is drawing to a close, but remains firmly entrenched. To the other, a new decolonizing paradigm based on empowerment and renewal has not yet taken hold, in spite of its lofty ideals to promote national reconciliation through "justice," "adaptation," and "workable intercultural relations" (Weaver, 1990, p. 15). This juxtaposition of bureaucracy with indigenization has proven both contradictory and confrontational, as new ways of thinking collide with the old without displacing the former.

Instead of a paradigm shift, in other words, what we appear to be witnessing is, arguably, a paradigm "muddle." Aboriginal–state relations are characterized by pervasive degrees of ambivalence as colonialist paradigms grind up against new patterns of thought (Weaver, 1991). It is not that the old paradigm refuses to disappear gracefully and make way for the new. Rather, as suggested by metaphors borrowed from plate tectonics and continental drift, diverse viewpoints are on a collision course as perspectives slide into each other, past each other, around each other, and over or under each other. Neither paradigm is strong enough to dislodge its conceptual opponent, with the result that the renewal process consists of discordant amalgams of progressive and traditional. Such a state of tension and conflict is likely to persist until conventional thinking accepts a "vision" of Canada as an asymmetrical pluralism of three founding peoples — aboriginal, French, and English — each sovereign in their own right, but Canadian nonetheless.

DISCUSSION QUESTIONS

1. Explain how debates over jurisdiction (that is, "who controls what") are central to many issues at the core of aboriginal–state relations in Canada.

2. Indicate what is meant by the concept of "debureaucratizing" with respect to aboriginal–state relations. Provide several examples of such developments within the Department of Indian Affairs, and in terms of its relationship with aboriginal peoples.

3. The "indigenization" of aboriginal policy and administration is perceived as critical to the process of decolonizing the aboriginal agenda. Describe some of the barriers that interfere with the process of "indigenizing" aboriginal–state relations.

4. It has been suggested that people may use the same words but speak a different language. Demonstrate the validity of this statement by pointing out how state perspectives (as conveyed by the Indian Affairs Department) compare with aboriginal visions for an appropriate level of self-government and autonomy.

5. Compare and contrast the different stages in the evolution of the Department of Indian Affairs, from an agent of bureaucratic control to a developmental agency for aboriginal empowerment. Employ the categories of goals, means, and outcomes as criteria for comparison.

6. The logic of bureaucracy does not sit well with aboriginal values and goals. Explore the validity of this statement by looking at how the Department of Indian Affairs is caught in the middle between aboriginal concerns and the mandate of a federal bureaucracy.

FURTHER READINGS

Boldt, Menno. 1993. *Surviving as Indians: The Challenge of Self-Government.* Toronto: University of Toronto Press. The author argues that only a revival of traditional values and practices can ensure the survival of aboriginal peoples as a distinct Indian society. The book examines the roots of injustice to aboriginal peoples, analyzes Canadian policy and aboriginal leadership, and proposes five channels for reopening aboriginal dialogue with Canadians at large.

Deputies Council for Change. 1991. *Towards Managing Diversity: A Study of Systemic Discrimination at DIAND.* Ottawa: Supply and Services. This superb case study on DIAND reveals how efforts to restructure aboriginal–state relations by "indigenizing" the bureaucracy have fallen short of the mark because of systemic institutional barriers. A must-read for anyone who still thinks that organizational change is a straightforward process.

Fleras, Augie and Jean Leonard Elliott. 1992. *The Nations Within: Aboriginal–State Relations in Canada, the United States, and New Zealand.* Toronto: Oxford

University Press. This book compares developments in Canada with those in other regions of the world. It not only traces the evolution of aboriginal policy and administration in three white settler colonies, but also explores the resurgence of aboriginal consciousness and the importance of traditional structures as a basis for renewal. The authors conclude that Canada may offer the greatest potential for national conciliation and aboriginal healing.

Levin, Michael D., ed. 1993. *Aboriginality and Ethnicity: Case Studies in Ethnonationalism.* Toronto: University of Toronto Press. This book offers a more advanced understanding of aboriginality from a global perspective. Eight leading scholars in the field examine some of the contradictions between state-building and nation-building in Canada and countries in Africa. The different strategies to reconcile national with aboriginal interests are especially intriguing, especially when aboriginal nationalism challenges the very legitimacy of the state itself.

Little Bear, Leroy, Menno Boldt, and J. Anthony Long, eds. 1984. *Pathways to Determination: Canadian Indians and the Canadian State.* Toronto: University of Toronto Press. This classic book on the subject of aboriginal self-government may be slightly dated in places, but it continues to reward the reader with insights into the barriers that preclude implementation of inherent aboriginal self-government. Many of the articles are written from an aboriginal perspective, and demonstrate the wide gap that sometimes separates aboriginal from non-aboriginal "visions" of the just society.

Weaver, Sally. 1981. *Making Canadian Indian Policy: The Hidden Agenda 1968-1970.* Toronto: University of Toronto Press. This book provides an insider's account of the politics behind the ill-fated white paper of 1969. It also points out how aboriginal reaction to the white paper culminated in the gradual overhaul of aboriginal–state relations. The Social Science Council acknowledged Weaver's analysis of the circumstances and personalities surrounding the events by selecting the book as one of Canada's twenty best social scientific works over the past 50 years. The award came as little surprise, but serves only to intensify the loss created by her untimely death.

Wotherspoon, Terry and Vic Satzewich. 1993. *First Nations: Race, Class, and Gender Relations.* Scarborough, Ont.: Nelson. This book, unlike many in the field of aboriginal–state relations, is organized around an explicit theoretical framework. The major theme is fairly straightforward. The authors contend that an understanding of aboriginal issues must occur within the context and dynamics of capitalist societies. The use of a "political economy" perspective may not appeal to everyone, and their attempts to be inclusive of race and gender do not always match the rhetoric, but this text furnishes fresh insights in an already crowded field.

REFERENCES

Angus, Murray. 1990. "And the Last Shall Be First: Native Policy in an Era of Cutbacks." Aboriginal Rights Coalition.

Asch, Michael. 1984. *Home and Native Land: Aboriginal Rights and Canadian Constitution.* Toronto: Methuen.

Assembly of First Nations (AFN). 1992. "To the Source." In First Nations Circle on the Constitution, *Commissioner's Report.* Ottawa: Assembly of First Nations.

Bienvenue, Rita. 1985. "Colonial Status: The Case of Canadian Indians." Pp. 199–216 in *Ethnicity and Ethnic Relations in Canada*, ed. Rita Bienvenue and Jay Goldstein. Toronto: Butterworths.

Boldt, Menno. 1993. *Surviving as Indians: The Challenge of Self-Government*. Toronto: University of Toronto Press.

Bull, Sam. 1994. "Federal Government Pursues Assimilation Policies Through Devolution Process." *Solidarite* (newsletter by Aboriginal Rights Coalition) 4(2).

Burger, Julian. 1987. *Report from the Frontier: The State of the World's Indigenous Peoples*. New Jersey: Zed Books.

Canadian Human Rights Commission. 1994. *Canadian Human Rights Commission: Annual Report*, comp. Max Yalden.

Cassidy, Frank. 1994. "British Columbia and Aboriginal Peoples: The Prospects for the Treaty Process." *Policy Options* (March): 10–19.

Clark, Bruce. 1990. *Native Liberty, Crown Sovereignty: The Existing Aboriginal Right of Self-Government in Canada*. Kingston, Ont.: McGill-Queen's University Press.

Comeau, Pauline and Aldo Santin. 1990. *The First Canadians. A Profile of Canada's Native People Today*. Toronto: James Lorimer and Sons.

Connor, Walker. 1973. "The Politics of Ethnonationalism." *Journal of International Affairs* 27(1): pp. 1–21.

Deloria Jr., Vine and Clifford Lytle. 1984. *The Nations Within: The Past and Future of American Indian Sovereignty*. New York: Pantheon.

Deputies Council for Change. 1991. *Towards Managing Diversity: A Study of Systemic Discrimination at DIAND*. Ottawa: Supply and Services.

Eckholm, Erik. 1994. "The Native and Not-So Native American Way." *New York Times Magazine* (February 27): pp. 45–52.

Elliott, Jean Leonard and Augie Fleras. 1991. *Unequal Relations: An Introduction to Race and Ethnic Dynamics in Canada*. Scarborough, Ont.: Prentice-Hall.

Fleras, Augie. 1989. "Inverting the Bureaucratic Pyramid: Reconciling Aboriginality and Bureaucracy in New Zealand." *Human Organization* 48(3): pp. 214–225.

———. 1992. "Managing Aboriginality: Canadian Perspectives, International Lessons." Paper presented to the Australian and New Zealand Association for Canadian Studies, Victoria University, Wellington, New Zealand. (December 6.)

———. 1994. "Multiculturalism as Society-Building: Blending What Is Workable, Necessary, and Fair." Pp. 24–40 in *Cross-Currents: Contemporary Political Issues*, 2nd ed., ed. Mark Charleton and Paul Barker. Scarborough, Ont.: Nelson.

Fleras, Augie and Jean Leonard Elliott. 1991. *Multiculturalism in Canada: The Challenge of Diversity*. Scarborough, Ont.: Nelson.

———. 1992. *The Nations Within: Aboriginal–State Relations in Canada, the United States, and New Zealand*. Toronto: Oxford University Press.

Fleras, Augie and Vic Krahn. 1992. "From Community Development to Inherent Self-Government: Restructuring Aboriginal–State Relations in Canada." Paper presented at the Annual Meetings of Learned Societies, Charlottetown, Prince Edward Island. (June.)

Frideres, James. 1990. "Policies on Native Peoples in Canada." In *Race and Ethnic Relations in Canada*, ed. Peter S. Li. Toronto: Oxford University Press.

———. 1993. *Native Peoples in Canada: Contemporary Conflicts*, 4th ed. Scarborough, Ont.: Prentice-Hall.

Government of Canada. 1992–93. *Main Estimates: Part II*. Ottawa: Supply and Services.

———. 1994. "Federal Government Begins Discussions on Aboriginal Self-Government." *News Release* 1-9354.

Government of Canada, Department of Citizenship and Immigration (DCI). 1958. *A Review of Activities, 1948–1958: Indian Affairs Branch*. Ottawa: Supply and Services.

Government of Canada, Department of Indian Affairs and Northern Development (DIAND). 1969. *White Paper: Statement of the Government of Canada on Indian Policy*. Ottawa: the department.

———. 1993a. "Growth in Federal Expenditures on Aboriginal Peoples."

———. 1993b. "DIAND's Devolution from Direct Service Delivery to a Funding Agency."

Goffman, Erving. 1963. *Asylums*. New York: Anchor Press.

Gupta, Tania Das. 1994. "Multiculturalism Policy: A Terrain of Struggle for Immigrant Women." *Canadian Women Studies* 14(2): pp. 72–75.

Habermas, Jurgen. 1976. *Legitimation Crisis*. Boston: Beacon.

Hawkes, David C. and Marina Devine. 1991. "Meech Lake and Elijah Harper: Native–State Relations in the 1990s." Pp. 33–63 in *How Ottawa Spends*. Ottawa: Carleton University Press.

Hummel, Ralph. 1987. *The Bureaucratic Experience*. New York: St. Martin's Press.

Kaplan, William, ed. 1993. *Belonging: The Meaning and Sense of Citizenship in Canada*. Montreal and Kingston, Ont.: McGill-Queen's University Press.

Levin, Michael D., ed. 1993a. *Ethnicity and Aboriginality: Case Studies in Ethnonationalism*. Toronto: University of Toronto Press.

———. 1993b. "Introduction." Pp. 3–8 in *Ethnicity and Aboriginality: Case Studies in Ethnonationalism*, ed. Michael D. Levin. Toronto: University of Toronto Press.

———. 1993c. "Ethnicity and Aboriginality: Conclusions." Pp. 168–79 in *Ethnicity and Aboriginality: Case Studies in Ethnonationalism*, ed. Michael D. Levin. Toronto: University of Toronto Press.

Lewycky, Laverne. 1993. "Multiculturalism in the 1990s and into the 21st Century: Beyond Ideology and Utopia." Pp. 359–402 in *Deconstructing a Nation: Immigration, Multiculturalism and Racism in 90s Canada*, ed. Vic Satzewich. Halifax: Fernwood Press.

Little Bear, Leroy, Menno Boldt, and J. Anthony Long, eds. 1984. *Pathways to Self-Determination: Canadian Indians and the Canadian State*. Toronto: University of Toronto Press.

Macklem, Patrick. 1993. "Ethnonationalism, Aboriginal Identities, and the Law." Pp. 9–28 in *Ethnicity and Aboriginality: Case Studies in Ethnonationalism*, ed. Michael D. Levin. Toronto: University of Toronto Press.

McBride, Stephen and John Shields. 1993. *Dismantling a Nation: Canada and the New World Order*. Halifax: Fernwood Press.

McMillan, Alan D. 1988. *Native Peoples and Cultures of Canada*. Vancouver and Toronto: Douglas and McIntyre.

Miliband, Ralph. 1973. *The State in Capitalist Society*. London: Quartet Books.

Miller, J.R. 1989. *Skyscrapers Hide the Heavens: A History of Indian-White Relations in Canada*. Toronto: University of Toronto Press.

Morse, Bradford W. 1989. "Government Obligations, Aboriginal Peoples and Section 91(24)." Pp. 59–92 in *Aboriginal Peoples and Government Responsibility*, ed. David Hawkes. Ottawa: Carleton University Press.

Nagle, Patrick. 1994. "Manitoba Takes First Steps to Axe Indian Act." *The Toronto Star* (April 24).

National Proceedings. 1993. "Report of a Symposium for University Presidents on Institutional Strategies for Race and Ethnic Relations at Canadian Universities." Queen's University, Kingston, Ontario. (February 2–4.)

Nelson, Adie and Augie Fleras. 1994. *Social Problems in Canada: Conditions and Consequences*. Scarborough, Ont.: Prentice-Hall.

Offe, Claus. 1984. *Contradictions of the Welfare State*. London: Hutchinson.

Pal, Leslie. 1993. *Interests of State: The Politics of Language, Multiculturalism, and Feminism in Canada*. Montreal and Kingston, Ont.: McGill-Queen's University Press.

Panitch, Leo. 1977. "The Role and Nature of the Canadian State," Pp. 3–27 in *Canadian State: Political Economy and Political Power*, ed. Leo Panitch. Toronto: University of Toronto Press.

Perrow, Charles. 1980. *Complex Organizations*. New York: Random House.

Platiel, Rudy. 1994a. "Chretien Objects to Federal Paternalism in Indian Act." *The Globe and Mail* (March 11).

———. 1994b. "Talks to Focus on Mohawk Communities." *The Globe and Mail* (April 6).

Ponting, J. Rick, ed. 1986. *Arduous Journey: Canadian Indians and Decolonization*. Toronto: McClelland & Stewart.

Ponting, J. Rick and Roger Gibbins. 1980. *Out of Irrelevance: A Socio-Political Introduction to Indian Affairs in Canada*. Toronto: Butterworths.

Poulantzas, N. 1975. *Classes in Contemporary Society*. London: New Left Review.

Pratt, Alan. 1989. "Federalism in the Era of Aboriginal Self-Government." Pp. 19–58 in *Aboriginal Peoples and Government Responsibility: Exploring Federal and Provincial Roles*, ed. David C. Hawkes. Ottawa: Carleton University Press.

Prince, Michael J. 1987. "How Ottawa Decides Social Policy: Recent Changes in Philosophy, Structure, and Process." In *The Canadian Welfare State: Evolution and Transition*, ed. Jaqueline S. Ismael. Edmonton: University of Alberta Press.

Raphals, Philip. 1991. "Nations in Waiting." *Canadian Forum* 10(14): pp. 10–14.

Resnick, Philip. 1990. *The Masks of Proteus: Canadian Reflections on the State*. Montreal and Kingston, Ont.: McGill-Queen's University Press.

Royal Commission on Aboriginal Peoples (RCAP). 1992. *Framing the Issues*, Discussion Paper No. 1. Ottawa: Supply and Services.

———. 1993. *Overview of the Second Round*. Prepared for the Royal Commission on Aboriginal Peoples by Michael Cassidy, Ginger Group Consultants. Ottawa: Supply and Services.

Seguin, Rheal. 1994. "Native Self-Rule Talks Plunged into Disarray." *The Globe and Mail* (May 19).

Sharp, Andrew. 1990. *Justice and the Maori*. Auckland: Oxford University Press.

Shkilnyk, Anastasia. 1985. *A Poison Stronger Than Love*. New Haven, Conn.: Yale University Press.

Silman, Janet, ed. 1987. *Enough Is Enough: Aboriginal Women Speak Out*. Toronto: Women's Press.

Simmons, Alan B. and Kieran Keohane. 1992. "Canadian Immigration Policy: State Strategies and the Quest for Legitimacy." *Canadian Review of Sociology and Anthropology* 29(4): pp. 421–52.

Stea, David and Ben Wisner, eds. 1984. "The Fourth World: A Geography of Indigenous Struggles." *Antipodes: A Radical Journal of Geography* 16(2).

Tanner, Adrian. 1993. "History and Culture in the Generation of Ethnic Nationalism." Pp. 75–96 in *Ethnicity and Aboriginality: Case Studies in Ethnonationalism*, ed. Michael D. Levin. Ottawa: Carleton University Press.

Taylor, John P. and Gary Paget. 1989. "Federal/Provincial Responsibility and the Sechelt." Pp. 297–348 in *Aboriginal Peoples and Government Responsibility*, ed. David Hawkes. Ottawa: Carleton University Press.

Tennant, Paul. 1985. "Aboriginal Rights and the Penner Report on Indian Self-Government." Pp. 321–32 in *The Quest for Justice: Aboriginal Peoples and Aboriginal Rights*, ed. Menno Boldt and J. Anthony Long. Toronto: University of Toronto Press.

Tobias, John L. 1976. "Protection, Civilization, and Assimilation: An Outline History of Canada's Indian Policy." *Western Canadian Journal of Anthropology* 6(2): pp. 13–30.

Weaver, Sally M. 1984. "Struggles of the Nation-State to Define Aboriginal Ethnicity: Canada and Australia." Pp. 182–210 in *Minorities and Mother Country Imagery*, ed. G. Gold. Institute of Social and Economic Research No. 13. St. John's Nfld.: Memorial University Press.

———. 1990. "Self-Government for Indians 1980–1990: Political Transformations or Symbolic Gestures." Paper presented at the UNESCO Conference Proceedings on the Migration and the Transformation of Cultures in Canada.

———. 1991. "A New Paradigm in Canadian Indian Policy for the 1990s." *Canadian Ethnic Studies* 22(3): pp. 8–18.

———. 1993. "Self-Determination, National Pressure Groups, and Australian Aborigines: The National Aboriginal Conference 1983–1985." Pp. 53–74 in *Ethnicity and Aboriginality: Case Studies in Ethnonationalism*, ed. Michael D. Levin. Toronto: University of Toronto Press.

Webber, Jeremy. 1994. *Reimaging Canada: Language, Culture, Community, and the Canadian Constitution.* Montreal and Kingston, Ont.: McGill-Queen's University Press.

Weber, Max. 1947. *The Theory of Social and Economic Organization.* New York: Free Press.

Wotherspoon, Terry and Vic Satzewich. 1993. *First Nations: Race, Class, and Gender Relations.* Scarborough, Ont.: Nelson.

York, Geoffrey. 1994. "Self-Rule Discussions Yield Little." *The Globe and Mail* (March 29).

CHAPTER 8

Contemporary Demography of Aboriginal Peoples in Canada

Mary Jane Norris[1]

INTRODUCTION

An understanding of the demographic characteristics and processes of any population is fundamental to meaningful analyses of issues and the development of relevant policies and programs. Furthermore, demographic information is essential in evaluating and determining the success of various policies and programs and in determining what will be required for the future. Thus, the purpose of this chapter is to provide a profile of the demographic characteristics and trends — past, present, and projected — of the aboriginal population in Canada. The aboriginal population is demographically distinct from the overall Canadian population. Most notably, it is much younger and it experiences higher mortality and fertility levels. As a result, some of the issues facing aboriginal people differ from those for the rest of the population.

Although there may be a general awareness of Native–non-Native differences, there has been, until recently, considerably less focus on the demographic differences among the different aboriginal groups themselves. The diversity of aboriginal people must also be addressed if we are to understand the dynamics and needs of different aboriginal groups. This chapter profiles the different aboriginal groups, incorporating writings from an earlier work on longer-term trends. That work (Norris, 1990, pp. 33–59) demonstrated significant variation among aboriginal peoples in their demographic characteristics, and is updated here on the basis of more recent statistics and population projections.[2] The chapter also compares characteristics of aboriginal groups with those of the overall Canadian population.

The chapter begins with a look at the issue of defining and measuring aboriginal ethnicity, which is crucial to establishing who is an "aboriginal" and to an understanding of how the different aboriginal populations are defined. This discussion is followed by a section on data sources, quality, and comparability. Statistical information on aboriginal populations is based on a number of different sources, collected by federal government departments including Indian and Northern Affairs Canada (INAC), Health and Welfare Canada (HWC), and Statistics Canada, which undertakes a census every five years, collecting data from all Canadian residents. These data sets vary in coverage and quality, with the result that data comparability can be limited. The discussion shows the complexity in reconciling statistics from different sources or over time.

Following the review of data sources, a brief historical background is provided from the time of the first European settlement in North America. Then, on the basis of different data sources, we attempt to trace the size and growth of the different aboriginal populations over the past 50 years or so.

A more in-depth look is provided for the 1991-based aboriginal populations, particularly those who identify with their aboriginal ancestry — that is, those who consider themselves to be aboriginal, as opposed to simply having aboriginal ancestry. On the basis of available data, we can see that different patterns emerge in identification with aboriginal ancestry by aboriginal group, age and sex, rural/urban residence, and region.

The discussion on the share and geographic distribution of aboriginal populations across Canada presents a picture of distinct regional variation. This discussion also shows how the concentration of aboriginal people in rural and urban areas differs significantly from that of Canadians in general. An important dimension in the geography of registered Indians, the distinction between residence on- and off-reserve, is also profiled.

The next section, on the age–sex structure of aboriginal populations, clearly illustrates how demographically distinct the younger aboriginal population is from the Canadian population in general. This is followed by a major review and analysis of the components of population change that contribute to the size, age–sex structure, and growth of the different aboriginal groups. Trends and patterns are presented for four components of growth: fertility, mortality, migration, and the Indian Act's Bill C-31 legislation — the latter having an impact on the growth of both status and non-status Indian groups.

From an analysis of the components of change, we look to the future size and growth of aboriginal populations using population projection data. Given the continuation of current trends and patterns, this section presents a picture of what aboriginal populations could look like over the next 10 or 25 years, not only with respect to size, but also in terms of geographical distributions by rural/urban areas and on-/off-reserve, age–sex structure, and regional shares and distributions. Our analysis of population projection data also demonstrates the potential role that each component of change could play with respect to the demographic characteristics of aboriginal populations in the future, and their impact on emerging new issues for aboriginal people, such as aging and the growth of the working-age group, over the next 25 years.

CONCEPTS CONCERNING ABORIGINAL ETHNICITY

The measurement of ethnicity is not an easy task. But if a useful assessment of the growth patterns of aboriginal groups is to be made, it is important to understand the concepts involved in establishing the size and composition of Canada's aboriginal populations.

The difficulties involved in defining and measuring the size of Canada's aboriginal populations through the census have been discussed by a number of analysts (Boxhill, 1984; Kralt, 1990; Pryor, 1984). There are number of inherent limitations associated with ethnicity data, a main one being the "subjective" self-reporting of the respondent. Also, while a respondent may report more than one ethnic origin, the degree of importance of each of the ethnicities is not known. Are they all equally important to the respondent, or is one more relevant? The measurement of ethnicity in the census has generally been based on the concepts of ethnic origin or ancestry.

Another aspect of aboriginal ethnicity is "identity." In other words, even though one may report aboriginal origins, one may or may not necessarily identify with these origins — that is, consider oneself to be an aboriginal person. This form of "identity" is subjective, in that it is "self-definition" that lies in one's concept of self. This contrasts with the more objective, legal criteria of the Indian Act that established Indian status. As noted by Frideres in his discussion on Native identity:

> the identity of the individual lies in his/her conceptualization of self. We can attempt to measure this self-conceptualization in some form, but all it tells us is the degree to which an individual feels Native. It does not identify the defining attributes nor the relative importance of each of these attributes. (Frideres, 1993, p. 21)

Frideres concludes that Native identity has become complex and fragmented, with many meanings, including identity with culture, local group experiences, and legal definition of band membership (Frideres, 1993, p. 45).

In consultation with aboriginal organizations, Statistics Canada developed a post-censal survey of aboriginal populations in Canada, which incorporated the dimension of "ethnic identity" and "ethnic origin" (Statistics Canada, 1993c, p. 11). Following the 1991 census, the 1991 Aboriginal Peoples Survey (APS) asked those persons who had indicated aboriginal origin in the census whether or not they identified with this ancestry. For example, a respondent in the census who indicated Métis ancestry may or may not identify with this origin (Statistics Canada, 1993c, p. 6). Data from the 1991 APS are used in this report to examine and compare the demographic characteristics of these populations with aboriginal identity, by aboriginal group.

As we will see, there do appear to be significant differences between the aboriginal "identity" and "origin" populations. Those who do not identify with their aboriginal origins tend to be closer in characteristics with the mainstream population, whereas those who "identify" with their origins probably reflect more the core of the aboriginal population.[3] For example, the identity population is less urbanized than the overall aboriginal origin or ancestry population.

Canada's aboriginal population consists of four major ethnic groups: status Indians, who are registered under the Indian Act of Canada; non-status Indians, who have lost or never had status under the Indian Act; Métis, who are of mixed Indian and non-Indian ancestry; and Inuit, who reside mainly in Canada's Arctic, in the Yukon and Northwest Territories, northern Quebec, and Labrador. Further distinctions can be made within some of these groups. For example, the Métis of the Prairies are historically different from those of mixed Native ancestry elsewhere in Canada. Overall, however, these major groups represent the main ethnic origins and identities of Canada's aboriginal population.

DATA SOURCES, QUALITY, AND COMPARABILITY

Analyzing the similarities and differences among aboriginal groups and between aboriginals and non-aboriginals is not an easy task. The data presented in this demographic profile are drawn from a wide variety of studies and sources, including census data, APS data, Indian Register data from INAC, and medical services data from HWC. The census, which is the most comprehensive source of aboriginal data, is used to examine differentials in age–sex structure, fertility, mobility, and migration among groups of different aboriginal ancestry, as well as in comparison to the overall population. The census also provides historical aboriginal data. The 1991 APS differs from the 1991 census in that it provides data for the population that identifies with its aboriginal origins. Like the census, the APS also includes those persons who reported registered Indian status under the Indian Act (Statistics Canada, 1993a; 1993c). Medical services and register data provide information on trends in fertility and mortality for registered Indians and the Inuit of northern Quebec. Unfortunately, data collection systems on births and deaths do not exist specifically for Métis and non-status Indians. Population registers had never been established for these groups, because they were for registered Indians due to legal and administrative requirements.

Limitations of Data Sources

All of the present data sources are limited due to undercoverage, incomplete enumeration, and misreporting in the census or APS, or late and underreporting in the register. Census and APS data are based on self-reported counts and characteristics. As such, these data can be at variance with other estimates of aboriginal group populations, especially Métis and non-status Indians, since there are no population registers for these groups. In the case of status Indians, the census and register populations are different in a number of ways. For example, the register lists all persons who are legally status Indians under the Indian Act, including women of non-Native origin who have gained status by marrying status Indian males, those outside Canada, and those in institutions. The census excludes institutional[4] residents from its ethnic data, such as prison inmates, chronic-care residents, those in rooming homes, hotels, etc., and those no longer officially residing in Canada. Furthermore, census origin/identity data are based on self-reported counts, and "some respondents may not have reported being registered under the Indian Act because of a lack of under-standing/familiarity with the wording of a question or because of some objection to its terminology" (Statistics Canada, 1993a, p. 28).[5]

Measurement of Ethnicity in the Census

Caution must be used when interpreting census and other data on aboriginal people, because data are not directly comparable from one census to another. Changes in questions, instructions, single- and multiple-ethnic responses, and the ways in which data are captured a few of the factors that make comparing data a difficult task. For example, 1981 and 1986 census data on ethnic origin are not directly comparable because of differences concerning multiple responses. Fortunately, comparability between the most recent 1986 and 1991 censuses is relatively reliable, even though some changes were introduced (Statistics Canada, 1993a, p. xii). For example, in 1986, respondents were asked, "To which ethnic or cultural group(s) do you or did your ancestors belong?" In 1991, the phrase "do you" was removed. In both censuses, and in 1981, multiple responses were allowed.

Changing concepts and measures of ethnicity that have occurred in Canada's censuses since 1871 reflect the societal conditions concerning ethnicity. At the same time, ethnic data can have an impact on the image that Canadians have of their society (Kralt, 1990, p. 27). For example, before the 1981 census, only the paternal ancestry of the respondent was reported. Kralt suggests that the image painted by these data was that of "four large, generally mutually exclusive ethnic or cultural groups . . . the charter groups, persons whose ancestry originated in either France or the British Isles . . . and the Others . . . divided between those of European origin and the Native peoples" (Kralt, 1990, p. 27). The multiple-response ethnic origin data from more recent censuses provide a more realistic picture of Canada's ethnic composition, especially considering the extent to which intermarriage has taken place and our increasingly multiracial and multicultural society.

Apart from changes to questionnaires, it should be remembered that the measurement of ethnicity, and also identity, can be affected over time by various factors, including the respondent's social and personal aspects, family background, and ethnic awareness. For example, in the 1986 census, about 712 000 people reported aboriginal origins, compared with just over 1 million in 1991. It is speculated that public attention on aboriginal issues may have increased the reporting of aboriginal origins, affecting the social and personal considerations of respondents (Statistics Canada, 1993a, pp. i, xii). Clearly, respondents' choices affect counts of ethnic groups.

HISTORICAL BACKGROUND

Scholars estimate that at the time of the first European settlement in North America about five centuries ago, the Indian population numbered about 200 000 and the Inuit population around 10 000 (Graham-Cumming, 1967, p. 159). Other estimates (Kroeber, 1939) indicate that before the arrival of Europeans, the total Indian population of North America was about 900 000 people, of whom about 220 000 were in what is now Canada. The advent of the Europeans brought a sharp decline in the Native population. The effects of war (both international and European), famines (for example, that of 1879–80 on the Prairies (Siggner, 1980, p. 32; 1986b)) and disease (especially tuberculosis) took their toll; by the late 1870s, the Indian population had been reduced to some 80 000 (Graham-Cumming, 1967, p. 159). Other records indicate that shortly after Confederation in 1867, the Indian population was about 102 000 in what is now Canada (Siggner, 1980; 1986b). In the several decades following, the Native population was relatively stable, fluctuating between that level and about 122 000, which represented from 2.5 to 1.1 percent of the total Canadian population (Siggner, 1980; 1986b).[6]

It was not until the 1940s that the Native population experienced a significant growth. According to Graham-Cumming, it was around 1940 that Indians were increasing in number at about the same rate as other Canadians, and by the 1960s the aboriginal population had outstripped other ethnic groups, with a steadily accelerating pace. It reached some 220 000, about the same size as it had been at the beginning of European settlement.

In the 1991 census, just over 1 million people in Canada reported aboriginal origins, compared with some 712 000 people in 1986. Just over half (53 percent) of the 1 million in 1991 reported multiple origins — that is, they gave a combination of at least two of the following responses: North American Indian, Métis, Inuit, and non-aboriginal. About 78 percent (784 000) of respondents with either single or multiple origins reported a North American Indian origin, as either the only one (single) or in combination with a non-aboriginal one, followed by 21 percent (212 700) with Métis origin (single and multiple), and about 5 percent (49 255) with Inuit origins (see Table 8.1). In the following section, the rates of population growth are examined in more depth.

TABLE 8.1 Census Counts of Aboriginal and Total Canadian Populations, Canada, 1931–1991

Census year	Total Canadian population (millions)	Total aboriginal population	Aboriginal as % of total population	Population of aboriginal groups		
				Indian	Métis	Inuit
1931	10.4	128 900	1.2	n.a.	n.a.	n.a.[3]
1941	11.5	160 900	1.4	118 300	35 400	7 200
1951	14.0	165 600	1.2	155 900	n.a.	9 700
1961	18.2	220 100	1.2	208 300	n.a.	11 800
1971	21.6	312 800	1.5	295 200	n.a.	17 550
1981	24.1	491 500	2.0	367 800	98 300	25 390
1986[1,2]	25.3					
Single origins		373 260	1.5	286 230	59 745	27 290
Multiple origins		338 460[4]	1.3	262 730	91 865	9 180
Single and multiple combined		711 725[4]	2.8	548 960	151 610	36 470
1991[1,5]	27.3					
Single origins		470 610	1.7	365 375	75 150	30 085
Multiple origins		532 060[4]	2.0	418 605	137 500	19 165
Single and multiple combined		1 002 675[4]	3.7	783 980	212 650	49 255

n.a. Not available or not published.

[1] Excludes institutional residents.
[2] Figures for 1986 exclude population of incompletely enumerated Indian reserves and settlements, estimated at 45 000.
[3] Estimate from Robitaille and Choinière (1985) of Inuit population from 1931 census reported to be 6000.
[4] Multiple counts by aboriginal groups include multiple aboriginal origins; therefore, the sum of multiples across aboriginal groups is greater than total multiples.
[5] Figures for 1991 exclude population of incompletely enumerated Indian reserves and settlements estimated at approximately 37 600 (Norris et al., 1995).
1931: Includes Native Indian, Inuit, and persons of mixed Native and non-Native ancestry traced on the mother's side.
1941: Includes Native Indian, Inuit, and persons of mixed Native and non-Native ancestry traced on the father's side.
1951: Includes Native Indian, Inuit, and some persons of mixed Native and non-Native ancestry living on Indian reserves or traced on the father's side.
1961: Includes Native Indian, Inuit, and some persons of mixed Native and non-Native ancestry living on Indian reserves or traced on the father's side.
1971: Includes Native Indian and Inuit only, traced on the father's side.
1981: Includes Native Indian, Inuit, and self-reported Métis, traced through both parents.
1986: Includes North American Indian, Inuit, and Métis traced through both parents.
1991: Includes North American Indian, Inuit, and Métis traced through both parents.

Sources: 1931 to 1981: Data and notes from Statistics Canada, The Daily, Table 1, February 1, 1983, cat. no. 11-001; 1986: Statistics Canada, 1986 Census of Canada — Summary Tabulations of Ethnic & Aboriginal Origins, Ottawa: Minister of Industry, 1987; 1991: Statistics Canada, 1991 Census, cat. no. 94-327, Ottawa: Minister of Industry, 1993.

SIZE AND GROWTH, 1931–1991

Tracing the size and growth of these Native groups, as well as the overall Native population, remains difficult owing to problems of comparability in census data, changes in definitions and reporting problems. The census, which is the only source of population data for some Native groups (Métis and non-status Indian), has differed over the years in the concepts and measurement of Native groups, as well as of ethnic groups in general (Kralt, 1990). Population counts of Native groups from 1931 to 1991, and cautionary notes on their degree of comparability, are provided in Table 8.1. Although 1986 and 1991 censuses are relatively comparable in terms of concept and measurement, comparability among earlier and even more recent censuses, 1981 and 1986, is limited.

Comparisons between 1986 and 1991 aboriginal counts indicate a 26 percent increase in single responses, from 373 000 in 1986 to 470 600 in 1991, and an even higher increase (57 percent) of multiple responses from 338 000 to 532 000. Overall, the population reporting aboriginal origins increased by 41 percent between 1986 and 1991, which, as noted earlier, could be related to increased public attention on aboriginal issues.

It is possible to assess the growth of the aboriginal population by comparing the 1941 and 1981 censuses, because "both made an explicit attempt to individually enumerate persons of mixed Native ancestry" (Statistics Canada, 1983, p. 6). Overall, the aboriginal population increased by 205 percent during this period, compared with 109 percent growth for the total Canadian population. Among the different Native groups, the Inuit had the highest increase (252 percent), followed by the North America Indian population (210 percent) and the Métis (177 percent). Indian Register data also show that between 1971 and 1981 the registered Indian population grew twice as fast as the general population, increasing 27 percent, compared with 13 percent for Canada's total population (Perreault et al., 1985).

These "relative" growth rates of aboriginal populations provided by the census data, albeit "crude," are corroborated by additional data sources on natural increase of registered Indians and Inuit. The growth of the Inuit population, which is due solely to natural increase,[7] has been the most rapid of the Native groups. Census data show that between 1931 and 1981 the Inuit population more than quadrupled, from 6000 to 25 000, at an annual rate of 2.9 percent. Recent estimates of crude birth and death rates by Robitaille and Choinière also suggest an annual rate of natural increase of 29 per 1000 for 1981 (Robitaille and Choinière, 1985, p. 5). In comparison to the Inuit, the slower growth for Indians indicated by the census is also confirmed by INAC's data on registered Indians. Estimates of 1981 crude birth and death rates for registered Indians (Ram and Romaniuc, 1985; Rowe and Norris, 1985) show a lower rate of natural increase of 23 per 1000 (due largely to the higher Inuit crude birth rate of

35 per 1000 versus the Indian birth rate of 29 per 1000). In contrast, low rates of natural increase are responsible for the much slower growth of the Canadian population as a whole, despite the contribution by immigration. In 1981, the annual total growth rate for the Canadian population was 1.2 percent, while the rate of natural increase was under 1 percent.

The size and growth of aboriginal groups in our discussion thus far have been based on ethnic origin or ancestry. The following account provides another picture on the size of the aboriginal groups as defined instead by ethnic identity rather than ancestry alone.

POPULATION WITH ABORIGINAL IDENTITY

The aboriginal identity population is a subset of the population reporting aboriginal ethnicity. The identity population represents those persons who consider themselves to be aboriginal — that is, who identify with one of the four major aboriginal groups or who reported themselves as registered under the Indian Act (Statistics Canada, 1993a; 1993c).

Of the roughly 1 million Canadians who reported aboriginal origins in 1991, about 63 percent[8] (625 710) actually identified with their aboriginal ancestry. Of those indicating aboriginal identity, 99 percent identified with just one aboriginal group. Identification with more than one group occurred the most among Métis, with about 4 percent identifying with more than one group (Statistics Canada, 1993a, p. ii). Perhaps the greater propensity of the Métis to identify with more than one aboriginal group reflects the fact that Métis is also considered a combination of other aboriginal and non-aboriginal origins (for example, North American Indian and non-aboriginal). Also, the degree of intermarriage among Métis may be greater than that among other aboriginal groups.

The following analysis of the available census and APS data on origins and identity suggests that identification with aboriginal origins varies across aboriginal groups, age and sex, regions, and rural/urban locations. Only a basic comparison between origin and identity population can be undertaken here; a more accurate and complete picture would require detailed cross-classification of the identity population and its characteristics, including ethnic origins.

Identification by Aboriginal Group

Some caution is required when interpreting patterns of identity by aboriginal group from the separate census and APS data sets, since in terms of aboriginal groups, respondents are not necessarily consistent in their responses between origins and identities. For example, someone who reported North American Indian and non-aboriginal origins in the census could subsequently indicate in the APS that they identified with the Métis; another respondent could report Métis origins in the census, but in the APS indicate that they identify with North American Indian. Thus, to the extent that these crossovers in aboriginal groups occur between origins and identity, the following figures may be correspondingly over- or under-estimated by group; more accurate figures would require detailed cross-classification of aboriginal origins by identities.[9]

Census and APS data suggest that identification with aboriginal ancestry varies by aboriginal group, such that the Inuit identity population represents the highest proportion (74 percent) of its corresponding origin population, followed by Métis (64 percent) and North American Indian (60 percent). Given that those with registered Indian status are automatically included, by definition, in the identity population, the figure of 60 percent for North American Indians would indicate that the percentage for identity among non-status Indians must be lower. The estimated number of non-status Indians who identified with the North American Indian group represents only 25 percent of the non-registered population reporting North American Indian origins (single and multiple).

This variation among aboriginal groups in identifying with aboriginal origins[10] affects the group composition of the "identity" population. Estimates

TABLE 8.2

ABORIGINAL ORIGIN AND IDENTITY POPULATIONS BY SELECTED ABORIGINAL GROUPS, CANADA, **1991**

Total population with	North American Indian (NAI)[1]	Registered NAI[1,2]	Non-status NAI[1,2]	Métis	Inuit	Total[4]
	(thousands)					
Aboriginal origins (Single and multiple origins)	784.0	357.2	426.8	212.7	49.3	1002.7
Aboriginal identities	460.7	353.0[3]	107.6[3]	135.3	36.2	625.7

[1] Data for registered and non-status Indians are based on unadjusted counts derived from census and APS data. Identity-based counts are from a report on population projections of the identity population (Norris et al., 1995); origin-based counts are from unpublished census data on registered and non-status origins, including single and multiple responses.
[2] Respondents are not necessarily consistent in reporting their aboriginal group(s) or registration status between the census and APS. For example, some who reported North American Indian or registration status in the 1991 census may have responded differently in the APS.
[3] For the identity-based counts of registered and non-status Indians, the 4830 North American Indians with registration status not stated in the 1991 APS were distributed as follows: those living on-reserve (1465) were assigned to the registered group; those living off-reserve (3365) were assigned to the non-status group.
[4] The sum of the individual aboriginal groups, which include multiples, is greater than the total aboriginal count, which does not double-count multiples.

Source: Based on data from Statistics Canada, *1991 Aboriginal Data: Age and Sex*, cat. no. 94-327, Ottawa: Minister of Industry, Science and Technology, 1993. Reproduced by authority of the Minister of Industry, 1995. Includes unpublished census/APS data.

of registered and non-status Indians account for 56 percent and 17 percent respectively of the identity population, compared with 36 percent and 43 percent of the population with aboriginal origins (single and multiple) (Table 8.2). Corresponding shares of Métis (22 percent) and Inuit (6 percent) in the identity population are more similar to their corresponding shares (21 percent and 5 percent respectively) of the origin population.

Identification with Ancestry by Age and Sex

With respect to age, a higher proportion of persons in the older (55+) and younger (under 25) age groups tended to identify with their aboriginal origins than did adults in the 25–54 age groups. The proportion who identified with their aboriginal ancestry (for total aboriginal) was highest (70 percent) among those aged 55+ and least (58 percent) in the 35–54 age group (Table 8.3).[11] Perhaps the greater propensity of youth and seniors to identify with their aboriginal origins reflects the current revival among youth in awareness of their aboriginal origins and the increased and traditional importance of elders as a source of community strength.

Among aboriginal groups, those aged 35–54 consistently identified the least with their aboriginal origins, followed by the 25–34 age group.

TABLE 8.3

ABORIGINAL IDENTITY POPULATION AS A PERCENTAGE[1] OF ABORIGINAL ORIGIN POPULATION, BY SELECTED AGE GROUPS AND SEX, 1991

Age groups and sex	Total aboriginal	Total North American Indian	Non-status Indian	Métis	Inuit
		(percent)			
0–4	67	63	31	65	81
5–14	67	63	29	66	81
15–24	65	63	25	62	74
25–34	60	56	22	64	69
35–54	58	55	22	61	62
55+	70	68	24	66	71
Males	63	59	25	64	72
Females	64	61	26	63	75
Both sexes	63	60	25	64	74

[1] *Percentages reflect adjustments for incomplete enumeration of reserves and settlements in the APS identity population for approximately 20 000 respondents who were enumerated in the 1991 census but not the APS. For comparability, these respondents were removed from the aboriginal origin population, by age and sex, in order to calculate percentages for the affected populations.*

Source: Calculated from Statistics Canada, *1991 Aboriginal Data: Age and Sex*, cat. no. 94-327, Ottawa: Minister of Industry, Science and Technology, 1993. Reproduced by authority of the Minister of Industry, 1995. Includes unpublished data for non-status Indians.

However, the age group that had the highest proportion of persons identifying was not always in the older ages. For example, among Inuit origins, about 71 percent of those aged 55+ identified with their group, compared with 81 percent of children aged 0–14 and 74 percent of the 15–24 age group (Table 8.3).

In terms of gender, a slightly higher proportion of females than males identified with their origins for all aboriginal groups, with the exception of the Métis (Table 8.3).

Identification with Ancestry by Region

A comparison between identity and origin populations by region suggests that the extent to which people identify with their aboriginal group varies across Canada. The proportion who identified with their aboriginal ancestry was highest in the Northwest Territories (98 percent), followed by Saskatchewan (91 percent), Manitoba (86 percent), Alberta and Yukon (71 percent each), and British Columbia (62 percent). Just half of Atlantic and 49 percent of Ontario respondents identified with their origins, while Quebec had the lowest proportion (41 percent) of the aboriginal origin population identifying with its ancestry. These regional figures include adjustments for incomplete enumeration of reserves and settlements in the APS, which increase unadjusted percentages by one or two percentage points. Some of the regional variation in identification with aboriginal ancestry, in general, may be associated with differences in rural/urban and group composition of regional aboriginal populations, and could also be influenced by the size, awareness, and cohesion of a particular aboriginal group in a region. For example, the higher percentage of aboriginal identity in the Prairies compared to Ontario could include possible differences between the "historical" Prairie Métis and Métis elsewhere in Canada in identifying with their aboriginal ancestry.[12] Again, a more accurate picture and better understanding of these regional variations would require a more detailed analysis of APS data.

Identification with Ancestry by Rural/Urban Area

Identity with aboriginal origins appears to be higher in reserve and rural areas than in urban areas, due to the impact of registered Indians. Among persons reporting aboriginal origins in 1991, nearly three-quarters (74 percent) of the 426 000 residing in reserve and rural areas identified with their aboriginal ancestry, compared with just over half (54 percent) of the 576 000 living in urban areas.

SHARE AND DISTRIBUTION
Share

Although aboriginal populations make up a small proportion of Canada's total population (see Table 8.1), their share has been increasing, from 1.4

percent in 1941 to 2.0 percent in 1981 to 3.7 percent in 1991 (based on unadjusted population data). This latter share rises to 3.9 percent if adjusted for incomplete enumeration and undercoverage. Persons of single-only aboriginal origins represented 1.7 percent; those of multiple origins, 2.0 percent. In 1991, the population that identified with its aboriginal ancestry, adjusted for incomplete enumeration and undercoverage, made up about 2.6 percent of the total Canadian population.

The proportion of a provincial or territorial population that is aboriginal varies considerably across Canada. In 1991, 61 percent of the population in the Northwest Territories and 23 percent of the Yukon population were of aboriginal origin. Among the provinces, Manitoba and Saskatchewan had the highest proportions of persons reporting aboriginal origins — around 10 percent. In Alberta and British Columbia, aboriginal people represented between 5 and 6 percent of the population. In central and eastern Canada, around 2 percent of the population reported aboriginal origins. Similar shares of aboriginal ancestry population were observed in earlier censuses, 1981 and 1986. The proportions of provincial or territorial populations that identify with aboriginal ancestry are similar to, but lower than, those observed for the aboriginal ancestry population.

Regional Distribution

As was the case in 1981 and 1986, Ontario claimed the largest number of people with aboriginal origins, followed by British Columbia and Alberta. Moreover, almost one in four Canadians who reported aboriginal origins (single or multiple) in 1991 resided in Ontario. Together, British Columbia (17 percent) and Alberta (15 percent) accounted for nearly a third of Canada's Native population, while another 21 percent resided in Manitoba and Saskatchewan. Quebec's share was 14 percent, while the Atlantic region had 5 percent, Northwest Territories 3.5 percent and Yukon 0.6 percent (Figure 8.1).

The 1991 regional distribution of the population identifying with aboriginal origins differs from that observed for the population reporting aboriginal origins. In general, differences in regional distributions between the origin and identity populations are accounted for by regional variations in aboriginal group composition and identification with aboriginal ancestry. Ontario's share of the aboriginal identity population is smaller (18 percent) than its share of nearly one-quarter of the aboriginal origin population. In contrast, the Prairie provinces of Manitoba and Saskatchewan account for nearly 30 percent of those who identify with their aboriginal origins, compared with just 20 percent of the population reporting aboriginal origins.

Similarly, in comparison to the ancestry-based distribution, regional shares of the identity population are higher for Alberta (17 percent), the Northwest Territories (5.5 percent), and Yukon (0.7); and lower in the Atlantic region (4 percent), Quebec (9 percent), and British Columbia (16 percent).

FIGURE 8.1

REGIONAL DISTRIBUTION OF POPULATIONS WITH ABORIGINAL ANCESTRY OR ABORIGINAL IDENTITY, CANADA, 1991

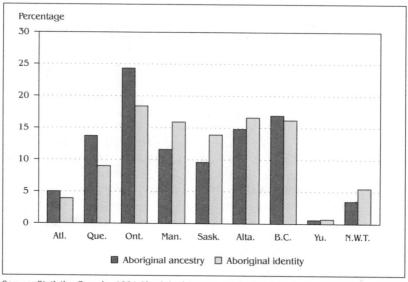

Source: Statistics Canada, *1991 Aboriginal Data: Age and Sex*, cat. no. 94-327, Ottawa: Minister of Industry, Science and Technology, 1993. Reproduced by authority of the Minister of Industry, 1995.

Rural/Urban Distribution

A significant proportion of Canada's Native people continue to reside in rurally situated reserves and settlements for a variety of social, economic, and political reasons. Even though they experience a high degree of geographic mobility, it is not surprising that the concentration of Native people in rural and urban areas is much different from that of the general population.[13] Table 8.4 shows that in 1991, 57 percent of the population with aboriginal origins lived in urban areas compared with about 77 percent of the nation's population. Moreover, among those who identified with their aboriginal origins, only half resided in urban areas — significantly lower than the more than three-quarters of the Canadian population in general. (Figures from Table 8.4 are not adjusted for incomplete enumeration of reserves and settlements, hence percentages on-reserve are underestimated, and, correspondingly, percentages off-reserve are overestimated.)

Among the different groups with aboriginal identity, the Inuit population had the highest proportion, 78 percent, residing in rural areas, followed by 59 percent of registered Indians, 35 percent of Métis, and 30 percent of non-status Indians (figures include reserves in rural classification) (Table 8.4).

TABLE 8.4
POPULATION DISTRIBUTION AND SEX RATIOS, BY PLACE OF RESIDENCE,[1]
ABORIGINAL AND TOTAL CANADIAN POPULATIONS, CANADA, 1991

	Percentage distribution of total population by place of residence			Sex ratios by place of residence			
	On-reserve	Off-reserve		On-Reserve	Off-reserve		Total
		Rural	Urban		Rural	Urban	
	(males per 100 females)						
Aboriginal							
Origin	18.0	24.5	57.5	107.4	100.9	89.4	95.2
Identity	29.3	21.1	49.5	106.1	96.9	84.4	93.0
Identity population by group:							
North American Indian	38.8	13.7	47.5	106.0	91.0	80.3	91.0
Registered Indian	49.6	9.6	40.8	106.0	82.3	77.5	91.1
Non-status Indian	3.3	27.0	69.7	104.5	102.3	85.8	90.6
Métis	3.4	31.7	64.9	115.4	100.9	95.1	97.5
Inuit	1.7	76.4	21.9	86.6	104.6	81.5	98.8
Total Canadian population	n.a.[3]	23.5	76.5	n.a.[3]	105.4	95.4	97.7

[1] Distribution and ratios based on data not adjusted for incomplete enumeration and undercoverage.
[2] Because both origin and identity data are not adjusted for the incomplete enumeration of reserves and settlements, the percentages of populations residing on-reserve, particularly for registered Indians, are underestimated, and correspondingly, percentages off-reserve are overestimated.
[3] For Canadian population in general, reserves have been classified under rural areas.

Source: Statistics Canada, 1991 census and APS data, unpublished tabulations.

On-/Off-Reserve Distribution

An important dimension of the geography of North American Indians is the distinction between residence on- and off-reserve. Taking into account adjustments to 1991 census data for undercoverage and incomplete enumeration, 58 percent of the registered Indian population lived on reserves and settlements. This figure is similar to the proportion of status or registered Indians living on-reserve, based on adjusted 1981 and 1986 census data, of about 60 percent. Data from INAC's Register also indicated a similar proportion (60 percent) of registered Indians living on-reserve in 1990, although INAC proportions of on-reserve residence for 1981 and 1986 were higher, at about 70 percent.

Register data from INAC show a decline in residence on reserves since the 1960s and higher proportions of women than of men living off-reserve. The proportion of registered Indians residing on-reserve declined from 85 percent in 1966 to 72 percent by the mid-1970s, and then stabilized at around 70 percent during the late 1970s and early 1980s.

Since 1985, a new factor in the distribution of Indians living on- and off-reserve is the reinstatement to Indian status of those Indians eligible under the amendment to the Indian Act. According to INAC data, between 1985 and 1994, nearly 96 000 persons have gained Indian status under these amendments (Norris et al., 1995). The majority of the reinstated population (70 percent) live off-reserve, according to 1991 APS data. Given that mostly non-status Indian women and their children were affected by Bill C-31, the age–sex distribution of Bill C-31 registrants differs from that of the overall status Indian population. Over time, the reinstated population has been characterized by a majority of women, especially at older ages (by 1987, 60 percent of the reinstated population were women). In 1987, inclusion of reinstated Indian women lowered the overall proportion of registered Indian women on-reserve from 69 percent to 62 percent. In recent years, the reinstated population has become more symmetrical, although women still continue to outnumber men.

AGE–SEX STRUCTURE

Age Structure

As the contrasting pyramids in Figure 8.2 clearly demonstrate, Canada's aboriginal population has a much younger age structure than that of the general population in Canada. The aboriginal population pyramid is much wider at the base, representing the younger ages, and narrower at the middle and old ages, compared with the population pyramid of Canada overall, which is more rectangular. In 1991, the median age of the aboriginal origin population was 22.3, compared with about 34 for Canadians as a whole — that is, half the aboriginal population is under the age of 22, while half the population in general is under the age of 34 (Nault et al., 1993, p. 17). As shown in Table 8.5, 36 percent of the total population with aboriginal ancestry is aged 0–14, compared with 23 percent of Canadians overall. In contrast, the proportion of the aboriginal population 55 years of age and over is only 6.6 percent, compared with 19 percent in the general population. Comparison between the aboriginal identity and origin populations shows that the identity population has slightly higher shares of children and seniors: children aged 0–14, and seniors (55+) represent 38 percent and 7 percent respectively of the identity population; while the adult population aged 25–54 comprise a slightly smaller proportion (36 percent) of the identity population than the origin population (38 percent). Overall, however, the age distribution of the identity population is fairly

FIGURE 8.2
PERCENTAGE DISTRIBUTION BY AGE GROUP AND SEX OF TOTAL CANADIAN, ABORIGINAL ANCESTRY, AND ABORIGINAL IDENTITY POPULATIONS, CANADA, 1991

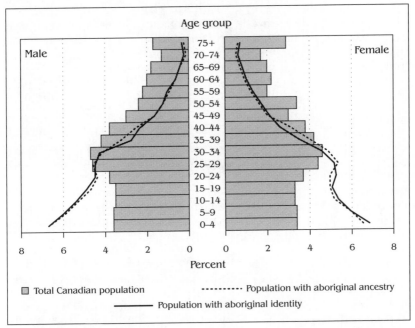

Note: All populations have been adjusted for undercoverage. The aboriginal populations have also been adjusted for incomplete enumeration.

Sources: Total Canadian population: Statistics Canada, Revised *Intercensal Population and Family Estimates, 1971–1991*, cat. no. 91-520, Ottawa: Minister of Industry, 1994; Aboriginal ancestry population: Loh, 1995; Aboriginal identity population: Norris et al., 1995.

similar to that observed for the aboriginal ancestry population as a whole, with a slightly higher median age of 22.6 for the identity population.

Among Native groups, the Inuit clearly have the youngest age structure. Estimated median ages by aboriginal group for the origin population are: 21.9 for registered Indians, 23.4 for non-status Indians, 21.8 for Métis, and 20.7 for Inuit (Nault et al., 1993). Comparable figures for the identity population tend to be even younger for non-status Indians and Inuit, at 19.4 and 18.8 respectively, and similar for registered Indians (22.6) and Métis (21.4). As shown in Table 8.5, among non-status Indians, 42 percent of those who identified with their North American Indian origins were under the age of 15, compared with 35 percent of the non-status population reporting Indian origins; similarly, for Inuit, 43 percent of the identity population is under the age of 15, compared with 38 percent of all persons of Inuit origin.

TABLE 8.5

PERCENTAGE DISTRIBUTION OF POPULATION BY SELECTED AGE GROUPS,
FOR ABORIGINAL AND TOTAL CANADIAN POPULATIONS,[1] CANADA, 1991

| | Age groups | | | | | | |
	0–4	5–14	15–24	25–34	35–54	55+	Total
	(percent)						
Total Aboriginal							
Origin	13.5	22.6	18.8	18.8	19.7	6.6	100.0
Identity	14.2	23.7	19.2	17.7	18.0	7.1	100.0
North American Indian							
Registered							
Origin	13.3	23.1	20.0	17.5	18.2	7.8	100.0
Identity	13.2	22.8	20.0	17.8	18.4	7.8	100.0
Non-registered							
Origin	13.4	22.1	17.5	20.1	21.5	5.5	100.0
Identity	16.5	25.5	17.3	17.1	18.4	5.2	100.0
Métis							
Origin	13.8	22.8	19.1	18.4	19.3	6.7	100.0
Identity	14.1	23.6	18.6	18.4	18.3	6.9	100.0
Inuit							
Origin	15.3	23.2	20.2	17.8	16.9	6.5	100.0
Identity	17.0	25.6	20.3	16.6	14.2	6.3	100.0
Total Canadian Population	8.7	13.8	13.9	17.6	26.7	19.3	100.0

[1] *Populations have not been adjusted for incomplete enumeration of reserves and settlements or undercoverage.*

Source: Calculated from Statistics Canada, *1991 Aboriginal Data: Age and Sex*, cat. no. 94-327, Ottawa: Minister of Industry, Science and Technology, 1993. Reproduced by authority of the Minister of Industry, 1995. Includes unpublished 1991 census and APS tabulations.

The much younger age structure of the aboriginal population, in comparison to the structure of the total Canadian population, is a reflection of the historically high fertility levels of the aboriginal population. Given that aboriginal fertility has been declining, the aboriginal population is aging, but at a slower pace than the Canadian population in general. For example, median age data from INAC's Register indicate an aging trend among Indians, from 16.5 years in 1971 to 19 in 1981, reaching 23 by 1990 (Nault et al., 1993). In comparison, the median age among the total Canadian population rose from 26.2 in 1971 to 33.2 by 1991 (Statistics Canada, 1994b, p. 2).

Sex Ratios

As with the Canadian population in general, women outnumber men in the aboriginal population as a whole.[14] Among the aboriginal ancestry population in 1991, there were 95.2 males for every 100 females, with fewer males, 93, per 100 females in the corresponding identity population, perhaps in part a reflection of the slightly higher propensity of females to identify with their aboriginal origins (see Table 8.4). The sex ratio of males to females for the Canadian population in 1991 was higher, at 97.7, than the overall aboriginal identity and origin populations. However, for the population with Inuit origins, men continue to outnumber women, with a sex ratio of 102 males per 100 females in 1991. Similar, but higher, ratios were also observed for Inuit in 1986 (103) and 1981 (105) (Norris, 1990). Yet, among those who identified with their Inuit origins, the sex ratio drops to 99, probably due to the higher proportion of females (75 percent) identifying than males (72 percent). For both registered and non-status Indian populations, the sex ratios of their respective identity population were also lower than for the corresponding origin populations. The reverse was true for the Métis, who had a slightly higher percentage of males (64 percent) than females (63 percent) identifying.

In a phenomenon that occurs among both aboriginal and non-aboriginal populations, the ratio of males to females is usually higher in rural than in urban areas, and for some groups, males tend to outnumber females in rural areas. Among the rural population with aboriginal identity in 1991, there were 96.9 males for every 100 females, compared with 84.4 in urban areas. Comparisons are similar for other groups, but sometimes more pronounced. For non-status Indians, Métis, and Inuit, males outnumber females in rural areas.

The comparison is the same but more pronounced for Indians between on- and off-reserve areas. In 1991, there were 106 males per 100 females on-reserve, compared with ratios of 82.3 and 77.5 for rural and urban areas, respectively, off-reserve. Corresponding ratios for status Indians were similar in 1986 (108 versus 85) and 1981 (107 versus 86) (Norris, 1990, p. 44).

Differences between urban/rural and on-/off-reserve sex ratios could be explained by two factors: male–female differentials in migration and, to a lesser extent, the higher fertility and, hence, younger populations in rural and reserve areas compared with urban areas. In the case of migration, women are much more inclined than men to move off-reserve or to leave rural areas, particularly in the more mobile, young adult age groups. In 1991, for every 100 Indian women aged 20 to 34 living off-reserve, there were only 70 men in the same age group. Women moving from reserve or rural areas to a greater extent than men may reflect a number of factors, such as the increased availability of traditional female occupations like administrative or clerical positions in urban areas, and the generally younger age at marriage of females than males.

With respect to fertility, among the aboriginal populations, sex ratios tend to be higher in areas with higher fertility, such as reserves and rural areas (see fertility section). "Young" populations and populations with high birth rates tend to have higher overall sex ratios than "old" populations and populations with low birth rates because of the higher rate of male births and the deficit of men among older persons (Shryock and Siegal, 1975, p. 194). However, this comparison does not hold between the "younger" aboriginal population and the "older" Canadian population in general in that the younger aboriginal population has the lower sex ratio. This deviation could be explained in part by a number of factors: an even greater differential in male/female mortality in the aboriginal than in the overall Canadian population; age-sex-specific immigration patterns; and male/female differentials in underenumeration and underreporting in census/APS.

COMPONENTS OF GROWTH

The following section looks at the components of growth — fertility, mortality, migration, and Bill C-31 amendments to the Indian Act — which affect the size, age–sex structure, and growth of aboriginal populations. The numbers of births and deaths in any population are a function of fertility and mortality rates, respectively, in combination with the age–sex structure of the population. The excess of births over deaths represents the natural increase in a population. With respect to trends in aboriginal fertility and mortality, Canada's earliest population can be characterized as undergoing what is referred to in the literature as a demographic transition, involving three stages, over the past century:

> The first stage was characterized by high fertility and high mortality rates during the first half of the 1900s. The second stage which took place during the 1950s and 1960s saw continued high fertility, however mortality dropped off rapidly due to advances in sanitation and medicine. The third stage, which took place in the 1970s, saw fertility rates decline as the effects of urbanization and modernization were felt, while mortality rates remained low. (Siggner, 1986a, p. 5; 1986b)

As a component of growth, migration between communities contributes to the changing size and distribution of the aboriginal population, within Canada[15] by place of residence, such as on- or off-reserve and in rural and urban areas, as well as by province and territory. In relation to migration, geographical mobility — that is, moving from one residence to another, but not necessarily to a different community — is also presented as a useful indicator of how transitory a population may be and its propensity to relocate.

The fourth component of growth is related to the amendments to the Indian Act, passed as Bill C-31 in June 1985, which restored Indian status and membership to those persons, mainly women and their children, who had lost them as a result of provisions in the earlier act, especially concerning the out-marriage of status women to non-status individuals. As a component of growth, Bill C-31 legislation affects the growth of both the registered and non-status Indian groups. These amendments, as noted earlier, have resulted in a significant addition of population to the registered or status Indian population. On the other hand, most of those reinstated are drawn from the non-status Indian population, thereby having the potential for reducing the population of this aboriginal group. However, in addition to the gains and losses of population associated with reinstatements, Bill C-31 legislation also includes a set of descent rules that establish entitlement to Indian status at birth based on the extent of out-marriage to non-status (aboriginal or non-aboriginal) individuals. As a result, some births to status Indian women will not be eligible for status, thereby producing a loss of population to the registered population and a potential gain to the non-status Indian group. Children may be categorized as non-status Indians, resulting in a population gain to the non-status group.

The next section reviews the trends, patterns, and group differentials associated with these various components of growth.

Fertility

Overall Trends

Over the past century, Canada's aboriginal people have undergone a transition in their fertility. Estimates of crude birth rates for Canadian Indians from 1900 to 1976 show that until the 1940s, the birth rate remained relatively stable, at around 40 births per thousand population. After the outbreak of World War II, the rate rose rapidly to a peak of 47 births per 1000 by 1960. Following this cycle of a rapidly increasing birth rate was a sharp downturn. Since the 1970s, the rate of decline has slowed.

For the Inuit of the Northwest Territories, estimates of crude birth rates from 1931 to 1981 indicate a similar pattern. From 1941, rates rose sharply from about 30 births per 1000 to a high of 60 per 1000 by the 1960s. The rates dropped off sharply after the mid-1960s, plummeting to 35 births per 1000 by the 1980s (Robitaille and Choinière, 1985).

A number of factors have been considered in assessing the rise and fall in Native fertility. The increase in Native rates between 1941 and 1961 was due in part to improved health conditions, since more pregnancies went full term and mothers had a better chance of surviving childbirth. Moreover, as part of the early stages of modernization, more Native women shifted to bottle feeding, birth intervals shortened, and the natural fertility rate increased (Romaniuc, 1981).

The decline in fertility since the 1960s largely reflected the growing use of contraceptives among the aboriginal population. Birth control was implemented in terms of both family size and timing of childbearing. As was the case for European populations entering the "demographic transition," family size consideration was the dominant issue for Natives using birth control, followed by considerations of when to have children and how far apart they should be spaced. Census data indicate not only that Native families are getting smaller, but also that Native women are having children later and spacing them further apart (Romaniuc, 1987). For example, the proportion of "ever-married" or not-single women aged 20–24 who had their first child dropped from 80 percent in 1961 to 74 percent by 1981. The proportion of those with at least two children in that age group dropped from 78 percent to 61 percent (Romaniuc, 1987, p. 78).

As with the population in general, factors such as smaller proportions getting married, later marriage, and increased marital instability play a role in aboriginal fertility.

Trends in Total Fertility Rates

As shown in Figure 8.3, there has been a declining trend in total fertility rates (TFRs)[16] for both the registered Indian and Inuit populations over the past three decades. These trends and levels differ from TFRs observed for the general Canadian population, and are more pronounced. The TFR for the Canadian population as a whole dropped from 3.8 births per woman

FIGURE 8.3

TOTAL FERTILITY RATES FOR INUIT, REGISTERED INDIANS, AND TOTAL CANADIAN POPULATION, CANADA, 1961–1991

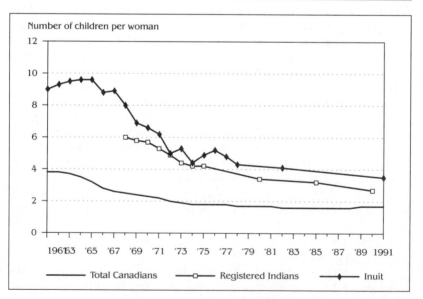

Sources: Total Canadian: Statistics Canada, *Vital Statistics*, Registered Indians: Nault et al., 1993, 1991; Norris et al., 1995; Inuit: Robitaille and Choinière, 1985, 1991; Norris et al., 1995.

in 1961 to 2.5 in 1968. It dropped to 1.8 by 1974, and thereafter gradually declined to 1.6 by 1987, followed by an increase to about 1.7 by 1990,
and has remained relatively stable through to 1993 (Statistics Canada,
1994b, p. 7). Over roughly the same period, Inuit fertility started decreasing from an estimated TFR of 9.2 in 1966 to 4.1 by 1983, and was projected to reach a possible TFR of about 3.4 by 1991 (Robitaille and
Choinière, 1985). Fertility of registered Indians declined from a TFR of 6.1
in 1968 to 3.1 by the early 1980s, with a further decline to 2.7 by 1990
(Nault et al., 1993). Between 1968 and 1981, the TFRs of Indians and Inuit
declined at a much faster rate than those for Canadians in general; both
Indian and Inuit fertility rates dropped by 48 percent, compared with 32
percent for the total population. These trends suggest a convergence of
Native fertility toward the overall Canadian fertility level.

Group Fertility Differentials

Among aboriginal groups, Inuit fertility rates have been and continue to
remain higher than those of registered Indians. In both 1981 and 1986,
census data rank the Inuit as having the highest fertility levels, followed by
status Indians, non-status Indians, and Métis. These rankings were derived
from indicators such as child–woman ratios and children aged 0–4 as a
percentage of total population. Child–woman data for aboriginal origin
groups also indicate that Inuit have the highest fertility, with 587 children
aged 0–4 per 1000 women, but that the lower fertility levels of the remaining three groups are about the same, at some 460 children per 1000
woman. However, for registered Indians on-reserve, the child–woman ratio
is similar to that observed for Inuit.

Fertility levels for 1991 were higher for the identity population, with a
child–woman ratio of 510 children aged 0–4 per 1000 women, compared
with 470 for the aboriginal origin population. The lower fertility of the origin-based population is consistent with the observation noted earlier that,
among the aboriginal origin population, the characteristics of those who
do not identify with their origins tend to be more similar to those of the
non-Native population; hence, the lower fertility. Estimates of TFRs (based
on 1991 census data) for the different identity populations support the
1981 and 1986 rankings, with the following TFRs: Inuit, 3.4; registered
Indians, 2.8; Métis, 2.4; and non-status Indians, 2.0 (Table 8.6).

Geographic Differentials

Fertility levels have been and continue to be significantly lower in urban
than in rural areas, and lower off-reserve than on-reserve. Both 1981 and
1986 census data show the higher fertility of reserve and rural populations compared with urban areas. These fertility differentials by place of
residence are also more pronounced among younger women (Norris,
1990). Both the child–woman ratios and TFR estimates indicate similar
differentials by place of residence among the aboriginal population. For

TABLE 8.6
ESTIMATED TOTAL FERTILITY RATES BY ABORIGINAL IDENTITY GROUPS, BY PLACE OF RESIDENCE, CANADA, 1991

	Place of residence			
Aboriginal identity	Reserve	Rural	Urban	Total
	(number of children per woman)			
North American Indian (registered)	3.3	2.5	2.2	2.8
North American Indian[1] (non-registered)	—	2.4	1.9	2.0
Métis[1]	—	2.8	2.3	2.4
Inuit[1]	—	—	—	3.4

[1] *For these groups, total fertility rates were not estimated for residence on-reserve, or, in the case of Inuit, for place of residence.*

Source: Norris et al., 1995.

example, in 1991, the aboriginal origin population had higher child–woman ratios for reserves (593 children for every 1000 women) and for rural areas (503) than for urban areas (429). Similarly, identity-based TFRs of registered Indian populations in 1991 are estimated to be 3.7 children per woman on-reserve, 2.4 for rural, and 2.2 for urban areas. TFRs for non-status Indians and Métis are also higher in rural than in urban areas (Table 8.6). Census data also suggest that the fertility level of Inuit residing in southern Canada is lower than that of Inuit in the North (Robitaille and Choinière, 1985).

Mortality

Mortality Trends

The mortality of both Indian and Inuit populations has declined significantly over the past century. Indian life expectancy[17] at birth increased from an estimated 33 years around the turn of the century to about 67 years for males and 74 years for females by 1991 (Table 8.7). Available estimates for the Inuit of northern Quebec indicate that life expectancy increased by some 30 years, from a life expectancy of 35 years (for both sexes) in 1940 to the present 1991 estimate of 58 and 69 years for males and females respectively (Table 8.8). In comparison, the life expectancy of the male and female Canadian population in general increased by about 12 and 15 years respectively over the last 50 years, to 74.6 years for males and 80.9 years for females in 1991 (Table 8.7). The 1991 discrepancy between male and female life expectancy is greater in both Indian and Inuit populations (7 and 11 years respectively) than in the population in general (6.3 years) (Tables 8.7 and 8.8).

TABLE 8.7
ESTIMATED LIFE EXPECTANCY AT BIRTH FOR REGISTERED INDIANS AND TOTAL CANADIAN POPULATIONS, FOR SELECTED PERIODS, CANADA, 1900–1991

Period	Registered Indian population		Year	Total Canadian	
	Both sexes			Males	Females
1900	33		1921	58.8	60.6
1940	38		1941	63.0	66.3
1960	56		1961	68.4	74.2
	Males	Females			
1960–64	59.7	63.5	1966	68.7	75.2
1965–68	60.5	65.6	1976	70.2	77.5
1976	59.8	66.3	1981	71.9	79.0
1981	62.4	68.9	1984–86	73.0	79.8
1982–85	64.0	72.8			
1991	66.9	74.0	1991	74.6	80.9

Sources: Registered Indian life expectancy: 1900, 1940, and 1960 from Romaniuc, 1981; 1960–64 and 1982–85 from Medical Services Branch, Health and Welfare Canada, 1976, 1981 and Rowe and Norris, 1985; 1991 from Nault et al., 1993; Canadian life expectancy: Statistics Canada, *Vital Statistics: Canadian Life Tables*, cat. no. 84–203, Ottawa.

TABLE 8.8
ESTIMATED LIFE EXPECTANCY AT BIRTH[1] FOR THE INUIT AND TOTAL CANADIAN POPULATIONS, CANADA AND REGIONS, 1940 TO 1991

Inuit Population						General Population	
Labrador		Northern Quebec		Northwest Territories		Canada	
Period	e_0	Period	e_0	Period	e_0	Period	e_0
		1941–51	35	1941–50	29	1940–42	65
		1951–61	39	1951–60	37	1950–52	69
						1955–57	70
		1961–71	59	1963–66	51	1960–62	71
						1965–67	72
1971–80	60	1971–81	62			1970–72	73
						1975–77	74
		1991	58 M	1978–82	66	1980–82	75
			69 F				
						1991	74.6 M
							80.9 F

[1] *Unless otherwise indicated, life expectancies (e_0) are shown for both sexes combined.*

Sources: Inuit: Robitaille and Choinière, 1985, p. 23; 1991: Létourneau, 1994; Canadian life expectancy: Statistics Canada, *Vital Statistics: Canadian Life Tables*, cat. no. 84-203, Ottawa.

Infant Mortality

Infant mortality, which refers to the deaths of babies under the age of one, is used as an indicator of a population's standard of living, such that the lower the mortality rate, the better the standard of living. A large part of the increase in Native life expectancy is attributable to the rapid decline in infant mortality. At the turn of the century, infant mortality rates (IMRs) of registered Indians were estimated to be some 240 infant deaths per 1000 live births, about 200 around World War II, declining to around 30 by the late 1970s (Romaniuc, 1981). Estimates based on data adjusted from INAC's Register indicate a substantial decline in IMRs from 39 per 1000 live births in 1975 to 12 by 1990 (Nault et al., 1993). Over the same period, Canadian rates decreased much more gradually, from 14.3 to 6.8. These comparisons suggest a convergence of Indian rates toward Canadian levels.

More recent data from Health and Welfare Canada suggest that the decline in registered Indian infant mortality rates may be levelling off, that the downward trend may have slowed or dropped. The 1992 rate of 12.6 per 1000 is even slightly higher than that observed for earlier years by HWC (Bobet and Dardick, 1995), and is also higher compared with the 1990 INAC-based estimate of 12.0 (Table 8.9). Among infant deaths, the largest discrepancy between Indian and Canadian rates in general appears to be with post-neonatal deaths — that is, between the ages of 28 days and one year — as compared with neonatal deaths of infants fewer than 28 days old. The Indian post-neonatal death rate is more than three times the national average: 7.8 per 1000 as compared with 2.1.

Declines in infant mortality of roughly the same magnitude as those of registered Indians have also occurred among the Inuit. Since the 1950s, the infant mortality of Inuit has decreased substantially, from 300 per 1000 to around 50 per 1000 by 1981 (Robitaille and Choinière, 1985). Levels of infant mortality remain higher than those of registered Indians. For example, Inuit infant mortality rates in the mid-1960s were estimated to be about twice as high as Indian rates, with 100 deaths per 1000 live births for Inuit compared with 50 for Indians (Webb, 1973).

Causes of Death

While infant mortality rates of aboriginal people have dropped significantly, declines in mortality at other ages are much less pronounced. An analysis of age-specific death rates of the registered Indian population for 1971, 1976, and 1981 indicated hardly any decrease for some ages over the period, or, in some cases, even slight increases in mortality (Rowe and Norris, 1985).

This pattern of relatively little decline in mortality at older ages, compared with the great strides made in infant survival, reflects the fact that the major causes of death for registered Indians are associated not with disease but with accidents, poisoning, and violence, and many of these deaths are alcohol-related (Jarvis and Boldt, 1982). Since 1960, improvements in health care have resulted in significant decreases in the number of deaths from respiratory conditions, digestive disorders, infection, and parasitic diseases as well as perinatal causes. For almost 300 years, tuberculosis was a major threat to Native health. Among Indians around Hudson Bay and James Bay, tuberculosis accounted for 30 percent of all deaths as early as 1885. In 1950, the incidence of tuberculosis among Indians and Inuit was estimated to be twelve times the national rate (Graham-Cumming, 1967). Currently, accidents, poisoning, and violence are the leading causes of deaths. Rates increased dramatically from 139 per 100 000 population in 1960 to 253 per 100 000 in 1978 (Murdock, 1983), then dropped to 174 per 100 000 in 1983 (Siggner, 1986) — still three times the rate for the Canadian population. Similarly, injuries and poisoning were the leading causes of death among the Inuit over the 1970–80 period: 21 percent in Northern Quebec, 34 percent in the Northwest Territories, and 40 percent in Labrador, compared with only 9 percent among Canadians as a whole (Robitaille and Choinière, 1985).[18]

More recent data on the health of registered Indians from Health and Welfare Canada for 1992 indicate that injury and poisoning is still the leading cause of death, with motor vehicle accidents and suicide accounting for the two main types of trauma. Indian death rates due to injury continue to be at least three times the Canadian average and, notably, four times in the case of males only. However, death rates for injury have fallen over the 1979–88 period, although they now seem to be slowing their downward trend and levelling off. For example, the 1992 Indian death rates due to injury and poisoning[19] were 169 per 100 000 population, compared with the 1983 rate of 174. The 1992 suicide rate itself is still at least three times the national average, with 40 deaths due to suicide per 100 000 Indian population, compared with 12 for Canadians in general (Bobet and Dardick, 1995).

The predominance of injuries and poisoning as the leading causes of death among aboriginal people overall also reflects the impact of the high proportion of young adults in the aboriginal population. The effect of the young age-structure can be demonstrated by controlling for differences in age structure between aboriginal and non-aboriginal populations. A "standardized" death rate is calculated for the aboriginal population, showing what the aboriginal rate would be if it had the same age composition as the overall Canadian population. For example, because the registered Indian population is much younger, its crude (unstandardized) death rate in 1981 was 6.1 deaths per 1000 population, compared with 7.0 for the overall Canadian population, while its death rate standardized to the Canadian population was 9.5 (Rowe and Norris, 1985). Similarly, causes of deaths associated mainly with young adults, such as accidents and injuries, are more liable to account for a higher proportion of deaths in the younger Indian population than in the older general population. It is worth noting that when rates by cause from 1978–86 were standardized according to the older Canadian age structure, diseases of the circulatory system become the leading cause of death among Indians, followed by injuries and poisonings (Harris and McCullough, 1988). This calculation clearly shows the importance of age structure in determining the overall leading causes of death in a population. One might expect, therefore, that as the population ages, the leading causes of death overall will shift.

Group Differentials

The mortality of aboriginal populations in Canada continues to remain much higher than that of the general population for reasons just outlined. Estimates of life expectancy at birth for registered Indians in the early 1980s and for Inuit as of 1991 are comparable to overall Canadian levels during the 1940s, when life expectancies ranged between 65 and 69 years of age (for males and females combined). Life expectancies of these Native groups are about 10 years less than for the overall population. In the case of Métis and non-status Indians, direct data on mortality are not available. However, given that these two groups are more urbanized than registered Indians or Inuit, one might speculate that mortality levels of Métis and non-status Indians would be more similar to that of the general population and, hence, lower than those of registered Indians and Inuit. In fact, estimates[20] of life expectancies for all four aboriginal groups reflect this relation. Life expectancies are highest for non-status Indians (71 and 78 years for male and females respectively), the most urbanized identity group, followed by Métis (70 and 77), registered Indians (67 and 74) and Inuit (58 and 69) (Table 8.9).

TABLE 8.9

ESTIMATED LIFE EXPECTANCY AT BIRTH BY ABORIGINAL IDENTITY GROUP, BY PLACE OF RESIDENCE, CANADA, 1991

| | Place of residence | | | | | | | |
| | Reserve | | Rural | | Urban | | Total | |
Aboriginal identity	M	F	M	F	M	F	M	F
North American Indian (registered)	62.0	69.6	68.5	75.0	72.5	79.0	66.9	74.0
North American Indian (non-registered)[1]	—	—	69.0	75.5	72.5	79.0	71.4	77.9
Métis[1]	—	—	68.5	75.0	71.5	78.0	70.4	76.9
Inuit[1]	—	—	—	—	—	—	57.6	68.8
Total aboriginal	—	—	—	—	—	—	67.9	75.0

[1] For these groups, life expectancies were not estimated for residence "on-reserve," or by place of residence for Inuit.

Source: Norris et al., 1995.

Geographic Differentials

Life expectancy estimates for the aboriginal population by place of residence indicate higher life expectancies for urban populations than those of rural or reserve areas. For example, 1991 life expectancy for registered Indians is estimated to be highest in urban areas, at 72.5 and 79 years for males and females respectively, lower in rural areas (68 and 75) and lowest on reserves (62 and 70) (Table 8.9).

Mobility and Migration

Propensity to Move or Migrate

Aboriginal people tend to move to a greater extent than Canadians in general. Those who identify with their aboriginal ancestry have a slightly greater tendency to change residences, but are less inclined to change communities, compared with the overall population with aboriginal origins. According to 1991 census and APS data, 58 percent of the aboriginal origin and 60 percent of the aboriginal identity populations had moved (changed residences) over the past five years (1986–91), compared with 47 percent of all Canadians (43 percent if external migration is excluded). In the case of migration, 25 percent of the aboriginal origin and 21 percent of the aboriginal identity populations had moved from one community to another, compared with 20 percent of Canadians[21] (Table 8.10). Similar comparisons were made for the aboriginal origin population with 1981 and 1986 census data (Norris, 1990).

By Aboriginal Group. Among the aboriginal identity groups, 1991 mobility rates were highest for the Métis and non-status Indians, with about 64 percent of their respective populations having changed residences over the five-year period (1986–91). The registered Indian population had the lowest mobility rate, 57 percent, while the rate for the Inuit was 62 percent. Migration rates were highest for non-status Indians (27 percent), followed by Métis (24 percent), registered Indians (21 percent), and Inuit (15 percent) (Table 8.10).

By Place of Residence. In general, aboriginal people who live outside the regions of their Native communities and settlements tend to be more transient than the general population, whereas within their own communities they are far less transient. A study based on 1981 census data showed that in the south, the aboriginal population had higher mobility rates than non-aboriginals, while in the far north, where mobility is high for both populations, non-aboriginals were more mobile than aboriginals (76 percent had moved compared with 54 percent of Natives). In the mid-north, 45 percent of the aboriginal population had moved over the 1976–81 period, compared with 69 percent of aboriginal people residing in metropolitan areas in the south (Norris and Pryor, 1984, p. 33). Another study of Inuit mobility and migration, based on 1981 census data, showed

TABLE 8.10
MOVERS AND MIGRANTS BY TYPE OF MOVE, ABORIGINAL AND TOTAL CANADIAN POPULATIONS, CANADA, 1991

Populations	Movers as a percentage of the population[1] aged 5+	Internal migrants as a percentage of the population aged 5+	Percentage distribution of migrants by type of move				Total number of internal migrants
			Rural-to-rural	Urban-to-urban	Rural-to-urban	Urban-to-rural	
	(percent)	(percent)	(percent)				(thousands)
Aboriginal							
Origin	58.1	25.3	10.0	48.9	18.9	22.2	217.9
Identity	59.8[1]	21.4	11.7	44.0	21.6	22.7	114.9[4]
North American Indian							
Registered identity[2]	56.8	19.6	14.1	36.2	25.7	24.0	60.2
Non-registered identity	64.1	27.4	6.7	61.0	13.1	19.2	24.6
Métis							
Identity	64.3	24.0	7.3	51.0	19.3	22.4	27.8
Inuit							
Identity	61.9	15.3	33.0	24.0	23.2	19.8	4.0
Total Canadian Population	46.7[3]	19.8	5.9	62.6	12.8	18.7	4947.6

[1] Clatworthy, 1996.

[2] For the purposes of comparison, reserves are classified as rural in the case of registered Indians.

[3] For total Canadian population, the figure of 46.7%, which includes external migrants (from outside Canada), drops to 43.0% if moves are restricted to within Canada.

[4] The sum of migrants for the individual identity aboriginal groups, which includes multiples, is greater than the total aboriginal identity count.

Source: Statistics Canada 1991 census and 1991 APS unpublished data; Clatworthy, 1996; Statistics Canada, 1993b.

FIGURE 8.4
FIVE-YEAR PERIOD AGE–SEX SPECIFIC MOBILITY RATES FOR REGISTERED INDIANS, ON- AND OFF-RESERVE, AND ALL CANADIANS, CANADA, 1986–1991

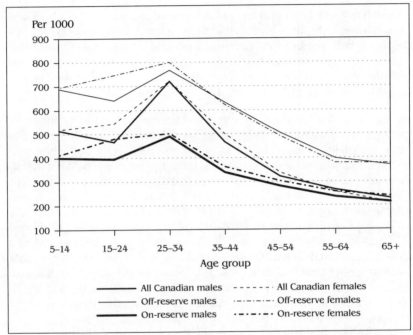

Sources: Registered Indians: Statistics Canada, 1991 census and 1991 APS unpublished data; All Canadians: Statistics Canada,"Mobility and Migration," *1991 Census*, cat. no. 93-322, Ottawa: Minister of Industry.

that among the Inuit, the rate of migration was low in northern regions, between 10 and 15 percent in 1981, but much higher in the south, at 38 percent, while that of the general population was 23 percent (Robitaille and Choinière, 1985). Census data indicate that while Indians living on-reserve were less mobile than Canadians in general, those who lived off-reserve were highly transient, moving both within and between communities to a greater extent than the general population over a five-year period (Norris, 1985; 1990).

Similar findings occur with 1991 census data, showing the higher mobility and migration of off-reserve Indians. For example, between 1986 and 1991, for every 1000 registered Indian women aged 15–24 living off-reserve, close to 750 had moved at some point over the five-year period, compared with about 475 per 1000 among those living on-reserve, and 540 for Canadians in general (Figure 8.4). Similarly, in the case of migration, 380 per 1000 registered Indian women aged 15–24 living off-reserve had migrated, compared with 150 on-reserve, and 240 for Canadians of the same age. Overall, mobility and migration rates of registered Indians off-reserve (670 and 310 per 1000 respectively) are much greater than the corresponding on-reserve rates (390 and 120) and higher than those for the Canadian population in general (406 and 172).

The higher mobility and migration rates of the off-reserve aboriginal population is only partly attributable to movement from reserves and settlement. Their higher mobility rates in general, which reflect movement within the same community as well as from different communities, demonstrate the impact of living outside Native communities and settlements on the propensity of aboriginal people to relocate.

By Age and Sex. Young adults, especially females, tend to be the most mobile in a population, and the aboriginal population is no different in that respect. Mobility rates follow the standard age pattern for both aboriginal and all Canadians, decreasing over the school age groups, peaking during the young adult years 25–29, and then declining fairly steadily thereafter. Young women, particularly those in the 20–24 age group, move and migrate to a greater extent than their male counterparts (Norris, 1985; 1990). For example, between 1986 and 1991, among the population aged 15–24, 750 per 1000 registered Indian women living off-reserve had moved, compared with 640 males; similarly, for Canadians, the female rate was higher than that for males (540 versus 465) (Figure 8.4). Some of this gender difference among youth and young adults is attributable to younger ages at marriage and earlier entry into the labour force of females, factors that are associated with geographical movement.

Women predominate in the movement to and from reserves; they are far more mobile than men, especially in their out-migration from reserves. The phenomenon of young Indian women leaving reserves to a greater extent than men is similar to, but much more pronounced than, the higher out-migration of women than men from rural areas among the general population. For example, according to the 1986 census, out-migration rates from rural areas for young adult women (aged 15–24) were only about one and a third times greater than those of males in the general population, whereas among aboriginal populations the out-migration rates of women from rural and reserve areas are about twice as high as those for men (Norris, 1990). Census data on registered Indians for 1991 show that among youth aged 15–24, rates of migration from reserve communities are significantly higher for females (86 per 1000) than for males (50) (Figure 8.5). Overall, five-year rates of out-migration from census data for males and females are 59 and 46 per 1000 respectively.

A number of studies by Gerber (1977), Clatworthy (1980; 1996), Norris (1985; 1990) have documented the fact that women are over-represented in the aboriginal migrant population. Aboriginal women, especially on reserves, experience push–pull factors in their moves that are different from or additional to those experienced by non-aboriginal women. The

FIGURE 8.5
FIVE-YEAR PERIOD AGE-SEX SPECIFIC OUT-MIGRATION RATES FOR RESERVE COMMUNITIES, REGISTERED INDIANS, CANADA, 1986–1991

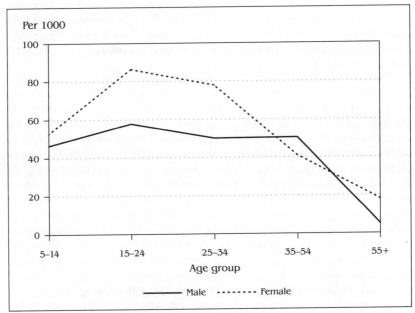

Source: Norris et al., 1995.

previous discrimination against women in the Indian Act, the high incidence of lone parenthood, and the economic conditions on reserves and opportunities in urban areas are important influences in the decision to move. In his study of aboriginal migration and mobility patterns, Clatworthy found that females, younger families, and lone-parent families are overrepresented in the migrant population (Clatworthy, 1994). An earlier study also found that aboriginal youth move to a greater extent than their non-aboriginal counterparts (Priest, 1985).

Migration Patterns by Place of Residence

Rural/Urban Migration. Aboriginal groups differ not only in their propensity to move or migrate, but also in the types of moves. There are significant differences in the rural/urban migration patterns among aboriginal groups. For example, according to 1991 APS data, over the 1986–91 period, the majority (61 percent) of non-status Indian migrants moved mainly between urban areas (like Canadians in general, 63 percent), compared with 51 percent of Métis migrants, 36 percent of registered Indians, and only 24 percent of Inuit (Table 8.10). A third of Inuit migrants had moved between rural communities, compared with only 7 percent of non-status Indians and Métis and 14 percent of registered Indians (for this latter group, reserves are classified as rural for comparison). Migration from rural (and reserve) to urban areas accounted for a larger share of registered Indian and Inuit migrants than non-status Indians and Métis. Over the 1986–91 period, both Métis and non-status Indians had relatively small net losses of migrants from urban areas, while registered Indians and Inuit recorded small net gains to urban areas.

Migration to and from Reserves. An important aspect of the migration patterns of registered Indians that distinguishes them from other aboriginal groups is the movement to and from reserves, especially between reserves and cities. Reserves have always been a source of Indian migrants who leave in search of better social or economic opportunities. Cities, both large and small, have become destinations for a significant proportion of migrants from reserves, with the result that the majority of migrants moving to reserves come from urban areas. Between 1986 and 1991, more than two-thirds (68 percent) of migrants from reserve communities moved to urban areas (35 percent to large urban centres or metropolitan areas [CMAs] and 33 percent to smaller urban areas), and in the opposite direction, the majority (61 percent) of in-migrants moving to reserves came from urban areas (26 percent from CMAs and 35 percent from smaller cities).

Overall, regardless of origin (from reserves or other communities), the major destination of one in three registered Indian migrants in 1991 was large urban or city areas (accounting for 35 percent of all in-migrants), followed by smaller cities (27 percent) and reserves (26 percent), with the remaining 12 percent moving to non-reserve rural areas (Table 8.11).

Over four census periods, it appears that large cities have attracted an ever-increasing share of Indian migrants, rising from 26 percent over the 1966–71 migration period to 35 percent over the 1986–91 period. Over the same intervals, the proportion of migrants moving to rural areas declined from 21 percent over 1966–71 to about 12 percent over

TABLE 8.11

Percentage Distribution of In-Migrants by Place of Destination, Registered Indians, Canada, Selected Five-Year Periods, 1966–1991

Place of destination	1966–71	1976–81	1981–86	1986–91
	(percent)			
Reserve	27	28	30	26
Rural	21	16	12	12
Urban CMA	26	29	30	35
Urban non-CMA	26	27	29	27
Urban total	52	56	59	62

Source: Calculated from unpublished tabulation of census migration data (1981, 1986, and 1991) and Siggner, 1977.

TABLE 8.12
FIVE-YEAR OUT-MIGRATION RATES BY PLACE OF RESIDENCE, PER THOUSAND
POPULATION, REGISTERED INDIANS, CANADA, SELECTED YEARS, 1966–1991

Place of residence	1966–71	1976–81	1981–86	1986–91
	(migrants per 1000 population)			
Reserve	28	52	47	53
Rural	232	410	463	465
Urban CMA	193	335	284	228
Urban non-CMA	263	415	422	373
Total migrants per 1000 population	187	186	178	197

Source: Calculated from unpublished tabulations of census migration data (1981, 1986, and 1991), and Siggner, 1977.

1981–86, and remained at the same level over 1986–91. Shares of in-migrants to reserves and smaller cities increased slightly between 1971 and 1986, followed by slight decreases to present 1991 proportions of 26 percent and 27 percent respectively[22] (Table 8.11).

Since the 1970s, the migration rate of registered Indians moving from non-reserve communities in rural areas has increased significantly, from 230 per 1000 over 1966–71 to 465 per 1000 over 1986–91. Thus, between 1986 and 1991, nearly half of registered Indians in rural areas migrated to other communities, usually in urban areas. In comparison, out-migration from reserves has remained fairly stable since 1976–81, at about 50 per 1000, while migration rates from large cities have declined from 33 percent to 23 percent and from smaller cities from 42 percent to 37 percent (Table 8.12).

Overall, nearly 70 percent of registered Indian migrants over the 1986–91 period, can be classified into three major flows: urban-to-urban (36 percent), rural-to-urban (17 percent), and urban-to-reserve (16 percent). The flows from small urban areas to the larger metropolitan areas account for the largest proportion of migrants (11 percent), followed by flows between communities within metropolitan areas themselves (10 percent) and flows from smaller cities to reserves (9 percent). Over time, some types of origin–destination combinations of migration flows have clearly decreased, while other combinations have increased, oscillated, or remained relatively stable. For example, from 1971 to 1991, the proportion of migrants moving between communities within reserve and rural areas has declined, from 12 percent to 3 percent and from 10 percent to 3 percent, while the proportion of migrants moving from small to larger cities has increased steadily from about 8 percent to 11 percent.

Net Migration Patterns of Registered Indians. The overall effect of registered Indian migration patterns for the 1986–91 period is a net inflow of about 9000 migrants[23] to reserves, a net outflow of some 9000 from rural areas, a net gain of 3800 to large cities, and a net loss of 4000 from the smaller cities. Although the major migration flows are between cities and reserves, the impact in terms of net gain or loss of population is most significant in rural areas. Rural areas lost registered Indian population largely through migration to urban areas. Large inflows of migrants to urban areas overall were practically negated by almost equally large outflows to reserves. Net migration rates over the 1986–91 period indicate the extent of the impact of migration on population by place of residence. The impact was extremely negative for the rural population, with a net loss of about 260 migrants per 1000 rural residents, and minimal for reserves, with a net gain of some 50 migrants per 1000 population. For large metropolitan urban areas, the impact was slightly more positive than for reserves, with a net gain of 67 migrants per 1000 residents, while the effect for smaller cities was just the opposite, with a net loss of 68 migrants per 1000 population. From 1971 to 1991, rural areas sustained increasingly significant net losses of migrants relative to their population, with net out-migration rates per 1000 of about 115 in the 1970s reaching about 260 in the 1980s. In contrast, the impact of net inflows for reserves has been relatively small, ranging between 40 and 50 migrants per 1000 population from 1976–81 on (Figure 8.6).

FIGURE 8.6
FIVE-YEAR PERIOD NET MIGRATION RATES BY PLACE OF RESIDENCE, REGISTERED INDIANS, CANADA, SELECTED PERIODS, 1966–1991

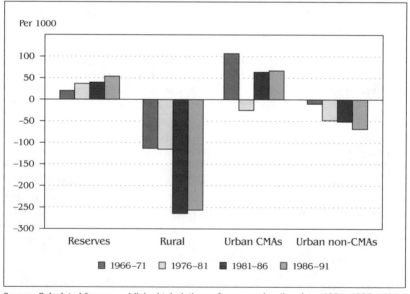

Source: Calculated from unpublished tabulations of census migration data (1981, 1986, 1991), and Siggner, 1977.

Unlike rural and urban areas off-reserve, reserves have consistently experienced net inflows of registered Indian migrants, largely from urban areas. At times of high unemployment or a slowdown in the economy, registered Indians may be more inclined to migrate to reserves than remain in cities. Unlike most other migrants, especially immigrants, registered Indians usually do have a "home" community, the reserve, to which they can return.

Bill C-31 Reinstatements and Births

As noted earlier, the Indian Act's Bill C-31 legislation can affect the population growth of both registered and non-status Indian groups, both positively and negatively. Reinstatements have increased the registered Indian population, and are probably reducing the size of the non-status Indian group, since most of those reinstated are drawn from this population. The second impact of Bill C-31 on population growth is due to the bill's set of descent rules, which establish entitlement to Indian status at birth on the basis of out-marriage to non-registered individuals.

> The 1985 amendments to the Indian Act (specifically Section 6) contained a set of descent (inheritance) rules which establish entitlement to Indian status. These rules result in two classes of Indian. . . . In general terms, children born to parents, both of whom are currently registered (or entitled to be registered) acquire entitlement under Section 6(1). Children born to parent combinations involving a parent registered (or entitled to be registered) under section 6(1) and a non-registered parent acquire entitlement under Section 6(2). Offspring from parental combinations involving a non-registered parent and a parent registered (or entitled to be registered) under Section 6(2) are not entitled to Indian registration. (Clatworthy, 1994, p. 3).

Thus, Bill C-31 births to status Indian women that are not entitled to status will result in a population loss to the registered Indian group, but a potential gain to the non-status Indian group.

Bill C-31 Reinstatements

Over the past decade, about 96 000 persons were reinstated as a result of the 1985 amendments. The annual number of registrants is projected to decline gradually, from about 6000 registrants in 1995 to some 1800 by 2002; the number is expected to drop to 1000 by 2006 and remain constant thereafter for the projection period to 2016 (Norris et al., 1995). Consequently, the registered Indian population, which by 1995 had already gained close to 100 000 persons through Bill C-31 reinstatements, is expected to have gained a grand total of some 143 000 by 2016.

It is thought that most of the reinstated persons have been, and will continue to be, sourced from the non-status Indian population. Projections of the aboriginal identity population assumed that of the some 63 000 persons who would be added as reinstatements to the registered

Indian group between 1991 and 2016, about a quarter of them (16 500) would be sourced from the non-status identity population, and the remaining three-quarters would come from the non-status origin population (Norris et al., 1995).

Bill C-31 Births

Given that the impact of Bill C-31 births is more a long-term than an immediate proposition, reference is made here to the assumptions developed for projections of the aboriginal identity population. The projected impact of Bill C-31 births is based on assumptions about out-marriage and the subsequent assignment of affected births from the registered Indian population directly into the non-status population:

> the out marriage rate has a substantial impact upon the percentage expected to retain status at birth, . . . on the assumption that the out marriage rate remains constant at 25 percent. Clatworthy estimated that the percentage retaining status at birth would decline from about 92 percent at the beginning of the projection period through to about 75 percent by the end; in other words, the percentage of births to status Indian women that are allocated to the non-status population are projected to increase from 8 percent to 25 percent. On this basis, . . . close to 43,000 births to status Indian would be transferred to the non-status Indian population over the 25-year projection period, under the continuation of current trends. (Norris et al., 1995)

ABORIGINAL POPULATION PROJECTIONS

Projections of aboriginal population represent the future trends that aboriginal populations are likely to follow if underlying assumptions with respect to fertility, mortality, migration, and Bill C-31 prove to be correct. However, projections are not predictions and it is for this reason that more than one projection scenario is developed in any set of projections, in order to provide a range of plausible options for the future aboriginal population. The assumptions related to the components of growth, particularly fertility and mortality, are based on an analysis of past trends.

The census- and APS-based projections presented here are derived from a cohort component approach. That is, the base population for 1991 is projected by age and sex (adjusted for incomplete enumeration and undercoverage) using assumptions of fertility, mortality, migration, and Bill C-31 over a 25-year period from 1991 to 2016. Results from two sets of aboriginal projections prepared by Statistics Canada are discussed: those from projections of the population with aboriginal origins based on the 1991 census prepared for the Employment Equity Data Program (Loh, 1995); and those from projections of the population with aboriginal identity based on the 1991 APS data prepared for the Royal Commission on Aboriginal Peoples (Norris et al., 1995). Assumptions in the identity-based projections about the mortality and fertility components and about Bill C-31 reinstatements are similar to those used in the origin-based projections. In the case of the identity-based projections, two additional components have been incorporated. They include assumptions about the impact of out-marriage of registered Indians on the eligibility of future generations for registration under the Indian Act (Bill C-31), and the projection of migration by both place of residence and regions. The main focus is on the future growth and structure the identity population, along with some highlights from projections of the aboriginal origin population.

As indicated earlier, projections can provide Native leaders, policymakers, and program analysts with crucial information on what the future size and growth of the aboriginal population and groups is likely to be over the next ten or twenty years. Moreover, population projections can also show us: the role the various components are expected to play over the next two decades in determining the size and growth of the different aboriginal groups; the distribution of aboriginal populations by place of residence on- and off-reserve, in rural and urban areas; what the age–sex structure of future aboriginal populations will look like in twenty-five years as the population ages; and the regional distributions of aboriginal populations across Canada and what their share of the overall Canadian population could be by the year 2016.

It should be remembered that the accuracy of these projections depends on the reliability of the base population and the degree to which the underlying assumptions about each component represent the actual trend. Both factors should be considered in assessing future trends. For example, analyses of past census results show how volatile the response to ethnic origin is. Furthermore, the new concept of "self-identity" on which these projections are based is probably also vulnerable to fluctuations in response over time. It is impossible to predict what the response will be in future censuses. It is assumed in these projections that identity is inherited, and can be gained but not lost over the projection period.

Projected Population Size and Growth, 1991–2016[24]

The population with aboriginal ancestry is expected to increase by almost 50 percent from around 1 million in 1991 to about 1.6 million by the year 2016 under a medium-growth scenario. The range in projected population by 2016 is from 1.5 million under a slow-growth scenario to 1.7 million under a rapid-growth scenario (Table 8.13).

Most of the projection results cited for the identity population are based on a medium–low-growth scenario (projection 2, Table 8.14), which reflect a continuation of current trends — that is, a rapid decline in fertility and a decline in mortality, combined with a continuation of current (1986–91) residential and regional migration patterns, along with Bill C-31 birth and reinstatement assumptions.

TABLE 8.13
TOTAL POPULATION WITH ABORIGINAL ANCESTRY, BY SELECTED PROJECTION,
CANADA, 1991, 2001, AND 2016

	Rapid growth	Medium growth	Slow growth
		(*thousands*)	
1991	1084.0	1084.0	1084.0
2001	1208.9	1295.0	1274.6
2016	1681.1	1615.8	1515.3

Source: Loh, 1995. Reproduced by authority of the Minister of Industry, 1995.

The population with aboriginal identity is projected to increase from an estimated 720 600 in 1991 to 890 500 by the turn of the century under the medium–low-growth scenario. Under the continuation of current trends and migration (projection 2, Table 8.14), by 2016 the population will have increased by 52 percent to about 1 093 400.[25] The range in projected population by 2016 is from 1 071 300 under the low-growth scenario (projection 4) to 1 207 100 under the high-growth scenario (projection 3).

Growth rates of the total aboriginal identity population are projected to decline steadily throughout the projection period, as with the aboriginal origin population (Loh, 1995). For example, if current trends continue, the annual growth rate will decline from 2.5 percent between 1991 and 1996 to 1.3 percent between 2011 and 2016.

Projected Impact of Components of Population Growth

At the national level, the components of growth include births, deaths, and, in the case of registered and non-status Indians, Bill C-31 assumptions about births and reinstatements. At the residential level, migration is an additional component of growth.

Natural increase (births minus deaths) is the major component of annual growth in the population with aboriginal identity. The reinstatement of persons to Indian status under Bill C-31 could also affect the growth of the total identity population, because a substantial number of the projected C-31 status Indians (75 percent) are assumed to come from the ancestry-based aboriginal population — that is, outside the aboriginal identity population. Under the continuation of current trends (projection 2), natural increase accounts for about 79 percent of annual growth at the beginning of the projection period (1991–92) and Bill C-31 reinstatements account for the remaining 21 percent. By the end of the projection period (2015–16), natural increase accounts for 95 percent of the annual growth in the total aboriginal population as a result of the projected decline in Bill C-31 reinstatements. Overall, annual growth is projected to

TABLE 8.14
POPULATION[1] WITH ABORIGINAL IDENTITY, BY ABORIGINAL TOTAL AND GROUP,
BY SELECTED PROJECTION, CANADA, 1991, 2001, AND 2016

	Projection 1 (current with zero migration)	Projection 2 (current with migration)	Projection 3 (high)	Projection 4 (low)
	(thousands)			
Total aboriginal[2]				
1991	720.6	720.6	720.6	720.6
2001	890.6	890.5	914.4	887.9
2016	1095.9	1093.4	1207.1	1071.3
North American Indians				
Registered				
1991	438.0	438.0	438.0	438.0
2001	561.5	561.3	575.8	559.5
2016	667.7	665.6	727.0	650.6
Non-status				
1991	112.6	112.6	112.6	112.6
2001	126.0	126.1	130.0	125.8
2016	178.6	178.4	204.1	176.0
Métis				
1991	139.4	139.4	139.4	139.4
2001	165.0	165.0	169.2	164.6
2016	199.5	199.4	219.1	196.2
Inuit				
1991	37.8	37.8	37.8	37.8
2001	46.6	46.6	48.1	46.4
2016	60.3	60.3	68.1	58.6

[1] Base populations of projections have been adjusted for incomplete enumeration and undercoverage.
[2] The total aboriginal population has been adjusted for multiple identities to avoid double-counting. Therefore, the sum for the individual aboriginal groups, which include multiples, is greater than the total aboriginal count.

Source: Norris et al., 1995.

decline over the projection period, owing mainly to the increase in annual deaths as the population ages, and to the decrease in births, thereby reducing the absolute size of natural increase.

For the registered Indian population in particular, Bill C-31 reinstatements represent a major component of projected growth, especially at the beginning of the projection period. In 1991–92, reinstatements represent about 39 percent of total growth, with natural increase accounting for the remaining 61 percent. Given the projected decline in the number of Bill C-31 reinstatements, their contribution to total annual growth would decrease to 16 percent by 2015–16. On the other hand, transfers of births to status Indian women to the non-status Indian classification under Bill C-31 will have a negative impact on the growth of the registered Indian population.

As with the registered Indian population, the projected growth of the non-status population is affected both positively and negatively by Bill C-31, but in opposite directions. Reinstatements from non-status to status Indians will have a negative but declining impact, while births assigned from status to non-status Indians will have a positive and more pronounced impact. Unlike the case with other aboriginal groups, the annual number of births in the non-status population is projected to increase, with 46 percent of non-status Indian births attributable to the inflow of Bill C-31 births over the entire projection period.

Projections by place of residence involve the additional component of migration. For the registered Indian population, about 27 percent of projected annual growth in the number of Indians living on-reserve is attributable to gains due to migration. Losses of population due to migration have a larger and more significant negative impact on rural growth relative to other components but a smaller negative impact on urban growth, not enough to offset the positive growth from natural increase. For non-status Indians, migration tends to be of lesser importance relative to the other components (natural increase and Bill C-31), and more pronounced in urban than in rural areas. For the Métis, migration has a greater impact in rural than in urban areas.

Projected Growth by Aboriginal Group

Aboriginal Identity Group

Significant population increase is projected for every aboriginal identity group. Over the 25-year projection period, the Inuit population is projected to grow the most rapidly, followed closely by the non-status Indian population (each with an increase of about 59 percent). Corresponding growth for the registered Indian group is slightly lower at 52 percent, and projected growth of the Métis is lowest at 43 percent. Under the continuation of current trends, the registered Indian population is projected to grow from an estimated 438 000 in 1991 to 665 600 by 2016; the non-status Indian population from 112 600 to 178 000; Métis from 139 400 to 199 100 and the Inuit from 38 000 to 60 000 (Table 8.14, Figure 8.7). The Inuit have the highest increase because of higher fertility in comparison to other aboriginal groups. Growth of the non-status Indian population is positively influenced by the net effects of the Bill C-31 assumptions — that is, the gain due to births reallocated from registered to non-status Indians outweighs the loss of population resulting from reinstatements of non-status Indians to the registered population.

FIGURE 8.7

POPULATION WITH ABORIGINAL IDENTITY BY ABORIGINAL TOTAL AND GROUP, BY PROJECTION, CANADA, 1991–2016 (IN THOUSANDS)

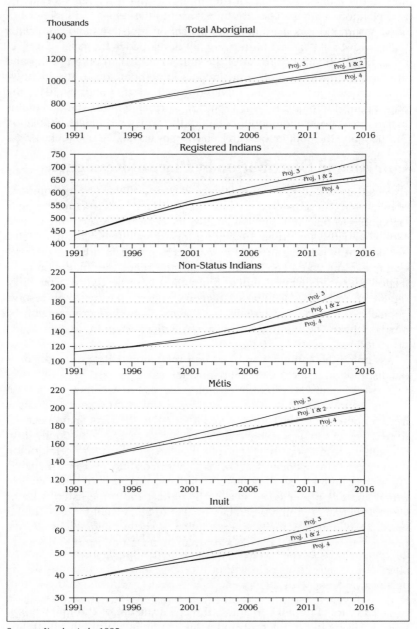

Source: Norris et al., 1995.

Aboriginal Origin Groups

Among the four aboriginal origin groups, highest growth is projected for the Inuit because of their high fertility, and lowest growth is projected for non-status Indians because of the impact of Bill C-31 reinstatements, whereby non-status Indians are transferred to the registered Indian category. Assumptions concerning the impacts on registered and non-status Indian growth of Bill C-31 births were not developed in these set of projections, hence the lower growth of the non-status Indian origin group and the higher growth of registered Indians in comparison to the identity-based projections. Under the medium-growth assumption, by 2016, the population with Inuit origins is projected to reach 84 600, the non-status Indian origin population about 508 000, the registered Indian population 747 000, and the population with Métis origins about 276 000 (Loh, 1995).

Growth and Distribution by Place of Residence

Projected growth by place of residence is clearly affected by assumptions of migration. For registered Indians, the projected pattern of migration is favourable to reserves, highly negative for rural non-reserve areas, and slightly negative for urban areas; and for non-status Indians and Métis, the pattern is positive in rural areas and negative in urban areas. For example, assuming a continuation of current trends with migration (projection 2), the registered Indian population is projected to grow most rapidly on reserves, by some 64 percent, whereas the rural non-reserve population of registered Indians is expected to decline dramatically, by nearly a third. The number of registered Indians living in urban areas is projected to increase by 50 percent.

Assuming the continuation of current migration patterns, the residential distribution of the aboriginal population can be expected to shift over the next 25 years. If current migration patterns are assumed (projection 2), the percentage of registered Indians residing on reserve increases from 58 percent in 1991 to 63 percent by 2016, the rural share declines from 8 percent to 4 percent, and the urban decreases only slightly from 34 percent to 33 percent. If current trends continue with no migration (projection 1), residential distributions shift negligibly by 1 or 2 percentage points. In the case of non-status Indians, the proportion residing in urban areas is projected to decline by almost the same extent with or without migration, from 69 percent in 1991 to 58 percent by 2016, under constant migration. Under the assumption of current migration patterns, the percentage of Métis residing in urban areas is projected to decrease from 65 percent in 1991 to 61 percent by 2016 (Table 8.15).

Age and Sex Structure

After 25 years of population aging, the age structure of aboriginal populations will be quite different under the continuation of current trends (projection 2), shifting to an older population. The proportion of young

TABLE 8.15
RESIDENTIAL DISTRIBUTION OF POPULATION WITH ABORIGINAL IDENTITY BY
ABORIGINAL TOTAL AND GROUP[1] FOR CURRENT TREND PROJECTIONS (WITH AND
WITHOUT MIGRATION), CANADA, 1991, 2001, AND 2016

	1991	Projection 1, 2001 (without migration)	Projection 2, 2001 (with migration)	Projection 1, 2016 (without migration)	Projection 2, 2016 (with migration)
			(percent)		
Total aboriginal					
Reserve	35.3	35.1	37.7	34.3	38.2
Rural	20.3	20.3	18.5	22.3	20.0
Urban	44.4	44.5	43.8	43.5	41.8
Total	100.0	100.0	100.0	100.0	100.0
North American Indians					
Registered					
Reserve	58.1	55.8	59.8	56.3	62.9
Rural	8.0	8.5	4.4	8.4	3.6
Urban	33.9	35.7	35.8	35.2	33.5
Total	100.0	100.0	100.0	100.0	100.0
Non-status					
Rural	31.0	33.0	35.8	40.8	41.8
Urban	69.0	67.0	64.2	59.2	58.2
Total	100.0	100.0	100.0	100.0	100.0
Métis					
Rural	35.4	35.3	37.5	35.9	38.8
Urban	64.6	64.7	62.5	64.1	61.2
Total	100.0	100.0	100.0	100.0	100.0

[1] *The Inuit population was not projected by place of residence.*

Source: Norris et al., 1995.

children (age 0–14) in the identity population is expected to decline from 37 percent in 1991 to 25 percent by 2016, the labour-force age group (15–64) to increase from 60 percent to 69 percent, and seniors (65+) to increase from 3 percent to 7 percent (Norris et al. , 1995). Similar shifts in age structure also occur for the projections of the overall population with aboriginal ancestry (Loh, 1995).

The age and sex structures projected for both the aboriginal identity and origin populations are contrasted with their corresponding 1991 structures in Figures 8.8 and 8.9. The 2016 pyramids are generally narrower at the base and wider at the middle and old ages. The evolution of the age structure from a pyramidal to a rectangular shape reflects the aging process.[26]

FIGURE 8.8
AGE AND SEX STRUCTURE OF THE POPULATION WITH ABORIGINAL IDENTITY, CANADA, 1991 AND 2016

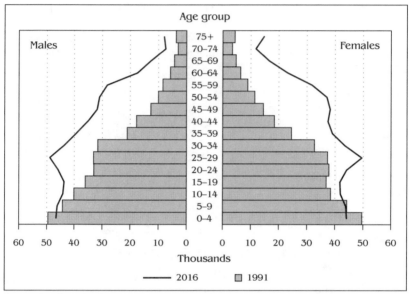

Source: Norris et al., 1995.

Median Age

The median age of the population with aboriginal identity is projected to increase over the projection period, a reflection of the aging trend. In 1991, half of the aboriginal identity population was under the age of 22; if current trends continue, this median age could rise to 30 by 2016. The median age of the population with aboriginal ancestry is also expected to increase over the projection period, from 22.3 in 1991 to 30.0 by 2016 under the medium-growth scenario.

Sex Ratios

Overall the male–female sex ratio for the aboriginal identity population remains constant throughout the projection period, with 96 males per 100 females, but the size and trend of the ratio vary by aboriginal group and place of residence. For example, the Inuit sex ratio, which was the highest among aboriginal groups overall, at 104 males per 100 females, in 1991, is projected to decline to 97 by 2016. Among registered Indians, the sex ratio on-reserve is also projected to decline, from 111 in 1991 to 102 by 2016. The combined effects of aging, excess male mortality in later life, residential migration patterns, and Bill C-31 births and rein-statements can contribute to these variations.

FIGURE 8.9
AGE AND SEX STRUCTURE OF THE POPULATION WITH ABORIGINAL ANCESTRY, CANADA, 1991 AND 2016

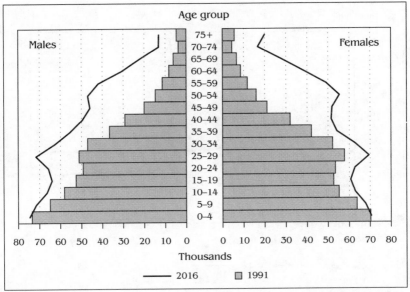

Sources: Loh, 1995; Statistics Canada, report prepared by Demography Division for Employment Equity Data Program. Reproduced by authority of the Minister of Industry, 1995.

Selected Age Groups

If current trends continue, the number of children under the age of 15 with aboriginal identity is likely to increase by only 1.5 percent, from 263 000 in 1991 to 267 000 in 2016. This small increase is a reflection of the rapid decline in fertility and its impact on the size of future childbearing cohorts (Figure 8.10).

The working-age (15–64) population is expected to grow substantially (73 percent), from 434 000 in 1991 to 753 000 by 2016. Among the three subgroups of the labour force — 15–24, 25–34, and 35–64 — the last is projected to increase the most (147 percent) and the first to increase the least (23 percent).

The aboriginal identity population aged 65 and over, numbering some 23 000 in 1991, is expected to more than triple to almost 74 000 by 2016. The projected growth of seniors varies by aboriginal group and place of residence. The increase is projected to be most pronounced among urban populations (Norris et al., 1995).

In the case of the population with aboriginal origins, the number of people in the working-age group, 15–64, is projected to increase substantially (59 percent) to 1.1 million by 2016 (under the medium growth

FIGURE 8.10

TOTAL POPULATION WITH ABORIGINAL IDENTITY BY SELECTED AGE GROUP,
PROJECTION 2, CANADA, 1991 TO 2016 (IN THOUSANDS)

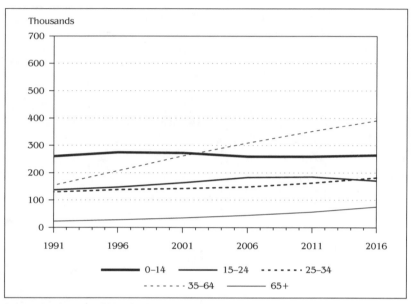

Source: Norris et al., 1995.

projection), while seniors ages 65 and over are expected to more than
triple between 1991 and 2016 to 113 000. Youth are projected to increase
slightly (6 percent) to 413 600 (Loh, 1995).

Share and Regional Distribution

The relative sizes of regional populations are projected to shift over the
projection period. In 1991, Ontario was clearly the province with the
largest aboriginal identity population (about 143 000), followed by British
Columbia (121 000) and Alberta (118 000). By 2016, under the continuation of current trends and migration, the aboriginal populations of both
Ontario and Alberta are projected to surpass 200 000, followed by
187 000 in British Columbia. Ontario's share of aboriginal population is
projected to decrease from 20 percent in 1991 to 18.6 percent by 2016,
while Alberta's share is projected to increase from 16.4 percent to 18.6
percent.

If current trends are retained but no interprovincial migration is
assumed (projection 1), projected regional populations and shares would
differ from those in projection 2 (with migration), most notably for British
Columbia, with a projected share of 15 percent without migration instead

of 17 percent under projection 3, and Saskatchewan with almost 15 percent without migration instead of 13 percent (Norris et al., 1995).

Canada's share of population with aboriginal origins and identities is expected to increase over the next 25 years. Given the continuation of current trends, the proportion of Canada's population with aboriginal identity could increase from 2.6 percent in 1991 to 3 percent by 2016 (under Statistics Canada's medium-growth national projection) (Norris et al., 1995). In comparison, under the medium-growth scenario, the proportion of the Canadian population with aboriginal ancestry could increase from 3.9 percent in 1991 to 4.5 percent by 2016 (Loh, 1995).

In the Atlantic region, Ontario, and Quebec, the population with aboriginal identity made up about 1 percent of the respective regional population in 1991, and is projected either to increase slightly or to remain stable by 2016. If current migration trends continue (projection 2), the aboriginal identity population is projected to increase in Manitoba from 9 percent to 12.5 percent, in Saskatchewan from 9 percent to 14 percent, in Alberta from 4 percent to 6 percent, and remain constant at 3.6 percent in British Columbia. In Yukon, the aboriginal population accounted for

FIGURE 8.11

POPULATION WITH ABORIGINAL IDENTITY AS A PERCENTAGE[1] OF GENERAL CANADIAN POPULATION, PROJECTION 2, CANADA AND REGIONS, 1991 AND 2016

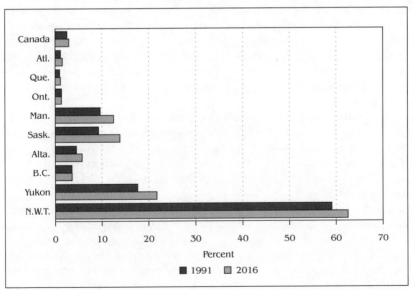

[1] *Proportions for 1991 based on populations adjusted for incomplete enumeration and undercoverage.*

Source: Norris et al., 1995.

almost 18 percent in 1991 and is projected to increase to around 22 percent by 2016. Persons with aboriginal identity represented the majority (59 percent) of the population in the Northwest Territories, with a projected share of 62 percent by 2016 (Figure 8.11).

CONCLUSION

This demographic profile of aboriginal people shows how distinct this population is from the rest of the Canadian population. It is a much younger, faster-growing population, with fertility and mortality levels higher than the overall Canadian levels. Fertility rates of aboriginal people are almost twice those of non-Natives, while Native life expectancies at birth are some 10 years less than those of the average Canadian. Unlike the rest of the Canadian population, the majority of aboriginal people live in rural areas. Aboriginal people who do not reside in their own Native communities or on-reserve tend to change dwellings and cities to a greater extent than Canadians in general, while those living in Native communities move considerably less. As well, women are much more likely than men to move away from reserves and rural communities to cities.

Demographic differences also exist among aboriginal groups themselves. The Inuit are the youngest and fastest growing, most "rural," and least mobile of the aboriginal populations, with fertility and mortality levels higher than those of registered Indians. Non-status Indians and Métis tend to be the closest in their demographic characteristics to the non-Native population. North American Indians, particularly status Indians, are distinct from the other two groups in terms of settlement and migration patterns associated with reserves. However, all these major groups are similar in their rural/urban differentials, such that Native populations in urban areas have higher concentrations of young adults and lower fertility, and are highly transient.

Within the aboriginal population, we see that the extent to which people identify with their aboriginal origins varies across age, sex, region, and residence, as well as by aboriginal group. In comparison to the total population with aboriginal origins, the identity population has higher fertility, is less urbanized, and is less inclined to migrate from one community to another.

As we move to the future, we can see that issues confronting aboriginal people will change over the next 25 years simply by virtue of their changing demographics. Population projections clearly show the impact of declining fertility and mortality levels on the aging of the aboriginal identity population overall. The most significant changes due to aging are the projected increases in the number of working-age aboriginal people expected to reach by 2016 three-quarters of a million among the identity population and 1.1 million among the ancestry population, representing close to 70 percent of their respective populations. At the same time, the identity population aged 65+ is projected to triple in size to some 74 000, representing about 7 percent of the identity population. However, the projected increased share of seniors to 7 percent of the population is still not as high as the current (1993) 12 percent share observed for the Canadian population in general, which is projected to increase to some 16 percent by 2016 (Statistics Canada, 1994a). Although both the aboriginal and Canadian populations are aging, they are experiencing different patterns. As Frideres notes:

> As both the Native and Canadian populations continue to age, the starting points are different: in the case of the general population, they are aging into retirement, while Natives are aging from youth to the working age group. (Frideres, 1993, p. 143)

The implications of aging for the aboriginal population are most pronounced for the growth of the working-age population and what that suggests in terms of the growing importance of education and job training for the future. Unemployment is already high among the aboriginal population, and clearly the projected increase of people with aboriginal identity or ancestry in the labour-force age groups is an issue that must be addressed by Native leaders and policy-makers alike.

There are other implications of an aging aboriginal population. For example, we will probably see a gradual shift in the leading causes of death for the population overall, from injuries and poisoning (associated more with youth and young adults) to diseases of the circulatory system (associated more with the older population). This shift due to aging would also be more affected if accompanied by a continuation of the decline in injury rates among young adults. In addition, given that the propensity to move and migrate is higher among youth and young adults, we may well see a slowdown in the mobility of the aboriginal population overall. Because of aging, the aboriginal population overall may become less transient and less inclined to relocate, even when living in cities and other non-Native communities off-reserve. However, this is difficult to predict, particularly in the movement to and from reserves, which can be associated with entry into and exit from the labour force. Many factors can affect future migration, such as economic and employment opportunities, housing availability on reserves, and educational levels.

In terms of the projected growth of the different aboriginal groups, the two components of fertility and Bill C-31 legislation are significant in accounting for group differentials. The Inuit population is projected to grow the most rapidly over the next 25 years because of its higher fertility in comparison to other groups, followed by non-status Indians, registered Indians, and Métis. With the impacts of Bill C-31, the non-status Indian identity population is projected to grow almost as rapidly as the Inuit. The gain in population for non-status identity Indians due to Bill C-31 births is projected to outweigh the loss from reinstatements to the registered population. Conversely, growth of the registered Indian population is expected to be slightly lower than that of non-status Indians, owing mainly to the assumed impacts of Bill C-31, which are opposite in their effects. If the impact only of Bill C-31 reinstatements is considered, and not the transfer of births between the two populations, the registered Indian population would grow faster than the non-status population, because of its higher fertility and the inflow of population due to reinstatements. Clearly, both demographics and legislation are important considerations in the future size and growth of both the registered and non-status Indian populations.

Obviously, there are many factors and implications associated with the projected growth of each aboriginal group. How current differentials in fertility and mortality, combined with migration and Bill C-31, play out over the next couple of decades will determine the make-up of the aboriginal population with respect to the size, structure, and identity of the different aboriginal groups across Canada, and their share of the Canadian population.

NOTES

1. The views expressed in this chapter are those of the author and do not necessarily represent the views of Statistics Canada. I would like to acknowledge with thanks the technical assistance provided by Hugues Basques, the late Stephanie Coyne, Dawn Warner, Mike Whalen, and the word processing by Danielle St-Germain. I am also grateful to François Nault, Andy Siggner, and Dr. Bali Ram for their comments on this paper.

2. The author gratefully acknowledges Dr. John Flood, director and general editor of Carleton University Press, for permission to use excerpts of this article.

3. In a preliminary analysis of socio-economic characteristics of identity and non-identity aboriginal population, Siggner has noted that the non-identity population is closer in its characteristics to the non-Native population (personal communication, 1995).

4. The exclusion of institutional residents from the census count of registered Indians could be a significant factor in relation to the comparability with the registered count since institutional residents represent a relatively high proportion of the Indian population compared with non-Natives.

5. See Cora Voyageur's discussion of Bill C-31 in Chapter 5 for an elaboration of the relationship between Indian Act legislation and population issues.

6. See Chapter 9 for a discussion of health-related population declines and increases.

7. Natural increase represents growth due to the difference between births and deaths in a population.

8. This figure, as well as those shown in Table 8.3, reflects adjustments for incomplete enumeration of some 20 000 respondents in the APS (for details, see Statistics Canada, 1993c).

9. Detailed cross-classification data were not available at the time of writing.

10. Registered Indians are automatically included in the APS identity population, and some may have aboriginal origins other than North American Indian (for example, Métis and registered), while a small proportion may have reported no aboriginal origins at all.

11. Figures on identity as a percentage of origin incorporate adjustments for incomplete enumeration of reserves and settlements in the APS.

12. In his discussion on "who is a Native," Frideres notes the distinction made between "historical Métis" and the "pan Métis." The historical Métis, who live predominantly in the Prairies, tend to be more established in terms of aboriginal title, whereas the "pan Métis" are dispersed throughout Canada, without aboriginal title (Frideres, 1993, p. 43).

13. See Chapter 11 for an extensive discussion of issues facing Natives in urban contexts.

14. The ratio of males to females varies significantly by aboriginal group and place of residence.

15. Unlike migration within Canada, known as "internal migration," "external migration" (migration to and from Canada) is not considered a significant component of growth for the aboriginal population.

16. Total fertility rate: The sum of single-year age-specific fertility rates during a given year. It indicates the average number of children that a woman would have if the current age-specific fertility rates prevail over her reproductive period.

17. Life expectancy: A statistical measure derived from the life table indicating the average years of life remaining for a person at the specified ages, if current age-specific mortality rate prevail for the remainder of that person's life (e_0 refers to life expectancy at birth).

18. This paragraph is based on Norris (1990).

19. Age–sex standardized to 1981 population of Canada.

20. Estimates of life expectancy for aboriginal groups by place of residence were developed in relation to previously established registered Indian life expectancy, using education — the level of schooling attained — as a proxy (Norris et al., 1995).

21. For comparison purposes, migration rates refer to internal movement only; external migration (to and from Canada) is excluded.

22. Some caution is required in the comparison of these migration data over time, because the population of registered Indians is not directly comparable over census periods in terms of concepts and measurement (see the earlier section on data sources, quality, and comparability).

23. If incompletely enumerated reserves and settlements are included as place of origin five years ago (but not as a destination since they were not enumerated), then the net inflow to reserves drops to +8000 (Norris et al., 1995).

24. Most of the following discussion is derived from the report "Projections of the Population with Aboriginal Identity in Canada, 1991–2016" (Norris, Kerr, and Nault, 1995), prepared by Statistics Canada for the Royal Commission on Aboriginal Peoples. The author is grateful to Andy Siggner, adviser with the Royal Commission, for permission to use the results presented in this report.

25. Although the two sets of aboriginal origin and identity projections are not directly comparable, it is interesting to note that overall, by the year 2016, the projected aboriginal identity population under the assumption of current trends (a medium–low-growth scenario) would represent 68 percent of the aboriginal origin population projected under a medium-growth scenario (based on adjusted-base populations for 1991, the identity population represents about 66 percent of the origin population).

26. The extent of aging is not always the same for all aboriginal/residential groups because of additional effects of migration or Bill C-31 assumptions.

DISCUSSION QUESTIONS

1. What are your ethnic origins or ancestry? To which ethnic or cultural groups do you or your ancestors belong? Do you identify with any or all of your origins? What personal and socio-economic considerations could be involved in reporting origins and whether or not a respondent identifies with his or her ancestry?

Among those persons reporting aboriginal ancestry, which factors — such as awareness of aboriginal origins, place of residence (large cities, aboriginal communities, region), age and gender, history and size of aboriginal original group — do you think play the most significant role in the extent to which people identify with their aboriginal ancestry? Why?

2. How does the age–sex pyramid of the aboriginal population differ from that of the Canadian population in general? How do the shapes of the pyramids differ between the two populations? What are the factors behind these differences? What will the age–sex structure of the aboriginal population look like in 25 years if current demographic trends continue?

3. In 1991, half of the aboriginal population was under the age of 22, while half of the Canadian population in general was under the age of 34. By 2016, it is expected that half of the aboriginal population will be under the age of 30. As the aboriginal population ages from youth into the working-age groups over the next 25 years, what impact do you think this could have on the issues facing aboriginal people? For example, what implications do you see for aboriginal issues as increasing numbers of aboriginal people enter the labour-force age groups?

4. Aboriginal people, especially youth, who live outside reserves, settlements, or other aboriginal communities, tend to move or migrate to a greater extent than the general population, as well as their own counterparts in aboriginal communities. Why do you think this is so? What are some of the push–pull factors facing aboriginal people today in their decision to move or relocate to other communities? What are some of the age- and gender-related considerations affecting mobility?

5. The growth of the registered Indian population is positively affected by the addition of reinstated persons through the Indian Act's Bill C-31 legislation, but negatively affected by the loss of children who are not entitled to Indian registration, because they are offspring of registered (Section 6(2)) and non-registered parents. How could the non-status Indian group, besides the registered Indian population, be affected in terms of population growth by Bill C-31? If the out-marriage rate of registered Indians to persons who are non-registered increases, what impact could this have on the population growth of registered and non-status Indian groups under the current Indian Act?

FURTHER READINGS

Clatworthy, S.J. 1996. "The Migration and Mobility Patterns of Canada's Aboriginal Population." Prepared for the Royal Commission on Aboriginal Peoples. Ottawa: Canada Mortgage and Housing Corporation, and the Royal Commission on Aboriginal Peoples. This report discusses the nature, scale, and implications of recent migration and mobility among Canada's aboriginal population. It identifies the geographic patterns of migration and describes the locational patterns of the aboriginal population residing in specific urban areas. It documents the characteristics of migrants and non-migrants, exploring the factors that contribute to or influence migration, and also explores the housing characteristics of aboriginal movers and those factors that contribute to or influence mobility. Data reported in this study are derived from both the Aboriginal Peoples Survey and the 1991 Census of Canada.

Frideres, James S. 1993. *Native Peoples in Canada: Contemporary Conflicts*. Scarborough, Ont.: Prentice-Hall. This book provides discussion of various recent events such as the constitutional negotiations and the Oka conflict, as well as a historical and statistical review. In particular, the chapters on "Who Is a Native," concerning Native groups and identity, and "Demographic and Social Characteristics" of aboriginal people are suggested for further reading.

Halli, Shiva S., Frank Trovato, and Leo Driedger, eds. 1990. *Ethnic Demography: Canadian Immigrant, Racial and Cultural Variations*. Ottawa: Carleton University Press. This volume on ethnic demography includes three relevant contributions: "Ethnic Origins in the Canadian Census, 1871–1986" (J. Kralt), which discusses the relation between census data on ethnic origins and the perception of Canadian society; "The Demography of Aboriginal People in Canada" (M.J. Norris), a synthesis of major works in aboriginal demography; and "The Emergence of Multiethnicities in the Eighties" (K.J. Krotki and D. Odynak), which considers the processes of assimilation and intermarriage in relation to multi-ethnicity and the relative importance of each ethnicity.

Loh, S. 1995. "Projections of Canada's Population with Aboriginal Ancestry, 1991–2016." Report prepared by Population Projections Section, Demography Division for Employment Equity Data Program, Housing, Family and Social Statistics Division, Statistics Canada. This report provides discussion on the projection methodology, base populations, assumptions, and results for each of the four aboriginal ancestry groups: registered Indians, non-status Indians, Métis, and Inuit. Projections are based on population data from the 1991 census data on aboriginal origins.

Norris, M.J., D. Kerr, and F. Nault. 1995. "Projections of the Population with Aboriginal Identity in Canada, 1991–2016." Report prepared by the Population Projections Section, Demography Division, Statistics Canada, for the Royal Commission on Aboriginal Peoples. This report provides discussion on projection methodology, base populations, assumptions, and results for each of the four aboriginal identity groups. Projections are based on population data from Statistics Canada's 1991 Aboriginal Post-Consal Survey. Ottawa: Canada Mortgage and Housing Corporation, and the Royal Commission on Aboriginal Peoples (Summary report publication also available).

Ponting, J. Rick, ed. 1986. *Arduous Journey: Canadian Indians and Decolonization*. Toronto: McClelland & Stewart. This book presents a comprehensive description and critical analysis of the situation faced by Canadian Indians in their journey toward self-determination. Its contributions provide historical, demographic, and public opinion data and discussion of pivotal events such as the James Bay agreement and Bill C-31 legislation. A.J. Siggner's "The Socio-Demographic Conditions of Registered Indians" provides an overview of social, demographic, and economic changes since the mid-1970s.

Robitaille, N. and R. Choinière. 1985. *An Overview of Demographic and Socio-Economic Conditions of the Inuit in Canada*. Ottawa: Indian and Northern Affairs Canada. This report provides an analysis of various socio-economic and demographic aspects of the Inuit population, based on data from censuses (1931–81), vital statistics, and the Register of the Inuit Population of Northern Quebec, maintained by the University of Montreal.

Romaniuc, A. 1987. "Transition from Traditional High to Modern Low Fertility: Canadian Aboriginals." *Canadian Studies in Population* 14(1): pp. 69–88. This paper documents the sharp decline in fertility among aboriginal people in Canada. A number of factors underlying this fertility transition are analyzed, such as delays in childbearing and greater time between children. The study provides a valuable data source on the fertility behaviour of aboriginal people, although not for each separate aboriginal group.

REFERENCES

Bobet, E. and S. Dardick. 1995. "Overview of 1992 Indian Health Data." Document, Medical Services Branch, Health and Welfare Canada, January.

Boxhill, W. 1984. "Limitations to the Use of Ethnic Origin Data to Quantify Visible Minorities in Canada." Working paper, Housing, Family and Social Statistics Division, Statistics Canada.

Clatworthy, S.J. 1980. "The Demographic Composition and Economic Circumstances of Winnipeg's Native Population." In *Indian Demographic Workshop: Implications for Policy and Planning*. Ottawa: Department of Indian Affairs and Northern Development and Statistics Canada.

————. 1994. "Revised Projection Scenarios Concerning the Population Implications of Section 6 of the Indian Act." Prepared by Four Directions Consulting Group, Winnipeg, for Research and Analysis Directorate, Department of Indian and Northern Affairs, Ottawa.

————. 1996. "The Migration and Mobility Patterns of Canada's Aboriginal Population." Prepared for the Royal Commission on Aboriginal Peoples. Ottawa: Canada Mortgage and Housing Corporation, and the Royal Commission on Aboriginal Peoples.

Frideres, J. S. 1993. *Native Peoples in Canada: Contemporary Conflicts*. Scarborough, Ont.: Prentice-Hall.

Gerber, L.M. 1977. "Community Characteristics and Out-Migration from Indian Communities: Regional Trends." Paper presented at the Department of Indian Affairs and Northern Development.

Graham-Cumming, G. 1967. "Health of the Original Canadians, 1867–1967." *Medical Services Journal Canada* 23(2): pp. 115–166.

Harris, J. and R. McCullough. 1988. "Health Indicators Derived from Vital Statistics for Status Indian and Canadian Population, 1978–1986." National Health and Welfare. (September.)

Jarvis, G.K. and M. Boldt. 1982. "Death Styles Among Canada's Indians." *Social Science and Medicine* 16: 1345–1352.

Kralt, J. 1990. "Ethnic Origins in the Canadian Census, 1871–1986." In *Ethnic Demography: Canadian Immigrant, Racial and Cultural Variations*, ed. Shiva S. Halli, Frank Trovato, and Leo Driedger. Ottawa: Carleton University Press.

Loh, S. 1995. "Projections of Canada's Population with Aboriginal Ancestry, 1991–2016." (Revised version of Nault and Jenkins, 1993.) Report prepared by Population Projections Section, Demography Division for Employment Equity Data Program, Housing, Family and Social Statistics Division, Statistics Canada.

Murdock, A.I. 1983. "Mortality Rates in Indian and Inuit Population: Changes in Trends and Recent Experience." Pp. 22–31 in *Proceedings of a Workshop on Indian Demographic Patterns and Trends and Their Implications for Policy and Planning, 20 June 1980*. Ottawa: Department of Indian Affairs and Northern Development and Statistics Canada.

Nault, F., J. Chen, M.V. George, and M.J. Norris. 1993. "Population Projections of Registered Indians, 1991–2016." Report prepared by the Population Projections Section, Demography Division, Statistics Canada for Indian and Northern Affairs Canada (INAC).

Nault, F. and E. Jenkins. 1993. "Projections of Canada's Population with Aboriginal Ancestry, 1991–2016." Report prepared by the Population Projections Section, Demography Division, Statistics Canada for the Department of the Interdepartmental Working Group on Employment Equity.

Norris, D.A. and E.T. Pryor. 1984. "Demographic Change in Canada's North." Pp. 117–39 in *Proceedings — International Workshop on Population Issues in Arctic Societies*. Co-sponsored by the Greenland Committee on Northern Population Research, Gilbjerghoved, Gilleleje, Denmark, May 2–5, 1984.

Norris, M.J. 1985a. "Migration Patterns of Status Indians in Canada, 1976–1981." Paper prepared for the session, Demography of Northern and Native Peoples in Canada, Statistics Canada. (June).

———. 1985b. "Migration Projections of Registered Indians, 1982 to 1996." Research Branch, Indian and Northern Affairs Canada.

———. 1990. "The Demography of Aboriginal People in Canada." In *Ethnic Demography: Canadian Immigrant, Racial and Cultural Variations*, ed. Shiva S. Halli, Frank Trovato, and Leo Driedger. Ottawa: Carleton University Press.

Norris, M.J., D. Kerr, and F. Nault. 1995. "Projections of the Population with Aboriginal Identity in Canada, 1991–2016." Report prepared by the Population Projections Section, Demography Division, Statistics Canada, for the Royal Commission on Aboriginal Peoples. Ottawa: Canada Mortgage and Housing Corporation, and the Royal Commission on Aboriginal Peoples.

Perreault, J., L. Paquette, and M.V. George. 1985. *Population Projections of Registered Indians, 1982–1996*. Ottawa: Indian and Northern Affairs Canada.

Priest, G.E. 1985. "Aboriginal Youth in Canada: A Profile Based upon 1981 Census Data." Statistics Canada.

Pryor, E.T. 1984. *Profile of Native Women: 1981 Census of Canada*. Ottawa: Supply and Services.

Ram, B. and A. Romaniuc. 1985. *Fertility Projections of Registered Indians, 1982 to 1996*. Ottawa: Indian and Northern Affairs Canada.

Robitaille, N. and R. Choinière. 1985. *An Overview of Demographic and Socio-Economic Conditions of the Inuit in Canada*. Ottawa: Indian and Northern Affairs Canada.

Romaniuc, A. 1981. "Increase in Natural Fertility During the Early Stages of Modernization: Canadian Indians Case Study." *Demography* 18(2): pp. 157–72.

———. 1987. "Transition from Traditional High to Modern Low Fertility: Canadian Aboriginals." *Canadian Studies in Population* 14(1): pp. 69–88.

Rowe, G. and M.J. Norris. 1985. *Mortality Projections of Registered Indians, 1982 to 1996*. Ottawa: Indian and Northern Affairs Canada.

Shryock, H.S., J.S. Siegel, and Associates. 1975. *The Methods and Materials of Demography*. Vol. 1. Washington, D.C.: U.S. Department of Commerce, Bureau of the Census.

Siggner, A.J. 1977. "Preliminary Results from a Study of 1966–71 Migration Patterns among Status Indians in Canada." Ottawa: Department of Indian Affairs and Northern Development.

———. 1980. "A Socio-Demographic Profile of Indians in Canada." Pp. 31–65 in *Out of Irrelevance: A Socio-political Introduction to Indian Affairs in Canada*, ed. J.R. Ponting and R. Gibbins. Toronto: Butterworths.

———. 1986a. "The Socio-Demographic Conditions of Registered Indians." *Canadian Social Trends* (Winter), Statistics Canada, Cat. no. 11-008.

———. 1986b. "The Socio-Demographic Conditions of Registered Indians." In *Arduous Journey: Canadian Indians and Decolonization*, ed. J.R. Ponting. Toronto: McClelland and Stewart.

Statistics Canada. 1983. *The Daily* (February 1).

———. 1987. *1986 Census of Canada — Summary Tabulations of Ethnic and Aboriginal Origins*. Ottawa: Supply and Services.

———. 1993a. *Aboriginal Data: Age and Sex*. Cat. no. 94-327.

———. 1993b. *Mobility and Migration: 1991 Census*. Cat. no. 93-322.

———. 1993c. *Users Guide — 1991 Aboriginal Data*. Ottawa: Supply and Services.

———. 1994a. *Population Projections for Canada, Provinces and Territories, 1993–2016*. Cat. no. 91-520, occasional.

———. 1994b. *Revised Intercensal Population and Family Estimates, July 1, 1971–1991*. Cat. no. 91-537.

Webb, M.L. 1973. "Maternal and Child Health, Indian and Eskimo." Parliamentary Enquiry 724 Ottawa.

CHAPTER 9

Circles of Healing: Illness, Healing, and Health among Aboriginal People in Canada

David Alan Long and Terry Fox

INTRODUCTION

> Health is the core of the well-being that must lie at the centre of each healthy person and the vitality that must animate healthy communities and cultures. Where there is good health in this sense, it reverberates through every strand of life. (RCAP, 1993a, p. 51)

In this chapter we explore the relationship between healing and health in the lives of aboriginal people in Canada. We do so by examining past and present ways in which Native and non-Native people have contributed to the health status of aboriginal individuals, families, and communities in this country. We note that many Native people who have walked a path of healing have until quite recently felt fear, anger, frustration, and even despair in relation to the physical, social, and spiritual ills that have afflicted them and their people. The picture we will paint, however, is not merely one of despairing people living in unhealthy and physically and socially destructive environments. Despite the ways in which colonization has ravaged much of their life, Native people in Canada have survived. We suggest that this is due in no small part to a spiritual, holistic approach to healing and health in Native life. Along with our description of various health-related issues and problems, we therefore also examine ways in which spiritual/cultural renewal continues to bring healing and hope to many Natives in Canada.

We address one of the central themes of this book by examining the ways in which past and many current Native health-care policies and services bear the imprint of colonialism. We begin our study by noting the differences between allopathic and holistic approaches to health and healing. We suggest that along with the allopathic perspective being imported, a deeper problem has been the tendency of western practitioners and policy-makers to fragment and dehumanize the healing process. They do so by viewing health as the absence of physical disease, by awarding the status of expert to westernized health-care practitioners, and by focussing most policies and programs on alleviating the symptoms of health problems rather than their underlying causes. Our analysis begins with a brief socio-historical examination of state-supported, health-related policies and practices. Included in this section is a description of the ways in which current socio-economic conditions contribute to typical physical and social health problems experienced by Native people in this country. We then provide a general picture of Native family violence. Following this is our case study of health in Stoney country, in which Terry Fox tells the story of how members of the Stoney First Nation in Morley, Alberta understand the health of their people. The case study also highlights recent efforts by many members of this community to focus on the medicine wheel and embark on a path of healing. We include these accounts to illustrate that addressing health-related problems means understanding complex connections between mental, emotional, physical, and spiritual dimensions of life. In holistic terms, we refer to the whole picture as the circle of healing. The two concluding sections of this chapter outline healing efforts from grass-roots to national levels, and point to some of the major obstacles that hinder the healing process.

The perspective underlying the following chapter assumes that awareness and understanding of the circle of healing involving Native people in Canada will grow to the extent that Native and non-Native people are able to:

1. appreciate the difference between western and aboriginal conceptions of illness, healing, and health;

2. identify the physiological as well as socio-cultural causes and consequences of ill-health that have long plagued Native people in Canada;

3. recognize that there are many points of contact between healing defined in terms of physiological outcomes and healing imagined as cultural rebirth;

4. become aware of efforts by those concerned to bring about healing, whether such efforts be those of individuals at the grass-roots level or those of multi-organizational coalitions working toward national or global change; and

5. name the many obstacles to healing faced by Natives and their supporters.

Fundamentally, understanding the circle of healing will be possible to the extent that we openly reflect on the thoughts, perspectives, and actions of those who have experienced or contributed to the physical, social, and spiritual ill-health of Native people in Canada. With this in mind, we turn to a brief comparison of western and aboriginal conceptions of illness, healing, and health.

PERSPECTIVES ON ILLNESS, HEALTH, AND HEALING

Aboriginal and Western Allopathic Medicine

One of the major difficulties in addressing problems of healing and health in aboriginal lives and communities is the different meanings these concepts hold for different people. As we note below, part of the difficulty in bringing about healing is that Native people experience and understand colonization in a multitude of ways. While many have adopted non-Native ways and values, others have not. Indeed, a growing point of tension both within and outside aboriginal communities in Canada has involved the rekindling of traditional, aboriginal ways of thinking and doing. Regardless of the perspective one has, Native people in Canada are faced with the fact that colonialism has profoundly affected how they think, act, and are able to live. As Long notes in Chapter 14, many Native people across Canada have responded to the problems of colonization over the past 30 years by seeking to revitalize the spiritual and cultural sources of their identities. Our case study of the Stoney people illustrates that, for Native people, health implies being in harmony with all of creation. Understanding and addressing the effects of colonization are therefore important steps in the healing process.

In contrast, western Europeans have long understood health in allopathic, interventionist terms. As Alice Hanson (1986, pp. 2–3) notes, "modern physicians in North America are trained to observe, assess and act. . . . Modern medical training in the Western world leaves little scope for the physician who is aware that physical symptoms often spring from an emotional or spiritual base. Time is money for today's practitioner, and the whole atmosphere of a crowded waiting room, the physician rushing into the sterile examination cubicle, and the speed with which the person is asked to state his problem reinforce those feelings of pressure." Research into Native health problems and health care has also had a notably interventionist focus. For example, researchers have examined the health problems of Native people in association with the relatively low birth weights of Indian children (Morrison et al., 1986), their higher rates of vitamin deficiency (Valberg et al., 1979), neonatal mortality (Evers and Rand, 1982), infectious diseases (Morrison et al., 1986, p. 272), non-infectious diseases (Shah and Farkus, 1985), respiratory diseases (Houston et al., 1979), digestive diseases (Ellestad-Sayed et al., 1979) and disability rates (Tervo, 1983). These and other similar studies suggest that biological, social, and environmental factors contribute to a number of physical health problems of aboriginal people in Canada. Nonetheless, they implicitly and often explicitly continue to support an allopathic agenda by focussing on the need for improvements in basic programming and services that address physical health problems and needs.

Illness in Relation to Physical, Health, and Lifestyle Factors

Researchers now agree that many factors contribute to the apparently low physical health status of Native people in Canada. Consequently, they alert us to the need to use caution in translating certain data. For example, Evers and Rand (1982, p. 252) found that the Indian patients in their study were twice as likely to be admitted to hospital as their non-Native counterparts. They note that "this difference was not necessarily related to the fact that Indian infants had more serious problems. Geographic and economic factors may have influenced the decision to admit an infant to hospital. . . . [Thus], environmental influences, health-care behaviour, and geographic constraints to seeking medical intervention, rather than ethnic differences, were probably the main factors influencing the higher incidence of health problems in the Indian infants." With such cautionary notes in mind, researchers have also examined the relationship between health status and lifestyles. These researchers did find a relationship between a number of gastrointestinal illnesses affecting newborn children, poor infant-feeding patterns, and children being fed non-nutritious food. Links have also been found between pre- and postnatal health problems for mothers and their children and lower maternal ages (Evers and Rand, 1982, p. 251), lower birthweight babies (Morrison et al., 1986, p. 272; McBride and Bobet, 1990, p. 7) and parental attitudes toward western medical care (Evers and Rand, 1982, p. 282). Communicable diseases, recurring infection, injuries, and chronic lifestyle diseases such as diabetes, sexually transmitted diseases, tuberculosis, and cancer are all regarded as principle causes of ill health. The most common communicable diseases such as hepatitis, shigella, and amoebiasis are all associated with environmental conditions (Kramer, 1990, pp. 14–15). Moreover, gastrointestinal and respiratory infections, which are endemic on most reserves, are directly related to poor housing, sanitation, and environmental conditions (McBride and Bobet, 1990, p. 14). Alcohol abuse has long been known to be a primary contributing factor to many problems in the lives of Native people and their communities, including incidents leading to injuries to oneself or others that demand medical attention. According to Callegari et al. (1989, p. 16) alcohol abuse and addiction, coupled with low employment rates and high rates of violence turned both inward and outward, are indicative of the hazardous lifestyle of many Native people, especially young Indian males living on reserve (Mao et al., 1986, pp. 266–67). The relatively high accidental death rate among young Native people similarly suggests more hazardous lifestyles than most of their non-Native counterparts (Connop, 1983, p. 78). Moreover, respiratory problems and accidental deaths among Native youth have been linked to fires, while high mortality rates among Native adults with respiratory complications have been connected to high rates of smoking (Morrison et al., 1986, p. 272).

There is now widespread agreement that social, economic, and political factors have profound effects on the relationship between lifestyles and health of Native peoples in Canada (HWC, 1992, p. 21). Although there have increasingly been calls for change over roughly the past fifteen years, government policies and practices have for the most part continued to support an allopathic approach to health care. Most of those directly or indirectly involved in Native health care recognize the need to do much more than simply expand health-care budgets or widen the delivery of services. McBride and Bobet (1990, p. 19) note that due to demographic, cultural, and socio-economic conditions, the health needs of Indian women have to be considered separately from Indian males. In their reports to the Royal Commission on Aboriginal Peoples (RCAP), spokespersons for the Métis National Council, the National Aboriginal Network on Disability, and the Canadian Association of Gerontology underlined the low priority being given to the people they represent by federal and provincial governments, as well as by aboriginal bands, organizations, and tribal governments (RCAP, 1994, pp. 43–44). Unfortunately, health needs are diverse and complex, and the wheels of bureaucratic change turn slowly.

Indeed, Health and Welfare Canada's own definition of health suggests that healing and health are complex phenomena:

> A state of feeling well in body, mind and spirit, together with a sense of extra strength; based upon normal functioning of the tissues, a practical understanding of the principles of healthy living and a harmonious adjustment to the environment (physical and psychological). (HWC, 1992, p. 2)

Nonetheless, government health policies and program initiatives indicate that, practically speaking, health continues to be primarily viewed in medical-physical terms. According to the Medical Services Branch (MSB) of Health and Welfare Canada, preventive health care for First Nations people means ensuring that registered Indians have the best possible access to health services. MSB representatives thus see it as their primary responsibility to coordinate: (1) community health (public health) services administered by nurses, dental therapists, and environmental health officers; (2) treatment services offered by physicians, nurses, and dental therapists; and (3) other services such as the provision of eyeglasses and prescription drugs, dental services, transportation to health services not available in the community, aids to daily living such as crutches, wheelchairs, etc., and other allied health services (HWC, 1992, p. 9). Although the MSB defines health in broad terms, its health-care policies and initiatives continue to display the overly medicalized, bureaucratic approach to healing and health that has informed much of the history of

Indian health services in Canada. Unfortunately, problems with the medicalization and bureaucratization of Native health care go beyond questions of perspective and means of treatment.

A BRIEF HISTORY OF NATIVE HEALTH-CARE DEBATES IN CANADA

Questions of Federal and Provincial Responsibility

Disputes over who is responsible for providing health care to aboriginal people in Canada pre-date Confederation. After Confederation, disputes emerged over whether responsibility for services should rest primarily on the shoulders of the federal or provincial governments. Legislation served to cloud the issue; the British North America Act of 1867 placed "Indians and lands reserved for Indians" under full legislative authority of the federal government, while at the same time placing health and social services under provincial jurisdiction. Although the provinces have been responsible for providing health care to the vast majority of Canadians, the federal government has for the most part overseen the delivery of health care to the country's status Indians and Inuit.

Dispute over who is responsible for providing health care to Native people in Canada is only one aspect of the problem. Equally vague and under dispute has been the extent to which the federal government should provide health care to First Nations people. Only Treaty Number 6, signed in 1876 by the government of Canada and the Cree of central Alberta and Saskatchewan, mentions government provision of health care:

> In the event hereafter of the Indians . . . being overtaken by any pestilence, or by general famine, the Queen . . . will grant to the Indians assistance . . . sufficient to relieve them from the calamity that shall have befallen them. . . . A medicine chest shall be kept at the house of each Indian Agent for the use and benefit of the Indians at the discretion of such Agent.

According to T. Kue Young[1] (1984, p. 258), Indian negotiators did request that their health care be provided for their people before signing Treaty Number 8, and possibly treaty numbers 10 and 11.[2] However, there has been much dispute over the meaning and limitations of the government's responsibility to provide a "medicine chest," in spite of the fact that the Indian Act of 1876 clearly acknowledges the government's responsibility to "prevent, mitigate, and control the spread of diseases on reserves . . . , to provide medical treatment and health service for Indians, to provide compulsory hospitalization and treatment for infectious diseases . . . , and to provide for sanitary conditions . . . on reserves."

Many status Indian, Inuit, and some non-status and Métis communities have asserted that their inherent right to self-government includes responsibility over all aspects of health. First Nations peoples who signed treaties also maintain that they have treaty rights to comprehensive health care (RCAP, 1994, p. 42). Furthermore, many Native people argue that they are "citizens plus," meaning that they are entitled to the full range of health services available to non-Native Canadians.

The federal government has assumed a very different view of the matter. It has maintained that under section 92(7) of the Constitution Act, health, including Native health, is a provincial responsibility. It has further contended that because all Native people are included in the calculation of transfer payments to the provinces, Natives should be afforded the same health services available to other provincial residents. The federal government has also claimed that federal programs and services have been provided to Indian and Inuit people as a matter of policy and custom rather than out of any statutory or treaty requirement (Kramer, 1990, p. 4). The government complicated the matter by passing authority for Indian health care from the Department of Indian Affairs (DIA) to the federal Department of Health in 1945. This not only made it difficult for status Indians to know who exactly had authority over their health care, it more fundamentally contributed to the fragmentation of Indian health services. All other responsibilities, including land, housing, education, and welfare, and even what is referred to as sanitation and hygiene, remained with the DIA. Consequently, responsibility for the provision of services that govern health, such as adequate housing, sewage disposal, and safe drinking water, rests with a branch of the government that is not directly responsible for the health of Canada's largest group of Native people — status Indians. Government representatives have further argued that since section 91(24) of the Constitution does not apply to Métis or non-status Indians, the government is not responsible for providing specific funding for their health care. Such legislative and bureaucratic confusion has only served to exacerbate the problems in Native health care.

Administration of Native Health Care

Before 1945, the Department of Indian Affairs controlled Indian health services. Although Dr. Peter Bryce lobbied and worked for over twenty years for more effective government control of Indian medical services, the DIA did not appoint a medical superintendent until 1927. The department's first superintendent, Colonel E.L. Stone, described the department's bureaucratized approach to Indian medical care in a 1935 medical journal article. Notably, all medical officers were under the supervision of Indian agents, who were directly accountable to their Ottawa head office. Specifically, Indian agents were to be consulted before patients were admitted to hospital. Furthermore, approval had to be received from the departmental office in Ottawa if a medical officer recommended that a patient needed to be sent to a sanatorium, deemed it necessary to evacuate someone by airplane, or thought it was warranted to quarantine people in order to prevent the spread of communicable diseases. It was not until 1945, the year after Parliament passed the Department of National Health and Welfare Act, that Indian health services were transferred from the DIA to the federal Department of Health. The postwar period was a time of change for the Inuit as well. It was during this time that the government of Canada recognized Inuit people as full citizens and began providing them with a complete range of social services (HWC, 1992, p. 16).

By 1960, about 10 percent of the total federal health budget was spent on Indian health services. Relatively minor administrative changes have occurred since the department was reorganized in 1962, when seven independent service areas were amalgamated under the Medical Services Branch directorate. However, service delivery has changed dramatically over the past 30 years. During this time, the MSB closed down most of the active treatment hospitals it operated, opting instead to increase support for nursing stations and health centres. Increasingly over the past twenty years, nursing stations have been supplemented by a network of modern health-care facilities. As we note in our section on healing programs and initiatives, the 1979 Indian Health Policy was the beginning of the end of full federal government support for Indian health care. Much like the way in which the 1969 government white paper provided an issue basis for large-scale resistance by Native people and their supporters, the government's 1979 health policy spurred new debate over Native health care in Canada.

OVERVIEW OF DEMOGRAPHICS AND LIVING CONDITIONS

Demographic Characteristics

Most commentators agree with Morrison et al. (1986, p. 272) that the most serious factors that contribute to the physical health problems of Native people from infancy to adulthood are social in origin. They also note that social factors which contribute to problems of physical health are not merely a matter of freely chosen lifestyles. As we note below, living conditions on many reserves and urban dwellings have long included overcrowded and low-quality housing, as well as poor sewage disposal and lack of proper heating. Similarly, low employment and a high incidence of alcohol abuse reflect as well as contribute to unhealthy social and physical conditions. As Long notes in Chapter 14, it has taken over 30 years of non-violent and violent political activity for non-Native Canadians to begin to ask why the living conditions of many Native people in this country continue to be so different from those in which other Canadians live. Faced with such inequality of condition, many non-Native Canadians have also begun to question the ways in which the governments of Canada continue to respond to such conditions. Given the size and growth of the aboriginal population of Canada, these questions are becoming ever more pressing.

A recent report by the Department of Indian Affairs and Northern Development (DIAND) (1993, p. 29) estimates that the aboriginal population in Canada of about 958 000 in 1991 represented 3.5 percent of the total Canadian population. Between 1961 and 1991, the annual population growth for the aboriginal population averaged roughly 3 percent (Frideres, 1993, pp. 129–30). DIAND also estimates that most aboriginal groups will increase their proportion of the total population into the year 2001, growing to roughly 1 145 000 at an annual rate of 1.8 percent and with a mean age ten years younger than that of the rest of the Canadian population (DIAND, 1993, p. 30). These slow but steady increases in Native population growth, due in part to the lowering of their infant mortality rates and an increase in their life expectancy, is also decreasing demographic gaps between Native and non-Native people in this country. From 1960 to 1991, the infant mortality rate among registered Indians in Canada decreased from 79 deaths per 1000 population to 13 per 1000, while for the same period the overall Canadian population decreased from 27.3 to 8. Moreover, the same period saw an increase in average life expectancy for registered Indian females and males from 63.5 and 59.7 respectively to 73.1 and 68, compared with an increase from 74.3 and 68.5 to 80 and 74 for non-Native Canadian females and males (Frideres, 1993, p. 136). Although the gaps between Native and non-Native infant mortality rates and life expectancy have lessened over the past three decades, the rates continue to differ significantly. The same is true of causes of death: unlike the rest of the Canadian population, the majority of Native people in Canada continue to die as a result of violence or accidents (HWC, 1992, p. 33).

Socio-Economic and Living Conditions

Along with problems linked to increases in population, aboriginal people have long experienced the worst socio-economic and living conditions of any group in the country. Hawthorn (1966) reported that the average yearly income of Native Indians in Canada at the time was $1361, compared with $4000 per year for non-Natives. By 1981, the average First Nations income was $8326, compared with $14 044 for others in Canada. Moreover, these differences may mask the real poverty experienced by many Native people, for there is a high degree of socio-economic diversity among Canada's aboriginal people. For example, in 1978, the per capita annual income in various First Nations bands across the country ranged from over $10 000 for those living on oil-rich reserves to as low as $550 (Frideres, 1988, p. 162), a relative distribution that has continued into the 1990s. According to DIAND (1991) data, throughout the 1980s, 40 percent of Native Indians of working age living on-reserve were unemployed; the unemployment rate in the rest of Canada ranged from 7 to 10 percent. Frideres (1993, p. 160, 164), who places the unemployment figures even higher, near 55 percent, argues that even these figures are lower than they should be since underemployed, seasonal, and part-time workers are included in the calculations.

Although comparing living conditions must be done with caution since people have different priorities, about 3 in 10 homes on Native reservations had a furnace by the late 1980s (Comeau and Santin, 1990, pp. 26–27). Nevertheless, certain living conditions have shown substantial improvement: in 1991, 88 percent of homes on reserves had adequate water supplies and 80 percent had adequate sewage disposal; in 1978, these figures were 53 percent and 47 percent. Conditions for Native people living in urban centres are often just as bad as or worse than those on some reserves (Frideres, 1988). Although living standards and experiences vary widely, there is much evidence that many aboriginal people in Canada have long experienced relatively impoverished living conditions. A number of analysts suggest taking such conditions into account as they relate to social and physical health problems. For example, Bachmann (1993, p. 57) asserts that long-term economic deprivation, coupled with hopelessness, frustration, and anger, contributes to the potential for physical and social problems. Perhaps nowhere is this problem of the adverse relationship between social conditions and physical/social/spiritual health of Native people more in need of examination than in relation to Native family violence.

NATIVE FAMILY VIOLENCE: ESTIMATES OF INCIDENCE AND CONTRIBUTING FACTORS

Given that research on family violence among aboriginal people in Canada is relatively recent, it is difficult to know just how recent a phenomenon it is, the extent of violence in "family" situations that occurs, and to what extent the incidence has increased, stayed level, or decreased over the past 30 years. It is for many reasons — changing perceptions of what constitutes assault; the economic, physical, and sometimes emotional dependency of the woman on the man she lives with, and for aboriginal women the cultural expectations of loyalty to one's community; the fear of reprisal by family or community members; the fear of having one's children taken away or one's sole source of support put in jail; lack of awareness of available services; fear of the police, threats, and loss of privacy — that family violence remains hidden from public view and from sources of support for those involved (Frank, 1993, p. 15–18). As a result, it is estimated that for the Canadian population as a whole, police become aware of family violence in only about 50 percent of assaults by a spouse or former spouse (Appleford, 1989, p. 3). A study on family violence in the

Northwest Territories estimated that "only between 10 to 30 percent of assaults ever come to the attention of social services. For the many more who never seek help, violence is simply a part of their everyday experience" (RGNWT, 1986, p. iii). As one woman told the Yukon Task Force on Family Violence (1985, p. 3), she had wished at times that her abusive husband would kill her, since she felt like little more than "a well-programmed robot." It is therefore difficult to estimate, let alone know, the extent of family violence that occurs in the Canadian population as a whole and is experienced by Native people in particular.

MacLeod's (1980) "conservative estimates" of 10 percent were based on her study of the number of women in transition homes, combined with the number of women filing for divorce on the grounds of physical cruelty. In a subsequent study, MacLeod (1987) estimated that almost 1 million women are abused in Canada each year. It was reported by members of a recent inquiry in Manitoba that one in six women in that province have been abused and that the figure for aboriginal women in the province is much higher. Another report to the same inquiry stated that spousal homicides account for 40 percent of all homicides in Canada (MAWS, 1989). For Native women in Canada, the situation is believed to be worse. Not only is the incidence of family violence among these women believed to be much higher, but the pressure to be loyal to one's spouse and community is felt very strongly by those who are in or who are aware of abusive situations (Frank, 1993, p. 16). In a 1989 study on family violence involving Native women in Ontario, 42 percent of the respondents indicated that when family violence occurs in their communities, it is not talked about publicly. In the same study, only 48 percent of respondents stated that family violence is reported when it occurs, 28 percent stated that it is not reported, and 24 percent said they did not know. More than half of questionnaire respondents (54 percent) also indicated that they thought very few aboriginal women who experienced family violence actually sought social, medical, or legal help (ONWA, 1989, p. 21). A representative of the Child Protection Centre of Winnipeg estimated that while only 10 percent of non-aboriginal women testify in court against their abusive partners, even fewer aboriginal women are willing to take their cases to court. Frank (1993, p. 18) reports that 67 percent of respondents to a Helping Spirit Lodge survey stated that many Native people are discouraged from receiving medical treatment because of the fear of reprisal from the abuser or the abuser's family. Moreover, about 65 percent of the aboriginal population in Canada lives in rural and remote parts of the country where information and services are lacking because of inadequate government funding and program development, financial hardship, and language and other cultural differences (NADC, 1988, p. 8). In many respects, the struggle against family violence by aboriginal women and men represents just one more struggle against oppression and toward self-understanding and determination (Frank, 1993, p. 7).

Estimates vary widely as to the extent of victimization among Native women in Canada. A study in British Columbia indicated that 86 percent of Native respondents had experienced family violence. In a study carried out by the Ontario Native Women's Association (1989, pp. 18–20), 84 percent of respondents indicated that family violence occurred in their communities, and a further 80 percent indicated that they had personally experienced family violence. In the same study, 78 percent of respondents indicated that more than one member of the family was a victim of regular abuse. A similar study carried out by the Yukon Task Force on Family Violence estimated that roughly 700 women in the Yukon are assaulted each year (1985, p. 13). In contrast, other research has suggested that, overall, one in three aboriginal women in Canada is abused by her partner (Aboriginal Justice Inquiry of Manitoba, 1990). Statistics Canada's Aboriginal Peoples Survey (1993) reported that 40 percent of respondents said that family violence is a problem in their community. Based on RCMP statistics, the incidence of spousal assaults in the Yukon in 1985 was 526 per 100 000 population, substantially higher than the national average of 130 per 100 000, although substantially lower than the one in three cited in the Manitoba study. In their report to the Yukon Task Force on Family Violence (1985, p. 15), representatives from the Transition Home in Whitehorse reported that their organization provided shelter, on average, to 160 women and 170 children per year. They also noted that 80 percent of their clients had fled a violent home situation. According to one study, these statistics suggest that physical abuse has become an "acceptable way of resolving conflict and of getting one's own way" that is being passed from generation to generation in many Native communities (YTFFV, 1985, p. 4). Given the findings of MacLeod (1987), however, viewing physical abuse as an acceptable means of resolving conflict is not necessarily unique to Native communities.

Family violence, as an intensely isolating experience and a disturbingly social phenomenon, is as difficult to understand as it is to address. Rates of victimization and offence, while important for our understanding of the pervasiveness of family violence involving Native people in Canada, barely scratch the surface of the physical, emotional, psychological, and spiritual pain and suffering that are involved. Moreover, the fact that the available statistics show considerable variance and are at times contradictory points to the need for research that is more collaborative, rigorous, and comprehensive in nature.

As the following discussion of health in Stoney country suggests, Native people in Canada are learning to understand the varied sources of their health problems and are working together to bring about positive change. It also suggests that research, policies, and program initiatives that highlight the need for healing and harmony among the physical, social, and spiritual aspects of Native life are vital if the Stoney and other Native people in Canada are to experience true healing.

ILLNESS, HEALTH, AND HEALING IN STONEY COUNTRY[3]

Stoney Definitions of Health and Healing

When I gaze westward to view the magnificent countryside of rolling hills, wide open grassy fields, and beautiful majestic mountains, I take pride in calling this place home. This exquisite location is the Stoney Reserve in southwestern Alberta, where I grew up. The Stoney Nation is of Sioux-Assiniboine descent. Our dialect and mother tongue is Nakoda. Currently, 3000 members make up the Stoney Nation. The three bands that comprise our nation are the Wesley, Chiniki, and Bearspaw, all of which took part in the signing of Treaty Number 7 in 1877.

Since the signing of the treaty, our people have gone through many changes. Oppressive European forces have contributed to the deterioration of our ways of life and the disintegration of our social structures. Over the past 100 years, a previously independent and healthy people gradually became dependent, depressed, and uncertain of their future as a nation. Signs of desolation have included physical, social, and spiritual pain and illness. Although the effects of colonization can still be seen today, it is also exciting to witness the gradual rebuilding of our nation. The Stoneys have now chosen a path of healing and wellness. In this section I will share my people's definitions of health and healing, as well as our cultural understanding of health. Then I will provide a short description of the history of Stoney health before and immediately following European contact, focussing on how health among my people has related to our social conditions. As we believe that a people cannot remain in oppression forever, I conclude by discussing efforts by the Wesley-Stoney people to restore our nation to wellness and independence.

Interviewees responded in a variety of ways when they were asked to define health. Some saw health as a state of individual well-being, while others defined health from a community perspective. There were those who viewed health from a traditional Native perspective, while others held more contemporary viewpoints. Despite these variations, the common thread in all definitions of health was the importance and meaning of the medicine wheel for our people. Although Native tribes throughout North America differ in their understanding of some aspects of the medicine wheel, we do share a common thread of meaning. In *The Sacred Tree*, it states that "the medicine wheel teaches us that we have four aspects to our nature: the physical, the mental, the emotional, and the spiritual. Each of these aspects must be developed in a healthy, well-balanced individual through the development and use of volition" (Bopp et al., 1984, p. 6). In other words, the medicine wheel represents the self, and all four components of the self must be nurtured and balanced in order for an individual to achieve or maintain health in a holistic sense. Neglecting one area of the wheel creates an imbalance, which results in the unwellness of the individual. All of the Stoney people I spoke to mentioned the medicine wheel, and understood that health meant all four areas needed to be in balance and harmony. Despite the fact that people in my community have different ways of defining and describing health, most of those I spoke with noted how the power of the medicine wheel enables people to have hope amid even the destructiveness of colonization. Indeed, most of the people in my community believe in the ancestral wheel and that balancing the components of the wheel will ensure the overall health of our people.

Along with comments about the medicine wheel, people also viewed health from individual and community perspectives. For some, health meant that individuals experienced the harmony and equilibrium of the medicine wheel. Others saw health as a well-balanced and productive community of physically, socially, and spiritually healthy people. Those with a community focus were undoubtedly speaking in relation to our community's current efforts to work toward overall community wellness. These efforts, which consist of a variety of personal-training workshops, job training, and employment opportunities, have contributed to a growing sense of pride among my people. Finally, people I spoke with associated health with the physical well-being of individuals. Being free of disease, eating well, having a clean and fit body, and having a relaxed attitude toward life were all viewed as important to one's physical health. The emphasis that many members of my community placed on their physical health is no doubt related to the promotion of physical health by members of the Stoney medical professions.

Underlying the different definitions and concerns were connections made by traditional people in my community between health, the environment, and spirituality. They believe that since the earth enables our people to survive, the environment must be respected and maintained. A healthy environment nurtures healthy people and communities. As long as the earth remains healthy, the people remain healthy. Our spirituality goes hand in hand with the respect we have for Mother Earth. Many people I spoke with believe that spiritual strength is related to good fortune and health. As I reflected on this, it occurred to me that our spiritual leaders are in good overall health in spite of their old age.

I also asked people if they thought there was a difference between health and healing. Most of them responded by saying that health is a state of being, while healing is the process we go through to achieve health. Essentially, health is seen by my people as the end product of physical, emotional, mental, and spiritual healing. For example, should a person become physically ill, he or she will likely see a doctor for diagnosis and treatment. Others recognize that efforts to bring about inner healing are just as important. Specifically, this means focussing on the emotional and mental aspects of our being by "look[ing] at unresolved issues and ways to resolve those issues."[4] Furthermore, "healing enables individuals to resolve past hurts, address needs, and to break down those barriers that hold us from going beyond where we are. Healing enables people to build on interpersonal strengths such as self-esteem and confidence."[5] Others also stated that a person's mental outlook and negative thinking have the ability to create diseases in the body. They believe, for example, that a person who holds on to their anger over a long period of time can experience serious illnesses such as strokes or heart disease. As Wesley band councillor Tina Fox stated, "healing one's self from childhood hurts, abuse, etc. through inner healing workshops, counselling, psychotherapy, and so on may release the anger and thereby lead to physical healing."[6]

Just as meaningful as physical healing to the Stoneys is the experience of spiritual healing. People indicated having strong spiritual beliefs and practices, and utilizing the services of medicine people was itself viewed as a form of healing. Instead of seeing a physician, many Stoney people see medicine men and women when seeking cures for their illnesses. Medicine people provide remedies in the form of herbal drinks and baths, roots, special smudges, leading sweat lodge ceremonies, and offering different prayers and other rituals. People often bring their offerings to our sacred Sundance ceremonies for the purpose of ensuring renewed or continued good health. There are also instances in which spiritual healing has brought about miraculous physical healing. We also believe that spiritual healing benefits the mental and emotional aspects of our being by clearing the mind and giving a person focus in their life. While we trust and depend on our medicine people for our health and well-being, they often refer their patients to members of the medical profession when they feel ill-equipped to deal with particular illnesses or health problems requiring special skills.

Nonetheless, it is apparent that there is a significant difference between how my people view health and how they view healing. Healing is a lifelong journey that even healthy people must travel in order to maintain their health. Fortunately, the Stoney people have begun the healing journey together, and the positive changes within our community have been remarkable. People are becoming more aware of the effects of colonization, especially the relationship between current health problems and assimilation. Having identified the problems, our people are now actively seeking healing solutions. These healing solutions involve most everyone in our community, though they are as diverse as our people. The most popular means being used to address mental and emotional scars are healing workshops. As Tina Fox noted, the role of such workshops is "to free people from shame and low self-esteem, and to address abuses." We are learning that healing can stop the cycles of abuse that have gone on for generations, and that through these workshops we become able to identify self-defeating behaviours that contribute to poor physical health. We also learn to see how changing our behaviours is an important part of solving our health problems. People are also learning that healing must come from within, which means being less dependent on others for our well-being. We are taught that facilitators cannot heal those who are broken; their role is to provide tools and encouragement by starting others on their own healing path.

As Danny Rabbit put it, healing "provides the community with a means of achieving healthier lifestyles," which is integral to the redevelopment and growth of our nation. In this respect, most of the people I spoke to suggested that there is a direct relationship between health and cultural understanding. However, I believe that actual health problems are not culture-specific. Although the media tend to label certain issues such as alcoholism and suicide as "Native problems," illness is illness. Actual health problems are not related to cultural beliefs and practices since Native people experience all of the same health problems as non-Natives. Moreover, no one I know thinks suicide or alcoholism should be an important part of our culture. They are outward signs of inner sicknesses.

The Stoney People's Understanding of Health and Colonization

Our elders teach us that although our ancestors did not have problem-free lives, our people were in excellent health before European contact. We are told that long ago people died mainly from such things as old age, complications for mothers and infants during and immediately after childbirth, and fatal injuries inflicted in battles with warring tribes. Moreover, our ancestors were very spiritual and ethical in dealing with self and others. This strength of mind and heart contributed to the wellness of our people. So too did their healthy diet. All food was truly natural and pure. There were no such things as iodized salt, refined sugar, and chemically treated food. Babies developed strong bones and immune systems as a result of being breastfed until they were three years of age. There was no trace of contemporary childhood diseases such as measles, mumps, and chicken pox. Being a migrating nation meant that everyone was physically active and generally in good physical condition. People walked for many miles during times of migration, hauling necessities such as water and wood by hand. Together with a strong sense of spiritual purpose, these factors contributed to the excellent physical, intellectual, emotional, and communal health of the Stoney people. Even today, our people experience a deep sense of pride in knowing that our ancestors were healthy and well-organized, and that they had the ability to survive in harsh environmental conditions.

Our elders also tell us that physical illness was rare before European contact, and when necessary there were medicine people to address most health needs. Medicine people still gain their healing powers and cures through visions that enable them to learn which herbs and roots to pick and combine for certain illnesses. Common physical illnesses of the past included infections from cuts and common colds, which could easily be treated by medicine people. Nowadays, our medicine people can treat many physical ailments from skin disorders to heart disease. One could speculate that our ancestors experienced common illnesses such as pneumonia. Whatever the case may be, health problems before European contact were dealt with by our competent medicine people. Support for this is evident in that our medicine exists and is used to this day.

Although our people were generally healthy, our elders also tell of many destructive diseases that followed European contact. There are many vivid, disease-related stories of the past, and the devastation that occurred as a result of these diseases is still clear in our people's minds. We also have heard stories of the hundreds of thousands of Native people who died as a consequence of European settlement in North America. Health-related deaths were the result of deliberate assaults on our physical well-being, as well as the consequence of the loss of our ways of life. Our elders speak of terminally ill and disease-ridden people being brought over from Europe to North America. Stories of explorers and settlers giving our people disease-tainted blankets are also well known. Our ancestors had never been in contact with foreign diseases such as smallpox and diphtheria, which meant their bodies had not developed immunities to them. As a result, families, clans, and even tribes were decimated or totally wiped out after European contact.

Along with the introduction of fatal, foreign diseases, the process of colonization contributed in a major way to health-related problems among our people. As we note elsewhere in this chapter, these problems are still very evident. Fundamentally, colonization resulted in the loss of our ways of life. Colonizers brought with them new foods and eating habits. The buffalo population, which for hundreds of years had sustained our people, was decimated through mass slaughtering. Refined foods like sugar, salt, and flour were added to our diets. Our people suffered from tooth decay and stomach problems in many respects because of these changes to our diets.

Furthermore, colonizers gradually outlawed our traditional, spiritual, and medicinal beliefs and practices. It therefore became next to impossible for our elders to teach our people about the medicine wheel. The loss of spirituality, combined with neglect of the physical, mental, and emotional aspects of our lives, resulted in increased stress, sadness, and overall unwellness. Corralling our people onto small pieces of land called reservations was another means of colonization. We were forced to move out of our teepees and into wooden houses. This put an end to migration and meant that we had to adapt to a more sedentary lifestyle. Our people no longer needed to manufacture hides, as buckskin and fabric shelters were replaced by wooden ones. Although houses eventually became equipped with heat and water, this also meant that people no longer experienced the physical benefits of hauling water and chopping wood. Changes in diet, lack of mobility, and an overall decrease in physical activity contributed to obesity and other physical health problems. Fur traders, explorers, and early settlers attacked our social structures in addition to bringing various physical diseases to our people. Within a relatively short period of time after contact, we were no longer a proud and independent people. We had become a dependent people ravaged with many physical, social, and spiritual problems.

Native people have thus suffered immensely as a result of colonization. Often, recovery has seemed a hopeless dream. However, the recent fulfilling of a Hopi prophecy made in the early 1900s has brought back hope to Native people all across North America. As Maggie Hodgson, director of Poundmaker-Nechi in St. Albert, Alberta, recounted it to me, a Hopi elder had a vision that Native people would rise above the darkness and move toward a path of healing when "the eagle lands on the moon." In 1969, when the American space craft first landed on the moon, the message sent back to earth was "the Eagle had landed." Since the landing of the Eagle, many First Nations in North America have slowly embarked on a path of healing. The Stoney people are no exception, for we too saw the need to address our problems of suffering and pain.

The loss of our way of life, our values, heritage, and pride have contributed to serious health and social problems across all generations. Stoney people have experienced addictions, physical violence, depression, and dependency on government agencies. Abuses continue to occur in the areas of family, children, finances, and politics. All of these have long contributed to a state of unhealthiness and unhappiness in our community. Nonetheless, many of our people have begun to walk a path of healing. Leading us along this path has been our current chief, Ernest Wesley, a wise man whom I've long respected. Mr. Wesley had long recognized that our people had been disempowered and our social systems disintegrated through years of colonization. When Mr. Wesley was first elected chief in 1992, he actively pursued the dream of rebuilding the Wesley-Stoney First Nation. Concretely, his dream was to bring wellness and a sense of independence back into our community.

The S.I.T.E. Program

One means of achieving wellness and independence that Chief Wesley introduced was a plan he called S.I.T.E. (Self-Improvement Through Empowerment). According to Chief Wesley:

> In order for First Nation people to say we are a nation, we must understand the concept of a nation.
>
> People are built around their history, customs, spirituality, language, and traditions. With stories and legends, our history is passed down through our generations through our language. This provides our youth with a solid culture, rather than a fractured culture we now live in.
>
> For us as a First Nation to rebuild, we must develop a framework for a process that would allow us to examine the things I have mentioned.
>
> S.I.T.E. is a process. Self-Improvement Through Empowerment. Word for word, they go hand in hand. It is to develop themselves in the five areas that I have mentioned, to step beyond being reactive, and up into the strength of understanding others, their weaknesses and strengths, and consequently they become proactive.

If you are empowered, the self-improvement comes, then the rest follows in sequence.

I believe that before we can talk about nationhood or rebuilding, we must address individual needs. These needs need to be focussed on our history, tradition, customs, spirituality, and language. In turn, once the individual can grasp this, then it will change the family. Once the family is well, then our community becomes well also. With our community well, the nation becomes one.

Overall, the purpose of S.I.T.E. is "to achieve family well-being and community wellness through the attainment of Self-Improvement Through Empowerment whereby a prosperous, independent, united, and self-reliant future is secured" (Wesley, 1994, p. 11).

Basic to the perspective of S.I.T.E. is a holistic approach to life, healing, and community-building. The process begins with the building up of the individual, then families, and finally the community as whole. The four steps in the S.I.T.E. program are: (1) healing, (2) lifeskills, (3) upgrading, and (4) work placement and employment. Although each step is designed to build upon the previous step, healing is the backbone of the entire process. The healing component of S.I.T.E. is usually addressed through a series of personal-growth workshops whereby participants learn to explore and rebalance their personal medicine wheels. Individuals learn to build strong spiritual relationships, take care of their bodies, think rationally and positively, and, finally, release old pains and express feelings in a healthy manner. Through healing, participants become able to deal with obstacles to their own healing. These include past pains that have in a variety of ways contributed to their mental, emotional, and physical illnesses. Once individuals become involved in healing workshops, they become more open and able to take part in lifeskills, training, and work placements.

Changes in the lives of those who have participated in the S.I.T.E. program have been incredible. Depression, negativity, and dependence have been replaced with certainty and cheerfulness as the people have begun to hope for the future and work eagerly toward it. Through the S.I.T.E. program, the overall health of our people has improved dramatically. Nonetheless, we are also realistic. As Chief Wesley noted, "we may never see 100 percent improvement, but if 50 percent [of our people] can improve, that is a step. That is success in a colonized world."

Although the Stoney people have a long way to go, the important thing is that we have begun the process of bringing wellness and health back to our nation. Despite our losses and the destruction of our ways through colonization, Native people in Stoney country and across North America have managed to survive. We are thankful that our cultures, languages, and spiritual ways have not been totally lost, and that we are now able to use them to regain our health and rebuild our nations. We still face many obstacles in achieving the vision of a healthy and independent nation. Often, these obstacles come from our own people who benefit from the sickness of the past. There are still those among us who do not wish to become well. From my own federal lobbying experiences, it also appears that many government representatives do not want our people to become healthy in a holistic sense. Perhaps it appears to them that it is easier to administer control over unwell, dependent people.

In spite of these and other obstacles, the circle of healing in Stoney country is growing. With guidance from our wise and respected leaders such as Chief Ernest Wesley and Councillor Tina Fox, we are rising above the confusion of the past and are becoming able to understand the many ways in which colonization has affected our community. We are seeing that along with understanding comes solutions. Most important, "we have started down the path to community wellness and community self-reliance, and [we know that] each day will bring new hopes, challenges, and prosperity for our people" (Wesley, 1994, p. 18).

HEALING PERSPECTIVES, POLICIES, AND INITIATIVES

Perspectives on Health and Healing

> [T]he wounds of the past run deep. Although many aboriginal people retain a strong sense of their roots and a positive identity, many others are almost lost to themselves and their people. Perhaps no one is undamaged. (RCAP, 1993a, p. 52)

As is noted in Chapter 14, some of the paths taken by Native people in Canada over the past 30 years have had violent consequences while others have not. Our discussion of health in Stoney country outlined two related dimensions of Native life that have contributed in a fundamental way to the positive directions taken by many Native people since the mid-1960s. These include the revitalization of Native spirituality and the rediscovery of some almost forgotten cultural traditions. Together, these have contributed to the strengthening of Native identities, the integrity of efforts to bring about social and political change, and their belief that change toward healing is possible. These dimensions of renewal are evident at the community level in the increasing call upon Native elders and traditional speakers to conduct sweetgrass ceremonies, speak at conferences, and lead aboriginal and non-aboriginal people in sweat lodge ceremonies and spiritual workshops (Peng, 1989, pp. 1–2). In pursuing their goals of self-determination and self-sufficiency, aboriginal communities have also increasingly taken control of their own schools, child welfare programs and agencies, economic development, crisis intervention programs, and justice systems (RCAP, 1993b). At the organizational level, friendship and healing centres and other aboriginal organizations have incorporated traditional teachings in their programs and decision-making processes (Supernault, 1993, pp. 24–25). Toward more political ends, aboriginal organizations and communities have increasingly conducted their own research and lobbied various levels of government with their findings and policy recommendations, as well as engaged in demonstrations, protest marches, and armed confrontation (Long, 1992, pp. 123–25).

It is evident to many of those living and working in aboriginal communities that no one solution will address the needs of all aboriginal children, women, men, families, and communities (ONWA, 1989, p. 114). Increasingly, the shared sentiment is that "if solutions are going to work, they have to be made by, and within, the community, however that community may be defined" (Frank, 1993, p. 17). The main bureaucratic difficulty with differences between Native communities, however, is that they confound what would otherwise be the uncomplicated application of generic therapies, community-development strategies, and national action plans. Recognizing this, many people working in community and health-related areas have designed programs that are easily adaptable to different needs and circumstances (HWC, 1988, p. 74–79). Such initiatives also often take into account the history of the community and the fact that those most likely to intervene at the community level will be para-professional volunteers, many of whom are Natives who are sensitive to the cultures of the people they are serving (Council for Yukon Indians, 1992, p. 8).

One of the main reasons offered in support of community-based health programs run by and for Native people is that "the system" has historically worked against rather than for Native people. As Dr. Jonathan Sheehan, health practitioner at the Sagkeeng First Nation, told the Royal Commission on Aboriginal Peoples, many potential Native clients fall through the cracks and are denied services to which they are entitled, because the provincial and federal health-care systems share responsibility for aboriginal people and both seem more concerned about saving money than about addressing people's needs. Specific concerns relating to the planned devolution of health and other services for aboriginal peoples have centred around three main questions: who will control the policies, funds, and other resources; what is the underlying agenda of those who control the health, justice, community development, and other budgets for aboriginal peoples in Canada; and, perhaps most important, will those who are most in need have their needs met? The answers that have been given to the first two questions provide a sense of the possible directions that policy and program initiatives, and possibly even legislative developments, could take in the future.

There are those who propose that if the immediate and long-term needs of Native people are to be met, Native people themselves must have absolute control over policy agendas and program implementation. In the words of Dr. Chris Durocher of the Yukon Medical Association, "self-determination for aboriginal peoples is a prerequisite for healing and the development of wellness — wellness meaning of body, mind and spirit. Control of their cultural rights, land resources, education, justice system and health care delivery must come into the hands of aboriginal people first." Central to this self-determination position is the view that the philosophies underlying health, family, justice, social, political, economic, and other agendas need to reflect the traditional worldviews and lived experiences of the aboriginal people involved. Advocates of this view note that unlike most westernized, government-supported approaches to healing, the traditional, holistic aboriginal approach seeks to integrate the physical, spiritual, mental, and emotional aspects of health (RCAP, 1993b, p. 52). Socio-economic problems such as poverty, unemployment, welfare dependence, and poor housing are understood in terms of the direct effects they have on the well-being of individuals, communities, and whole societies (Agenda for First Nation and Inuit Mental Health, 1991). From this perspective, "abuse and other imbalances of life cannot be healed by attempting to heal isolated aboriginal individuals apart from their family and their community. To get to the root cause of abuse and neglect, the entire system that allowed it to occur must be restored to balance. This means that the accumulated hurt of generations, carried to our families and our communities, needs to be released through a healing process" (The Nechi Institute et al., 1988, p. 4).

Cultural Issues

Similar reports and testimonies from those sensitive to the spiritual and cultural dimensions of aboriginal life acknowledge the uniqueness of aboriginal nations and communities and the need to restore communal balance and spiritual harmony (YTFFV, 1985, p. 10). Advocates of the self-determination view also underscore the importance of grass-roots developments in aboriginal communities and focus on the healing that needs to occur within every individual and community. The most strident of these recommend that resources and efforts be directed primarily toward community-based programs and initiatives (RCAP, 1993b, p. 59). They also assert that respect for their traditional ways in all areas where healing is needed is vital, and that tinkering with parts of a fundamentally flawed socio-political system will not alleviate the root causes of violence by and against their people (Nuu-Chah-Nulth Tribal Council, 1989).

Many others who support traditional, Native beliefs and practices also strongly believe that aboriginal individuals and communities can benefit from the knowledge and expertise of non-aboriginal people. Especially in health- and justice-related initiatives, these new traditionalists maintain that aboriginal perspectives and practices need to be combined with non-aboriginal conflict resolution, support-group therapies, and community health and development programs (Frank, 1993, p. 17). They maintain that combining different perspectives, strategies, and techniques will enable aboriginal people to rediscover and strengthen their identities in community while learning to co-exist with others in the modern world (RCAP, 1993b, p. 60). For example, suggested ways of responding to family violence in Native communities include: greater enforcement of wife assault policy and subsequent use of the criminal justice system;

assurances from police that they will in fact respond to their calls and take appropriate action; alternative approaches to the justice system (based on traditional values); more transition houses, second-stage housing, and safe homes as well as easier access for Native women and children to these facilities; greater accessibility to counselling both in aboriginal communities and within mainstream services; enhanced or holistic support services throughout the justice system; increased access to legal aid; cross-cultural training of justice personnel; cultural awareness through public education; the development of wife assault intervention models and men's violence prevention programs; and family counselling and mental health teams that are sensitive to the many different experiences and perspectives of Native people (Frank, 1993, p. 17). Advocates of this perspective accept that aboriginal perspectives and traditions must play a central role in the healing process. However, they also believe that addressing the hydra-headed problems related to physical violence requires the type of specialized knowledge and training that most aboriginal people do not yet have. Accordingly, they call for understanding and patience during this time of transition in which aboriginal people are learning, among other things, to rekindle their traditional awareness and practices, to strengthen relations with their own people, and to build co-operative, healthy relationships with non-aboriginal people (RCAP, 1993b, p. 60).

Central to all discussions regarding policy development and implementation is the issue of program effectiveness, with everyone involved in the "healing debates" maintaining that they have the best interests of Native people in mind. In contrast to those who support the inclusion of Native perspectives and people in the healing process, there are many others who illustrate through their actions that they believe Native people are best left out of the dialogue (Boldt, 1993, pp. 18–21). Advocates of this position may pay lip-service to the idea that aboriginal cultures and traditions are a valid part of the healing process, but their policies and practices suggest that they do not support the fundamental, systemic changes advocated by many Native people and their supporters. Testimonies and reports given over the last 30 years in relation to aboriginal life in Canada suggest that many non-Natives and Natives who benefit from supporting the status quo have been able to maintain their positions of power and influence, thus enabling them to stifle meaningful change in the healing process and to perpetuate the oppressiveness of colonizing structures, policies, and practices.

Structural Issues

Although DIAND and other federal and provincial government departments have often worked with Native people in developing and initiating "healing-related" policies and programs, the majority of these initiatives have been neither preventive in nature nor arrived at through an inclusive, consensual process (Barnaby, 1992, p. 40). The analysis presented above suggests that the problem has not merely been a lack of political will or resources. Rather, there have been and continue to be (at least) two significant factors hindering positive, meaningful changes. First, most dialogue and efforts to implement meaningful structural changes continue to be constricted by an underlying paternalistic, bureaucratized perspective that views aboriginal peoples in Canada as wards of the state who, after well over 200 years of colonial administration, continue to be in need of protection and help (Boldt, 1993, p. 21). As a result, many aboriginal people have taken the stand that nothing short of violent protest will bring awareness to those who continue to view Canada's aboriginal peoples from a colonial perspective (Long, 1992). Compounding the problem of paternalism is the unwillingness or inability of many aboriginal and non-aboriginal people to admit that they do not like the prospect of change, or that they fear reprisal from their colleagues or community members for making honest, dissenting comments (Dyck, 1993, p. 194). Numerous RCAP intervenors echoed the words of the Native women interviewed by Silman (1987), most of whom noted that political interference by the political leadership in Native communities inhibited healing on their reserve since they refused to grant aboriginal women an equal place and voice in their communities. They point out that many aboriginal people, especially women, have often had to be satisfied with programs and services that at best have served to meet only their most basic needs (HWC, 1990, p. 106), and at worst have ignored the needs of some altogether (Silman, 1987, p. 125).

The cultural and organizational changes in Native life mentioned above have therefore also been accompanied by continued demands by aboriginal people and their supporters for structural changes in health care, criminal justice, politics, and economic development policies. For well over 30 years, one of the key assumptions underlying these demands is that aboriginal people are best suited to identify and develop policies and programs that serve their needs. Although many government representatives have deemed that such an arrangement is impossible or at best unlikely to occur in the immediate future, aboriginal people have continued to assert that those who have suffered and those who have perpetuated the violence need to be an integral part of the healing process if violence is to be stopped and healing is to occur. Along with major political and legal changes, Native people and their supporters have therefore also proposed, among other things, that:

1. all aboriginal people should be able to take responsibility for making changes in their own lives;

2. Native peoples in this country should have more control over policy development, funding, and program implementation in all areas of their lives (RCAP, 1993a, p. 35);

3. national forums should be established to address the myriad of issues involved in the areas of physical violence, criminal justice, and community development as they relate to aboriginal people;

4. expert advisory committees should be appointed by the federal government to facilitate discussions, program implementation, and policy changes in all areas where physical violence is a problem;

5. the federal government should enact a child welfare act and establish a child welfare system by the year 2000;

6. the federal government should establish a mental health policy for aboriginal peoples by the year 2000 (HWC, 1990, pp. 108–9);

7. prevention, intervention, and postvention policies and programs should take into account the unique experiences and perspectives of the aboriginal people they are meant to serve (RCAP, 1993a, p. 35);

8. comprehensive education programs in family violence, suicide, and criminal justice should be established for leaders and other members of aboriginal communities, as well as professionals and lay practitioners working with aboriginal people in these areas (HWC, 1990, p. 108);

9. there should be cross-national education for non-Native people in education and work-related areas;

10. there should be support for community-based alternatives to the formalized systems of justice, health care, family and child welfare, and economic development that incorporate customary law and traditional practices and that, where needed, facilitate healing and reconciliation (RCAP, 1993a, pp. 35–63);

11. social, educational, health, and justice-related services should be implemented for aboriginal people living in urban areas (RCAP, 1993a, p. 3);

12. there should be more positions created in formalized settings, such as Native court-workers and prison elders, that provide culturally sensitive assistance and support to aboriginal people in those settings (HWC, 1990, p. 109);

13. the federal and provincial governments should address all outstanding land claims with integrity and as expeditiously as possible; and

14. the governments and courts of Canada should work with aboriginal people in making self-government and self-sufficiency a reality for aboriginal peoples all across Canada (RCAP, 1993a, p. 41).

These examples provide some indication that the ideas and activities of those concerned with health and healing among aboriginal people in Canada are as varied as the people themselves. Whatever the theoretical reasons for personal illness and unhealthy aboriginal communities may be, those who refuse to accept the status quo say that they will continue to fight for change. They assert that positive changes in the conditions of life for aboriginal people will fail to materialize to the degree that Native people lack control over their own lives, families, communities, and nations. Accordingly, they believe that only the implementation of aboriginal self-government and the restoration of Native traditions will stop the cycles of violence and brokenness and allow for meaningful changes and healing to begin. The often painful truth for many, however, is that self-government, community-based control over health and other services, and traditional beliefs and practices do not, in and of themselves, ensure healing and growth (YTFFV, 1985, p. 318). This is not to deny the importance of community-level programs, for many of them have resulted in positive social change (HWC, 1988, p. 74). As community workers and mental health-care practitioners note, however, countless aboriginal individuals and communities continue to experience illness and violence, whether or not programs are implemented and people are educated about the problems. Again, many political activists assert that nothing short of fundamental changes in the cultural and structural relations between Native and non-Native people in Canada will help bring healing. Given that Native people in this country have experienced and responded to health-related problems in a wide variety of ways, the picture of what these and many other healing efforts may bring in the future remains cloudy, though hopeful for many of those involved.

OBSTACLES TO NATIVE HEALTH AND HEALING

Perhaps the most significant obstacle to health and healing among aboriginal people in Canada is the dispute between federal and provincial governments over Native health-care responsibilities. Currently, most Native health programs are initiated and supervised by provincial representatives. This has always been the case for non-status Indians and the Métis under the terms of the Indian Act, but it also appears to be increasingly the case for status Indians because the federal government seems to be offering fewer programs directly to status Indians. Instead, programs and services are offered through provincial bodies with transfer support from federal funding.

A difficulty associated with the transfer of responsibilities from federal to provincial levels is the resulting fragmentation of program planning and delivery. Every level of government has specific departments and offices, each of which organizes a number of service-delivery units designed to address a particular problem. On First Nations reserves, fragmentation is often compounded by jurisdictional divisions between federal and provincial governments. Moreover, many aboriginal people live in small, isolated communities where the differentiation of service delivery creates more problems than it solves. Services in these areas are frequently delivered by one resident staff person or by a shared staff person who may be responsible for service delivery in several locations. These health-service deliverers are for the most part accountable to decision-makers who live a distance from the service-delivery area. Professionals work without collegial support and, frequently, without the authority to adjust services according to the needs of the people they are meant to serve. Members of the communities often find it difficult to make sense of the differentiation of programs and services. When one is thinking of the well-being of 30 battered women in a community, the question of which program best suits each woman easily clouds and even displaces the more important question of how programs might be developed to address both the needs of each woman and their communities.

One solution to the problem of ineffective health-care delivery, which has been proposed recently by the government of Alberta, is to transfer responsibility for service delivery to local authorities. However, even this solution is not without its difficulties and problems. In some provinces, such as Ontario, the existence of a highly formalized policy process prevents easy devolution to more grass-roots programs and solutions. Moreover, the promises of grass-roots programming, while enabling Native people to organize and control services and programming within their own communities, are not without their dangers. By working with provincial or federal government representatives on an individual basis, aboriginal communities may indirectly contribute to the waning of solidarity and lessening of political influence. Possible economic consequences include the reduction in health-care budgets for communities with the greatest need. It is perhaps a case of Native people having to fight many small battles within and outside their communities, knowing as they do that each battle is an important part of a larger war against the many vestiges of colonization. As Halfe (1993, pp. 9–10) describes the healing process, "When the Indigenous people are allowed to dance their journey by reclaiming their visions, their personhood, their families, their societies, and all which they encompass, perhaps then we shall see a decrease in self-destructive behaviour." Their hope, it appears, rests on the continued revitalization of Native spirituality, holistic traditions of healing, cultural rebirth, and reconciliation with non-Natives who share this land. For the circle of healing to become whole, Native and non-Native people in Canada must therefore learn to walk the sometimes painful path of healing together.

NOTES

1. Much of the following discussion is a summary of Young's (1984) detailed socio-historical analysis of Indian health services in Canada.

2. Young's claim is based on references to such discussions made by treaty commissioners in their reports. Although the reports do refer to medicine chest discussions, Young notes that the provision of health services was only mentioned in the written text of Treaty Number 6.

3. By Terry Fox. It is truly gratifying to be given the opportunity to co-author this chapter, because it allows me to share the stories of my people. Since this

chapter is about health in aboriginal communities, my research involved interviewing numerous people in my community. My findings confirmed some of what I knew about health in Stoney country, although the people I spoke with also taught me many things of which I was unaware.

4. Interview with Danny Rabbit, member of the Stoney Nation, August 1994.

5. Interview with Sara Gissing, member of the Stoney Nation, August 1994.

6. Interview with Tina Fox, Wesley Band councillor, August 1994.

DISCUSSION QUESTIONS

1. What are the main differences between the traditional aboriginal and the western European perspectives on health and healing?

2. What do you think were the most important aspects of European colonization that affected the health of aboriginal people in the past? What do you think are the most important health-related issues currently facing aboriginal people in Canada? In what ways might these be similar to and different from the health-related issues facing non-aboriginal people in this country?

3. In what ways do you think the story of the Stoney First Nation is typical of Native experiences? In what ways is it unique?

4. How are the problems associated with Native family violence similar to and different from problems experienced by non-Natives?

5. What do you think are the most significant personal, cultural, and structural obstacles faced by Native and non-Native people who want to work toward health and healing in the lives of Canada's aboriginal peoples?

FURTHER READINGS

Alexei, Sherman. 1994. *The Lone Ranger and Tonto Fistfight in Heaven*. New York: Harper Collins. A collection of humorous, poignant, and disturbingly realistic stories about life and death in Native communities.

Bachmann, Ronet. 1993. *Death and Violence on the Reservation: Homicide, Family Violence, and Suicide in American Indian Populations*. New York: Auburn House. Detailed theoretical and empirical analysis of three extreme forms of criminal violence on American Indian reservations.

Ontario Native Women's Association. 1989. *Breaking Free: A Proposal for Change to Family Violence*. Thunder Bay, Ont.: ONWA. Discussion and analysis of controversial findings from a large-scale study on Native family violence commissioned by the ONWA.

Supernault, Esther. 1993. *A Family Affair*. Edmonton: Native Counselling Services of Alberta. Supernault, a Native counsellor, outlines her perspective on how Native individuals, families, and communities can bring about inner and outer healing.

REFERENCES

Agenda for First Nation and Inuit Mental Health. 1991. Ottawa: Assembly of First Nations.

Appleford, Barbara. 1989. *Family Violence Review: Prevention and Treatment of Abusive Behaviour*. Ottawa: Correctional Service Canada.

Bachmann, Ronet. 1993. *Death and Violence on the Reservation: Homicide, Family Violence, and Suicide in American Indian Populations*. New York: Auburn House.

Barnaby, Joanne. 1992. "Culture and Sovereignty." Pp. 39–44 in *Nation to Nation: Aboriginal Sovereignty and the Future of Canada*, ed. Diane Englestad and John Bird. Toronto: Anansi Press.

Boldt, Menno. 1993. *Surviving as Indians: The Challenge of Self-Government*. Toronto: University of Toronto Press.

Bopp, Judy, Michael Bopp, Lee Brown, and Phil Lane, compilers. 1984. *The Sacred Tree*. Lethbridge, Alta.: Four Worlds Development Project.

Callegari, P.R., J.D.M. Allen, H.A Sankowsky, and M.G.A. Grace. 1989. "Burn Injuries in Native Canadians: A 10 Year Experience." *Burns* 15(1): pp. 15–19.

Comeau, Pauline and Aldo Santin. 1990. *The First Canadians: A Profile of Native People Today*. Toronto: James Lorimer and Company.

Connop, Peter J. 1983. "A Canadian Indian Health Status Index." *Medical Care* 21(1): pp. 67–81.

Council for Yukon Indians. 1992. "Council for Yukon Indians Family Violence Project." *Transition* 4(4): pp. 1–2.

Department of Indian Affairs and Northern Development (DIAND). 1993. *Growth in Expenditures*. Ottawa: Supply and Services.

Dyck, Noel. 1993. "Telling It Like It Is: Some Dilemmas of Fourth World Ethnography and Advocacy." Pp. 192–212 in *Anthropology, Public Policy and Native Peoples in Canada*, ed. Noel Dyck and James B. Waldram. Montreal and Kingston, Ont.: McGill-Queen's University Press.

Ellestad-Sayed, J., F.J. Coodin, L.A. Dilling, and J.C. Haworth. 1979. "Breast-Feeding Protects Against Infection in Indian Infants." *Canadian Medical Association Journal* 120: pp. 295–98.

Evers, Susan E. and Charles G. Rand. 1982. "Morbidity in Canadian Indian and Non-Indian Children in the First Year of Life." *Canadian Medical Association Journal* 126: pp. 249–52.

Frank, Sharlene. 1993. *Family Violence in Aboriginal Communities: A First Nations Report*. Report to the Government of British Columbia. Victoria: Queen's Printer.

Frideres, James. 1988. *Native Peoples in Canada: Contemporary Conflicts*, 3rd ed. Scarborough, Ont.: Prentice-Hall.

———. 1993. *Native Peoples in Canada: Contemporary Conflicts*, 4th ed. Scarborough, Ont.: Prentice-Hall.

Government of Canada. 1969. *Statement on Indian Policy* (the white paper). Ottawa: Supply and Services.

Halfe, Louise. 1993. "Healing from a Native Perspective." *Cognica* 26(1): pp. 7–10.

Hanson, Alice. 1986. "Traditional and Western Medicine in the North." Paper presented at the Aboriginal Health Conference, Edmonton, July. (unpublished.)

Health and Welfare Canada (HWC). 1988. *Suicide in Canada: Report of the National Task Force on Suicide in Canada*. Ottawa: Supply and Services.

———. 1990. *Reaching for Solutions: Report of the Special Advisor to the Minister of National Health and Welfare on Child Sexual Abuse in Canada*. Ottawa: Supply and Services.

———. 1992. *Aboriginal Health in Canada*. Ottawa: Supply and Services.

Houston, C.S., R.L. Weiler, and B.F. Habbick. 1979. "Severity of Lung Disease in Indian Children." *Canadian Medical Association Journal* 120: pp. 1115–21.

Kramer, Joyce. 1990. "Native Health Issues: Proposed Principles and Goals." Report prepared for Federal and Provincial Ministers, Ottawa.

Long, David. 1992. "Culture, Ideology and Militancy: The Movements of Native Indians in Canada 1969–1992." Pp. 18–34 in *Organizing Dissent: Contemporary Social Movements in Theory and Practice*, ed. William B. Carroll. Toronto: Garamond.

Mao, Yang, Howard Morrison, Robert Semenciw and Donald Wigle. 1986. "Mortality on Canadian Indian reserves 1977–1982." *Canadian Journal of Public Health* 77: pp. 263–68.

MacLeod, Linda. 1980. *Wife Battering in Canada: The Vicious Circle*. Ottawa: Canadian Advisory Council for the Status of Women.

———. 1987. *Battered But Not Beaten: Preventing Wife-Battering in Canada*. Ottawa: Canadian Advisory Council on the Status of Women.

Manitoba Association of Women's Shelters (MAWS). 1989. *Report to the Manitoba Royal Commission on Family Violence*. Winnipeg: the commission.

McBride, Catherine and Ellen Bobet. 1990. "Health of Indian Women." Paper presented at the Canadian Public Health Association Conference, Toronto.

Morrison, H.I., R.M. Semenciw, Y. Mao, and D.T. Wigle. 1986. "Infant Mortality on Indian Reserves 1976–1983." *Canadian Journal of Public Health* 77: pp. 269–73.

The Nechi Institute, The Four Worlds Development Project, The Native Training Institute, and New Direction Training. 1988. *Healing Is Possible: A Joint Statement on the Healing of Sexual Abuse in Native Communities*. Alkalai Lake, B.C.: The Nechi Institute.

Northern Alberta Development Council (NADC). 1988. *Family Violence in Northern Alberta*. Edmonton: the council.

Nuu-Chah-Nulth Tribal Council. 1989. *Nuu-Chah-Nulth First Family Proposal.* Vancouver: Nuu-Chah-Nulth Tribal Council.

Ontario Native Women's Association (ONWA). 1989. *Breaking Free: A Proposal for Change to Family Violence.* Thunder Bay, Ont.: ONWA.

Peng, Ito. 1989. "Minobimadiziwin: An Examination of Aboriginal Paradigm and Its Policy Implications." Department of Social Work, McMaster University.

Report to the Government of the Northwest Territories (RGNWT). 1986. *Choices: A Three Year Program to Address Family Violence in the Northwest Territories.* Yellowknife: Queen's Printer.

Royal Commission on Aboriginal Peoples (RCAP). 1993a. *Public Hearings: Overview of the Second Round.* Ottawa: Supply and Services.

———. 1993b. *Public Hearings: Focusing the Dialogue.* Ottawa: Supply and Services.

———. 1994. *Public Hearings: Toward Reconciliation.* Ottawa: Supply and Services.

Shah, C.P. and C.S. Farkas. 1985. "The Health of Indians in Canadian Cities: A Challenge to the Health Care System." *Canadian Medical Association Journal* 133: pp. 845–59.

Silman, Janet. 1987. *Enough Is Enough: Aboriginal Women Speak Out.* Toronto: Women's Press.

Supernault, Esther. 1993. *A Family Affair.* Edmonton: Native Counselling Services of Alberta.

Tervo, R. 1983. "The Native Child with Cerebral Palsy at a Children's Rehabilitation Centre." *Canadian Journal of Public Health* 74: pp. 232–42.

Valberg, L.S., N. Birkett, J. Haist, J. Zamecnik, and O. Pelletier. 1979. "Evaluation of the Body Iron Status of Native Canadians." *Canadian Medical Association Journal* 120: pp. 285–89.

Wesley, Chief Ernest. 1994. *S.I.T.E Proposal.* Morley, Alta.: Wesley-Stoney Band.

Young, T. Kue. 1984. "Indian Health Services in Canada: A Socio-Historical Perspective." *Social Science and Medicine* 18(3): pp. 257–64.

Yukon Task Force on Family Violence (YTFFV). 1985. *Report of the Task Force on Family Violence.* Whitehorse: Queen's Printer.

CHAPTER 10

Aboriginal Education at the Crossroads: The Legacy of Residential Schools and the Way Ahead

Jean Barman[1]

A boriginal education in Canada is at the crossroads. Despite the fact that children are staying in school longer and other measures of improvement, the legacy of residential schools endures. For many families, negative attitudes toward schools today are grounded in their own experience, or that of parents and grandparents, in residential schools that were meant to assimilate aboriginal children into mainstream society but that in reality educated them for inequality. It is not only aboriginal people who must heal themselves; members of the dominant society must also acknowledge this educational misadventure as part of our common history. Four factors ensured that residential schools, and their lesser counterpart of federal day schools, would not educate children to compete with non-aboriginal counterparts but for inequality: the government's assumption of aboriginal peoples' sameness across Canada; pupils' lesser time in the classroom than their non-aboriginal counterparts in public schools; the generally poor quality of teaching; and the lack of federal funding for the operation of schools. Only in the mid-twentieth century did aboriginal families acquire other educational options, and only in the past two decades have bands been taking charge of schooling on reserves. This chapter uses first-person accounts from British Columbia to make its argument, but, given the federal nature of schools for aboriginal children, the findings would likely be the same whatever the accounts' province of origin.

ABORIGINAL EDUCATION AT THE CROSSROADS

Conditions of schooling are improving for aboriginal peoples across Canada. Children are staying in school longer. The proportion of pupils living on-reserve who remained in school to grade 12 has risen from

3 percent in 1960–61 and 15 percent in 1970–71 to 20 percent in 1980–81 and 47 percent in 1990–91 (DIAND, 1995, p. 39). By 1993–94, fully 78 percent of on-reserve aboriginal children were still in school to grade 12. More and more bands are taking charge of their children's schooling. Whereas in 1975–76 there were only 2842 pupils in 53 band-operated schools on reserves across Canada, by 1993–94 there were 53 312 students in 372 band-operated schools (DIAND, 1995, pp. 45, 47). About half of the on-reserve elementary pupils in 1991 reported being taught in part in an aboriginal language, as did a quarter of all secondary pupils (Statistics Canada, 1993, pp. 70, 66). Aboriginal educators are taking the lead in planning curriculum and other aspects of school life as they respond to aboriginal peoples' needs (Battiste and Barman, 1995; as an example, BCME, 1995).

Yet all is not well. Disquiet persists in aboriginal education. Far too many aboriginal pupils lag behind their non-aboriginal counterparts. Stories of families whose lifestyles and other factors interfere with or work against their children's education are all too commonplace. One very significant reason is not difficult to locate. The legacy of residential schools still hangs heavy in the air, tainting the very concept of schooling. School for many aboriginal people is much more an object of fear to be avoided than a place of learning.

The time has come to clear the air. Aboriginal people themselves have begun to do so. Recent initiatives range from individuals having the courage to face up to past abuses inflicted on them to organizations taking the lead in the healing process, as with the Assembly of First Nations' (1994) interpretive study *Breaking the Silence*. It is also essential for the dominant society, those of us untouched by residential schools, to grasp their full meaning. And perhaps most of all, we need to acknowledge that residential schools had no possibility of "success" in terms of their declared mandate of assimilating aboriginal peoples into mainstream society. However much missionaries, federal bureaucrats, and other interested parties might have proclaimed lofty goals, residential schools were doomed to failure. They never functioned as more than a holding operation, an institution ensuring that the dominant society maintained a status quo created by, controlled by, and utterly favourable to themselves. Even if the outcomes of residential schools were not consciously so planned or understood by contemporaries, they were inevitable. To lay the legacy of residential schools finally to rest, not only must aboriginal peoples heal themselves, but members of mainstream society also must come to recognize their complicity in the misadventure. Only then will the way ahead be assured for aboriginal education.

Critics of residential schools have very persuasively drawn attention to a range of unacceptable practices, from prohibitions on speaking aboriginal languages to incidents of physical and sexual abuse, and to their consequences for the quality of aboriginal life in Canada into the late twentieth century (Satzewich and Mahood, 1995; AFN, 1994; Purvis, 1994;

Jaine, 1991, 1993; Harper, 1993; Archibald, 1993; Knockwood, 1992; Millward, 1992; Sterling, 1992; Furniss, 1992; Bull, 1991; Hodgson, 1991; Fiske, 1991; Lascelles, 1990; Johnston, 1988; Haig-Brown, 1988). "Subjugation has taken its toll on our cultures. Indigenous peoples have the highest rates of impoverishment, incarceration, suicide and alcoholism in Canada. Much of this can be traced back to the abuse received at the residential schools" (Jaine, 1993, p. x). In *Breaking the Silence*, the Assembly of First Nations divided aboriginal children's experience at residential schools into the emotional, mental, physical, and spiritual realms, and demonstrated through individual recollections how pupils were wounded by having their feelings ridiculed, creativity and independent thinking stifled, bodily needs ignored or violated, and ways of life denied. Recognition, remembering, resolving, and reconnecting are all essential for "breaking the silence" and enabling the healing process to begin.

The legacy of residential schools takes on an element of tragedy when set in the context of their initial, publicly enunciated goal. The schools' origins in the late nineteenth century lay in a federal policy of assimilating aboriginal peoples into mainstream Canadian society. "The Indian problem exists owing to the fact that the Indian is untrained to take his place in the world. Once teach him to do this, and the solution is had" (DIA, 1895, p. xxi). By taking children away from the old ways and "civilizing" them into European ways, so the argument ran, "the Indian problem" would be solved. The initial goal of residential schools, and of their less favoured counterpart, federal day schools, was the absolute opposite of what occurred. Instead of becoming agents of assimilation, the schools served as vehicles for marginalizing generations of young men and women both from the Canadian mainstream and from home environments.

This chapter does not pretend to assess the rightness or wrongness of the federal goal of assimilation; it rests with aboriginal scholars to tackle this fundamental historical question. Instead, this chapter explores the reasons why the principal means of assimilation, the residential schools, were such a dismal failure with far-reaching consequences for aboriginal education. The reasons had to do less with the actions of individual teachers or administrators than with a federal policy that legitimized and even compelled aboriginal children to be schooled not for assimilation but for inequality. They were educated not to compete with their non-aboriginal counterparts on any basis of equity or rough parity, but to ensure that they could not do so. And neither could most students comfortably return home to take up traditional ways. Although teachers and administrators of good will were able to ameliorate the worst aspects of the system for their pupils, all of the individual good will in the world could not have rescued a system that was fundamentally flawed.

The character of residential schools becomes particularly evident when examined from the perspective of its participants. Personal testimony is used in this chapter not to set apart individuals or schools but rather to demonstrate how federal policy constructed aboriginal pupils' experience of education regardless of individual or institution.[2] The chapter draws on published recollections of residential schools in British Columbia, but, given that residential schooling was imposed throughout the country, any other province would almost certainly, as a variety of scholars attest, yield the same conclusions (Archibald, 1993; Barman, Hébert, and McCaskill, 1986–87; Bull, 1991; Coates, 1984–85; Fiske, 1989, 1991; Gresko, 1979; Haig-Brown, 1988; Miller, 1991; Titley, 1984, 1986, 1993).

RESIDENTIAL SCHOOL ATTRIBUTES ENSURING INEQUALITY

The inequality inherent in federal schools for aboriginal children rested in four complementary attributes of the system as devised and overseen by the Department of Indian Affairs. First, it was assumed that aboriginal peoples were the same across Canada. Differences among tribes, bands, and individuals played no role in a federal policy that viewed aboriginal peoples as a singular "object" to be acted upon. In parts of Canada, such as British Columbia, some aboriginal families were already sending their children to public school when federal policy intervened to declare residential schools, and their lesser complement, day schools, to be their sole educational options. Second, despite a curriculum in federal schools that paralleled the curriculum in provincial schools where other Canadian children were educated, aboriginal children were allotted less time in the classroom than were their non-aboriginal counterparts. The difference was particularly marked in the residential schools that formed the federal system's showcases. Third, until the mid-twentieth century, residential school instruction was based on voluntarism, the traditional style of teaching, rather than the newer and growing professionalism of public school teachers across Canada. With few exceptions, aboriginal schooling was carried on by Christian missionaries who were concerned primarily with saving souls, and only secondarily with literacy education. Fourth, federal funding levels of schools for aboriginal children quickly fell below provincial funding levels for public schools. However fine a school's intentions may have been, they became unrealizable. For these four reasons, as well as others, generations of aboriginal children were effectively, if not always deliberately, schooled for inequality.

Assumption of Aboriginal Peoples' Sameness

At the time of Confederation under the British North America Act in 1867, aboriginal peoples still occupied much of the land on which newcomers hoped to settle. The rhetoric of the day, premised on biological determinism, assumed that persons who were non-white were inferior by virtue of their race and so incapable of using the land to best advantage or otherwise determining their own destiny (Francis, 1992; Fisher, 1992;

Berkhofer, 1978). The British North America Act was consistent with this thinking. Its provisions made aboriginal peoples "wards" of the federal government, eligible for federally sponsored schooling, health care, and other services on their agreeing to treaties that surrendered traditional lands for much smaller reserves. The British North America Act made no attempt to distinguish aboriginal peoples in all of their diversity and individuality, but simply reduced them to a single dependent condition, captured in the word "status." Consistent with gender assumptions of the day, descent was traced through the male line and all persons with male aboriginal ancestry were registered as status Indians subject to federal control.

Schooling soon became viewed as something of a panacea by the new Department of Indian Affairs (DIA), which was charged with overseeing all aspects of federal policy on status Indians. Using reasoning similar to that gaining force in the United States, policy-makers looked to the civilization of aboriginal peoples "so as to cause them to reside in towns, or, in the case of farmers, in settlements of white people, and thus become amalgamated with the general community" (DIA, 1887, p. lxxx). Given the reluctance of adults to change their ways, attention turned to children, who were perceived to be more malleable. By separating the young from their families and thereby from the old ways for years on end, residential schools would, so contemporaries argued, achieve the federal goal of assimilation within a single generation:

> The Indian youth, to enable him to cope successfully with his brother of white origin, must be dissociated from the prejudicial influences by which he is surrounded on the reserve of his band. And the necessity for the establishment more generally of institutions, whereat Indian children, besides being instructed in the usual branches of education, will be lodged, fed, clothed, kept separate from home influences, taught trades and instructed in agriculture, is becoming every year more apparent. (DIA, 1880, p. 8)

Two types of residential schools were established in Canada in the late nineteenth century: boarding schools for younger children and industrial schools for their older siblings. Not only did the latter put greater emphasis on occupational training, but they also tended to be larger and located further away from pupils' home reserves (Titley, 1986). Over time, the distinction between the two types of schools broke down, and they all became known as residential schools. Day schools also existed, but were perceived as less acceptable than either boarding or industrial schools, to be established only where circumstances did not permit their preferred counterparts.

When the British colony of British Columbia entered the Canadian Confederation in 1871, it became subject to the provisions of the British North America Act and, a decade or so later, to the emerging federal policy favouring residential schools for aboriginal children. For aboriginal peoples in British Columbia, the policy's consequences were particularly poignant, for it removed an educational option that was beginning to give their children rough parity with non-aboriginal counterparts. Ever since free non-denominational public schools were legislated, shortly after British Columbia became a province, some aboriginal children had enrolled alongside their neighbours and, to an extent, had found acceptance there. Another narrative might well be constructed today about British Columbia's aboriginal peoples, and very likely also those elsewhere in Canada, had not federal policy intervened.

Part of the explanation for the educational circumstances of British Columbia lies in demographics and part in aboriginal peoples' everyday lives. When British Columbia entered Confederation, aboriginal peoples still formed the overwhelming bulk of the population. They totalled some 25 000 or more, as compared with about 1500 Chinese, almost all of them adult males, some 500 blacks, and about 8500 Europeans (Barman, 1991, p. 363). In many outlying settlements, aboriginal children were essential to secure the minimum enrollment necessary for a public school's establishment and survival.

Aboriginal children's acceptability in public school is also explained by the character of British Columbia's aboriginal population. Like their counterparts across North America, they possessed distinctive ways of life developed over many thousands of years. Particularly along the west coast, linguistic divisions were complex, economies self-sufficient, and cultures more sophisticated, in many respects, than in any other part of the continent north of Mexico (Barman, 1991, pp. 13–17). Generational continuity was assured through ongoing, lifelong education premised on the models of behaviour of the elders. By 1871, some aboriginal peoples had already been interacting with Europeans for two generations or more, initially in the fur trade and then during the gold rush beginning in 1858. The continued availability of such traditional staples as salmon, cedar, and game animals meant that British Columbia's aboriginal peoples were not experiencing the wrenching despair and utter dependency befalling their prairie counterparts. As the Department of Indian Affairs later phrased it with particular reference to British Columbia, "The Indians have been from the earliest times self-supporting, and the advent of white population, which in the west caused the complete disappearance of the buffalo, did not occasion any serious change in their source of food-supply" (DIA, 1910, p. 327). Contemporaries lauded the resourcefulness of the province's aboriginal population. A guide to prospective settlers asserted: "The intending settler may depend on finding the Indians peaceable, intelligent, eager to learn and industrious to a degree unknown elsewhere among the aborigines of America" (West Shore, 1884, quoted in Roy, 1984, p. 28). More than one settler was struck by how "the Indians differ toto caelo from the North West plains Indians. They are very well off" (Mair, 1892).

The published annual reports of the Department of Indian Affairs repeatedly praised British Columbia's aboriginal peoples. "The intelligence of the Indians of that province gives encouragement to the expectation that with liberal encouragement the Indians, who form so large a proportion of the population may, as they are not deficient in enterprise, be transformed into valuable members of the community" (DIA, 1874, p. 37). "The Indians of British Columbia exhibit more enterprise than those of any other Province in the Dominion" (DIA, 1880, p. 3). "The Indians of this Province, with but few exceptions, pursued their wanted course of manly independence, intelligent enterprise, and unflagging industry during the past year" (DIA, 1890, p. xxx). "Taking them altogether, the British Columbia Indians are remarkably industrious, enterprising, self-reliance, honest, sober and law-abiding. They are good neighbours, and friendly with the whites and with each other" (DIA, 1902, p. 283).

Perhaps, then, it is not surprising that as public schools became established across the far-flung province in the 1870s and 1880s, aboriginal children were sometimes among the first pupils to attend alongside their settler neighbours. The provincial superintendent of education received numerous letters from teachers and others inquiring about the government's policy toward "Indian children of school age in the immediate vicinity whose parents express a willingness to send to School" (Deans, 1876, in BCSE, IC). "There are a few bright-looking native children here. Would it be all right if I get them to attend the school?" (Hunter, 1886, in BCSE, IC). "There are numbers of Indian children . . . for whom no provision in the way of education has hitherto been made" (Petition, 1888, in BCSE, IC). "There are three Indian . . . children that wish to attend the school when it is established" (Hughett, 1891, in BCSE, IC).

The superintendent of education was consistently supportive.

> You are doing perfectly right in admitting Indian children so long as they are not taken [by force] & conduct themselves properly. . . . If they are troublesome or dirty the trustees must prohibit their attendance — Personally I am glad to hear of their attendance wherever circumstances will admit of it. (Jessop, 1876, in BCSE, OC)

The superintendent responded in 1886 to a query by some "parents of white children" about Indian children's attendance (Malpass, 1886, in BCSE, IC): "There is no authority given in the School Act to refuse them admittance. Since the inception of the present School system they have been admitted on an equality with other pupils" (Pope, 1886, in BCSE, OC).

Aboriginal children's attendance was for the most part accepted without question, as a matter of course, perhaps because they were often not that different in actions and even appearance from their non-aboriginal contemporaries. Some teachers encouraged aboriginal children into their schools. One young woman wrote the superintendent about a young aboriginal boy who "sent another boy to me to get a book as he wanted to learn to read. . . . I told him if he was so anxious to learn he could come to school as long as he behaved properly. He has come ever since and is acquitting himself creditably both to himself and me" (Trenaman, 1876, in BCSE, IC). The invitation may have started a trend. "Since then another

Indian boy has come to me wanting to come. I permitted him to do so on the same conditions" (Trenaman, 1876, in BCSE, IC). Another teacher wrote with particular reference to the aboriginal children in her classroom: "I love the children, black and white, are the same to me. I am an impartial Teacher. Act conscientiously and as long as I am able to impart instruction to them they shall all have it in equality" (Cordiner, 1875, in BCSE, IC).

Aboriginal families in British Columbia demonstrated a resourcefulness that would have served them well had not federal education policy assuming aboriginal peoples' sameness across Canada intervened. Although only a handful of treaties were ever made in British Columbia, similar federal services were gradually provided there as well. And despite the repeated comments in the annual reports of the Department of Indian Affairs on the distinctiveness of British Columbia's aboriginal people, they were treated no differently from their counterparts across Canada.

As the number of federal schools grew, it became increasingly difficult for aboriginal children to attend their local public schools. The shift in attitudes is visible from the late 1880s. A teacher noted concerning an "application to admit an Indian as a pupil" that the trustees "are of the opinion that the Dominion Government undertakes to provide for the educational interests of the Indians" (Shepherd, 1888, in BCSE, IC), to which the superintendent responded:

> Although Indian children are considered to be wards of the Dominion Government, yet it has not been the custom to refuse them admittance to Public Schools whose attendance is not over large. Of course they are required to comply with the Rules and Regulations as to cleanliness, supplying themselves with books etc. In all cases refer such matters to the Board of Trustees. (Pope, 1888, in BCSE, OC)

The superintendent was less sanguine a year later, considering that "Indian children are wards of the Dominion Government, and are not presumed to be entitled to attend the Public Schools of the Province" (Pope, 1889, in BCSE, OC).

Yet so many aboriginal children continued to enrol that the superintendent of education relented somewhat, stating in a circular in 1891 that "the matter of attendance of Indian children is left entirely in the hands of the [local] Board of Trustees" (Pope, 1893, in BCSE, OC; also Sheirs, 1891, in BCSE, IC). Almost all responses from individual teachers and boards of trustees supported the continued presence of aboriginal children. A teacher wrote that they were "quiet, tidy and much more devoted to study than the average child" (Sheirs, 1891, in BCSE, IC). Another commented that "the rate-payers seem to be of the opinion that it is of advantage to the community if the young Indians who reside here was [sic] educated" (McAdam, 1891, in BCSE, IC). The secretary of a school board reported that "the present Trustees all think the privilege of getting a better education should not be denied them especially as their parents seem grateful for it" (Cutler, 1892, in BCSE, IC). In the fall of 1893 the superintendent ruled that "if a single parent objects to the attendance of Indian pupils, they cannot be permitted to attend" (Pope, 1894, in BCSE, OC). In response, one trustee wrote indignantly that "it is desirable that in every locality the relations between Indians & settlers should be friendly but this ruling is not likely to secure it" (Cutler, 1893, in BCSE, IC).

Although some aboriginal children continued to attend individual public schools up to the time of World War I, and a few thereafter, they became the exceptions rather than the rule. Schools received no funding for aboriginal pupils, federal policy discouraged their attendance, and growing numbers of settlers meant that aboriginal pupils were no longer essential to the survival of most schools. In 1881 aboriginal peoples still formed the majority of British Columbia's population; by 1901 they had fallen to 16 percent and by 1911 to just 5 percent of a total provincial population approaching 400 000 (Barman, 1991, p. 363).

The moment of opportunity had passed. By 1900, British Columbia possessed 14 residential and 28 day schools, enrolling 675 and 893 pupils respectively. Two decades later, the totals had risen to 1 115 registered, or status, children in 17 residential schools and 1 197 in 46 day schools, and by 1940 to 2025 children in 15 residential schools and 2045 in 65 day schools. The relative importance of residential schools compared with federal day schools peaked during the interwar years when they enrolled about half of all aboriginal pupils in British Columbia, just as they did more generally across Canada.

Until the mid-twentieth century, federal policy toward aboriginal peoples — adults as well as children — refused to acknowledge their distinctiveness between geographical areas or as individuals. They were treated as a single category to be dealt with as expeditiously and economically as possible. The initiative demonstrated by British Columbia's aboriginal peoples, in political and economic matters as well as in schooling, only served to label them as nuisances for refusing to conform to their given role of dependency (Tennant, 1990).

Time in the Classroom

Logically, the shift of British Columbia's aboriginal children from provincial to federal schools should have made little or no difference to them academically, for in 1895 the newly established School Branch of the Department of Indian Affairs laid down a uniform curriculum based on provincial counterparts. Aboriginal pupils were to move between six "standards" or grades centred around readers similar to those being used in provincial systems (DIA, 1895, pp. 348–51; DIA, 1894, p. xxi). Instruction was to be offered in writing, arithmetic, English, geography, ethics, history, vocal music, calisthenics and religion. It was anticipated that "the work done and results obtained . . . [would] equal those of the common-schools of the rural districts" (DIA, 1896, p. xxxvii).

The new curriculum would have boded well for the proclaimed federal goal of assimilating aboriginal peoples had not children been expected somehow to get through it in less time each day than was allotted to their non-aboriginal counterparts in provincial schools. Although some flexibility existed in day schools, which were never that closely monitored by federal authorities, in residential schools usually only half of each day was spent in the classroom. Sometimes this occurred in segments. At one school, the hours of instruction were 9–11:30 A.M. and 2–3 P.M. (Gresko, 1986, p. 96). Regardless of format, the total was two to four hours per day compared with the five hours or longer that other Canadian children spent on the prescribed curriculum.

The reports on individual schools included in the annual reports of the Department of Indian Affairs often implied longer hours of instruction, but accounts from individual schools almost always reveal a shorter time period. Personal testimonies are damning. "We went to school in the mornings about ten o'clock. . . . I would stay there till dinner time. Twelve o'clock" (Tappage, 1973, p. 18). "We spent very little time in the classroom. We were in the classroom from nine o'clock in the morning until noon. Another shift [of children] came into the classroom at one o'clock in the afternoon and stayed until three" (Manuel and Posluns, 1974, p. 64; also Haig-Brown, 1988, p. 61). "We knew we had to do our chores, such as sweeping the dormitory, cleaning the washrooms, in the morning, and go to school half a day" (Baker, 1994, pp. 30–31). This pupil's daily round grew more onerous as he got older: "Our job was getting tougher. We went to school for half a day. One month you worked in the mornings and the next month you worked in the afternoons. We never went to school full-time until the last year, in grade eight" (Baker, 1994, p. 29). In his discussion of the academic subjects taught in British Columbia Catholic residential schools, Oblate historian Thomas Lascelles concluded:

> Usually they occupied the students several hours a day, the remainder being devoted to training in practical skills such as farming, shoemaking and housekeeping, an arrangement which was not abandoned until the 1940s or 1950s when pupils began to spend full time on academic subjects, and to follow Provincial curricula more closely. (Lascelles, 1990, p. 30)

Shorter time periods for classroom instruction existed even though many children were being forced to study in a second language. As part of their becoming "civilized," federal policy recommended that aboriginal children be "taught in the English language exclusively" (DIA, 1895, p. xxiii). The local aboriginal languages that most boys and girls brought with them to school were almost always prohibited, even for private conversations between pupils. "Teached us in English. She speak English to us all the time. I learn little bit of English from her. After a while I learn a little bit what she mean" (Mack, 1993, p. 19). "I entered knowing no English. I found that every time I used my native tongue I was punished" (Webster, 1983, p. 41). "Native languages were forbidden. English was the only allowable language" (Hall, 1992, p. 81). "What I could never understand, we weren't allowed to speak our language. If we were heard speaking Shuswap, we were punished. We were made to write on the board one hundred times, 'I will not speak Indian any more'" (Tappage, 1973, p. 7). "In my first meeting with the brother, he showed me a long black leather strap and told me, through my interpreter, 'If you are ever caught speaking Indian this is what you will get across your hands'" (Manuel and Posluns, 1974, p. 64).

The logic behind the limited time allotted to the formal curriculum was obvious to policy-makers. While it was important that aboriginal children be made literate in English, it was even more critical that they acquire the practical skills permitting their entry into mainstream society, but only at its very lowest rungs. Although assimilation was a desirable goal, its achievement should not challenge the status quo. During the second half of each school day boys learned how to do farm chores or some low-status trade such as shoemaking, girls to perform household tasks ranging from potato-peeling to dusting to needlework. As a pamphlet widely distributed by the Methodist church put the case in 1906:

> The girl who has learned only the rudiments of reading, writing and ciphering, and knows also how to make and mend her clothing, wash and iron, make a good loaf of bread, cook a good dinner, keep her house neat and clean, will be worth vastly more as mistress of a log cabin than one who had given years of study to the ornamental branches alone. . . . The Indian must be educated along industrial lines. It should be along the line of the physical rather than the mental. (Ferrier, 1906, pp. 17 and 25; also DIA, 1888, p. x; 1897, p. 60)

However much federal rhetoric might have maintained the illusion of assimilation, the Department of Indian Affairs was ensuring the failure of aboriginal peoples to compete socially or intellectually with their white neighbours. The gap in illiteracy rates between mainstream Canadians and aboriginal peoples remained overwhelming, indicating that many aboriginal children were still not in school at all. In 1921, about 2 percent of Canadian youth were illiterate, compared with fully 40 percent of aboriginal youth. Over the decade, the illiteracy rate for Canadian youth halved to 1 percent; that for aboriginal youth also fell, but still stood in 1931 at about 25 percent. The gap was comparable between non-aboriginal and aboriginal youth in British Columbia, and for adults both in the west coast province and more generally across Canada.

Aboriginal children in school may not have fared that much better in terms of becoming literate. Whereas most pupils in provincial schools reached the upper elementary grades by the end of World War I, the overwhelming majority of aboriginal children never got beyond Grade 1 or 2. Up to 1920, four out of every five aboriginal boys and girls attending a federal school across Canada were enrolled in Grade 1, 2, or 3 (DIA, school statements; Dominion Bureau of Statistics). This did not necessarily mean that they had been in school so short a time, but more likely that they were simply kept in the lower grades year after year for the sake of convenience or because the level of instruction was so poor. "We only had two hours of classes when I went to residential school. We worked . . . you had to get out as soon as you're sixteen. I didn't get much education, very little education" (F. Charlie, quoted in Lascelles, 1990, p. 44).

In any case, aboriginal pupils were long prohibited by law from going beyond the elementary grades. "There was a rule at that time that Indians could not go past Grade eight. I do not recall many boys staying around long enough to protest the education that was being denied us" (Manuel and Posluns, 1974, p. 66). "We had to stay in school until we were eighteen years of age to go as high as grade eight. And then no high school after" (Hall, 1992, p. 81). Until the mid-twentieth century, the proportion of aboriginal children in school across Canada who were in grades 1–3 stagnated at two-thirds or more. In sharp contrast, the percentage of their counterparts in provincial schools who were enrolled in grades 1–3 fell by mid-century to just over a third, indicating that almost all non-aboriginal children were by then completing the elementary grades. Similarly, whereas the proportion of children of the dominant society reaching Grade 7 or higher grew from less than one-fifth in 1920 to about one-third by 1950, the percentage of aboriginal children reaching Grade 7 moved up from none in 1920 to 3 percent a decade later, and then to just 10 percent by mid-century (DIA, school statements; Dominion Bureau of Statistics). Father Lascelles summed up the situation in this observation: "The half-day academic program in effect until the middle of this century ensured that the children did not receive an education on a par with that given in the public schools" (Lascelles, 1990, p. 83). Even then, a boy at school during the mid-1950s recalled that classes "were from nine in the morning until three in the afternoon, but many times we were taken from class to work outside" (Monk, 1994, p. 51).

Teachers and Teaching

The third attribute of federal policy ensuring that aboriginal children were schooled for inequality resulted from the remarkable symbiosis that developed between the federal government and the various religious denominations across Canada. Unlike education policy toward aboriginal peoples in the United States where missionaries were subordinated to the federal government (Szasz and Ryan, 1988), in Canada they were left in charge. By the time the federal policy on education emerged, the major churches had long since carved Canada up into spheres of influence for the purposes of aboriginal conversion. In British Columbia, as elsewhere, the different denominations each had their own spheres of influence. It was understood that the missionary group that got to a group of aboriginal peoples first would not be challenged, for there were, to put the matter somewhat crudely, enough "heathens" to go around. One of the first activities that most missionary groups initiated on arriving in a locality was the establishment of a school to inculcate basic literacy alongside Christian principles and practices.

So the federal government, instead of establishing its own system of aboriginal education in 1880s, decided to buttress those already in place. Existing day and residential schools were subsidized by per-pupil grants, and some funding was provided to build needed new schools. The Department of Indian Affairs restricted itself to general oversight, which included annual reporting by each school and periodic visits by local officials, known as Indian agents, and later also by federal school inspectors. The various Christian churches eagerly accepted the new challenge.

While the federal policy was justified as suitably acknowledging an already established school system, it was also an economical means of relieving the federal government of its responsibility to create and maintain its own institutions. "The department has fully recognized its inability to conduct such institutions as economically as can be done by denominations, and consequently it has endeavoured to have their management placed in the hands of the respective churches" (DIA, 1896, p. xxxviii). A student recalled, "One day Sister Catherine told us in the classroom, 'We work so hard for you, we don't get any pay at all for looking after you Indians'" (Hall, 1992, p. 81).

By leaving the ongoing operation of the schools to missionary groups, the federal government relieved itself of direct responsibility for the provision, payment, or supervision of teaching staffs. In residential schools, most teachers were missionaries principally motivated by a commitment to convert aboriginal peoples. "We had prayers ten, twenty times a day and when we weren't praying, we were changing clothes for prayers. We prayed when we got up, we prayed before breakfast and after breakfast, and we prayed when we got to the classroom and when we were in the classroom I lost count of how many times a day we prayed" (Monk, 1994, p. 57). "We had to listen, morning and night, to readings from the Bible. We did not understand any of it. Even today I cannot pronounce many of the words" (Webster, 1983, p. 42). One pupil shrewdly observed: "Mr. Hall wasn't paid to teach us, I don't think. I think he was just paid as a minister" (Nowell, 1941, p. 100). At their best teachers possessed, as one federal official phrased it, "infinite patience and tact, although without scholarly attainments" (Lejac school correspondence, 1910, quoted in Fiske, 1989, p. 243).

The situation was comparable between residential and day schools. One of the most perceptive critics of the schooling being accorded aboriginal children across Canada was Edward Ahenakew, a Cree who through extraordinary perseverance became an Anglican priest early in the twentieth century. Ahenakew was convinced that the frequent closure of federal day schools "for poor attendance" in favour of residential schools, while generally attributed to the indifference of aboriginal families, was in reality due to a paucity of "qualified teachers": "The teachers have been too often of the poorest type, and those who were good seldom stayed long, for they could always find more congenial work and higher pay elsewhere" (Ahenakew, 1973, pp. 127–28). Parents who sought a change of teacher were routinely rebuffed. A group of Fraser Valley parents informed the Department of Indian Affairs in 1936 that the "Indians of our Band are quite willing and anxious to do their part in educating their children, but we are asking the Department to give us a capable Instructor who will take a deeper interest in the progress of our children" (Chehalis band, 1936, quoted in Archibald, 1993, p. 101). Having considered the request, the department concluded: "While he is not a trained teacher, and the children do not make the same progress as they might with a modern highly trained instructor, he is rendering good service to the Department in a variety of ways." Although individual teachers at day schools, as at residential schools, were sometimes sympathetic to pupils' plight and so remembered by them, they were generally untrained.

The contemporary literature is replete with observations attesting to the poor quality of teaching at residential schools. A pupil of the 1920s has mused, "it is said by many that the teachers are not really teachers at all. They are not trained as the teachers are in the [local public] school" (John, 1988, p. 53–54). Conversely, a sister teaching at the same school recalled being informed by the federal inspector of Indian schools that there was "no training for your situation anyway, just for public schools" (unnamed teacher, quoted in Fiske, 1989, p. 244). An anonymous comment in DIA's internal files dated 1932 acknowledged that teaching positions are sometimes "merely posts provided for persons for whom billets had to be found" (Sluman and Goodwill, 1982, p. 157). Into the 1940s, the refrain was much the same, that teachers "were often unqualified to teach. They used to just send old missionaries to the village to try and do the best they could" (Sewid, 1959, p. 191). The situation continued largely unchanged into the mid-twentieth century, in sharp contrast to the growing professionalism distinguishing teachers and teaching in mainstream society.

Where an individual's religious commitment conflicted with his or her role as a teacher, the former usually triumphed. A local Indian agent observed in 1912 that "there is a disposition to devote too much time to imparting religious instruction to the children as compared with the imparting of secular knowledge, which is perhaps not unnatural when the teachers are employed and selected by the various churches" (DIA, 1912, p. 399). The pupil–teacher relationship outside the classroom was often determined more by religious than by didactic considerations:

> If you passed [the nuns] in the hall or anywhere, you're to stop and bow your head. They were really up on the pedestal. . . . They sure put themselves somewhere where you couldn't touch them. You couldn't reach them and you had to bow to them, . . . it made me to a certain extent very bitter by the time I left school. (M. Englund, quoted in Whitehead, 1981, p. 64)

Language sometimes compounded difficulties. Whereas aboriginal children were expected, once in school, totally to abandon their aboriginal tongue in favour of English, their teachers did not necessarily know the English language sufficiently well to speak it, much less teach it to others. "But them French teachers you know they don't really pronounce their sounds right. There was only Sister Patricia who was Irish" (C. Johnson, quoted in Whitehead, 1981, p. 50). The Department of Indian Affairs acknowledged a possible conflict in its observation that "the dual system of control between the department on the one hand and the church on the other, each with their different ideals, the one requiring a secular education, and the other looking more to the spiritual instruction of the children, is almost somewhat anomalous" (DIA, 1911, p. 374).

Federal Funding

The fourth and perhaps most fundamental reason why aboriginal children were schooled for inequality lay in the schools' low levels of federal financial support. Even taking into account the largely volunteer labour available as a consequence of schools' missionary ties, they were underfunded when compared with provincial institutions or even with the bare basics of survival. The per-pupil subsidy provided by the federal government assumed that much of the teaching would be volunteer, but even then it was inadequate to provide a minimum standard of everyday life for pupils, much less material conditions conducive to learning. The men and women who ran the schools were expected to scramble for donations simply to survive. Father Lascelles has made the critical link: "Crucial to the determined efforts [of Catholic residential schools to secure better qualified teachers], however, were dollars; dollars which were few and far between" (Lascelles, 1990, p. 42).

The published reports of the Department of Indian Affairs were very open in acknowledging the inadequacy of funding of residential schools, as in 1896: "The denominations interested in the last-named, owing to the smallness of the annual per capita grant, are forced to meet any shortage of the Government grant by contributions from outside sources" (DIA, 1896, p. xxxvii). A decade later the annual report stated bluntly that residential schools across the country were "all largely supplemented by the missionary societies" (DIA, 1906, p. 251). Father Lascelles concluded that between 1915 and about 1950, "funding for the education of Indian children by the Department [of Indian Affairs] remained at a relative standstill" (Lascelles, 1990, p. 42).

The half-day program adopted in most residential schools became little more than a means of having pupils provide the manual labour necessary for the survival of the institutions. From the beginning, federal officials hoped to see schools become "self-supporting" through the use of pupils raising crops, making clothes, and generally doing "outside work" (DIA, 1891, p. xiii). This meant that much of the supposed occupational training was in reality unpaid brute labour:

> The longer half of our day was spent in what the brothers called "industrial training." Industrial training consisted of doing all the kinds of manual labour that are commonly done around a farm, except that we did not have the use of the equipment that even an Indian farmer of those days would have been using. (Manuel and Posluns, 1974, p. 64)

The need for manual labour cut across the sexes, and many "an Indian girl washed, cooked, cleaned, and mended her way through residential school" (Mitchell and Franklin, 1984, p. 24). "We had to patch. We had to patch the boys' clothes. We had to wash and iron Mondays and Tuesdays. We had to patch and keep on patching till Saturday" (Tappage, 1973, p. 18). "We made all of the dresses and uniforms worn in the school, and socks, drawers, chemises, and aprons" (John, 1988, p. 45). The situation was, in this woman's view, even more detrimental for her male counterparts:

> The bigger ones spent almost no time in class. Instead, they were cutting down trees and pulling up stumps, or else they were up before daylight feeding the horses and milking the cows. Long after he left Lejac one boy said, "I'm just a human bulldozer!" (John, 1988, p. 44)

A male pupil at the same school confirmed this assessment: "I was up at five-thirty every morning either to serve as an altar boy for Mass or to work on the farm, milking cows, working the garden, and so forth" (Monk, 1994, p. 51). The memories of a boy at another school are similar:

> So I feed the horses, clean the barn, feed the cows and later even milk the cows. I get up at four o'clock in the morning sometimes and go look for them cows. . . . I also helped look after the farm, help with the potatoes, and helped cut the hay. I tried to go to school but there was not enough time. I worked most of the time. I went to Alert Bay for school and instead they put me in a job! (Mack, 1993, pp. 22–23)

From the perspective of some pupils, poor or too little food caused most everyday distress. "Hunger is both the first and last thing I can remember about that school. I was hungry from the day I went into the school until they took me to the hospital two and a half years later. Not just me. Every Indian pupil smelled of hunger" (Manuel and Posluns, 1974, p. 65). Particularly difficult for pupils to understand was their being expected to eat the barest of fare day after day while subjected to the smells and even the sight of school staffs dining far more sumptuously:

> After Mass we put our smocks over our uniforms and line up for breakfast in the hall outside the dining room. We can talk then because Sister goes for breakfast in the Sisters' dining room. They get bacon or ham, eggs, toast and juice. We can see when they open the door and go in for breakfast. We get gooey mush with powder milk and brown sugar. (Sterling, 1992, p. 24)

The food given to us daily was not of the best. I am saying the food for the staff was of better quality and more palatably prepared. (Hall, 1992, p. 83)

At school it was porridge, porridge, porridge, and if it wasn't that, it was boiled barley or beans, and thick slices of bread spread with lard. Weeks went by without a taste of meat or fish. . . . A few times I would catch the smell of roasting meat coming from the nuns' dining room, and I couldn't help myself —I would follow that smell to the very door. Apart from the summers, I believe I was hungry for all seven of the years I was at school. . . . We were on rations more suited to a concentration camp! (John, 1988, p. 39)

The comparison was apt for, according to the wife of the commander of a World War I camp in British Columbia for German prisoners of war, they were provided only with "cheap" food, the allocation being limited to "approximately seventeen cents per person per day," or just over $50 a year (Cash, 1977, p. 23).

Indeed, it may be that many aboriginal children fared less well than did prisoners of war. Until 1910, boarding schools received from the federal government a grant of $60 a year per qualifying pupil, which was intended to cover all costs, not just food. Industrial schools received double that amount or even a bit more, but the consequence for all residential schools was what one administrator termed "frugal maintenance" (All Hallows School, 1906, p. 538). Moreover, because most schools, as part of their religious commitment to service, accepted more children than were allotted to them by the Department of Indian Affairs, federal funds were usually stretched over a larger pupil body than intended.

From 1900 to 1908, the statements of income and expenditure of some industrial and boarding schools were published in DIA's annual reports. They make clear the extent to which schools struggled to make ends meet. Including donations, the average annual income per pupil at the three British Columbia boarding schools whose financial statements were published for 1900 was $94. Of this total, $41 comprised the government subsidy, which in theory was $60 per pupil but in practice much less due to most schools' greater enrollments than allotted by DIA. The remaining income consisted of donations, contributed primarily to further the schools' religious purposes. Housekeeping expenses alone, principally food, exceeded total federal funding at $44 per child. Physical upkeep of facilities added another $16 per pupil, and then came salaries for the minority of staff who received wages and miscellaneous expenses ranging from school books to clothing. In 1908, the average annual income per pupil at seven British Columbia boarding schools was $87, of which $46 comprised the federal subsidy and the remainder donations. Out of necessity, housekeeping expenses, including food, had fallen to $38 per pupil.

The parsimony of federal funding is particularly evident when comparison is made to private schools for children of the dominant society. At the turn of the century, even a relatively modest private day school in British Columbia had fees of $50 a year, roughly the amount on which the federal government expected aboriginal boarders to survive (advertisements in *News Advertiser*, 1902). In 1900, at the only British Columbia boarding school enrolling both aboriginal and white female students, the latter's families were charged $160 a year (All Hallows School, 1900).

Federal subsidies for aboriginal pupils were raised in 1910, but not to adequate levels. Moreover, "increased financial assistance" came at the cost of "greater demands" in the standard of buildings, care, and administration (DIA, 1911, xxvi, pp. 294–95). In the case of boarding schools for younger children, the per-pupil subsidy was doubled from $60 to $125, but only after schools met rigorous new requirements demanding more space per pupil, better physical facilities, and far higher health and sanitation standards — no easy matter, given that capital costs for upgrading were not integral to the revised policy. In comparison, in 1912 a British Columbia elite private school for white boys charged $470 a year for boarders and $150 for day pupils (University School, 1912).

The financial situation in aboriginal day schools was equally grim. Federal day schools in British Columbia initially received an annual federal grant of $12 per pupil. The paucity of the amount becomes evident when compared with neighbouring British Columbia public schools, whose budgets rose from an average of $15 per pupil at the turn of the century to double the amount by 1908 (British Columbia, Department of Education, tables A and D; DIA, school statements).[3] Federal day school grants were raised in 1910 to $17 per child, but by then the comparable allocation per pupil in the British Columbia provincial system had reached $34.[4] As the reports of Indian agents repeatedly emphasized, teachers' salaries were a central issue for day schools, which were often compelled to recruit from outside of religious orders. "Complaint is continually made of the small amount allowed for a teacher. The teachers of the public schools receive at least $80 per month, with a long summer vacation, and have fewer scholars than the teachers of Indian day schools" (DIA, 1912, p. 408; also DIA, 1911, p. 378). Another Indian agent noted that "the churches do not pay an adequate salary and trained teachers prefer to go to white schools, where social surroundings are always preferable to the isolated location among the Indians" (DIA, 1912, p. 399).

Within a few short years of the 1910 increase in subsidies, federal schools in British Columbia, and across Canada, were in even worse financial straits. A school inspector on the Prairies reported in 1915 concerning residential schools:

> Although the per capita grant given by the department was increased about four years ago, the religious bodies, under whose auspices these schools are operated, find the grant to be inadequate to meet the advanced cost of foodstuffs daily in use in these schools. Moreover, contributions toward the support of such institutions are said to have been diminished, owing chiefly to the financial stringency caused by the war in Europe. (DIA, 1915, p. 238)

Contributing to a deteriorating situation was growing interest on the part of some missionaries in converting Asians, who were viewed as more tractable and perhaps more glamorous than aboriginal peoples (Grant, 1984, p. 191). To some extent, aboriginal schools ended up with the left-overs — missionaries who lacked the zeal and determination to put themselves in the front line of Christianity's advance.

Federal stinginess was not lost on contemporaries. It was not just aboriginal leaders like the Rev. Ahenakew who realized the seriousness of the situation. The respected anthropologist Diamond Jenness made extensive personal observations throughout Canada during the 1920s before writing his landmark description of the country's aboriginal population. While damning the quality of teaching in many schools as "exceedingly poor," he was concerned that missionaries not be blamed since "they lacked the resources and the staffs to provide a proper education. . . . It was not the missions that shirked their responsibility, but the federal government, and behind that government the people of Canada" (Jenness, 1983, p. 162). Yet, as late as 1947, even as a joint parliamentary committee was finally being established to probe aboriginal affairs, the federal government was spending $45 a year per aboriginal pupil in federal day schools compared with about $200 allocated per pupil in British Columbia public schools. As Father Lascelles insightfully concluded, "Financial problems were one of the major handicaps the schools laboured under for more than half a century" (Lascelles, 1990, p. 83).

ABORIGINAL RESPONSES

Perhaps the most fundamental critique of federal policy was its deluding of aboriginal peoples. Certainly, not all parents sought formal schooling for their offspring. Concerning "a large no. of children of the pure Siwash [Indian in the widely spoken Chinook trade language] persuasion between the ages of 5 and 16 in the district," an early British Columbia public teacher reported that "it will be a difficult matter to get them to attend school as their respected progenitors believe them to be as well off without book learning as with it" (Leduc, 1876, in BCSE, IC). Many an Indian agent reported that "parents see in education the downfall of all their most cherished customs" (DIA, 1888, p. 104).

Other families accepted at face value that what they were given every reason to believe was, despite its obvious trade-offs, a genuine opportunity for their children. Aboriginal parents in British Columbia sent their children, first to public schools and then to federal schools, as one former pupil put it, "to learn White people's ways" (C. Clare, quoted in Barman, 1986, p. 112). Knowledge of the English language was recognized as having very real advantages. A man born in 1870 who attended one of the earliest boarding schools in British Columbia considered that "my little education in English helped me in all the jobs I got" (Nowell, 1941, p. 192).

Even his father saw value in the white man's schooling, as revealed in his deathbed instructions to his son:

> "Most of all I want to say is, I know you have been to school, and I think the only way for you to remember the main positions and all the ancestors is for you to write them down, because it seems to me that everybody is forgetting all their ancestors and names. I have often heard people make mistakes. The first thing, you will write down our ancestors till now." . . .
> So I did — all our ancestors right down to him. (Nowell, 1941, p. 107)

Similarly, a woman born two generations later, in 1931, remembered her mother's words: "You're going to have to learn to read and write because when you grow up you're going to have to get a job" (Cook, quoted in Haegert, 1983, p. 21). Other times, it was fathers who made their children aware of changing times. " 'It's going to get crowded in the valley in a few years,' he said. . . . 'You kids want to get yourselves an education. Get a job. That way you'll be okay' " (Sterling, 1992, p. 125).

The deception wrought on aboriginal parents was deliberate. Children and youth were often compelled to attend residential schools despite parents' wishes or through some form of moral coercion. "One day the Indian agent grabbed me by the hair and dragged me, pulled me up to my mother. He going [sic] to send me to poor kid's school at Alert Bay. Any poor kid around, they put them in that school" (Mack, 1993, p. 21). Once at school, children were sometimes admonished against giving their families details of what went on in school, and in some cases prohibited from doing so. As late as the 1950s, letters home, if allowed at all, were routinely censored. "Sister Theo checks our letters home. We're not allowed to say anything about the school. I might get the strap, or worse" (Sterling, 1992, p. 12).

British Columbia families became frustrated as they realized that their children were being treated unfairly. The refrain was the same regardless of geographical area or particular circumstances. "Children are not taught enough" (DIA, 1911, p. 381). "We wish our children taught the same as the whites. They go to school, maybe, five, six, seven years. They learn read a little. That's all. Not much use" (p. 381). "They just get nicely started — they just get their eyes opened the same as young birds and then they are turned out to fly. They don't get enough education for a livelihood nor are they taught a trade of any kind" (W. Sepass in 1916, quoted in Archibald, 1993, p. 100). "The boys are not learning how to hunt and trap and set a net for fish. . . . They are supposed to go to Lejac to be educated, but they are not in the classrooms. They are in the fields or the barns, and the girls are too much in the sewing room or the kitchen" (John, 1988, p. 53). "We all apply to have school at our own place. . . . Please look into matter soon as possible. We feed our children at home then" (Stoney Creek Council, 1917, quoted in Fiske, 1989, p. 240).

Just as British Columbia parents were not alone in recognizing the deceptive character of federal education policy, so they were not alone in pushing for change. Concerned to ameliorate the poor quality of teaching,

the Cree priest Edward Ahenakew drew a direct comparison between aboriginal families and the thousands of immigrants who had arrived in
Canada in the decade and a half before World War I. The newcomers were,
as Ahenakew observed, "supplied with the best of teachers" in the hopes of
making them "good citizens," whereas aboriginal children were ignored:

> Is it justice that the weak Indian nation, which gave of all its life blood to
> provide its loyalty [in World War I], should have to be satisfied with teachers
> who seldom have any qualifications to teach? . . . Schools, in the modern
> sense of that word, must have properly qualified teachers. If that is not so,
> then you may call the building in which the children congregate by any
> name you choose, but it is not a school. (Ahenakew, 1973, pp. 127–28)

> The world around us is too far advanced for any playing at education. Either
> close all our schools and let the children help at home and on the farms, or
> else supply properly qualified teachers. (Ahenakew, 1973, p. 135)

Not only were such voices unheard by federal policy-makers, but individual parents faced tremendous obstacles when they sought to intervene directly in their children's best interests. Two examples from
Vancouver Island are indicative. "I wanted my boys to go to high school,
so I went to see the Indian agent, M.S. Todd, and told him so. He said to
me, 'Nothing doing!' I asked him, 'Isn't it for everybody?' and he
answered me, 'Not for you people' " (Assu, 1989, pp. 95–96). A second
father was forced to desperate measures so that his children "would be
able to go to school a full term":

> The school at Village Island was run by the Indian Department and we used
> to have that schoolteacher for three months a year. . . . I went over to the
> Indian Office at Alert Bay and pleaded with the Indian agent to keep her on
> for another couple months. He told me that he had no authority to pay her
> for another month and that they had spent all that was allowed. So I went to
> the school teacher and asked if she would accept $50 to stay for another
> month. . . . So the next month Simon Beans paid her $50 to stay for
> another month. That's how hard it was. (Sewid, 1959, pp. 125–26)

Parents who resisted federal schools altogether in favour of their local
public school rarely succeeded. One exception was a North Vancouver
parent who, having spent a decade in residential school, was determined
that his children would not do so. Given that this was at the beginning of
World War II, it may be that the system was beginning to crack, or that he
was particularly determined:

> We didn't want to send them to no boarding school because I was working
> and we wanted them at home. We had quite a time to have them accepted
> into the public school. We finally got them admitted. Priscilla and Barbara
> were the first Indian children to be accepted into the public school. I had to
> struggle with Indian Affairs, the North Vancouver School Board, the West
> Vancouver School Board to get my children in school. . . . I had to pay their
> tuition fee myself for two years to have my children go to the public school.
> I paid five dollars a month per child. (Baker, 1994, p. 73)

It was not just adults but also children who became actors. In some cases, pupils through their own efforts were able to mitigate a school's worst attributes, not just for themselves but for their fellow pupils:

> Sometimes we used to help the ones who needed it. I always had that in my mind because I was brought up by my people, the teaching I got was to always try to help the other person. . . . I used to take the lower class out who were having problems, go for a walk. . . . I taught them about nature, making a bow and arrow, little canoes, to get their minds off problems. (Baker, 1994, p. 31)

More often, pupils simply refused to co-operate as they realized that residential school was not what it purported to be. "The boys often rebelled and I didn't blame them. They were supposed to be in Lejac to get educated, but instead they were unpaid laborers, living on poor food and no more freedom than if they were prisoners in a jail" (John, 1988, p. 44).

Pupils protested treatment that they deemed unfair and discriminatory, and in cases of desperation they ran away. "I ran away from the bus that was going to take me back to school and I hid in the bush until the priests and the police officers stopped looking for me" (Monk, 1994, p. 10). "Some were successful and managed to reach their parents' traplines, but more often, they were caught by the Mounties, brought back and whipped" (John, 1988, p. 44). Sociologist Celia Haig-Brown (1988) has argued that resistance was integral to everyday life in residential school.

CHANGING TIMES

Over time, aboriginal peoples did effect change, but extraordinarily slowly. Unlike the United States where federal policy began to encourage children into public schools during the interwar years (Szasz and Ryan, 1988; Hendrick, 1981; Szasz, 1977; Senese, 1991), in Canada the symbiosis between state and church was too comfortable to be altered until it became absolutely impossible for the federal government to ignore changing times. Only after World War II did increased awareness of aboriginal peoples lead to the creation of a select joint committee of the Senate and House of Commons, which in 1951 called for the integration of aboriginal peoples into the Canadian mainstream. Although aboriginal education remained under federal jurisdiction, children were encouraged to attend their local public school or possibly an integrated religious school. In British Columbia, where provincial schooling has always been non-denominational, the Catholic church was particularly concerned about losing its traditional clientele and so expended considerable effort in constructing new integrated parochial schools. Funding still came from the federal government, through tuition agreements negotiated with provincial governments or religious denominations.

Early integration was often top-down, with aboriginal children sometimes attending a local public or Catholic parochial school for grades beyond those available in an existing federal school. "Dorothy goes to classes at St. Mark's now, the Catholic high school in town. All the pupils in grade ten, eleven and twelve do. Father Pitt drives them in a yellow school bus every day" (Sterling, 1992, p. 41). Such piecemeal practice may have induced new forms of discrimination. "We still had to wear the residential school clothes and this made an obvious distinction between us and the other students who would taunt us" (A. Collison, in Jaine, 1993, p. 38). For individual aboriginal children, integration sometimes existed more in theory than in practice. "It was difficult going to [public] school, a lot of ideas and attitudes haven't changed much. Segregation is happening, not visibly but in the classes" (S.M. Grismer, quoted in Niehaus, 1978, p. 7). At this school, aboriginal children were seated separately, and it remained very much a "white man's school" (p. 7). Other children continued to attend federal schools where not that much had changed, at least in terms of teaching staffs, from previous decades. "Some of them were good, but others were young and didn't give a hell. The villagers, the chief, and the councillors had no say in the qualifications or lack of them in the teachers who were hired — we just took what we could get" (Monk, 1994, p. 103, referring to 1971). By 1970, almost three-quarters of the 12 500 registered Indian pupils in British Columbia, and 60 percent of the 66 000 in school across Canada, were attending integrated institutions.

At about the same time, in 1969, Prime Minister Pierre Trudeau issued a white paper, or policy document, calling for total aboriginal integration into his "just society." He proposed to repeal the Indian Act and abolish Indians' special legal status in Canada. The aboriginal response was overwhelmingly negative — a decade and more of growing awareness had awoken pride in aboriginal heritage and culture. The white paper was withdrawn in favour of aboriginal self-determination looking toward management of their own affairs. The fundamental policy shift agreed to by the federal government and aboriginal peoples was epitomized in the catchphrase "Indian control of Indian education." Federally funded, band-operated schools, whose numbers have steadily increased across Canada, were intended to encourage pride in aboriginal languages and cultures alongside the necessary skills to participate in mainstream society.

The official shift in aboriginal education policy did not bring about immediate change. As one band leader recalled about the 1970s, "We had to fight for every dollar and every bit of independence we could get for the education of our children. A policy of delay, delay, delay, was practiced and is still practiced" (Monk, 1994, p. 156). The proportion of registered, or status, children attending band schools grew from 12 percent in British Columbia in 1980 to 19 percent in 1985, and in Canada as a whole from 8 percent to 23 percent. In 1994, just over half of the children living on-reserve were attending a band school.

THE LEGACY OF RESIDENTIAL SCHOOLS

Although residential schools have disappeared from the Canadian educational landscape in favour of a mix of provincial, private, and band schools, their legacy endures. The consequences are still being lived across British Columbia and in the rest of Canada:

> If I had to pick one area where the federal government, through the Department of Indian Affairs, inflicted the most harm on my people, it would have to be in the field of education. . . . At the beginning of the white man's rule, Aboriginal people were confined to reserves, most of them far away from schools. When the government was finally forced to do something about the lack of educational facilities, the solution was a partnership between church and state to set up residential schools. Children were removed from their communities and placed in an alien environment that almost destroyed their culture and their language; we call it cultural genocide. (Monk, 1994, pp. 155–56)

The personal accounts used to ground this chapter have ranged through time and across British Columbia, but they all tell a similar story, one that would almost certainly have been little different had they been taken from any other province.

Half or fewer British Columbia aboriginal children of past generations actually attended residential school at any point in time, but numbers were sufficient for family life to deteriorate. A pupil has recalled her "inability to show love to my mom, brothers, and sisters" (R. Bell, in Jaine, 1993, p. 13). Students of different sexes were almost always separated in residential school, and siblings in the same school often could not even speak to each other for months and years on end. "I never did get to know my brothers. We were kept away from each other for too long. To this day I don't know much about my brothers. I just know that they are my brothers" (p. 10). "After a year spent learning to see and hear only what the priests and brothers wanted you to see and hear, even the people we loved came to look ugly" (Manuel and Posluns, 1974, p. 67). "Some of the most damaging things that resulted from my experiences at residential school was lack of nurturing as well as being denied learning parenting skills" (C. Thompson, in Jaine, 1993, p. 129). Subsequent generations have reaped the consequences:

> Although my older brother and I didn't attend residential school, we didn't really escape it either as it visited us every day of our childhood through the replaying over and over of our parents' childhood trauma and grief which they never had the opportunity to resolve in their lifetimes. . . . I grieve for the gentle man in my father who was never allowed to grow, and I grieve for my mother who never had the loving relationships she deserved, nor the opportunity to be the mother I knew she could have been. (V. Manuel in Jaine, 1993, p. 115)

Much the same deterioration occurred with language and culture. If not banned outright, both were so disparaged in school that they were among its casualties:

Those who were taken to the residential school and taught the English language and the European ways were told that ceremonies such as Oo-simch [an Ahousat practice in which knowledge of natural medicines used in healing is passed on within the family] were "superstitious." I guess this meant that the priests and nuns thought that these practices were "savage" or without meaning compared to the customs of the white man. This has always puzzled me. (Webster, 1983, p. 23)

It didn't matter that Carrier was the only language we knew — we were told not to use it and, if we did, wham! right now. I think now that it was the worst thing that happened to us. (Monk, 1994, p. 55)

In some cases families themselves were complicit in the disappearance of language and culture in order to protect their children. A father who spoke six languages in his job as a court interpreter deliberately refrained from teaching his children:

He speaks lots of Indian languages, but he won't teach us. Mom won't either. She says the nuns and priests will strap us. . . . The nuns strapped her all the time for speaking Indian, because she couldn't speak English. She said just when the welts on her hands and arms healed, she got it again. That's why she didn't want us to learn Indian. (Sterling, 1992, p. 36)

The practice may have been widespread. "Because my parents also attended residential school they didn't see the value in teaching us our language. The Indian Agent told them not to speak to their children in Haida because it would not help them in school" (R. Bell, in Jaine, 1993, p. 10).

The self-fulfilling prophecy inherent in racism came to fruition as aboriginal peoples deemed to be inferior were schooled for inequality and thereby largely did end up in the bottom ranks of Canadian society. Personal testimonies are revealing: "The residential school (not just the one I went to — they were the common form of Indian education all across Canada) was the perfect system for instilling a strong sense of inferiority" (Manuel and Posluns, 1974, p. 67). The reasons are not difficult to fathom:

For many of us our most vulnerable and impressionable years, our childhood years, were spent at the residential school where we had always been treated like dirt and made to believe that we weren't as good as other people. . . . I find it hard to believe that these schools claim to have groomed children for success when we were not allowed to be normal children. . . . The constant message [was] that because you are Native you are part of a weak, defective race, unworthy of a distinguished place in society. That is the reason you have to be looked after. . . . That to me is not training for success, it is training for self-destruction. (B. Sellers, in Jaine, 1993, p. 131)

I was frustrated about how we were treated, humiliated, and degraded, so I drank and took drugs to numb the frustrations of how my life had turned out. (A. Collison, in Jaine, 1993, p. 39)

A lot of us left residential school as mixed-up human beings, not able to cope with family or life. Many of us came out with a huge inferiority complex realizing something was missing, but not knowing what it was. Many searched for love and support in the wrong way. Girls became promiscuous,

> thinking this was the only way they could feel close to another person. Never having learned to cope with the outside world, many turned to drinking and became alcoholics. (L. Guss, in Jaine, 1993, p. 92)

For almost a century the federal government in Canada sought to control the lives and souls of aboriginal peoples. Outwardly espousing assimilation through education, the federal government neither took the leadership nor provided the resources to achieve any other goal than the self-affirming prophecy inherent in racist rhetoric. Religious denominations may have, in their view, acted from the highest of motives, but lives were damaged or destroyed nonetheless. The logic behind the concept of the residential school was muddled at best, duplicitous at worst. The system's attributes made possible no other goal than aboriginal peoples' absolute marginalization from Canadian life — a goal that schools achieved with remarkable success. Unable to consider aboriginal peoples as differing between time and place or capable of exercising control over their daily lives, federal policy deliberately bypassed the opportunity to integrate aboriginal peoples into the larger society at their own pace, a process that had begun at least in a small way in late nineteenth-century British Columbia. The Department of Indian Affairs may have saved a few dollars in the short run, but at the cost of generations of diminished and wasted lives.

THE WAY AHEAD

The past cannot be undone, but it can be better understood and acknowledged as part of our common history as Canadians. Only then can the cycle of the residential school be broken. "The silent suffering has to end. It is time for the healing to start and the only way that will happen is if we acknowledge the past, face it, understand it, deal with it, and make sure that nothing like that ever happens again" (B. Sellers, in Jaine, 1993, p. 129). The residential school was an educational misadventure in which we are all culpable.

Today the schooling of aboriginal children remains a federal responsibility overseen by the Department of Indian Affairs, although tuition agreements with provinces, bands, and churches mean that children in British Columbia, like their counterparts across Canada, no longer have a single educational option. Aboriginal children living on-reserve often attend a school operated by the local band, especially at the lower grade levels. Older children may go by bus to the nearest public school or possibly an integrated Catholic parochial school. Other on-reserve families have chosen to send their children from kindergarten on to a nearby public or parochial school. Most aboriginal children living in urban settings now attend school alongside their non-aboriginal contemporaries almost as a matter of course. Children in some urban areas also have alternative aboriginal-oriented facilities available to them. These shifts, as important as they are, only go partway. A paucity of aboriginal teachers, inadequate support for teaching aboriginal languages, and lack of appropriate aboriginal content in textbooks and in the classroom are only some of the difficulties yet to be resolved for the education of Canada's aboriginal children to become truly equal to that of other Canadian children (see Battiste and Barman, 1995).

NOTES

1. I am grateful to the Social Sciences and Humanities Research Council of Canada for funding the research on which this chapter draws, and to C. Evans, V. Giles, D. Penney, D. Whyte, and R. Wiebe for research assistance. An essay based on the same data and making many of the same points for a different audience appears in Barman, Sutherland, and Wilson (1995).

2. It is important to note that the recollections of residential schools used in this chapter do refer to a variety of schools: Ahousat (P. Webster), All Hallows (C. Clare), Christie (F. Charlie), Kamloops (G. Manuel, S. Sterling), Lejac (L. Hall, M. John, J. Monk), Port Alberni (V. Manuel, C. Thompson), St. Eugene's at Cranbrook (T. Hunter), St. George's at Lytton (S. Baker), St. Joseph's at Williams Lake (C. Johnson, B. Sellars, A. Tappage), St. Mary's Mission (M. Englund), St. Michael's at Alert Bay (C. Mack, C. Nowell), St. Paul's at North Vancouver (L. Guss), and Edmonton (R. Bell, A. Collison, sent from Haida Gwaii/Queen Charlotte Islands). Coleman (1993) used a comparable research base, consisting of just over a hundred recollections of aboriginal schooling in the United States and Canada (listed on pp. 203–8). The strengths and limitations of aboriginal first-person accounts are discussed in Brumble (1988).

3. The two years compare aboriginal and rural public schools operating in close geographical proximity: for 1899–1900, Alberni, Alert Bay, Comox, Quamichan, Saanich, and Somenos; and for 1907–08, Alert Bay, Bella Coola, Clayoquot, Hazelton, Lytton, Telegraph Creek, and Uculelet.

4. Because no breakdown of financial support for individual Indian day schools is included following the 1910 revision, mean support per pupil across British Columbia is compared with mean cost in rural public schools operating in geographical proximity to Indian day schools in Alert Bay, Bella Coola, Clayoquot, Hazelton, Lytton, Masset, Similkameen, Telegraph Creek, and Uclelet.

DISCUSSION QUESTIONS

1. In what ways did residential schools discourage aboriginal people from competing socially, economically, and intellectually with their non-aboriginal counterparts in mainstream society?

2. How did aboriginal families in British Columbia respond to residential schools?

3. What has been the legacy of residential schools for their pupils and for subsequent generations of aboriginal people who did not themselves attend the schools?

4. How has education for aboriginal people changed over the past several decades?

5. What are the strengths and weaknesses of first-person accounts for understanding aboriginal peoples' lives?

FURTHER READINGS

Assembly of First Nations. 1994. *Breaking the Silence: An Interpretive Study of Residential School Impact and Healing as Illustrated by the Stories of First Nations Individuals*. Ottawa: Assembly of First Nations. Based on thirteen interviews with former students, the Assembly of First Nations' study goes far beyond its small database in its sensitivity to the residential school experience and thoughtful recommendations for "breaking the silence."

Barman, J., Y. Hébert and D. McCaskill, eds. 1986–87. *Indian Education in Canada*, 2 vols. Vancouver: UBC Press. These companion volumes, subtitled *The Legacy* and *The Challenge*, bring together essays by aboriginal and non-aboriginal scholars and practitioners. They are concerned, respectively, with the years before and after the initiation of the Indian control of Indian education policy in the early 1970s.

Battiste, M. and J. Barman, eds. 1995. *First Nations Education in Canada: The Circle Unfolds*. Vancouver: UBC Press. Essays by aboriginal and non-aboriginal scholars conceptualize aboriginal education using a sacred circle or medicine wheel model, assess priorities, and offer perspectives on a variety of issues.

John, M. 1988. *Stoney Creek Woman: The Story of Mary John*, ed. B. Moran. Vancouver: Tillicum. This highly readable first-person account of a lifetime on a reserve in central British Columbia illustrates not so much the residential school's destructive impact as it does aboriginal peoples' resilience and strength.

Johnston, B.H. 1988. *Indian School Days*. Toronto: Key Porter. Using a powerful combination of anger and humour, the author recaptures his own residential school experience and, more generally, the broader meaning of assimilation rhetoric.

Sterling, S. 1992. *My Name Is Seepeetza*. Vancouver: Douglas & McIntyre. Shortlisted for the Governor General's award, this charming young people's novel is a fictionalized evocation of the author's years at the Kamloops Residential School.

REFERENCES

Ahenakew, E. 1973. *Voices of the Plains Cree*, ed. R.M. Buck. Toronto: McClelland & Stewart.

All Hallows School. Various years. *All Hallows in the West*. Yale, B.C.: All Hallows School.

Archibald, J. 1993. "Resistance to an Unremitting Process: Racism, Curriculum and Education in Western Canada." Pp. 93–107 and 223–27 in *The Imperial Curriculum: Racial Images and Education in the British Colonial Experience*, ed. J.A. Mangan. London: Routledge.

Assembly of First Nations (AFN). 1994. *Breaking the Silence: An Interpretive Study of Residential School Impact and Healing as Illustrated by the Stories of First Nations Individuals*. Ottawa: AFN.

Assu, H. with J. Inglis. 1989. *Assu of Cape Mudge: Recollections of a Coastal Indian Chief*. Vancouver: UBC Press.

Baker, S. 1994. *Khot-La-Cha: The Autobiography of Chief Simon Baker*, ed. V.J. Kirkness. Vancouver: Douglas & McIntyre.

Barman, J. 1986. "Separate and Unequal: Indian and White Girls at All Hallows School, 1884–1920." Pp. 110–31 in *Indian Education in Canada*, vol. 1, ed. J. Barman, Y. Hébert, and D. McCaskill. Vancouver: UBC Press.

———. 1991. *The West Beyond the West: A History of British Columbia*. Toronto: University of Toronto Press.

Barman, J., Y. Hébert, and D. McCaskill, eds. 1986–87. *Indian Education in Canada*, 2 vols. Vancouver: UBC Press.

Barman, J., N. Sutherland, and J.D. Wilson, eds. 1995. *Children, Family and Schools in the History of British Columbia*. Calgary: Detselig.

Battiste, M. and J. Barman, eds. 1995. *First Nations Education in Canada: The Circle Unfolds*. Vancouver: UBC Press.

British Columbia, Department/Ministry of Education. Various years. *Annual Report*. Victoria: the department/ministry.

British Columbia, Ministry of Education (BCME). 1995. *B.C. First Nations Studies 12: Integrated Resource Package 1995*. Victoria: the ministry.

British Columbia, Superintendent of Education (BCSE), Inward Correspondence (IC). British Columbia Archives and Records Service, Victoria, GR 1445.

Cordiner, C. (Granville). 1875. To J. Jessop. (September 16.)

Cutler, S. (Sooke). 1892. To S.D. Pope. (October 31.)

———. 1893. To S.D. Pope. (November 8.)

Deans, A. (Langley). 1876. To J. Jessop. (June 26.)

Hughett, O.N. (Genoa). 1891. To S.D. Pope. (September 21.)

Hunter, W. (Lillooet). 1886. To S.D. Pope. (August 7.)

Leduc, T. (Lillooet). 1876. To J. Jessop. (January 8.)

McAdam, W. (Port Hammond). 1891. To S.D. Pope. (November 2.)

Malpass, J. (North Cedar). 1886. To S.D. Pope. (May 17.)

Petition (Port Essington). 1888. To S.D. Pope. (August 27.)

Sheirs, M.E. (Port Kells). 1891. To S.D. Pope. (October 13.)

Shepherd, S. (Yale). 1888. To S.D. Pope. (December 2.)

Trenaman, J.E. (Hope). 1876. To J. Jessop. (October 25.)

British Columbia, Superintendent of Education (BCSE), Outward Correspondence (OC). British Columbia Archives and Records Service, Victoria, GR 450.

Jessop J. 1876. To J.E. Trenaman. (October 30.)

Pope, S.D. 1886. To J. Malpass. (May 20.)

———. 1888. To S. Shepherd. (December 15.)

———. 1889. To G. Hopkins. (July 29.)

———. 1893. To S. Cutler. (August 1.)

———. 1894. To H. Young. (March 27.)

Brumble, D.H. 1988. *American Indian Autobiography*. Berkeley: University of California Press.

Bull, L.R. 1991. "Indian Residential Schooling: The Native Perspective." *Canadian Journal of Native Education* 18 (supplement): pp. 1–64.

Cash, G. 1977. *Off the Record: The Personal Reminiscences of Canada's First Woman Reporter*. Langley, B.C.: Stagecoach.

Coates, K. 1984–85. " 'Betwixt and Between': The Anglican Church and the Children of the Carcross (Choutla) Residential School, 1911–1954." *BC Studies* 64 (Winter): pp. 27–47.

Department of Indian Affairs (DIA). Various years. *Annual Report*. Ottawa: the department.

Department of Indian Affairs and Northern Development (DIAND). 1995. *Basic Departmental Data: 1994*. Ottawa: the department.

Dominion Bureau of Statistics. Various years. *Annual Survey of Education*. Ottawa: the bureau.

Ferrier, T. 1906. *Indian Education in the Northwest*. Toronto: Department of Missionary Literature of the Methodist Church.

Fiske, J. 1989. "Life at Lejac." Pp. 235–72 in *Sa Ts'e: Historical Perspectives on Northern British Columbia*, ed. T. Thorner. Prince George: College of New Caledonia Press.

———. 1991. "Gender and the Paradox of Residential Education in Carrier Society." Pp. 131–46 in *Women and Education*, 2nd ed., ed. J. Gaskell and A. McLaren. Calgary: Detselig.

Furniss, E. 1992. *Victims of Benevolence: Discipline and Death at the Williams Lake Indian Residential School, 1891–1920*. Williams Lake, B.C.: Cariboo Tribal Council.

Grant, J.W. 1984. *Moon of Wintertime: Missionaries and the Indians of Canada in Encounter Since 1534*. Toronto: University of Toronto Press.

Gresko, J. 1979. "White 'Rites' and Indian 'Rites': Indian Education and Native Responses in the West, 1870–1910." Pp. 163–81 in *Shaping the Schools of the Canadian West*, ed. D.C. Jones, N.M. Sheehan, and R.M. Stamp. Calgary: Detselig.

———. 1986. "Creating Little Dominions Within the Dominion: Early Catholic Indian Schools in Saskatchewan and British Columbia." Pp. 88–109 in *Indian Education in Canada*, vol. 1, ed. J. Barman, Y. Hébert, and D. McCaskill. Vancouver: UBC Press.

Haegert, D. 1983. *Children of the First People*. Vancouver: Tillicum.

Haig-Brown, C. 1988. *Resistance and Renewal: Surviving the Indian Residential School*. Vancouver: Tillicum.

Hall, L. 1992. *The Carrier. My People*. Fort St. James, B.C.: [n.p.].

Harper, M. 1993. "*Mush-Hole*": *Memories of a Residential School*. Toronto: Sister Vision Press.

Hendrick, I.G. 1981. "The Federal Campaign for the Admission of Indian Children into Public Schools, 1890–1934." *American Indian Culture and Research Journal* 5: pp. 13–32.

Hodgson, M. 1991. Rebuilding Community After the Residential School Experience." Pp. 101–12 in *Nation to Nation: Aboriginal Sovereignty and the Future of Canada*, ed. D. Engelstead and J. Bird. Toronto: Anansi.

Jaine, L. 1991. "Industrial and Residential School Administration: The Attempt to Undermine Indigenous Self-Determination." *Journal of Indigenous Studies* 2: pp. 37–48.

———, ed. 1993. *Residential Schools: The Stolen Years*. Saskatoon: Extension University Press, University of Saskatchewan.

Jenness, D. 1983. "Canada's Indians Yesterday: What of Today?" Pp. 158–63 in *As Long as the Sun Shines and Water Flows: A Reader in Canadian Native Studies*, ed. A.L. Getty and A.S. Lussier. Vancouver: UBC Press. Originally published in 1954 in *Canadian Journal of Economic and Political Science* 20(1).

John, M. 1988. *Stoney Creek Woman: The Story of Mary John*, ed. B. Moran. Vancouver: Tillicum.

Johnston, B.H. 1988. *Indian School Days*. Toronto: Key Porter.

Knockwood, I. with G. Thomas. 1992. *Out of the Depths: The Experience of Mi'kmaw Children at the Indian Residential School at Shubenacadie, Nova Scotia*. Lockeport, N.S.: Roseway.

Lascelles, T.A. 1990. *Roman Catholic Residential Schools in British Columbia*. Vancouver: Order of OMI in British Columbia.

Mack, C. 1993. *Grizzlies and White Guys: The Stories of Clayton Mack*, ed. H. Thommasen. Madeira Park, B.C.: Harbour.

Mair, C. 1892. To George Denison, Okanagan Mission. December 5. In Mair Correspondence in possession of D. Thomson and used with permission.

Manuel, G. and M. Posluns. 1974. *The Fourth World: An Indian Reality*. Toronto: Collier Macmillan.

Miller, J.R. 1991. "Owen Glendower, Hotspur, and Canadian Indian policy." Pp. 323–52 in *Sweet Promises: A Reader on Indian–White Relations in Canada*, ed.

J.R. Miller. Toronto: University of Toronto Press. Originally published in 1990 in *Ethnohistory* 37(4).

Millward, M. 1992. "Clean Behind the Ears? Micmac Parents, Micmac Children, and the Shubenacadie Residential School." *New Maritimes* (March/April): pp. 6–15.

Mitchell, M. and A. Franklin. 1984. "When You Don't Know the Language, Listen to the Silence: An Historical Overview of Native Indian Women in BC." Pp. 17–35 in *Not Just Pin Money: Selected Essays on the History of Women's Work in British Columbia*, ed. B.K. Latham and R.J. Pazdro. Victoria: Camosun College.

Monk, J. 1994. *Justa: A First Nations Leader*, ed. B. Moran. Vancouver: Arsenal Pulp Press.

News Advertiser. 1902. Vancouver. August 10.

Niehaus, V. 1978. "Mrs. Sharon McIvor Grismer." *Nicola Valley Historical Quarterly* 1(4): p. 7.

Nowell, C.J. 1941. *Smoke from Their Fires: The Life of a Kwakiutl Chief*, ed. C.S. Ford. New Haven, Conn.: Yale University Press.

Purvis, R. 1994. *T'shama*. Surrey, B.C.: Heritage House.

Roy, P.E. 1984. "*The West Shore*'s View of British Columbia, 1884." *Journal of the West* 22(4): 26–32.

Satzewich, V. and L. Mahood. 1995. "Indian Agents and the Residential School System in Canada, 1946–1970." *Historical Studies in Education* 7: pp. 45–69.

Senese, G.B. 1991. *Self-Determination and the Social Education of Native Americans*. New York: Praeger.

Sewid, J. 1959. *Guests Never Leave Hungry: The Autobiography of James Sewid, a Kwakiutl Indian*, ed. J.P. Spradley. New Haven, Conn.: Yale University Press.

Sluman, N. and J. Goodwill. 1982. *John Tootoosis: A Biography of a Cree Leader*. Ottawa: Golden Dog Press.

Statistics Canada. 1993. *1991 Aboriginal Peoples Survey: Schooling, Work and Related Activities, Income, Expenses and Mobility*. Ottawa: Supply and Services.

Sterling, S. 1992. *My Name Is Seepeetza*. Vancouver: Douglas & McIntyre.

Szasz, M.C. 1977. *Education and the American Indian: The Road to Self-Determination Since 1928*. Albuquerque: University of New Mexico Press.

Szasz, M.C. and C. Ryan. 1988. "American Indian Education." Pp. 284–301 in *Handbook of North American Indians*, vol. 4, *History of Indian–White Relations*, ed. W.E. Washburn. Washington, D.C.: Smithsonian Institution.

Tappage, A. 1973. *The Days of Augusta*, ed. J.E. Speare. Vancouver: J.J. Douglas.

Tennant, P. 1990. *Aboriginal Peoples and Politics: The Indian Land Question in British Columbia, 1849–1989*. Vancouver: UBC Press.

Titley, E.B. 1984. "Duncan Campbell Scott and Indian Educational Policy." Pp. 141–53 in *An Imperfect Past: Education and Society in Canadian history*, ed. J.D. Wilson. Vancouver: Centre for the Study of Curriculum and Instruction, University of British Columbia.

———. 1986. "Indian Industrial Schools in Western Canada." Pp. 133–53 in *Schools in the West: Essays in Canadian Educational History*, ed. N.M. Sheehan, J.D. Wilson, and D.C. Jones. Calgary: Detselig.

———. 1993. "Industrial Education for Manitoba Natives: The Case of Rupert's Land Indian School." Pp. 371–403 in *Issues in the History of Education in Manitoba: From the Construction of the Common School to the Politics of Voices*, ed. R.C. Bruno-Jofee. Lewiston, Md.: Edwin Mellon Press.

University School. 1912. *Prospectus*. Victoria: University School.

Webster, P.S. 1983. *As Far as I Know: Reminiscences of an Ahousat Elder*. Campbell River, B.C.: Campbell River Museum and Archives.

Whitehead, M. 1981. *Now You Are My Brother: Missionaries in British Columbia*. Sound Heritage Series No. 34. Victoria: Provincial Archives of British Columbia.

CHAPTER 11

Aboriginal People in Urban Areas

Evelyn Peters

T here have always been aboriginal people living in urban areas in Canada, though for much of Canada's history since contact, non-aboriginal Canadians have tended to view the presence of aboriginal people in urban areas with misgivings. This chapter addresses the source of these misgivings, and suggests alternative views of aboriginal people and urban life.

The largest increase in the urban aboriginal[1] population has occurred since the early 1950s. After 1960, a substantial literature emerged that addressed the implications of this movement to cities. Although attention to the issue had declined by the late 1980s, the urban aboriginal population had not, and the 1991 census suggested that many cities had substantial numbers of people with aboriginal origins living in them. Now, public attention seems again to be drawn to urban aboriginal people. In 1992, the Royal Commission on Aboriginal Peoples identified urban aboriginal people as an important emphasis in their research. Urban aboriginal people have been featured in chapters in recent books on aboriginal people generally (Comeau and Santin, 1990; Frideres, 1993; Richardson, 1994), a bibliography (Kastes, 1993), and a book of "life stories" (Shorten, 1991).

There has been almost no writing by aboriginal people on the experience of migrating to and living in urban areas. Most of the available literature comes from non-aboriginal academics, consultants, researchers. From the beginning, aboriginal urbanization has been presented as problematic in this literature. The way this "social problem" was defined provided a framework for identifying appropriate policy responses. There is evidence that this framework is increasingly being challenged by aboriginal people. In this context, it is appropriate to provide a critical assessment of non-aboriginal writing about aboriginal urbanization.

The primary object of this chapter is not to explore the situation of aboriginal people in urban areas. The works cited above are available to interested readers, and there will be more information available in the near future from research published by the Royal Commission on Aboriginal

Peoples. Moreover, I am not an aboriginal person; I am an academic of Dutch and Ukrainian origins who is not qualified to speak about the urban experience for aboriginal people. What I do feel qualified to write about, in a critical way, is how I and my peers have conceptualized the situation of urban aboriginal people, what some of the implications have been, and what are some possible ways forward.[2]

The chapter begins with a brief profile of aboriginal people and organizations in urban areas. Next, it compares aboriginal urbanization patterns with cycles of public interest in their situation. The chapter then moves to an exploration of how aboriginal people in cities have been labelled problematic, and how this problem has been characterized. The final sections of the chapter present an alternative approach, and identify some ways to make cities better places for aboriginal people and cultures.

A PROFILE OF CONTEMPORARY URBAN ABORIGINAL PEOPLE

Population Characteristics

A brief profile of the characteristics of aboriginal people in urban areas cannot possibly do justice to all the important issues facing this population, nor can it depict the diversity of urban aboriginal populations or of urban areas. The following paragraphs highlight five themes: urbanization rates in 1991; socio-economic, legal, and cultural characteristics; and urban institutions.

In 1991, about half (49.5 percent) of those who identified themselves[3] as aboriginal people in Canada lived in urban areas (Table 11.1). Urbanization rates varied for different groups of aboriginal people. A little over 40 percent of registered Indians lived in cities. In comparison, the majority of non-registered Indians and Métis live in urban areas. The Inuit are the least urbanized of all the aboriginal groups.

Until recently, there was very little statistical information available on the socio-economic characteristics of urban aboriginal people across the country. Surveys conducted in 1978 and 1982 by the Institute of Urban Studies in Winnipeg provided information about aboriginal people in Winnipeg, Saskatoon, and Regina (Clatworthy, 1980; Clatworthy and Hull, 1983), but there was little in the way of more recent information that provided wider geographic coverage. Data from the Aboriginal Peoples Survey demonstrate that many of the attributes highlighted for urban aboriginal people in these prairie cities hold in other urban areas and in recent years. Table 11.2 shows that the urban aboriginal population tends to be younger than the total urban population, with a higher proportion of women, particularly in the main childbearing years. Unemployment rates are much higher for aboriginal people than for total metropolitan populations, and many more aboriginal people had relatively low incomes.

TABLE 11.1
LOCATION OF RESIDENCE, ABORIGINAL IDENTITY POPULATION,[1] 1991

	Total aboriginal[2]	Registered North American Indian[3]	Non-registered American Indian[4]	Métis[5]	Inuit
Total	625 710	351 590	104 260	135 260	36 215
On-reserve	183 600 (29.3%)	173 655 (49.4%)	3 600 (3.5%)	4 535 (3.4%)	620 (1.7%)
Off-reserve	412 105 (70.7%)	177 940 (50.6%)	100 660 (96.5%)	130 725 (96.6%)	35 590 (98.2%)
Urban,[6] off-reserve	309 940 (49.5%)	143 910 (40.9%)	72 150 (69.3%)	87 850 (64.9%)	7 151 (21.9%)

[1] These data have not been adjusted for incomplete enumeration or undercoverage.

[2] Because some respondents (about 1 percent) gave multiple aboriginal identities, summing identity categories will result in overcounting. The "Total aboriginal" category does not double-count those giving multiple aboriginal identities.

[3] The North American Indian population registered according to the Indian Act of Canada. This category excludes: 4830 North American Indians with registration status not stated in the APS; 17 060 Métis who reported being registered according to the Indian Act (they are counted as Métis); 2080 Inuit who reported being registered according to the Indian Act (they are counted as Inuit); and an estimated 58 000 persons residing on unenumerated Indian reserves or settlements.

[4] Those who identified themselves as North American Indian who were not registered according to the Indian Act.

[5] Those who identified themselves as Métis.

[6] This number does not include urban reserves.

Source: Privy Council Office, Royal Commission on Aboriginal Peoples, Research Directorate, Customized Data from the 1991 Aboriginal Peoples Survey, pp. 20-21, Ottawa: Minister of Supply and Services, 1994. Reproduced with the permission of the Minister of Supply and Services, Canada, 1995.

Although there were some aboriginal people earning incomes of $40 000 and more, the proportion was much lower than the total metropolitan population. Because of their low incomes, aboriginal people are more likely to live in poor housing. As other researchers have found, migration rates are similar for aboriginal and non-aboriginal people.

It is important to recognize, however, the variation in the characteristics of the aboriginal population in different urban areas. Table 11.3 compares major Canadian cities with respect to some characteristics of aboriginal residents. These data are based on the population that identified itself as aboriginal in the Aboriginal Peoples Survey (APS).[4] The number of aboriginal people varies from slightly more than 1000 in Halifax to over 35 000 in Winnipeg. Aboriginal people comprise the largest proportion of the

TABLE 11.2
Socio-Economic Characteristics of People Who Identify Themselves as Aboriginal in Selected Census Metropolitan Areas[1]

	Aboriginal identity population	Total metropolitan population
Total	159 945	16 665 360
Ages 0–14	35.9%	19.8%
Females in 25+ population	57.5%	52.1%
Unemployment rate	23.4%	9.4%
Adults 15+ with total income less than $10 000	48.4%	25.3%
Adults 15+ with total income greater than $40 000	6.4%	19.0%
Residence needs major repairs	12.8%	6.9%
Moved between 1986 and 1991	46.1%	50.4%
Moved in last 12 Months	20.4%	17.6%

[1] Data are available for Halifax, Montreal, Ottawa–Hull, Toronto, Winnipeg, Regina, Saskatoon, Calgary, Edmonton, Vancouver, and Victoria.

Sources: Statistics Canada, 1991 Census, cat. nos. 93-339 and 93-340, Ottawa: Minister of Industry, 1991; Royal Commission on Aboriginal Peoples, Aboriginal Peoples Survey, cat. no. 94-327. Ottawa, 1991.

metropolitan populations of Regina and Saskatoon. Cultural characteristics also vary. Prairie cities contain the largest number of Métis people. They also contain the most people who understand an aboriginal language. The latter dimension varies from 14.1 percent in Montreal to 61.1 percent in Saskatoon. With respect to socio-economic characteristics, unemployment rates are highest in Saskatoon (32.7 percent) and lowest in Toronto (11.2 percent).

Aboriginal people living in urban areas are subject to a complicated legal regime. According to the APS, Indians registered under the Indian Act of Canada constituted the largest legal category. The federal government has held that it was responsible only for registered Indians and that these responsibilities were limited to reserve borders (Morse, 1989). Only a few federally funded services are available to registered Indians generally, no matter where they live. The most notable of these are non-insured health benefits and post-secondary educational assistance. The federal government has regarded non-registered Indians and Métis as a provincial responsibility. In 1939, the courts ruled that the Inuit would be considered as Indians for the purposes of clarifying federal jurisdiction.

These categories are further complicated by differences between registration status and band membership. Under Bill C-31, passed in 1985, registration and band membership were separated. After Bill C-31, bands were given the opportunity to draw up and adopt codes governing

TABLE 11.3
SELECTED CHARACTERISTICS OF PEOPLE WHO IDENTIFY THEMSELVES AS
ABORIGINAL IN MAJOR METROPOLITAN AREAS,[1] 1991

	Number who identify as aboriginal	% of city population	% Métis	% who understand aboriginal language	Unemployment rate	% 15+ who moved since 1986
Halifax	1 185	0.3	—	—	—	38.2
Montreal	6 775	0.4	24.7	14.1[2]	13.1	42.1
Ottawa–Hull	6 915	0.8	20.6	22.2[2]	12.7	47.0
Toronto	14 205	0.2	5.6[2]	25.3[2]	11.2	36.1
Winnipeg	35 150	3.3	21.3	49.1	27.3	44.1
Regina	11 020	4.1	33.8	49.2	25.8	57.8
Saskatoon	11 920	3.8	46.9	61.1	32.7	44.2
Calgary	14 075	0.9	30.4	37.3	18.1	52.5
Edmonton	29 235	2.0	46.2	50.2	28.1	46.1
Vancouver	25 030	0.8	16.3	39.6	29.0	49.4
Victoria	4 435	1.2	7.8[2]	38.5[2]	19.5	40.2

[1] Data are available for Halifax, Montreal, Ottawa–Hull, Toronto, Winnipeg, Regina, Saskatoon, Calgary, Edmonton, Vancouver, and Victoria.
[2] The coefficient of variation of the estimate is between 16.7% and 33.3%. These estimates should be used with caution to support a conclusion.

Sources: Statistics Canada, 1991 Census, cat. no. 94-327, Ottawa: Minister of Industry, 1993; Royal Commission on Aboriginal Peoples, Aboriginal Peoples Survey, cat. nos. 94-327, 89-533, and 89-534, Ottawa, 1991.

membership, while registration continues to be governed according to (revised) Indian Act regulations. Band membership involves a variety of rights and privileges with respect to an individual's band of origin, including rights of residency on the reserve. Some urban aboriginal people are registered but are not band members, while some are band members but are not registered.

The complex amalgam of legal categories that has emerged has created inequalities for and among urban aboriginal people. Registered Indians living on-reserve have access to federally funded programs not available to urban Indians. Registered Indians in urban areas have access to some federally funded programs that other aboriginal people do not have. Band members have opportunities to participate in self-government through their bands of origin. These opportunities are denied to aboriginal people who do not have band membership.[5] Although some urban programs have been established through federal, provincial, and municipal funding, these initiatives are unevenly distributed, with short-term and often limited funding.

TABLE 11.4
ORIGINS OF THE ABORIGINAL POPULATION, REGINA, SASKATCHEWAN, 1982

First Nations

Reserve origins: 27 reserves in Saskatchewan plus others in other provinces

Treaty area of origin: Treaty numbers 1, 2, 3, 4, 5, 6, 7, and 9

First Nation of origin: Assiniboine, Blackfoot, Cree, Dakota, Ojibwa, and possibly others

Provincial origins: British Columbia, Alberta, Saskatchewan, Manitoba, Ontario, and Nova Scotia

Countries of origin: Canada and the United States

Métis

Provincial origins: British Columbia, Alberta, Saskatchewan, Manitoba, Ontario, and Nova Scotia

Countries of origin: Canada and the United States

Source: Peters, 1994.

The cultural diversity of aboriginal people in urban areas is not often recognized. Although published data on cultural origins are not available from the Aboriginal Peoples Survey, information about aboriginal people living in Regina in 1982 is suggestive (Table 11.4). First Nations people living in the city came from 27 reserves, eight treaty areas, at least five First Nations, six provinces, and two countries. Métis people came from five provinces and two countries. Many other cities must demonstrate comparable heterogeneity.

Researchers in the past commented on the paucity of aboriginal institutions representing or providing services for urban aboriginal people (Clatworthy and Gunn, 1981; Falconer, 1985, 1990; Frideres, 1984). At present, however, many large urban areas have a considerable number of organizations controlled and staffed by aboriginal people, whose focus is the permanent urban aboriginal population. Winnipeg appears to be among urban centres with the most well-developed set of urban aboriginal institutions (Table 11.5).[6] While some of these organizations have a very long history, many have been established only in recent years. Collectively, these organizations provide a fairly broad range of services to aboriginal people.

There are several features of the Winnipeg situation that appear to be unique. Unlike most urban areas with large aboriginal populations, Winnipeg has two organizations, the Aboriginal Centre Inc. and the Winnipeg Native Family Economic Development Corporation (WNFED), which have focussed on community development and attempted to provide inter-agency links and networks.[7] The Aboriginal Centre Inc. recently purchased Winnipeg's CPR station in the heart of Winnipeg's core area, with the

TABLE 11.5
ABORIGINAL INSTITUTIONS IN WINNIPEG, 1994

Organization	Primary focus	Year established
A-Bah-Nu-Gee Child Care	Child and family services	1984
Aboriginal Centre Inc.	Social service, community and economic development	1990
Aboriginal Council of Winnipeg	Political	1990
Aboriginal Literacy Foundation	Education	1990
Aiyawin Corporation	Housing	1983
Anishinabe Oway-Ishi	Employment	1989
Anishinabe RESPECT	Employment	1981
Bear Clan Patrol Inc.	Safety	1992
Children of the Earth High School	Education	1991
Indian Family Centre Inc.	Religious/social service	1973
Indian Métis Friendship Centre	Cultural/social service	1959
Iwkewak Justice Society	Justice	1986
Kinew Housing	Housing	1970
Ma Mawi Chi Itata Centre	Child and family services	1984
Manitoba Association for Native Languages	Language education	1984
MMF — Winnipeg Region	Political	n.a.
Native Clan	Inmates	1970
Native Employment Services	Employment	1972
Native United Church	Religious	n.a.
Native Women's Transition Centre	Housing	n.a.
Nee-Gawn-Ah-Kai Day Care Centre	Child care	1986
Neechi Foods Community Store	Economic Development	n.a.
Original Women's Network	Women's resource centre	n.a.
Payuk Inter-Trival Housing Co-op	Housing	1985
Three Fires Society	Cultural	1982
Winnipeg Council of First Nations	Political	1991
Winnipeg Native Families Economic Development Corporation	Social service, community and economic development	n.a.

n.a. Not available or unknown.

Source: Clatworthy et al., 1995; Peters, 1995.

objective of bringing under one roof a variety of aboriginal organizations. The building would provide a critical mass of aboriginal services, provide a place for aboriginal activities, and serve as a focal point for the urban aboriginal community. WNFED is an umbrella organization created to bring together a number of different projects in order to provide linkage and a support network within the aboriginal community. Winnipeg also

TABLE 11.6

TOTAL AND OFF-RESERVE REGISTERED INDIAN POPULATION, 1959–1991

	Registered Indian population	Off-reserve		Enfranchisements[1] per five-year period	
		Number[2]	Percent	Number	Percent
1959[3]	179 126	30 372	16.9		
1961	191 709			2077	1.1[4]
1966	224 164	43 746	19.5	3216	1.4
1971	257 619	69 106	26.8	3009	1.2
1976	288 938	79 301	27.4	1094	0.4
1981	323 782	96 290	29.6	40	0.01
1986[5]	415 898	123 642	31.9	14	0.00
1991	511 791	207 032	40.5		

[1] The Indian Register only records individuals who maintain their registration under the Indian Act. It is possible that a substantial number of Indians gave up their status under the Indian Act, or enfranchised, and moved to cities during this period. However, enfranchisement rates do not bear out this possibility. Department of Indian Affairs records indicate that enfranchisements between 1876 and 1948 totalled about 4000 (Canada, Joint Committee, 1960b, p. 539). Data available for 1959–85 indicate that, historically, the proportion of the registered Indian population opting for enfranchisement has been relatively low. Subsequent to Bill C-31, passed in 1985, enfranchisement is no longer an option.
[2] Not including those living on Crown land.
[3] Statistics on off-reserve residency began to be collected only in 1959 (Bradley, 1993).
[4] Figures for 1961 and 1966 are estimates based on DIAND's fiscal year; figures for 1971 to 1986 are based on the calendar year.
[5] In 1985, the Indian Act was amended by Bill C-31 to allow the restoration of Indian status to those who had lost it due to discriminatory clauses in the Indian Act.

Sources: Information Canada, *Perspective Canada: A Compendium of Social Statistics*, p. 244, Ottawa: Minister of Industry, 1974; DIAND, *Indian Affairs: Facts and Figures*, Ottawa: Indian Affairs Branch, 1967; DIAND, *Basic Departmental Data*, p. 5, Ottawa: Minister of Supply and Services, 1992; Powless, J., DIAND, personal communication, 1994.

appears to be unique in that it has Métis, First Nations, and pan-aboriginal political organizations functioning simultaneously. Like many other aboriginal political bodies, these organizations are exploring self-governance options (Helgason, 1995).

Urbanization Patterns

It is difficult to build up a reliable historical picture of the movement of aboriginal people to Canadian cities. Changing definitions of ancestry in census data (Goldman, 1993) make it difficult to compare population numbers over time. The Indian Register kept by the Department of Indian Affairs omits Métis and non-registered Indian people, dates only from 1959, and identifies residence on- or off-reserve, but not in particular cities.[8] Despite problems with finding accurate, comparable data, it

TABLE 11.7
ABORIGINAL PEOPLE IN MAJOR METROPOLITAN CENTRES, 1951–1991

	1951	1961	1971[1]	1981	1991[2]
Halifax	—	—	—	—	1 185
Montreal	296	507	3215	14 450	6 775[3]
Ottawa–Hull	—	—	—	4 370	6 915
Toronto	805	1196	2990	13 495	14 205
Winnipeg	210	1082	4940	16575	35 150
Regina	160	539	2860	6 575	11 020
Saskatoon	48	207	1070	4 350	11 920
Calgary	62	335	2265	7 310	14 075
Edmonton	616	995	4260	13 750	29 235
Vancouver	239	530	3000	16 080	25 030
Victoria	—	—	—	2 800	4 435

[1] The 1971 data do not include the Inuit.
[2] Individuals who identified with an aboriginal group in the Aboriginal Peoples Survey.
[3] The population for the Kahnawake and Kanesatake reserves, which are in the Montreal metropolitan area boundaries, were not enumerated in 1981 or 1991. Population estimates (5218 and 618 respectively) were included in 1981 counts but not included in the 1991 counts.

Source: Statistics Canada, Census and Aboriginal Peoples Survey, cat. no. 94-327, Ottawa: Minister of Industry, 1993; Statistics Canada, DIAND customized data, 1981; Information Canada, Perspective Canada: A Compendium of Social Statistics, p. 244, Ottawa: Minister of Industry, 1974.

appears that aboriginal urbanization is a comparatively recent phenomenon. In this section, data from the Indian Register, the Aboriginal Peoples Survey, and the census are analyzed to provide a picture of aboriginal populations in urban areas.

Although early studies show that, even in the 1950s, some aboriginal people had been relatively long-term residents of cities (Boek and Boek, 1959, p. 20; Davis, 1965, p. 372; Lurie, 1967), overall urbanization rates appear to have been low. There is no statistical information available about Métis urbanization trends, but it appears that relatively few registered Indians left their reserves between the turn of the century and the 1950s. In 1959, only 16.9 percent of registered Indians lived off-reserve, with probably an even smaller proportion resident in cities (Table 11.6). In 1981, 29.6 percent of registered Indians lived off-reserve, and by 1991 that proportion had increased to 40.5 percent.

Table 11.7 shows census statistics on the changing number of people with aboriginal ancestry in major metropolitan centres. Data for the years 1951 to 1981 in this table are based on answers to the census question on ethnic origin or ancestry. Although the data for various years are not directly comparable because of changing definitions and questions on census forms (Goldman, 1993), they present some rough estimates of the size of the urban aboriginal population. Changes in the census question on ancestry make it impossible to compare 1991 data with data for earlier years.[9] The 1991 statistics are from the Aboriginal Peoples Survey, which asked individuals who reported aboriginal ancestry in the census whether they identified with an aboriginal group. If the 1981 method of collecting information about ancestry had been used, these numbers would probably be greater.

In interpreting these statistics, it is important to remember that changes in census statistics on urban aboriginal populations are not only a function of migration, but also a reflection of changing patterns of self-identification as aboriginal, natural increase, and the addition of Bill C-31 populations,[10] as well as changing definitions of ancestry and methods of data collection. Despite these caveats, it is clear from Table 11.7 that, while the number of people with aboriginal origins in major cities was very low in 1951,[11] the numbers steadily increased in the following decades. By 1991, several prairie cities had very substantial populations of aboriginal people, and it is likely that for many cities, the absolute increase between 1981 and 1991 was greater than the increase between 1971 and 1981.

WRITING ABOUT ABORIGINAL URBANIZATION

Changes in the degree of public interest in urban aboriginal people do not reflect changes in their numbers in cities. Although issues concerning aboriginal people were very much in the public eye in the late 1800s, they seemed to fade in importance after the turn of the century (Tobias, 1983). As public interest in aboriginal issues revived in the mid-1900s, federal and provincial governments commissioned an array of studies into the conditions of aboriginal people (Davis, 1965, p. 519; Hawthorn et al., 1958, p. 84; Hawthorn, 1966–67; Lagasse, 1958). An overriding theme in many of these studies was the depressed social and economic conditions of reserves and rural Métis settlements. As these conditions came to public attention, policy-makers looked to urbanization for at least a partial solution. Even without public policy intervention, rapid population growth on reserves made out-migration seem inevitable.

The prospect of the rapid migration of aboriginal peoples to cities challenged academics, citizens' groups, and policy-makers to formulate what the "urban experience" meant for migrants and for cities. A large body of literature on the topic, academic and policy-oriented, emerged after the late 1960s and continued to the mid-1970s. A number of studies appeared in the early 1980s, many associated with statistical surveys of aboriginal people in Winnipeg, Regina, and Saskatoon conducted by the Institute of Urban Studies at the University of Winnipeg. Relatively little was published on urban aboriginal people after 1985. As a result, there is little current work available[12] with respect to urban aboriginal people, and Kastes's (1993, p. 56) recent overview of the literature on aboriginal urbanization concluded as follows:

The literature on urban Aboriginal issues in Canada is sparse, limited in scope, largely dated in relevance. . . . Given the significant changes which have occurred in Canada, as well as within the Aboriginal communities themselves since the mid 1980s, the existing literature is of limited use for contemporary policy and program development.

"Large numbers appear threatening," states Larry Krotz (1980, p. 50) in his journalistic account of urban aboriginal people in prairie cities. However, the interest in urban aboriginal issues does not appear to be related to numbers. Nor is the decline in interest due to the fact that urban aboriginal people were being integrated into the economic mainstream in urban areas. These factors suggest that it is not only the objective conditions and numbers of urban aboriginal people that contribute to public interest in aboriginal urbanization, but also interpretations of its significance and frameworks of meaning through which aboriginal peoples' migration to cities was understood. In what follows, I suggest that cycles and themes in writing about urban aboriginal people reflect ideas about the relationship between aboriginal culture and urban life.

Constructing Aboriginal Urbanization as a Problem

From the earliest writing on aboriginal people in cities, their presence was constructed as a problem.[13] Even in the 1950s, when very few aboriginal people lived in Canadian cities, many employers, municipal governments, and members of the general public viewed aboriginal migration to cities with apprehension. On the basis of his Manitoba survey, Lagasse (1958, p. 167) concluded that "the belief that an Indian's place is on the reserve is still very strong among the Canadian people." The Saskatchewan government's 1960 submission to the Joint Committee of the Senate and the House of Commons warned that "the day is not far distant when the burgeoning Indian population, now largely confined to reservations, will explode into white communities and present a serious problem indeed" (Canada, 1960c, p. 1083). Buckley's (1992, pp. 72–76) review of attitudes toward aboriginal employment in northern prairie resource towns in the 1950s and 1960s concluded that, in public opinion, there was no place for aboriginal people in these communities. Other writers also noted the intense hostility of townspeople in the mid-1900s to aboriginal residents and visitors (Braroe, 1975; Brody, 1983; Lithman, 1984; Robertson, 1970; Shimpo and Williamson, 1965; Stymeist, 1975).

Although materials from mid-century on demonstrate agreement that migration to cities would create problems for aboriginal people (Canada, 1960a, p. 369; Canadian Corrections Association, 1967, pp. 7–8; Regina Welfare Council, 1959), there were also worries about the state of cities — about how to maintain property values, keep down welfare rolls, and prevent inner-city decay (Hirabayashi, 1962; Indian-Eskimo Association, 1960; Lagasse, 1958, p. 167).[14] John Melling, former executive director of the Indian-Eskimo Association, chastised federal, provincial, and municipal governments for being concerned about First Nations peoples only when the conditions of inner cities were seen to be threatened. His statement, however, also reflects attitudes toward aboriginal urbanization at the time:

> One hundred and sixty thousand Indians may wither in their reserves. . . . But bring even one-quarter of that number into our towns, or to fester in city tenements and shanty slums . . . and that situation is quite intolerable. If the rot can be confined to the lives of Indians alone and if it can remain hidden from the rest of us, that is one thing; if it begins to affect the lives of others and becomes an open eyesore, that is another thing. (Melling, 1967, p. 72)

Aboriginal people were still conceptualized as a threat to cities in the 1970s. The introduction to a 1977 report for the city of Winnipeg stated:

> [A] major in-migration of generally low skilled, minimally educated . . . and relatively impoverished people will serve to exacerbate the increasing expenditure and services demands. Beyond this, native urbanization will pose specific and unique problems and situations for both the City of Winnipeg and native people themselves. (Reiber-Kremers, 1977, p. 1)

The government of Saskatchewan's urban Native initiative in the late 1970s linked urban aboriginal people and inner-city deterioration (Saskatchewan, 1979). More recently, Kastes (1993, p. 83) argued that the situation of aboriginal people constituted a serious challenge for prairie cities:

> In recent years, Aboriginal urbanization issues have received little attention from researchers despite the fact that the social, economic and political problems within the urban Aboriginal community represent, by all accounts, one of the most serious and complex set of issues currently affecting urban environments.

Assigning the Source of the Problem

The nature or source of the problem as identified by researchers and policy-makers has changed over time. A common theme in the literature on aboriginal urbanization before the 1980s was that aboriginal culture[15] presents a major barrier to successful adjustment to urban society. A 1957 Calgary conference on Aboriginal people in urban areas, organized by the National Commission on the Indian Canadian (later the Indian-Eskimo Association), clearly enunciated this view. Delegates representing churches, labour, government, and community groups concluded that as follows:

> Our Indian Canadian is faced or hampered with . . . his own personality. The Indian Canadian is different from his fellow Canadians of European descent. . . . These differences are from his cultural heritage. . . . For instance, his concepts of time, money, social communication, hygiene, usefulness, competition and cooperation are at variance with our own and can prove a stumbling block to successful adjustment. (Canada, 1957, p. 3)

TABLE 11.8
RESERVE-CITY CULTURAL DIFFERENCES

Reserve characteristics	City characteristics
• Cultural homogenity	• Cultural heterogeneity
• Economic activity requires generalized skills	• Occupational specialization
• Natural environment	• Manufactured environment
• Social life characterized by primary relationships, community, informality, personal relationships	• Social life characterized by class structure, formal relationships, anonymity
• Work is task-oriented; it is one aspect of life and does not confer status; it is independent and unsupervised	• Work is time-oriented, separate from personal life, and the main source of status and satisfaction; is supervised and directed
• Ties with kin and to the land result in a deep attachment to place and may interfere with geographic mobility	• Nuclear families and occupational specialization result in a weak attachment to place and do not inhibit economic and geographic mobility

Source: Zeitoun, 1969.

In *Indians in the City*, a book based on his Ph.D. research in Toronto, Nagler wrote:

> While urban living is not foreign to most European immigrants, it is a completely new way of life for the Indian. The highly generalized characteristics described as "being Indian" affect the Indian's ability to urbanize. . . . Indians thus experience difficulty in adjusting to a new environment because their conceptions of living do not involve punctuality, responsibility, hurry, impersonality, frugality, and the other social practices which are a part of the urban environment." (1970, p. 25)

Zeitoun's (1969) review for the Department of Manpower and Immigration contrasted reserve and urban cultures and identified these differences as underlying the dislocation of urban Indians (Table 11.8). Adaptation to the urban environment, according to Zeitoun and others, required a change in cultural values and orientation.[16]

These views were still current in the late 1970s. A consultant's report (Reiber-Kremers, 1977, p. 2) to the city of Winnipeg, for example, indicated that the problems of aboriginal people "stem from major cultural differences, lack of familiarity with wage economy participation as well as urban lifestyles." Although some writers challenged these interpretations (for example, Elias, 1975; Lurie, 1967; Price and McCaskill, 1974), the overriding emphasis in the literature of the 1960s and 1970s was on the incompatibility of aboriginal culture and urban life and the need to abandon cultural values in order to adapt to the urban setting.

The "problem" of aboriginal urbanization was largely redefined in work after 1980,[17] and explicit mention of issues concerning aboriginal culture virtually disappeared. Much of the work on urban aboriginal people during this period framed the issue as a problem of poverty stemming from lack of education and unemployment. Comeau and Santin (1990) focussed primarily on the poverty of urban aboriginal people. A series of studies based on statistical surveys of aboriginal people in prairie cities and published by the Institute of Urban Studies in Winnipeg demonstrated low incomes and high levels of unemployment and dependence on transfer payments. Summarizing much of this work, Kastes (1993, p. 78) illustrates that the needs of urban aboriginal people were seen to derive from their socio-economic status:

> Most studies describing the needs of the urban Aboriginal population develop a common integrated description of needs. They stem from a relative lack of formal education leading to unemployment or low-wage/low-skill jobs, insufficient levels of income, poverty and ultimately dependency on social assistance. The vast majority of needs in much of the urban Aboriginal population related to housing, health care, recreation and child care are not that dissimilar from other disadvantaged groups which make up the urban poor.

The main factors differentiating the urban aboriginal population from the other urban poor were the services required to adapt to urban life, the degree of their poverty, and the extent of their housing needs (Kastes, 1993, pp. 79–80).

Another approach to typifying the nature of the problem emphasized structural elements. One thread of this analysis identified the confusion over federal and provincial responsibility for making policy and funding programs for urban aboriginal people as an important element (Breton and Grant, 1984; Comeau and Santin, 1990, p. 43; Falconer, 1985).[18] Analysts noted the inconsistency in relationships between the federal government and various provinces, the inequities between various groups of aboriginal people, and the wrangling among governments about policy-making and financial responsibility. In their analysis of government programs for urban Indians in Manitoba, Breton and Grant (1984, pp. ix-xx) warned:

> The past ten years of circular jurisdictional squabbling have permitted the situation of Manitoba's Indians to become progressively worse. If we have ten more years of inconclusive action, the results, in human terms, will be too disastrous to contemplate.

Another theme was the inability of public service organizations to meet the needs of urban aboriginal people (Falconer, 1985; Frideres, 1988; Maidman, 1981; Reeves and Frideres, 1981). Frideres (1988) argued that public service organizations failed to adequately serve urban aboriginal peoples because of their assimilationist objectives, limited target groups, unclear mandates, and uncertain funding. Although aboriginal organizations were more successful in providing culturally appropriate services, they had relatively little success in "graduating" their clients.

The themes of the 1980s provide an important context for efforts to make urban areas better places for aboriginal people. However, they do not address the essential question of the relationship between aboriginal culture and urban life. In fact, the invisibility of aboriginal culture in this literature suggests that it has no role in urban life — that it is irrelevant. In this context, urban aboriginal people become just another socio-economically marginalized group in Canadian inner cities, with no distinct rights or needs.

Changing frameworks for interpreting aboriginal urbanization may explain cycles of public interest in aboriginal people in cities. When the source of the problem is defined as a cultural mismatch between aboriginal and urban cultures, a substantial literature emerges that focusses on urban aboriginal issues. When urban aboriginal people are viewed primarily as a socio-economically disadvantaged population, their situation can be subsumed under the general literature on urban poverty.

ALTERNATIVE CONCEPTIONS OF ABORIGINAL CULTURE IN URBAN LIFE

The ways in which aboriginal people have been defined in western thought have set up a fundamental tension between the idea of aboriginal culture and the idea of modern civilization (Berkhoffer, 1979; Francis, 1992; Goldie, 1989). Although the geographic implications of these deeply held images have not been well developed, Goldie (1989, pp. 16–17, 165) points out that, in non-aboriginal writing, "true" aboriginal culture is seen to belong either to history or to places distant from urban centres. The failure to address, critically, how researchers conceptualize aboriginal culture in relation to the city helps to reproduce a framework that defines aboriginal people as problematic and potentially disruptive of city life.[19] In this context, assumptions about the incompatibility between urban and aboriginal culture persist (Peters, forthcoming). As the Native Council of Canada recently noted, "There is a strong, sometimes racist, perception that being Aboriginal and being urban are mutually exclusive" (1992, p. 10).

In contrast to views of aboriginal culture as either incompatible with or irrelevant in an urban environment, aboriginal people have argued that supporting and enhancing aboriginal culture is a prerequisite for coping in an urban environment. These perspectives recognize that aboriginal cultures and the Euro-Canadian cultures that dominate Canadian cities are distinct in many ways, but they insist that aboriginal cultures can adapt to and flourish in urban areas, and that supporting aboriginal cultures will enrich cities as well as make them better places for aboriginal people.

Urban aboriginal people who spoke to journalist Lynda Shorten in Edmonton (1991) identified the process of regaining their cultural heritage as essential for survival in the city. At the National Round Table on Aboriginal Urban Issues sponsored by the Royal Commission on Aboriginal Peoples, speakers emphasized the importance of maintaining their cultural identities in urban areas, and passing them on to their children. Aboriginal participants at a 1994 workshop on urban self-government identified the process of healing from the effects of colonialism on their cultures as a priority for urban residents (Peters, 1995).

In their submissions to the 1992–94 public hearings of the Royal Commission on Aboriginal Peoples, participants stressed the need to enhance aboriginal cultures in urban areas. Nancy Van Heest, working in a pre-employment program for aboriginal women in Vancouver, told the commissioners:

> Today we live in the modern world and we find that a lot of our people who come into the urban setting are unable to live in the modern world without their traditional values. So we started a program which we call "Urban Images for First Nations People in the Urban Setting" and what we do is we work in this modern day with modern day people and give them traditional values so that they can continue on with their life in the city.[20]

Urban aboriginal people spoke to the commissioners of the need for a strong foundation in aboriginal culture for healing the urban aboriginal community. In Orillia, Ontario, Harold Orten outlined the relationship between recovering aboriginal cultures and healing:

> Recovering our identity will contribute to healing ourselves. Our healing will require us to rediscover who we are. We cannot look outside for our self-image, we need to rededicate ourselves to understanding our traditional ways. In our songs, ceremony, language and relationships lie the instructions and directions for recovery.[21]

In Saskatoon, Margaret King, representative for the Saskatoon Urban Treaty Indians, argued that

> our cultural heritage . . . formed the basic elements of individual empowerment, a solid foundation of cultural values and the knowledge of our history and traditions, our basic needs in the development of an individual before he or she becomes a productive member of society. As an assembly we believe in the value of individual self-esteem and will strive to empower our people through the development of culturally appropriate programs and services.

The assault on aboriginal cultures does not originate only in cities. It is part of the colonial legacy of our country. Yet urban areas present special challenges for the survival of aboriginal cultures. These challenges come in part because many of the traditional sources of aboriginal culture — contact with the land, elders, aboriginal languages, and spiritual ceremonies — are difficult to maintain in cities at present. Moreover, aboriginal people are continuously exposed to perceptions, either consciously or unconsciously held, that cities are not where aboriginal cultures belong and can flourish (RCAP, 1993a, p. 2). At the public hearings, David Chartrand, then president of the National Association of Friendship Centres, told the commissioners:

> Aboriginal culture in the cities is threatened in much the same way as Canadian culture is threatened by American culture, and it therefore requires a similar commitment to its protection. Our culture is at the heart of our people, and without awareness of Aboriginal history, traditions and ceremonies, we are not whole people, and our communities lose their strength. . . . Cultural education also works against the alienation that the cities hold for our people. Social activities bring us together and strengthen the relationship between people in areas where those relationships are an important safety net for people who feel left out by the mainstream.[22]

CHANGING CITIES TO WELCOME ABORIGINAL PEOPLES AND CULTURES

Making cities places where aboriginal cultures are welcomed and enhanced will require sustained effort. Aboriginal people must be involved in identifying and putting into place appropriate initiatives. The following, however, puts forward some suggestions to illustrate what it means to change long-standing views about the relationship between aboriginal cultures and urban places. These include cultural programming, building urban aboriginal communities, supporting urban self-government, and improving the representation of aboriginal people in urban areas.

Supporting Cultural Programming and Education

At present, there are many urban aboriginal institutions that attempt to meet the needs of urban aboriginal people, including the need to strengthen cultural identity. However, a survey of urban aboriginal institutions in Winnipeg, Toronto, and Edmonton (Clatworthy et al., 1995) showed that although organizations attempted to meet the cultural needs of their clients by incorporating aboriginal philosophies and cultures into their structures and program delivery, relatively few had as their primary mission the promotion or support of aboriginal culture and identity. Moreover, while organizations reported flexibility in delivery style and administrative matters, their activities were highly circumscribed by funding relationships with other parties, mostly non-aboriginal governments.

Friendship centres, which have existed in Canada's urban centres for over 30 years, have often become the main focus of cultural and social events and activities for aboriginal people living in cities. In many urban areas, the friendship centre has been the only major voluntary association available to meet the needs of aboriginal people for social and cultural development. Yet there is only funding to friendship centres for activities that support aboriginal cultures, such as celebrations, access to elders, and language education. The cultural work that friendship centres currently carry out is chronically underfunded and relies heavily on the work of volunteers who are already overcommitted. In the context of the sustained assault on aboriginal cultures in cities and the poverty of much of the urban aboriginal population, there is a need for substantial new institutional support to assist aboriginal people in maintaining and enhancing their cultural identity in urban areas. Teaching aboriginal languages is one area that needs to be stressed. The Aboriginal Peoples Survey showed that only about 15 percent of urban aboriginal people could speak their aboriginal language of origin. Yet 71 percent of aboriginal people who could not speak an aboriginal language would like to learn or relearn one. Other priorities include providing space for aboriginal activities and ceremonies and cultural education for children, youth, and adults.

Building Aboriginal Communities

The evolution of strong aboriginal communities in urban areas remains largely unfulfilled after 40 years of urbanization. In many cities, aboriginal people exist as an impoverished minority, without a collective cultural identity. Although there are now many cities with a variety of aboriginal organizations, they do not reflect and have not been able to create group solidarity and cohesion. A study of aboriginal organizations in Edmonton, Toronto, and Winnipeg found that only a small portion of the total urban aboriginal population participates as members or receives benefits or services from existing organizations (Clatworthy et al., 1995). The study also found that there were relatively few formal and effective inter-organizational structures with a focus on community-building and consolidation.

Community-building through the establishment of networks, institutions, and collective identity can enhance political strength and visibility and provide the support for resilient cultural identities. Community-building can also contribute to economic development and begin to address the pressing poverty of many aboriginal people living in cities (Rothney, 1992). In this context, some urban aboriginal people have emphasized the need to engage in a process of healing, and consensus- and community-building in urban areas.[23] David Chartrand, then president of the National Association of Friendship Centres, told the Royal Commission on Aboriginal Peoples that the most effective way to solve the problems that aboriginal people face in the city was to catch them before they start by strengthening individuals' identities and awareness of the urban aboriginal community.[24]

The challenges to community-building in urban areas are considerable. One challenge comes from the cultural diversity of urban aboriginal people. In his report for the Native Council of Canada, Morse (1993, p. 88) noted:

> In the urban setting, asking the individual members of the potentially very diverse urban group [sic], each with their own unique identity, traditions, language and culture, to put aside their differences and build a new community is a formidable task. It requires the rejection of the long history of federal intervention, and for the urban Aboriginal population to come to terms with their diversity.

Many people who live in urban areas retain ties with their non-urban communities of origin, and these ties represent an important component of their cultural identities. Moreover, some land-based First Nations communities are currently exploring ways of extending their jurisdiction over members who live in urban areas.

At the same time, urban aboriginal people need local access to places, people, and activities that support the celebration and enhancement of their cultures. In cities where there are relatively few people from any particular cultural group, these opportunities can only exist through co-operation and collective activities. The challenge for aboriginal people, then, urban and non-urban, is to explore ways of creating urban communities that will support a variety of cultural origins and, at the same time, protect the ties that some people have with their non-urban communities of origin. These approaches can only be designed by aboriginal people themselves, and they may vary from place to place.

Another challenge to community-building comes from the extreme poverty of many urban aboriginal people.[25] Poverty and economic marginalization work against community-building, the very thing that could begin to alleviate that condition. The majority of urban residents do not possess the financial resources to support institutional development. Moreover, many are faced with enormous daily challenges in trying to obtain an adequate standard of living, which leave little time or energy for participation in community-building. These struggles take place in the context of a political environment that does not support urban community-building. As representatives to the Royal Commission on Aboriginal Peoples' National Round Table on Aboriginal Urban Issues pointed out: "any sort of co-operative urban Aboriginal movement has been hamstrung by scarce resources, fragmented populations, unclear mandates, and a lack of . . . federal or provincial encouragement and support" (RCAP, 1993a, p. 79). In many cities, then, the processes of urban aboriginal community-building require the infusion of financial resources from other levels of government.

Supporting Self-Government

Until recently, most of the literature on the nature of and possibilities for aboriginal self-government focussed on land-based populations. Although there was some consideration of urban applications (see Dunn, 1986; Reeves, 1986; Weinstein, 1986), most researchers pointed out the difficulties of implementation off a land base and concentrated on land-base arrangements (see, for example, Penner, 1983; RCAP, 1993b, p. 44).

Urban aboriginal peoples' demands for self-government contradict the colonial legacy, which views aboriginal cultures, communities, and values as incompatible with or inappropriate in the urban industrial milieu. Self-government is also essential for the enhancement of aboriginal cultures in urban areas. In their study of aboriginal organizations in three major urban centres, Clatworthy et al. (1995) found that the activities of the organizations were highly circumscribed by the interests of funding organizations, which were, for the most part, non-aboriginal governments. Opekokew (1995) argues that cultural preservation and enhancement occur only when aboriginal people have control over their institutions.

A number of models of urban self-government for aboriginal peoples in urban areas have been put forward in recent years. Many First Nations support the extension of jurisdiction of land-based governments to urban citizens (Opekokew, 1995). The Native Council of Canada (now the Congress of Aboriginal Peoples) suggested options including governance over urban reserves or aboriginal neighbourhoods, self-determining aboriginal institutions, and pan-aboriginal governing bodies in urban areas (Native Council of Canada, 1993). Tizya (1992, p. 8) described an approach where urban residents would fall under the jurisdiction of the First Nation in whose traditional territory the urban centre lies. Métis organizations place governance for urban residents in a structure with urban and rural locals nested in provincial and national organizations (Young, 1995).

The issue is complex. In addition to debates over the scope of an inherent right to self-government in urban areas, some approaches to governance cannot be implemented in conjunction with others, and setting up different structures for each cultural group could result in impossible complexity (Peters, 1994). Yet extending opportunities for self-government is crucial for the large number of aboriginal people living in urban areas.

Representing Aboriginal Peoples in Urban Landscapes

Initiatives to change public perceptions about the relationship between aboriginal cultures and urban life are needed in addition to support for community-building, cultural programming, and self-government. These initiatives must occur in a wide variety of areas, and they must be sustained because they are part of changing very deeply held ways people have of organizing their view of the world. In this context, changing presentations of aboriginal peoples and histories in educational materials and the media would benefit urban aboriginal people. However, some initiatives that focus specifically on urban landscapes are also needed.

One important strategy in this regard has to do with changing the way aboriginal people are represented (or not represented) in urban landscapes. Symbols in urban landscapes reflect and reproduce societal values about what is and what is not valued and important. Contemporary urban landscapes offer little to valorize aboriginal cultures, affirm their relevance to contemporary life, or admit their continuing existence. There is little recognition that most cities are on aboriginal peoples' traditional territories or that urban development may affect sites that are important for spiritual or historic reasons.[26] There are few attempts at historic preservation of significant sites that bring the aboriginal heritage of the lands on which urban areas are built to public consciousness. There are few streets, parks, or buildings named after significant aboriginal people, whether historic or contemporary. Aboriginal heroes do not often appear in monuments dedicated to their memory. Making aboriginal people and cultures visible in urban landscapes would signal that they have a valued place in contemporary urban areas.

CONCLUSION

Support for the maintenance and enhancement of aboriginal cultures is not the only challenge facing aboriginal people in urban areas. Aboriginal people have also stressed other pressing needs. Participants at the Royal Commission on Aboriginal People's National Round Table on Aboriginal Urban Issues identified the need for economic development, more appropriate services, changes in government policies and jurisdiction, and a voice in governance and decision-making (RCAP, 1993a). I have focussed on cultural issues in this chapter for two reasons. The first has to do with a long history of denying that aboriginal cultures have an appropriate place in urban areas — a place that has challenged the identities of many urban aboriginal people. The second has to do with my sense that valuing and supporting urban aboriginal cultures in cities would contribute to meeting some of the other needs of urban aboriginal communities.

About half of the aboriginal people of Canada live in urban areas. Taking measures to support and enhance their cultures will make cities better places for aboriginal people and for non-aboriginal residents.

NOTES

1. By aboriginal peoples I mean the indigenous peoples of this country, including First Nations peoples, Métis, and Inuit. First Nations peoples are people who identify themselves as such, including people who are and are not registered under the Indian Act. I use the term "Indian" when I refer to Euro-Canadian constructions of First Nations peoples. Registered Indians are registered under the Indian Act.

2. The chapter takes a social constructionist approach to the issue of aboriginal urbanization (see Best, 1989; Spector and Kitsuse, 1987). This approach argues that people's sense of what is and what is not a problem is not simply the result of objective conditions, but has also been produced or constructed through social action and events. Typically, the social construction of an issue characterizes it as a certain type of problem. This characterization serves as a framework for identifying appropriate strategies for its management or solution.

3. The census question that collects information on Canadians' ethnic or cultural origins asked, "To which ethnic or cultural group(s) did this person's ancestor's belong?" In 1991, a postcensal survey, the Aboriginal Peoples Survey (APS), asked individuals who indicated they had aboriginal ancestry whether they identified with an aboriginal group. This "identity" population is smaller than the population that has aboriginal ancestry or cultural origins.

4. See note 3 for a description of the APS.

5. To date, federal negotiations have been held with bands and groups of bands.

6. This list does not represent all aboriginal organizations in the city, but those that are managed by aboriginal people and that are autonomous of other organizations, urban-based, and urban-focussed.

7. In Vancouver, URBAN is an umbrella organization for 54 non-profit societies that provide social services to aboriginal people in Vancouver.

8. Other limitations include changing definitions (Gerber, 1977, p. 4), the location of a number of reserves in urban centres, and failure to update records regularly (Canada, DIAND, 1992).

9. Before 1981, only one ethnic origin was captured in the census. In 1981, more than one origin was allowed, but respondents were not encouraged to identify more than one.

10. By 1991, about 87 000 had been added to the registered Indian population, increasing the total population by about 21 percent between 1985 and 1991. A substantial proportion of the peoples added to the Register would have lived in urban areas.

11. There are no published statistics on urban aboriginal people before 1951.

12. The Royal Commission on Aboriginal Peoples, established in 1992, has urban aboriginal peoples as one of its research focuses. However, this material is not available at present.

13. John MacLean, a missionary with a doctorate in history and author of *The Indians of Canada* (1889) and *Canadian Savage Folk* (1896), was considered to be an authority. Describing the Sarcees on a reserve near Calgary, he wrote (1896, p. 18):

    "Their close proximity to Calgary is injurious to the morals of the white people and Indians, as the natives of the plains always find the lower stratum of society ready to teach the willing learner lessons of immorality, and degradation is sure to follow any close relationship of Indians with white people in the early stages of their training."

14. Although I recognize that some of the concern may be spillover from events in inner cities in the United States during the 1960s, the definition of aboriginal

urbanization as problematic substantially pre-dates these events, and the themes and explanations are too persistent to be simply a reflection of the U.S. experience.

15. There is little recognition of the diversity of aboriginal cultures in this literature.

16. These quotations do not represent isolated opinions taken out of context, but reflect a general framework within which writers understood the nature of the urban experience for aboriginal migrants. See also, for example, Asimi, 1967, p. 94; Bond, 1967; Currie, 1966, p. 14; Indian-Eskimo Association, 1971, p. 6; Melling, 1967; Canada, 1960c, pp. 1034–39; Trudeau, 1969; Vincent, 1971, p. 13; Zentner, 1973, p. xii. At the same time, it is also important to note that there were writers who argued that urbanization did not represent a rejection of aboriginal culture (Lurie, 1967; McCaskill, 1981).

17. Clearly these dates are approximate, and there are works that fit into neither time period nor subject category as I have organized them. Moreover, some of the themes I associate with the post-1980 period were also present before then.

18. Ryan (1975) made similar points earlier.

19. It is important to note that aboriginal people are not the only group that has been so defined (see Ray, 1992; Sibley, 1981).

20. Nancy Van Heest, Vancouver, B.C., public hearing, June 2, 1993, p. 14.

21. Harold Orten, Orillia, Ontario, public hearing, May 13, 1993, p. 66.

22. Toronto public hearing, June 26, 1992, p. 565.

23. See, for example, presentations by Sylvia Maracle and Wayne Helgason to a workshop on urban self-government (Peters, 1995).

24. Toronto public hearing, June 26, 1992, p. 565.

25. It is important to emphasize that the economic marginalization of urban aboriginal people is not of their own making. Rather, it comes from a long history of their exclusion from the mainstream of society.

26. Rosalee Tizya, co-coordinator, Urban Perspectives, Royal Commission on Aboriginal Peoples, made this point at a workshop on self-government for urban aboriginal peoples held at Queen's University, May 25–26, 1994.

DISCUSSION QUESTIONS

1. What do you know about the culture and traditions of the aboriginal people living in your city (or the city nearest to you)?

2. On which nation's traditional territory is your city (or the city nearest to you) located?

3. How are aboriginal people presented in this city?

4. When you read your newspaper, how do articles present local aboriginal people? How often are they featured? How is the relationship between aboriginal culture and urban life conceptualized?

FURTHER READINGS

Maracle, L. 1992. *Sundogs*. Penticton, B.C.: Theytus Books Ltd. Lee Maracle's novel, about an aboriginal family during the time of the downfall of the Meech Lake accord and the Oka crisis, is one of the few pieces of fiction by an aboriginal person that is set in an urban area.

Peters, E.J. 1995. *Self-Government for Aboriginal Peoples in Urban Areas*. Kingston, Ont.: Institute of Intergovernmental Relations, Queen's University. This publication represents the proceedings of a workshop on urban self-government held at Queen's University in May 1995. Speakers included aboriginal people involved in urban political and service organizations, and representatives from municipal, provincial, and federal governments. Three background papers explore demographic characteristics of urban aboriginal people, urban aboriginal institutions, and models of urban self-government.

Richardson, B. 1994. "The Aboriginal City." Pp. 227–53 in *People of Terra Nullius: Betrayal and Rebirth in Aboriginal Canada*. Vancouver and Toronto: Douglas & McIntyre. Boyce Richardson reports on his interviews with urban aboriginal people, primarily in Winnipeg, highlighting a variety of issues that are of contemporary concern to them.

Royal Commission on Aboriginal Peoples. 1993. *Aboriginal Peoples in Urban Centres: Report of the National Round Table on Aboriginal Urban Issues*. Ottawa: Supply and Services. From June 21 to 23, 1992, the Royal Commission on Aboriginal Peoples hosted a national round table on urban aboriginal issues in Edmonton. The published proceedings of the round table include a summary of the issues raised, a report on the workshops on services, health and wellness, economics, and governance, and a series of short issue papers.

Ryan, J. 1979. *Wall of Words: The Betrayal of the Urban Indian*. Toronto: Peter Martin Associates. This classic book tells the story of the attempts of two Blackfeet men to provide services to First Nations people migrating to the city, and documents the federal government's consolidation of its stance that it was responsible only for reserve residents.

REFERENCES

Asimi, A.P. 1967. "The Urban Setting." Pp. 89–96 in *Resolving Conflicts — A Cross-Cultural Approach*. Winnipeg: Department of University Extensions and Adult Education, University of Manitoba.

Best, J. 1989. *Images of Issues: Typifying Contemporary Social Problems*. New York: Aldine de Gruyter.

Berkhoffer, R.F. 1979. *The White Man's Indian: Images of the American Indian from Columbus to the Present*. New York: Vintage.

Boek, W.E. and J.K. Boek. 1959. *The People of Indian Ancestry in Greater Winnipeg.* Winnipeg: Queen's Printer.

Bond, J.J. 1967. *A Report on the Pilot Relocation Project at Elliot Lake, Ontario.* Ottawa: Department of Indian Affairs and Northern Development.

Braroe, W.W. 1975. *Indian and White: Self-Image and Interaction in a Canadian Plains Community.* Stanford, Conn.: Stanford University Press.

Breton, R. and G. Grant. 1984. *The Dynamics of Government Programs for Urban Indians in the Prairie Provinces.* Montreal: The Institute for Research on Public Policy.

Brody, H. 1983. *Maps and Dreams: Indians and the British Columbia Frontier.* New York: Penguin.

Buckley, H. 1992. *From Wooden Ploughs to Welfare: Why Indian Policy Failed in the Prairie Provinces.* Montreal and Kingston, Ont.: McGill-Queen's University Press.

Canada, Department of Indian Affairs and Northern Development (DIAND). 1957. *The Indian News* 2(4): p. 3.

———. 1967. *Indian Affairs Facts and Figures.* Ottawa: DIAND.

———. 1992. Quantitative Analysis and Socio-Demographic Research. *Basic Departmental Data.* Ottawa: Supply and Services.

Canada, Information Canada. 1974. *Perspective Canada: A Compendium of Social Statistics.* Ottawa: Department of Industry, Trade and Commerce.

Canada, Joint Committee of the Senate and the House of Commons on Indian Affairs. 1960a. Brief of the Indian-Eskimo Association of Canada. *Minutes of Proceedings and Evidence.* Vol. 5: pp. 363–427.

———. 1960b. *Minutes of Proceedings and Evidence.* Vol. 14: pp. 537–42.

Canada, Joint Committee of the Senate and the House of Commons on Indian Affairs. 1960c. Submission by the Government of Saskatchewan. *Minutes of Proceedings and Evidence.* Vol. 12: pp. 1029–79.

Canadian Corrections Association. 1967. *Indians and the Law.* Ottawa: Canadian Welfare Council.

Clatworthy, S.J. 1980. *The Demographic Composition and Economic Circumstances of Winnipeg's Native Population.* Winnipeg: Institute of Urban Studies, University of Winnipeg.

Clatworthy, S.J. and J.P. Gunn. 1981. *The Economic Circumstances of Native People in Selected Metropolitan Centres in Western Canada.* Winnipeg: Institute of Urban Studies, University of Winnipeg.

Clatworthy, S.J. and J. Hull. 1983. *Native Economic Conditions in Regina and Saskatoon.* Winnipeg: Institute of Urban Studies, University of Winnipeg.

Clatworthy, S., J. Hull, and N. Loughran. 1995. "Urban Aboriginal Organizations: Edmonton, Toronto and Winnipeg." Pp. 25–81 in *Self-Government for Aboriginal People in Urban Areas,* ed. E.J. Peters. Kingston, Ont.: Institute of Intergovernmental Relations, Queen's University.

Comeau, P. and A. Santin. 1990. *The First Canadians: A Profile of Canada's Native People Today.* Toronto: James Lorimer.

Currie, W. 1966. "Urbanization and Indians." Address to the Mid-Canada Development Corridor Conference, Indian-Eskimo Association, Lakehead University, Thunder Bay, Ont.

Davis, A.K. 1965. *Edging into Mainstream: Urban Indians in Saskatchewan.* Bellingham: Western Washington State College.

Dunn, M. 1986. *Access to Survival: A Perspective on Aboriginal Self-Government for the Constituency of the Native Council of Canada.* Kingston, Ont.: Institute of Intergovernmental Relations, Queen's University.

Elias, P.D. 1975. *Metropolis and Hinterland in Northern Manitoba.* Winnipeg: Manitoba Museum of Man and Nature.

Falconer, P. 1985. "Urban Indian Needs: Federal Policy Responsibility and Options in the Context of the Talks on Aboriginal Self-Government." Discussion paper (unpublished).

———. 1990. "The Overlooked of the Neglected: Native Single-Mothers in Major Cities on the Prairies." Pp. 188–210 in *The Political Economy of Manitoba,* ed. J. Silver and J. Hull. Regina: Canadian Plains Research Centre, University of Regina.

Francis, D. 1992. *The Imaginary Indian: The Image of the Indian in Canadian Culture.* Vancouver: Arsenal Pulp Press.

Frideres, J.S. 1984. "Government Policies and Programs Relating to People of Indian Ancestry in Alberta." Pp. 321–517 in *The Dynamics of Government Programs for Urban Indians in the Prairie Provinces,* ed. R. Breton and G. Grant. Montreal: The Institute for Research on Public Policy.

———. 1988. *Canada's Indians: Contemporary Conflicts,* 3rd ed. Scarborough, Ont.: Prentice-Hall.

———. 1993. *Native Peoples in Canada: Contemporary Conflicts,* 4th ed. Scarborough, Ont.: Prentice-Hall.

Gerber, L.M. 1977. "Trends in Out-Migration from Indian Communities Across Canada: A Report for the Task Force on Migrating Native People." Ph.D. thesis, Harvard University.

Goldie, T. 1989. *Fear and Temptation: The Image of the Indigene in Canadian, Australian and New Zealand Literature.* Montreal and Kingston, Ont.: McGill-Queen's University Press.

Goldman, G. 1993. "The Aboriginal Population and the Census: 120 Years of Information — 1871 to 1991." Statistics Canada, Ottawa. (Unpublished.)

Hawthorn, H.B. 1966–67. *A Survey of the Contemporary Indians of Canada — A Report on Economic, Political and Educational Needs and Policies,* 2 vols. Ottawa: DIAND

Hawthorn, H.B., C. Belshaw, and S. Jamieson. 1958. *The Indians of British Columbia.* Toronto: University of Toronto Press.

Helgason, W. 1995. "Urban Aboriginal Issues, Models and Stakeholders Relative to the Transition to Self-Government." Pp. 131–40 in *Self-Government for Aboriginal Peoples in Urban Areas,* ed. E. Peters. Kingston, Ont.: Institute of Intergovernmental Relations, Queen's University.

Hirabayashi, G.K. 1962. *The Challenge of Assisting the Canadian Aboriginal People to Adjust to Urban Environments: Report of the First Western Canadian Indian-Métis Seminar.* Edmonton: University of Alberta Press.

Indian-Eskimo Association. 1960. "Proceedings of the National Research Seminar on Indians in the City," Queen's University. (Unpublished.)

———. 1971. *Final Report: Indians and the City*. Toronto: Contract with Secretary of State.

Kastes, W.G. 1993. *The Future of Aboriginal Urbanization in Prairie Cities: Select Annotated Bibliography and Literature Review on Urban Aboriginal Issues in the Prairie Provinces*. Winnipeg: Institute of Urban Studies, University of Winnipeg.

Krotz, Larry. 1980. *Urban Indians: The Strangers in Canada's Cities*. Edmonton: Hurtig Publishers.

Lagasse, J.H. 1958. *A Study of the Population of Indian Ancestry in Manitoba: A Social and Economic Study*. Winnipeg: Social and Economic Research Office, Manitoba Department of Agriculture and Immigration.

Lithman, Y.G. 1984. *The Community Apart: A Case Study of a Canadian Indian Reserve Community*. Winnipeg: University of Manitoba Press.

Lurie, N.O. 1967. "The Indian Moves to an Urban Setting." Pp. 73–86 in *Resolving Conflicts — A Cross-Cultural Approach*. Winnipeg: Department of University Extensions and Adult Education, University of Manitoba.

MacLean, J. 1889. *Indians of Canada: Their Manners and Customs*. Toronto: William Briggs.

———. 1896. *Canadian Savage Folk: The Native Tribes of Canada*. Toronto: William Briggs.

Maidman, F. 1981. *Native People in Urban Settings: Problems, Needs and Services*. Toronto: Ontario Task Force on Native People in the Urban Setting.

McCaskill, D.N. 1981. "The Urbanization of Indians in Winnipeg, Toronto, Edmonton and Vancouver: A Comparative Analysis." *Culture* 1(1): pp. 82–89.

Melling, J. 1967. *Right to a Future: The Native Peoples of Canada*. Toronto: T.H. Best Printing Co. Ltd.

Morse, B. 1989. "Government Obligations, Aboriginal Peoples and Section 91(24)." Pp. 59–92 in *Aboriginal Peoples and Government Responsibility: Exploring Federal and Provincial Roles*. ed. D.C. Hawkes. Ottawa: Carleton University Press.

———. 1993. *A Legal and Jurisdictional Analysis of Urban Self-Government*. Ottawa: Native Council of Canada Royal Commission Intervenor Research Project.

Nagler, M. 1970. *Indians in the City*. Ottawa: Canadian Research Centre for Anthropology, St. Paul University.

Native Council of Canada. 1992. *Decision 1992: Background and Discussion Points for the First Peoples Forum*. Ottawa: NCC.

———. 1993. *The First Peoples Urban Circle: Choices for Self-Determination*. Book 1. Ottawa: NCC.

Opekokew, D. 1995. "Treaty First Nations Perspectives on Self-Government of Aboriginal Peoples in Urban Areas." Pp. 168–72 in *Self-Government for Aboriginal Peoples in Urban Areas*, ed. E. Peters. Kingston, Ont.: Institute of Intergovernmental Relations, Queen's University.

Penner, K. 1983. *Indian Self-Government*. Ottawa: Supply and Services.

Peters, E.J. 1994. "Geographies of Self-Government." In *Implementing Aboriginal Self-Government in Canada*, ed. J. Hylton. Saskatoon: Purich Publishers.

——. 1995. *Self-Government for Aboriginal Peoples in Urban Areas*. Kingston, Ont.: Institute of Intergovernmental Relations, Queen's University.

———. forthcoming. "'Urban' and 'Aboriginal': An Impossible Contradiction?" In *Critical Approaches to Canadian Urbanism*, ed. J. Caulfield and L. Peake. Toronto: University of Toronto Press.

Powless, J. 1994. Department of Indian Affairs and Northern Development. Personal communication. (January 12.)

Price, J.A. and D.N. McCaskill. 1974. "The Urban Integration of Canadian Indians." *Western Canadian Journal of Anthropology* 4(2): pp. 29–45.

Ray, B.K. 1992. "Immigrants in a 'Multicultural' Toronto: Exploring the Contested Social and Housing Geographies of Post-War Italian and Caribbean Immigrants." Ph.D. thesis, Department of Geography, Queen's University.

Reeves, W. 1986. "Native Societies: The Professions as a Model of Self-Determination for Urban Indians." Pp. 342–58 in *Arduous Journey: Canadian Indians and Decolonization*, ed. J.R. Ponting. Toronto: McClelland & Stewart.

Reeves, W. and J. Frideres. 1981. "Government Policy and Indian Urbanization: The Alberta Case." *Canadian Public Policy* 7(4): pp. 584–595.

Regina Welfare Council. 1959. *Our City Indians: Report of a Conference*. Regina: Saskatchewan House.

Reiber-Kremers and Associates. 1977. "A Preliminary Overview of Native Migration into the City of Winnipeg." Discussion paper prepared for the City of Winnipeg, Environmental Planning Department.

Richardson, B. 1994. *People of Terra Nullius: Betrayal and Rebirth in Aboriginal Canada*. Vancouver and Toronto: Douglas & McIntyre.

Robertson, H. 1970. *Reservations Are for Indians*. Toronto: James Lewis & Samuel.

Rothney, R.G. 1992. *Neechi Foods Co-op Ltd.: Lessons in Community Development*. Winnipeg: Winnipeg Family Economic Development Inc.

Royal Commission on Aboriginal Peoples. 1993a. *Aboriginal Peoples in Urban Centres: Report of the National Round Table on Aboriginal Urban Issues*. Ottawa: Supply and Services.

———. 1993b. *Partners in Confederation: Aboriginal Peoples, Self-Government, and the Constitution*. Ottawa: Supply and Services.

———, Research Directorate. 1994. *Customized Data from the 1991 Aboriginal Peoples Survey*. Ottawa: Supply and Services.

Ryan, J. 1975. *Wall of Words: The Betrayal of the Urban Indian*. Toronto: Peter Martin Associates.

Saskatchewan. 1979. *The Dimensions of Indian and Native Urban Poverty in Saskatchewan*. Regina: Social Planning Secretariat.

Shimpo, M. and R. Williamson. 1965. *Socio-Cultural Disintegration Among the Fringe Saulteaux*. Saskatoon: Centre for Community Studies, University of Saskatchewan.

Shorten, L. 1991. *Without Reserve: Stories from Urban Natives*. Edmonton: NeWest Press.

Sibley, E. 1981. *Outsiders in Urban Societies*. New York: St. Martin's Press.

Spector, M. and J.I. Kitsuse. 1987. *Constructing Social Problems*. New York: Aldine de Gruyter.

Stymeist, D. 1975. *Ethnics and Indians*. Toronto: Peter Martin Associates.

Tizya, R. 1992. "Comments on Urban Aboriginals and Self-Government." Pp. 45–52 in *Aboriginal Governments and Power Sharing in Canada*, ed. D. Brown. Kingston, Ont.: Institute of Intergovernmental Relations, Queen's University.

Tobias, J.L. 1983. "Protection, Civilization, Assimilation: An Outline History of Canada's Indian Policy." Pp. 29–38 in *As Long as the Sun Shines and Water Flows: A Reader in Canadian Native Studies*, ed. A.L. Getty and A.S. Lussier. Vancouver: UBC Press.

Trudeau, J. 1969. "The Indian in the City." *Kerygma* 3(3): pp. 118–23.

Vincent, D.B. 1971. *The Indian-Métis Urban Probe*. Winnipeg: Indian-Métis Friendship Centre and Institute of Urban Studies, University of Winnipeg.

Weinstein, J. 1986. *Self-Determination Off a Land-Base*. Kingston, Ont.: Institute of Intergovernmental Relations, Queen's University.

Young, D. 1995. "Some Approaches to Urban Aboriginal Governance." Pp. 153–62 in *Self-Government for Aboriginal Peoples in Urban Areas*, ed. E. Peters. Kingston, Ont.: Institute of Intergovernmental Relations, Queen's University.

Zeitoun, L. 1969. "Canadian Indians at the Crossroads: Some Aspects of Relocation and Urbanization in Canada." Study for the Manpower Utilization Branch, Department of Manpower and Immigration, Ottawa. (Unpublished.)

Zentner, H. 1973. *The Indian Identity Crisis*. Calgary: Strayer Publications Ltd.

CHAPTER 12

Lessons in Decolonization: Aboriginal Overrepresentation in Canadian Criminal Justice

Patricia A. Monture-Angus[1]

> And it was rare for Crees to commit any crimes against one another at that time, even though there were so many people of different tribes, they did not very often commit violent crimes against one another, they lived together peacefully. (Peter Vandall, Cree elder, Atahk-akop's Reserve, Sandy Lake, Saskatchewan) (Ahenakew and Wolfant, 1987, p. 47)

INTRODUCTION

The loss of peaceful existence in many aboriginal communities has been the subject of many reports, inquiries, academic studies, and research. Much of this work has been funded by government dollars. Unfortunately, the analysis of the "problem" in aboriginal communities has a distinct and narrow focus. The majority of our understanding has been developed without a serious regard for the pattern of colonialism that is clear and pronounced in aboriginal communities and experiences including the experience of the criminal justice system. This has serious consequences for aboriginal peoples.[2]

The overrepresentation of aboriginal people in the system of Canadian criminal justice is all to often seen as an aboriginal problem (that is, a problem *with* aboriginal people). In 1983, Don McCaskill observed:

> The conventional explanation for this phenomenon views native offenders as members of a pathological community characterized by extensive social and personal problems. The focus is inevitably on the individual offenders. They are seen as simply being unable to adjust successfully to the rigors of contemporary society. They are part of a larger "Indian problem" for which various social service agencies have been created to help Indians meet the standards of the dominant society. The long-range goal is that, in time, with

sufficient help, Indians will lose most of their culture, adopt the values of the larger society, become upwardly mobile, and be incorporated into main-stream society. In short, Indians will assimilate. (McCaskill, 1983, p. 289)

Professor McCaskill made this observation more than a decade ago. Unfortunately, non-aboriginal people have taken little constructive action to reconstruct the theoretical parameters that house this particular analysis of the relationship of aboriginal peoples with the Canadian criminal justice system. It is important to question why a system that has so markedly failed aboriginal peoples (and people) has been allowed to continue to operate in an unjust and colonial manner for so many years and through so many reports and inquiries. In fact, McCaskill's point was made prior to the majority of justice reports that really proliferated after 1984 (Alberta, 1991, p. 4–3).

This failure to take responsibility for the continued perpetuation of colonial relations in current criminal justice practices and policies has not escaped the gaze or understanding of aboriginal people and our governments. It is a situation that magnifies the contempt that aboriginal peoples have for a system that is neither fair and just nor responsible. My purpose in agreeing to add my voice to the others in this collection is simple. I choose to name and expose the colonialism present in both Canada's criminal justice system and the literature about the overrepresentation of aboriginal people in that system. By naming and exposing, I hope to narrow the gap that exists between the understanding of justice relations in aboriginal communities and the academic (and research) communities.

It is curious to me that non-aboriginal people always think that aboriginal peoples have lost their culture. Having your culture interfered with (and even made illegal)[3] does not mean that your culture fails to exist. The response of non-aboriginal people to aboriginal people who are skilled at being bicultural (because our survival generally depends on this skill) is misinterpreted. Because I have learned to relate to you on terms that you have defined cannot lend itself to a reasonable construction of aboriginal culturelessness. Because I can understand non-aboriginal ways does not necessarily mean that I can no longer understand or, worse yet, that I reject aboriginal ways of doing, thinking, and being. All that can be concluded is that non-aboriginal people have not been as successful (as a group) at understanding aboriginal culture as we have been successful at understanding Canadian culture and ways.

As the opening quotation indicates, there were few problems of crime and disorder among aboriginal populations at the time of contact and for some years after. This reality is well documented but infrequently given the respect or position in the discourse that it deserves (see Newell, 1965; Upton, 1979, pp. 142–52). Any curious mind considering this fact can easily conclude that aboriginal people had systems to maintain order in our communities. This is true despite the fact that we did not have prisons, punishment, and all the trappings that Canadians recognize as the characteristics of an organized and formal justice system. The crux of the problem is Canada's failure (that is, non-aboriginal people including policy-makers, researchers, prison administers, politicians, and lawyers) to own up to and address the fact that aboriginal overrepresentation in the justice system is not necessarily the individual failure of particular aboriginal people but also the impact and vestige of colonialism.

Colonialism is not difficult to understand. It is easily conceptualized:

> Colonialism involves a relationship which leaves one side dependent on the other to define the world. At the individual level, colonialism involves a situation where one individual is forced to relate to another on terms unilaterally defined by the other. The justice system becomes a central institution with which to impose the way of life of the dominant society. (McCaskill, 1983, p. 289)

Recognizing colonialism as a central explanation (if not *the* central explanation) for aboriginal overrepresentation in the justice system is essential. At the same time, we must recognize that the process of colonization requires colonizers, not just the colonized. The process of decolonization is not just an aboriginal responsibility but must also involve the colonizers' learning new ways of relating to enclaved peoples. It is very difficult to honour my commitment to live in a decolonized way when I survive in an environment where others (aboriginal and not) continue to remain committed to the entrenchment of the colonizers' ways. So far, my efforts to decolonize my own life and mind have proven to be a long and difficult process.

THE MANY JUSTICE REPORTS

The situation of aboriginal people and Canada's criminal justice system has been studied by commissions, inquiries, and task forces since 1967. In 1990, the Alberta Cawsey commission noted:

> The real proliferation in reports began in the mid-1980's. . . . Seventeen of the twenty-two reports were released between 1984 and 1990 (and note that this does not include the anticipated Blood and Manitoba Inquiry Reports). In 1988 and 1989, alone, eleven reports were published. This suggests that, in the last five to six years, something has occurred to make all levels of Government acutely aware and concerned with Native involvement in the Criminal Justice System. Considering the repetition of recommendations it could be speculated that this "something" is an awareness that earlier recommendations were not implemented, or that current strategies are not effective (but perhaps with a hope that more of the same might be). (Alberta, 1991, p. 4-4)

Since 1991, in addition to the reports that were expected, the Royal Commission on Aboriginal Peoples has published a volume of collected justice papers (RCAP, 1993) and the Law Reform Commission of Canada has studied and reported on the impact of the criminal sanction on aboriginal peoples (LRCC, 1991).

There is a haunting repetition throughout the two decades of reports and the corresponding 1500 recommendations.[4] The Cawsey commission makes these comments on the trends in the recommendations:

> Despite the patterns of recommendations, there have been changes in the type of recommendations made over the years. The Reports between 1967 and 1978 made wide-ranging recommendations that put the Criminal Justice System in a wider societal context. These recommendations included alcohol treatment, diversion, economic development and recreation as crime prevention strategies.
>
> Of the later reports, only *Policing in a Pluralistic Society* (1989) includes such recommendations. Later reports tend to be very Criminal Justice System-specific and frequently focus on only one component, such as the Police (especially the Police), the Courts, or corrections. It should be noted that: 1) only one report deals with Native victims of crime; and, 2) recommendations dealing with specific services are concentrated in certain reports (e.g. the policing studies). In addition to these reports there have been an increasing number of reports on discrimination, education and socio-economic conditions which may account for the decrease in contextual recommendations in the Criminal Justice reports. (Alberta, 1991, pp. 4–6)

The work of the Cawsey commission has been the only attempt to rigorously analyze the existing recommendations.[5] The problem is not one of not knowing what is happening to aboriginal people in the justice system. The problem is not a failure of new ideas that are meant to ameliorate the situation. The failure is a clear failure to implement what is already known.

The Royal Commission on Aboriginal Peoples has reviewed eight of the major justice reports and noted that "the extent to which recommendations have been implemented is a matter for concern; certainly the release of an inquiry report has not necessarily signified the beginning of change and amelioration of the problem" (Blackburn, 1993, p. 16). The realization that few reports have been substantially implemented raises a series of questions. This is an area where systematic research of government responses would benefit our understanding. It is not aboriginal communities that need to be further studied. There are two sides to the justice problems aboriginal people face, and the truth is that very little is known about why the knowledge we have has not been fully implemented. Rather, our communities need to be resourced so that crime and justice projects can be begun or be strengthened. After all, one of the things we do know is that (in the words of Justice Cawsey): "Everything that has worked for natives has come from natives" (RCAP, 1993, p. 12).

The most important realization is that aboriginal people's struggle with the criminal law sanction is not manifest only in our overrepresentation. Aboriginal struggles with the criminal law sanction in Canada is also not a new phenomenon. It did not begin in 1967 when Canadians began to study the issue. It is a historic relationship that finds its origins in the time of contact (see Backhouse, 1991; Kly, 1991; Schuh, 1979; Stonechild, 1986). The historical understanding that is accessible concerning the relationship of aboriginal peoples and the criminal justice system is at best rudimentary.

Criminal justice experts (who tend to be non-aboriginal people) minimize the historic relations between aboriginal people and the state as a source of the problems that aboriginal people currently face in the existing criminal justice system. This is a significant difference that continues to separate aboriginal and non-aboriginal understandings of the problem. As an aboriginal woman who struggles to understand decolonization, I am aware of the impact of the history of my people in this country. I know that the Royal Canadian Mounted Police were actively involved in the suppression of our traditional forms of government and the insistence that we follow the Indian Act model of non-democratic elected rule. These facts ground my response to the criminal sanction in such a way that I cannot view the Canadian system as a just one. Many other justice scholars (generally non-aboriginal individuals) possess the luxury and ability to begin their scholarly undertakings by presuming the system is just. This is a fundamental difference in the two forms of justice scholarship.

THE CONTOURS OF OVERREPRESENTATION WITHIN INSTITUTIONS OF CRIMINAL JUSTICE

The overrepresentation of aboriginal people in the Canadian criminal justice system has been the starting place of every Canadian justice inquiry mandated in the last three decades. In keeping with this well-established preoccupation with documenting the current situation, this chapter also considers the statistics. Truly, the picture revealed is bleak. No commission or inquiry has managed to move fully beyond this fixation with numbers. Even the Royal Commission on Aboriginal Peoples based almost its entire research agenda on this preoccupation with numerical documentation. We all admit there is a problem. This documentation preoccupation is a trend that must not be continued, because it ensures that no meaningful change can occur. This chapter adds the theory of decolonization to the statistical picture that is overwhelmingly available.

It is difficult to rely on existing data to provide a clear and complete picture of aboriginal involvement and experience of the justice system.[6] Data collection methods are inconsistent across various components of the justice system. The federal–provincial sharing of criminal jurisdiction also complicates the problem by adding a further level of inconsistency. National police statistics were abolished three decades ago. In police data, only gender is specified; age, race, and other socio-demographic data are not consistently available (Johnson and Rodgers, 1993, p. 95). In the 1980s, Statistics Canada abandoned efforts to collect national court data (Johnson and Rodgers, 1993, p. 96). All of this raises concerns about the reliability of the statistical pictures we have all been insistently drawing. In 1967, the authors of the report *Indians and the Law* experienced difficulties in data collection that they described as follows:

> Since collection of such data by the provincial agencies required special report forms not ordinarily used, the information was difficult to obtain. Indeed, serious difficulties were encountered in practically all agencies because very few differentiate between Indians and non-Indians when recording arrests, court appearances or sentences. Consequently, the statistics are not as complete as would be desirable although they do indicate trends that cannot be ignored. (Laing and Monture, 1967, p. 12)

After almost three decades of looking at the problem of aboriginal overrepresentation, the bleak statistical picture remains incomplete. Perhaps this is one of the reasons that researchers remain preoccupied with examining the statistical backdrop. Nonetheless, both situations are barriers to meaningful change in the experiences of aboriginal people in Canada's justice system.

It is helpful to understand the patterns that emerge when statistical information is examined. These patterns help us understand the shape of the discrimination that aboriginal people experience in current criminal justice experiences. We know more about federal offenders than we do about provincial offenders or young offenders. It is difficult to make interprovincial comparisons for young offenders and provincial offenders. It must be understood that the statistical picture is incomplete and perhaps inaccurate. What is known absolutely is that aboriginal people are clearly and dramatically overrepresented in the Canadian justice system. This alone is sufficient evidence to question the justness of that system. Aboriginal overrepresentation is only a window through which the existing system can begin to be examined and understood.

The overrepresentation of aboriginal people in Canadian prisons is a well-acknowledged fact. In Manitoba, aboriginal people account for 12 percent of the population but represent half of the admissions to correction institutions (Manitoba, 1991, p. 85). The overrepresentation of aboriginal offenders in the federal system is most marked in the prairie region (Alberta, Saskatchewan, and Manitoba). As of November 1994, aboriginal inmates accounted for 75 percent of the individuals incarcerated federally. In the fiscal year 1989–90, the overrepresentation was greatest in the province of Saskatchewan (Correctional Service of Canada, 1994a, p. 1). In and of itself, the overrepresentation is a disturbing fact. It is, however, a superficial and incomplete portrait of the reality that faces aboriginal people caught by the Canadian criminal justice system.[7]

The data provided by the Aboriginal Justice Inquiry of Manitoba is an informative place to start looking in detail at the experience of aboriginal people in the justice system. Data for the other western provinces are not unlike those for Manitoba. The Manitoba report notes that in 1989 40 percent of the population at Stoney Mountain prison were aboriginal men.[8] This figure has steadily increased since 1965, when aboriginal men accounted for 22 percent of the federal admissions at the same prison (Manitoba, 1991, pp. 9–10, 101).[9] Despite attempts in the last two decades to address the problem of overrepresentation, there has been no meaningful decrease in the ratio of overrepresentation. In fact, the situation has steadily worsened in this federal prison.

In Saskatchewan, the situation is even worse. Aboriginal prisoners account for 55 percent of the population at Saskatchewan Penitentiary. There is reason to question the accuracy of this statistic since "some managers suggest that the official figures . . . underestimate the number of Aboriginal inmates in their Institutions" (Correctional Service of Canada, 1994a, p. 1). Compare this with the realization that in the 1920s, only 5 percent of all provincial inmates in Saskatchewan were aboriginal (School of Human Justice, 1991). This is despite a number of well-intentioned attempts to address aboriginal overrepresentation. The reforms attempted have not been successful if the standard is a decrease in overrepresentation. Reforms may have changed, perhaps even improved, the individual experience of aboriginal offenders. The failure of past reforms must be taken seriously and form a basis for the conclusion that a new direction in correctional reform is required.

The statistical evidence that is available clearly indicates that the situation is not going to improve in the next decade. The overrepresentation of aboriginal youth in Manitoba's provincial institutions is more pronounced than in the federal population. In 1990, "64 percent of the Manitoba Youth Centre population and 78 percent of Agassiz's population were Aboriginal youth" (Manitoba, 1991, p. 10). Provincial offenders in Manitoba are also overrepresented. In 1989, 47 percent of the admissions to Headingley Institution were aboriginal. The same pattern of increasing disproportional representation in youth and provincial offender populations over the last decade must be noted. The many attempts at amelioration have been failures if the reduction in overrepresentation is the measure of meaningful change.

Those involved in corrections understand that there is a pattern in the progression of individuals from youth to provincial to federal institutions. Since the overrepresentation of aboriginal people is most pronounced in youth offender populations, and more marked in provincial than in federal institutions, there is no relief to be seen from the disproportional representation of aboriginal people in custodial institutions in the next few years. If youth overrepresentation were notably lower than provincial and federal overrepresentation, there would be some immediate hope for a decrease in overrepresentation in provincial and federal inmate populations in the future. The concern is deepened when it is noted that the portion of the aboriginal population between the ages of 15 and 24 is greater than that found in Canadian population. This is further evidence that suggests that we will see a continued increase of overrepresentation of aboriginal people in Canadian prisons, jails, and youth facilities.

The figures presented thus far have largely involved only the overrepresentation of aboriginal men. Men account for the majority of all adult offenders. On any given day, the head count in federal prisons tallies around 18 400 men (Correctional Services of Canada, 1994c); women number only 500.[10] The number of individual lives of women *directly* affected by incarceration is far lower than men. However, the overrepresentation of aboriginal people in the criminal justice system is most noted among aboriginal women. In a recent Saskatchewan study, it was found a treaty Indian woman is 131 times more likely, and a Métis woman 28 times more likely, to be incarcerated than a non-aboriginal woman (Jackson, 1988, p. 3). In Manitoba, 67 percent of the 1989 admissions to Portage jail (for women) were aboriginal women (Manitoba, 1991, p. 10). The impact of incarceration on aboriginal people must include a gendered analysis.

The impact of incarceration on aboriginal women must be understood through an analysis of the development of correctional policy in Canada. The system was created to house prisoners, the vast majority of whom were and are men. Until 1934, when the federal Prison for Women was opened in Kingston, women were housed in prisons alongside men. Women's incarceration was an afterthought in corrections. The system of incarceration in Canada is a system designed and developed for men, by men, and is directed at male crime. Just as women were an afterthought in corrections, so were aboriginal people. It is equally true that the system of corrections in Canada was designed and developed for white men, by white men. Aboriginal women are, therefore, an afterthought within an afterthought (Correctional Service of Canada, 1990, pp. 17–18). This situation must be seen to be unacceptable. The Task Force on Federally Sentenced Women, mandated in 1989, was the first to be charged with examining the situation of women (as women) in federal prisons. Because of a strong aboriginal women's lobby, our views were included in this work. The task force report, *Creating Choices*, did not examine the overall situation of women in conflict with the law. It examined only the situation of women sentenced to federal terms of imprisonment. In this way, the report is narrowly focussed and no clear national picture is available on the way in which women experience the full range of the criminal justice sanction.

The figures that document the drastic overrepresentation of aboriginal people in contact with the Canadian criminal justice system measure only the experience of those who have come into direct contact with the penal system. This particular focus can diminish the overall impact that the criminal justice sanction has on aboriginal people and our communities. For example, it is known that aboriginal men are more likely than non-aboriginal men to be federal prisoners (at a ratio of more than 20:1). It is a serious error to conclude that the problem of overrepresentation is borne only by our men. Those men are brothers, fathers, husbands, and sons of aboriginal women. Statistics indicate that in one urban centre, Winnipeg, 43 percent of aboriginal families are headed by single women compared with 10 percent of non-aboriginal families (Manitoba, 1991, p. 481). It is unnecessary to wonder where *all* of these men have gone. We know, logically, that some of them are incarcerated. Aboriginal women may not be directly affected by the criminal justice system as frequently as men, but the impact of the system on our lives is equally extreme.

It is not just the fact of overrepresentation and the repercussions felt in our families and communities that must become publicly noted and concern-evoking. The depth of the disparity in the treatment of aboriginal and non-aboriginal offenders must also be noted. The Aboriginal Justice Inquiry of Manitoba concluded that every aspect of the criminal justice system is problematic for aboriginal people. The inquiry conducted a survey as well as reviewed provincial court records and made some startling observations. Aboriginal people are more likely to be charged by police with multiple offences. Twenty-two percent of aboriginal people appearing in court face four or more charges, compared with only 13 percent of non-aboriginal people. Once arrested, aboriginal people are 1.34 times more likely than non-aboriginal people to be held in jail before their court appearances, and once in pretrial custody, aboriginal people spend 1.5 times longer in custody before their trials. When preparing for court appearances, aboriginal people see their lawyers less frequently and for less time than do non-aboriginal people: "Forty-eight percent of Aboriginal people spent less than an hour with their lawyers compared to 46 percent of non-Aboriginal inmates who saw their lawyers for more than 3 hours" (Manitoba, 1991, p. 102).[11] Although statistics from one jurisdiction cannot be assumed to apply to other areas, there is no information that suggests that the majority of aboriginal offenders do not face the same kinds of difficulties in other parts of the country. Furthermore, the overrepresentation of aboriginal people in correctional institutions is clearly and obviously linked to these factors.

In the Manitoba courts, the disparity in treatment of aboriginal people is also remarkable. Sixty percent of aboriginal people entered guilty pleas compared with 50 percent of non-aboriginal people. Aboriginal people received jail terms in 25 percent of the cases while non-aboriginal people were incarcerated in 10 percent of the cases. Aboriginal people receive longer sentences and receive absolute or conditional discharges less frequently (Manitoba, 1991, p. 103). These statistics also enhance our understanding of the patterns of and reasons behind the grave overrepresentation of aboriginal people in Canadian prisons. The pattern exposed reveals that there are important systemic patterns within the justice system that contribute to aboriginal overrepresentation in prisoner populations. Aboriginal overrepresentation is not properly explained by theories of individual aboriginal pathology.

After documenting the pattern of overrepresentation of aboriginal people in Canadian prisons, courts, and police contacts, the commissioners of the Aboriginal Justice Inquiry came to this poignant conclusion:

> These statistics are dramatic. There is something inherently wrong with a system which takes such harsh measures against an identifiable minority. It is also improbable that systemic discrimination has not played a major role in bringing this state of affairs into being.

The recognition that the problem of corrections is in fact systemic has yet to be fully incorporated into the thinking of those with the power to change correctional relations. An analysis of the reforms to date indicates that the vast majority of reforms have expected aboriginal people to change to fit into the system (that is, most efforts at reform have been individualized as opposed to systemic). Reforms such as provincial court workers or legal education projects have been established to assist aboriginal people in understanding the foreign system of Canadian laws and justice relations. Why is it that aboriginal people are expected to change to accommodate the system, rather than the system changing in such a way that aboriginal people are fundamentally respected by that system? A system of justice that is capable of singling out any identifiable group to receive special and excessive contact cannot be seen to be just and fair. However, this situation has not only existed in Canada since at least 1967, it has continued to worsen.

Once incarcerated, aboriginal offenders continue to receive unequal treatment. The Aboriginal Justice Inquiry of Manitoba again provides an interesting window on the shape of the problems within correction institutions. The inquiry surveyed 258 inmates (60 aboriginal and 198 non-aboriginal). The aboriginal inmates reported that they felt that aboriginal spirituality was not respected in their institution (81 percent). Fewer than 5 percent of these inmates indicated that they had regular access to these activities (Manitoba, 1991, p. 444). In fact, the commissioners of the inquiry concluded that aboriginal spirituality is not being encouraged in institutions, it is being actively discouraged (Manitoba, 1991, p. 445).

Aboriginal inmates also report that programming in the institutions is not acceptable. In most cases, appropriate programming that addresses their needs is not available.[12] "Yet, if they do not participate in the programs that are offered, that fact appears on their record and harms their chances for parole" (Manitoba, 1991, p. 447). Aboriginal offenders are forced to engage in programs that have little personal (cultural) worth if they wish to have any opportunity to secure a parole. Logically, the statistics available on parole indicate that aboriginal people are less likely to be granted parole. In 1994, 60 percent of non-aboriginal offenders were granted parole compared with only 44.5 percent of aboriginal offenders. These release rates are an improvement over the 1980 figures. For several years now, and particularly in the prairie region, aboriginal inmates have been able to have elder-assisted parole hearings. Studies indicate that this has not significantly improved the rate of granting of parole to aboriginal offenders, but parole board members report that it has provided aboriginal inmates with the opportunity to have "hearings that are more relaxed and informal which many find is conducive to openness and sincerity" (Correctional Service of Canada, 1994b, pp. 25–26). It is not documented whether aboriginal offenders would agree with this conclusion.

As equally remarkable as the overrepresentation of aboriginal people as clients in the criminal justice system is the exclusion (or underrepresentation) of aboriginal people from any place of authority in the criminal justice system (Manitoba, 1991, p. 663). There are very few aboriginal lawyers, police officers, court personnel, corrections workers, or parole officers. There is usually no one in our communities employed in the system to turn to if we are confused by what is happening to us in that system. As a result, aboriginal people view the justice system as a system that belongs to Canada and not to aboriginal people. We understand that as the clients of that system, we "support" the system. In fact, the system is built on the backs of many aboriginal offenders and their families. Aboriginal people see little if any benefit accruing to our communities. We do not earn our livelihood by involvement in that system. Instead, we pay fines and see dollars (and individuals) going out of our communities and know that the benefit is received by the government or Canadians in general (Manitoba, 1991, p. 420). It is little wonder that aboriginal people have little respect for the Canadian criminal justice system.

The overrepresentation of aboriginal people in penal institutions, their disparate treatment in prisons, and the chronic underrepresentation in positions of employment within the justice area are merely glimpses at the way in which justice relations negatively affect aboriginal people. Although it would be unfair to stereotype all reserves as having high crime rates, there is a greater statistical likelihood that an individual living on-reserve will be victimized by crime.[13] The national crime rate is 92.7 crimes per 1000 population. The Department of Indian Affairs reports that the crime rate on reserves is 165.6 per 1000 population, or 1.8 times the national average (Manitoba, 1991, p. 87). Even more troubling is the fact that the rate of violent crime is greater on Indian reserves. The violent crime rate on reserves is 3.67 times the national rate (Manitoba, 1991, p. 87). Indian people are more likely to be victims of crime and the "opportunity" to be a victim of violent crime is even greater. The need to address the difficulties in the Canadian criminal justice system as it is applied to aboriginal people is a concern that is much broader than the mere jailing of our citizens. It is a reflection of the life experiences of aboriginal people and has a negative impact on the quality of life in our communities. The impact of the Canadian criminal justice system and its failure to provide meaningful correctional and criminal justice services to aboriginal offenders also create additional burdens on our communities and on victims.

An equally disturbing pattern of exclusion (underrepresentation) is evident in the scholarly papers that have been completed to date. In

1992, Robert Silverman and Marianne Nielson (neither of whom self-identify as aboriginal people)[14] edited a collection of papers entitled *Aboriginal People and Canadian Criminal Justice*. Of the contributors to this book, I can identify three of 21 who are aboriginal people.[15] The editors themselves note:

> As our primary goal was to span the criminal justice process with empirically based materials, it became evident that we would not be able to include many Aboriginal authors. There is a literature, but it tends to be based on oral tradition or is very narrowly cast. We were fortunate in finding a few articles by Native authors. In order to better represent a Native point of view, we have included appropriate newspaper excerpts. (Silverman and Nielson, 1992, p. vii)

The editors chose to produce a text that was based on the structure of the existing justice system. This must be understood to have been a choice. Because the analyses in the text were based on existing components of the criminal justice system, there was no place left for an aboriginal analysis or understanding. This does not reflect a weakness in aboriginal analysis, but a weakness in the theoretical presumptions that grounded the development of the book. Even more troubling is the minimization of the importance of oral histories in a manner that perfectly mirrors the Eurocentric biases in academia. Because the material in this book was preoccupied with documentation, it was dated before it was published. This book is not the only collection that suffers these kinds of difficulties.[16] It is long past time for a change in how research and writing that fundamentally affect the lives of aboriginal people are completed.[17]

UNDERSTANDING THE COLONIAL IMPACT OF CANADIAN JUSTICE INSTITUTIONS

The situation of over- and underrepresentation of aboriginal people in the Canadian criminal justice system must be understood to create the situation where aboriginal people can have no respect for Canada's system of criminal law and correction. This is not the fault[18] of aboriginal people but must be seen to be a systemic problem that is the responsibility of the Canadian justice system and those who support it. Canadians must also come to understand colonization and, more important, decolonization. It is very difficult for aboriginal people to live in a decolonized manner when the practice of colonialism is still alive and well in Canada.

Since 1967 and the release of the report of the Canadian Corrections Association, social scientists, often in partnership with government departments, have searched for the cause of aboriginal criminality. In the 1967 report, the discussion concluded with a realization "that much of whatever trouble these people were having with the law could be understood only in light of economic conditions, culture patterns, minority group status and other underlying factors" (Laing and Monture, 1967, p. 9). Since 1989 and the release of the Donald Marshall inquiry report, the factors analyzed to produce an understanding of aboriginal criminality became individualized. This is troubling. Economic disadvantage, underemployment, substance abuse, and other factors that are used to explain aboriginal overinvolvement in crime are not the source of the problem but symptoms of the problems of a society that is structured on discriminatory values, beliefs, and practices. The outcome of the individualized analysis of aboriginal patterns of crime conceals the true relationship.

Commissioners Hamilton and Sinclair note in the Report of the Aboriginal Justice Inquiry of Manitoba (1991) two immediate answers to the reasons for the shocking overrepresentation of aboriginal people in the criminal justice system. Either aboriginal people commit disproportionately more crimes than do non-aboriginal people, or aboriginal people are the victims of a discriminatory justice system. They add:

> We believe that both answers are correct, but not in the simplistic sense that some people might interpret them. We do not believe, for instance, that there is anything about Aboriginal people or their culture that predisposes them to criminal behavior. Instead, we believe that the causes of Aboriginal criminal behavior are rooted in a long history of discrimination and social inequality that has impoverished Aboriginal people and consigned them to the margins of Manitoban society. (Manitoba, 1991, p. 85)

In particular, discrimination in the justice system cannot be simply understood. Discrimination comes in many forms. Aboriginal people experience discrimination in the courts and jails, and in our communities where we have a greater statistical likelihood of being victimized; and we recognize familiar patterns of exclusion in the lack of opportunity to be employed within the justice system. The two causes of aboriginal overrepresentation identified by the Manitoba commissioners lead to several logical conclusions about reforming the justice system.

I have never thought that reform of the existing system would be a full and complete remedy. This became a hardened opinion during my years as a volunteer in the Kingston-area penitentiaries.[19] This lesson is reaffirmed every time I consider the government-sponsored justice reports. It saddens me to think that it is even a necessary remedy, but it is. Reform of the existing system is most necessary. Many aboriginal prisoners are currently serving sentences in Canada's prisons and jails. These are relatives and friends on whom I cannot turn my back. I am very much convinced that even if the existing system were reformed in such a way that aboriginal people were proportionately represented and received equal treatment, aboriginal people would still continue to report that they perceive the Canadian criminal justice system as unfair.

There is another factor that affects the perception of aboriginal people that they are treated unfairly by the existing system. This factor has largely been ignored in the academic literature and multiple reports, but I have heard it mentioned by many aboriginal people. This forgotten factor is history. There is a long history of the criminal law sanction being used to control, oppress, and force the assimilation of aboriginal peoples. This is carefully remembered by some aboriginal people. There are a number of examples of the historic relationship.

Examining the introduction of alcohol to aboriginal populations provides an important example of the way that an understanding of historic relations must complement present-day understandings. The abuse of alcohol has been demonstrated to influence the participation in criminal activity. This is true across most categories of offences and is particularly true for aboriginal offenders. Alcohol was introduced into aboriginal nations by European traders who learned that they could accumulate great profits when they relied on alcohol as a trade commodity. In the Cypress Hills area (southern Saskatchewan), for example, it has been reported that

> [t]he trading of whiskey could boost a trader's profits substantially. In 1854 a clear profit of 45 cents could be made on trading a $9.67 gun for $416.00 worth of buffalo robes. Proof alcohol cost the trader $3.25 to $6.00 a gallon — diluted and spiced up it could bring up to $50.00 in hides. In one rate of exchange, two robes were traded for one large glass of "rot-gut" whiskey. (Hildebrandt and Hubner, 1994, p. 36)[20]

Today, the history of aboriginal people's introduction to alcohol consumption is forgotten. It is within this relationship that one of the seeds of aboriginal overrepresentation in the criminal justice system was firmly rooted.

The Aboriginal Justice Inquiry of Manitoba is the first Canadian report to have developed a consistent focus on the effect of racism, individual and systemic, in the overrepresentation of aboriginal people within the criminal justice system. This focus on racism and criminal sanction extends back in time to the period of contact and is manifest today in the overrepresentation of aboriginal offenders in the criminal justice system. In their own words, the commissioners explain:

> Historically, the justice system has discriminated against Aboriginal people by providing legal sanction for their oppression. This oppression of previous generations forced Aboriginal people into their current state of social and economic distress. Now, a seemingly neutral justice system discriminates against current generations of Aboriginal people by applying laws which have an adverse impact on people of lower socio-economic status. This is no less racial discrimination; it is merely "laundered" racial discrimination. It is untenable to say that discrimination which builds upon the effects of racial discrimination is not racial discrimination itself. Past injustices cannot be ignored or built upon. (Manitoba, 1991, p. 109)

The work of the Aboriginal Justice Inquiry introduced a new level of analysis to an old question. The question of aboriginal overinvolvement in all relations of criminal justice in Canada is analyzed at a systemic level.

Racism is understood as the central factor in understanding the over-representation of aboriginal people in Canadian prisons.

Racism is in fact an incomplete explanation of what is happening in the Canadian criminal justice system. Racism does not emphasize enough the historic relationships that appear when the overrepresentation of aboriginal people in Canadian jails is placed in context. In fact, colonialism is also a necessary component of the explanation. The Canadian justice system is now the central institution that reinforces colonial relationships against aboriginal people. This fact must influence the way that any reformation of Canadian criminal justice systems proceeds.

When I think about reforming the Canadian criminal justice system, I often find myself reflecting on my experiences of the struggle that individuals have faced to keep out of prison. Learning to walk on this side of the prison wall has been difficult for many people with whom I have shared small parts of this experience. Little in the way of programming within the prison system has prepared them for the journey that they face on this side of the prison wall. Little is known in a scholarly sense about what works in the "after-care" field. Few resources are devoted to providing postincarceration services and programs. The question, how do we keep our people out, has become central in my thoughts on criminal justice and aboriginal peoples. Intuitively, I know the answer. Caring and connection keeps people out. This does not surprise me because I understand that the vast majority of aboriginal law is nothing more than rules about kinship and caring. Aboriginal law is relational. The question, how do we keep our people out, is the question I wish to leave you with.

NOTES

1. Mohawk Nation, Grand River Territory, currently residing at the Thunderchild First Nation, Saskatchewan. Associate Professor, Department of Native Studies, University of Saskatchewan. The chapter is written for my brothers and sisters in iron cages. It is written with prayer that meaningful change is not far away.

2. In recent writings I have chosen to adopt constitutionally prescribed language. "Aboriginal peoples" include the Indian (status and not), Inuit, and Métis. I intend this language to include all indigenous peoples of the territory now known as Canada.

3. For example, in 1886 section 114 of the Indian Act provided for a term of imprisonment not to exceed six months (and not less than two months) for anyone engaging in the "festival" known as the potlatch or the dance known as the *tamanawas*. A similar provision existed in the Indian Act until the 1951 amendments. Since it was first enacted, the section was broaden to include many other Indian ceremonies and dances.

4. A systematic and detailed analysis of these recommendations has never been undertaken and made accessible. Disappointingly, the Royal Commission on Aboriginal Peoples did not attempt such a project, even though it was well within its mandate and resources. Rather, every study replicates the ones that

came before. Part of this is a problem of the multiple jurisdictions involved in criminal justice matters and the fragmentation of services from prevention and policing to corrections.

5. The Cawsey commission notes (Alberta, 1991, pp. 4–7) that the top ten recommendations are (in no particular order): "cross-cultural training for non-Native staff; employ more Native staff; have more community-based programs in corrections; have more community-based alternatives in sentencing; have more special assistance to Native offenders; have more Native community involvement in planning, decision-making and service delivery; have more Native advisory groups at all levels; have more recognition of Native culture and law in Criminal Justice System service delivery; emphasize crime prevention programs; and, self-determination must be considered in planning and operation of the Criminal Justice System." The report also notes that there "has been very little focus at the front-end of the system." Little attention has been paid to victim services and prevention (pp. 4-9).

6. The most complete picture available is found in the Aboriginal Justice Inquiry of Manitoba. This study focusses on justice relations and experiences in the province of Manitoba only. No comprehensive national picture is available.

7. I believe justice to be a much larger relation than just one involving the criminal law sanction. This chapter will, however, focus on the consequences of aboriginal overrepresentation in the existing justice system. Discussions of the broader meaning of justice can be found in Monture-Okanee, 1994 and 1992.

8. Stoney Mountain is a federal penitentiary operated by the Correctional Service of Canada. It houses prisoners who are serving sentences of longer than two years. Provincial prisons (discussed in the next paragraph of the text) are prisoners who are serving sentences of less than two years. Youth offenders are under the age of 18.

9. It must be noted that these statistics are open to criticism. Part of the increase in the overrepresentation may be accounted for by the fact that it has become more acceptable to admit aboriginal ancestry. Federal data rely solely on self-report figures.

10. These numbers were provided to the members of the Task Force on Federally Sentenced Women.

11. Part of this phenomenon may be explained by the greater number of guilty pleas that aboriginal people enter.

12. The aboriginal inmates indicated what kind of programs they would like to see in the Manitoba institutions. The most desired programs were educational or vocational (43 percent), followed by programs involving spirituality and culture (29 percent). Also in demand were life-skills programs (14 percent). Also mentioned as important were "alcohol and drug dependency, stress management, crafts, parenting, marital counseling and Native languages" (Manitoba, 1991, p. 449).

13. Figures such as these are available only for registered Indians.

14. My concern is not simply whether researchers are aboriginal. I am concerned to see that individuals who attempt to explain aboriginal people's understanding and experience of criminal justice in fact understand aboriginal worldview(s) and histories. Unfortunately, this has been the exception in the work completed to date.

15. One of the difficulties in determining whether an author is of aboriginal ancestry is that it is accepted academic practice to list only degrees and institutional affiliations. It is not "proper" for an academic to list her nation or clan. There is no non-aboriginal equivalent to such a reference. This can make it difficult to determine who is doing the writing, but who is doing the writing *does* make a difference. In the aboriginal worldview(s), lived experience is at least as important as book knowledge.

16. The other collection that is held out as a watershed work on aboriginal people and criminal justice in Canada is a volume of the *Canadian Journal of Criminology*, also published in 1992. The same pattern of exclusion of aboriginal authors is noted. Again, only professional credentials are identified and it is difficult to identify the aboriginal authors.

17. A new work that meets this challenge is Gosse, Henderson, and Carter, 1994.

18. I do not believe that assigning blame is necessarily part of the solution to the problems that exist in the justice system.

19. I lived in the Kingston area from 1983 to 1988. I was actively involved in the prisons during those years and have maintained many of the friendships after I left the area. My involvement with the Task Force on Federally Sentenced Women also reinforced this view.

20. Similar figures and the tale of a trader can be found in Weekes, 1994, pp. 9–18.

DISCUSSION QUESTIONS

1. What knowledge is gained from the many justice reports commissioned in the last decade?

2. Why is it essential to include the "perspective" of aboriginal people in an analysis of overrepresentation within the criminal justice system?

3. What inequalities do aboriginal people face in the Canadian criminal justice system?

4. Why have reforms to the criminal justice system in the last decade not been fully successful?

5. What "reforms" do you believe would be more successful?

FURTHER READINGS

Correctional Service of Canada. 1990. *Creating Choices: Report of the Task Force on Federally Sentenced Women*. Ottawa: Supply and Services. This is a ground-breaking report, the first to look specifically at the situation of women in federal corrections. The report concludes that women were an afterthought in federal corrections — a system developed by men for men and about men. The report also focusses on the situation and experiences of aboriginal women in the federal prison system and their grave overrepresentation as offenders.

Fox, Lana and Fran Sugar. 1989–90. "Nistum Peyako Seht'wawin Iskwe-wak: Breaking Chains." *Canadian Journal of Women and the Law* 3(2): pp. 465–82. This research paper compiled for the Task Force on Feder-ally Sentenced Women tells the stories of 42 aboriginal women who have served federal sentences. It is a valuable report both for its infor-mation and as an example of the research possibilities that exist when research is sensitive to aboriginal worldviews.

Gosse, Richard, James Youngblood Henderson, and Roger Carter. 1994. *Continuing Poundmaker and Riel's Quest: Presentations Made at a Conference on Aboriginal Peoples and Justice*. Saskatoon: Purich Pub-lishing. This collection of papers is the most recent publication on abo-riginal peoples and the Canadian justice system. It is also unique in that it combines the views of correctional workers, politicians responsi-ble for running correctional systems, and aboriginal peoples.

Monture-Angus, Patricia. 1995. *Thunder in My Soul: A Mohawk Woman Speaks*. Halifax: Fernwood. This book does not focus solely on issues of criminal justice but on the perspectives of one aboriginal woman academic. The book contains papers on justice from a holistic (or abo-riginal) perspective, child welfare, education, and feminism. This text will help readers understand some specific justice concerns as well as providing a larger context in which to consider the issues.

Royal Commission on Aboriginal Peoples. 1993. *Aboriginal Peoples and the Justice System: Report of the National Round Table on Aboriginal Justice Issues*. Ottawa: Supply and Services. In 1992, the royal com-mission brought together a group of aboriginal people and a number of non-aboriginal people involved in various components of the crimi-nal justice system to discuss the direction in which the commission could take its work. The people brought together were lawyers, aca-demics, justice employees, and politicians. This text canvasses a num-ber of issues that surround the establishment of aboriginal justice systems from a number of different perspectives.

Solomon, Arthur. 1990. *Songs for the People: Teachings on the Natural Way*. Toronto: NC Press.

————. 1994. *Eating Bitterness: A Vision Beyond the Prison Walls*. Toronto: NC Press. These are inspiring texts by an elder who has worked tirelessly for aboriginal people incarcerated in the Canadian criminal justice system. Dr. Solomon's vision will touch every reader.

REFERENCES

Ahenakew, Freda and H.C. Wolfart, eds. 1987. *waskahikaniwiyiniw — acimowina* (Stories of the House People). Winnipeg: University of Manitoba Press.

Alberta. 1991. *Report of the Task Force on the Criminal Justice System and Its Impact on the Indian and Métis People of Alberta.* Vol. III. *Working Papers and Bibliography.* Edmonton: Solicitor General.

Backhouse, Constance. 1991. *Petticoats and Prejudice: Women and Law in 19th Century Canada.* Toronto: Women's Press.

Blackburn, Carole. 1993. "Aboriginal Justice Inquiries, Task Forces and Commissions: An Update." Pp. 15–41 in *Aboriginal Peoples and the Justice System,* Royal Commission on Aboriginal Peoples. Ottawa: Supply and Services.

Correctional Service of Canada. 1990. *Creating Choices: Report of the Task Force on Federally Sentenced Women.* Ottawa: Supply and Services.

———. 1994a. "Aboriginal Issues," Internal CSC newsletter. (nd)

———. 1994b. *Care and Custody of Aboriginal Offenders.* Ottawa: Solicitor General.

———. 1994c. *Inmate Profile* (June 29).

Gosse, Richard, James Youngblood Henderson, and Roger Carter, eds. 1994. *Continuing Poundmaker and Riel's Quest: Presentations Made at a Conference on Aboriginal Peoples and Justice.* Saskatoon: Purich Publishing.

Hildebrandt, Walter and Brian Hubner. 1994. *The Cypress Hills: The Land and Its People.* Saskatoon: Purich Publishing.

Jackson, Michael. 1988. *Locking Up Natives in Canada: Report of the Canadian Bar Association Committee on Imprisonment and Release.* Toronto: Canadian Bar Association.

Johnson, Holly and Karen Rodgers. 1993. "A Statistical Overview of Women and Crime in Canada." Pp. 95–116 in *In Conflict with the Law: Women and the Canadian Justice System,* ed. Ellen Adelburg and Claudia Currie. Vancouver: Press Gang Publisher.

Kly, Yussuf. 1991. "Aboriginal Canadians, the Anti-Social Contract, and Higher Crime Rates." Pp. 81–94 in *Criminal Justice: Sentencing Issues and Reform,* ed. Les Samuelson and Bernard Schissel. Toronto: Garamond Press.

Laing, Arthur and Gilbert C. Monture. 1967. *Indians and the Law.* Ottawa: Canadian Corrections Association.

Law Reform Commission of Canada (LRCC). 1991. *Aboriginal Peoples and Criminal Justice.* Report 34. Ottawa: LRCC.

Manitoba. 1991. *Report of the Aboriginal Justice Inquiry of Manitoba: The Justice System and Aboriginal People.* Vol. I. A.C. Hamilton and C.M. Sinclair, Commissioners. Winnipeg: Queen's Printer.

McCaskill, Don. 1983. "Native People and the Justice System." Pp. 288–98 in *As Long as the Sun Shines and Water Flows: A Reader in Canadian Native Studies,* ed. Ian A.L. Getty and Antoine S. Lussier. Vancouver: University of British Columbia Press.

Monture-Okanee, Patricia. 1992. "The Roles and Responsibilities of Aboriginal Women: Reclaiming Justice." *Saskatchewan Law Review* 56(2): pp. 237–66.

———. 1994. "Aboriginal Peoples and Canadian Criminal Justice: Myths and Revolution." In *Continuing Poundmaker and Riel's Quest: Presentations Made at a*

Conference on Aboriginal Peoples and Justice, ed. Richard Gosse, James Youngblood Henderson, and Roger Carter. Saskatoon: Purich Publishing.

Newell, William B. (Ta-io-wah-ron-ha-gai). 1965. *Crime and Justice Among the Iroquois Nations*. Montreal: Caughnawaga Historical Society.

Royal Commission on Aboriginal Peoples (RCAP). 1993. *Aboriginal Peoples and the Justice System*. Ottawa: Supply and Services.

School of Human Justice, University of Regina. 1991. Brief submitted to the Saskatchewan Indian and Métis Justice Review Committee.

Schuh, Cornelia. 1979. "Justice on the Northern Frontier: Early Murder Trials of Native Accused." *Criminal Law Quarterly* 22: pp. 74–111.

Silverman, Robert and Marianne Nelson, eds. 1992. *Aboriginal People and Canadian Criminal Justice*. Toronto: Butterworths.

Stonechild, Blair. 1986. "The Uprising of 1885: Its Impacts on Federal/Indian Relations in Western Canada." *Saskatchewan Indian Federated College Journal* 2(2): pp. 81–96.

Upton, L.F.S. 1979. *Micmacs and Colonists: Indian–White Relations in the Maritimes, 1713–1867*. Vancouver: UBC Press.

Weekes, Mary. 1994. *The Last Buffalo Hunter*. Saskatoon: Fifth House Publishers.

CHAPTER 13

Aboriginal Peoples' Vision of the Future: Interweaving Traditional Knowledge and New Technologies

Simon Brascoupé

In the past century, the locus of aboriginal peoples' economic activity has shifted from the primary sector to the service sector. In some regions, this transformation occurred in only the past quarter century. The end result is that aboriginal peoples in Canada have been pushed to the margins economically and socially. Will this continue to be the pattern for the future? Can we put an end to this trend? Since the 1970s aboriginal peoples' political and economic influence has been growing in Canada. This new, although limited, autonomy provides aboriginal peoples with an opportunity to build a new economic, cultural, and social sustainable future. This chapter argues that through education, training, planning, and traditional knowledge, aboriginal peoples can expand upon an economical and environmental strategy that consists of seven elements:

1. education based on science, technology, and traditional knowledge;

2. training directed toward the environment, leading-edge technology, and resource management;

3. development of traditional knowledge institutions controlled by aboriginal peoples;

4. policy and development support for aboriginal environmental employment strategies;

5. sharing of information, stories, and knowledge around present initiatives in remote sensing and geographic information systems (GIS) in aboriginal communities to manage resources;

6. development of partnerships between aboriginal traditional ecological knowledge institutions, universities, colleges, and governments; and

7. a short-term education, training, and internship program supported by federal and provincial governments to attract aboriginal peoples into key sectors of environmental fields, including business, resource management, research, and science.

Change for the coming generations of aboriginal peoples is likely to be just as dramatic as the change from the fur trade to an industrialized economy. This time, though, there appears to be a number of favourable conditions for aboriginal peoples. First, they have greater political autonomy (self-government and land claims) and therefore are able to negotiate for greater control over their lives and resources. Second, in the current restructuring of the world economy, with its emphasis on resolving the environmental crisis, there is a place for traditional ecological knowledge. Third, society demands more environmentally sound solutions to production and development. Fourth, there is a growing awareness that a serious environmental strategy does not conflict with education, employment, and training programs.

It is now important that aboriginal peoples regain control over their economy and traditional territories through a strategy that includes sustainable resource harvesting, restoration of the environment, land claims, traditional knowledge, and new technologies. It appears that there are some sectors in which aboriginal peoples should pursue development in the future. Tourism, forestry, business, and new technologies are the main ones reviewed in this chapter.

There are several barriers, however, to realizing this strategy:

1. lack of understanding of the traditional economy and traditional knowledge of aboriginal peoples;

2. lack of models for the strengthening of traditional economies as a viable alternative to the present exploitive models of economic development; and

3. lack of understanding of how to link traditional environmental knowledge and science.

Removing the barriers will involve research and education directed at improving Canadians' understanding of their own fur trade history, as well as validating indigenous knowledge and traditional areas of work such as fishing, hunting, and trapping.

LEARNING FROM ABORIGINAL PEOPLES

This section argues that the world will have to change its basic value system to save the planet. This is not to say that westerners should become like aboriginal peoples. But western society needs to learn from indigenous peoples about respecting and living harmoniously with Mother Earth, and return to its own religious teachings with their ancient systems of knowledge, customs, and practices that respect Mother Earth. This process and reflection will emerge into a dialogue between western society and aboriginal peoples based on respect.

Without a fundamental and profound change in our value systems, culture, and social relations, the survival of human beings is threatened. Evidence of this abounds. Vaclav Havel, playwright, human rights campaigner, and former president of the Czech Republic (formerly Czechoslovakia) identifies overpopulation, AIDS, the greenhouse effect, holes in the ozone layer, depletion of biodiversity (for example, fisheries, trees, and medicines), nuclear terrorism, commercial television culture, racism, and regional wars as some of the threats we face at the close of the twentieth century.

Parents may find it disquieting that we have to keep our children out of the direct sun to prevent skin cancer, but even more worrying is the unknown impact of clear-cutting, fisheries depletion, pollutants, and garbage disposal. Increasing the awareness of and care for the environment by all people, all over the world, is our greatest challenge.

The Seventh Generation

One of the aboriginal peoples' teachings that is having an impact on the west is the Seventh Generation. Simply put, it refers to the fact that when indigenous communities make a decision, they must think about the impact it may have on the seven generations to come. Society is responsible for leaving future generations with a continuous cycle of resources, and a habitable and safe environment. This contrasts with western planners, who often think that all they are only morally responsible for the planning period, usually five years.

Aboriginal culture is endowed with a rich diversity of teachings, rituals, and ceremonies that continuously remind us of our responsibility to Mother Earth. When I was ten years old, I had a garden next to our house on the Tuscarora Indian Reservation. It was mid-summer in 1958. I remember it was quite dry and I had to water my growing plants every day. I asked my grandmother if she knew of a way I could make it rain. She said I could go and sing in my garden. It did not matter what song I sang, but it would help. I did as she said. I do not remember if it rained, but I do remember carrying more water to my garden that summer.

Years later when I was doing research, I found there was a song Seneca women sang to Mother Earth apologizing for disturbing her skin, explaining that they needed to cultivate to survive. I have since experienced and learned that indigenous peoples all around the world have this sacred relationship with Mother Earth. This respect, honouring, and responsibility according to our teaching extends to the seventh generation. In the words of Oren Lyons, faithkeeper of the Onondaga Nation:

> In our way of life, in our government, with every decision we make, we always keep in mind the Seventh Generation to come. It's our job to see that the people coming ahead, the generations still unborn, have a world

no worse than ours — and hopefully better. When we walk upon Mother Earth we always plant our feet carefully because we know the faces of our future generations are looking up at us from beneath the ground. We never forget them. (Wall and Arden, 1990, p. 68)

The Seventh Generation teaching is also a prophecy that predicts that the world will eventually come to indigenous peoples, when westerners relearn how to live in harmony with the earth. The prophecy says there would be a time when the air would make a person's eyes water, a time when the water would be undrinkable. It described large black snakes, which our elders have interpreted as roads, that stretched across the land. The World Commission on Environment and Development, also known as the Bruntland commission (WCED, 1987), saw the importance of indigenous teachings, and recommended that indigenous peoples be consulted to learn how to live sustainably with the earth. Indigenous peoples have laws or original instructions given to them by the Creator. The first principle, "natural law," identifies the relational quality of all life:

> Our ancestors developed ways and means of relating to each other and to the land, based upon simple and pragmatic understanding of their presence on this earth. If they failed to consider what the environment had to offer, how much it could give, and at what times it was prepared to give — they would simply die. This basic law held for every living thing on the earth. All living creatures had to be cognizant of the structure of the day, the cycle of the seasons, and their effects on all other living matter. (Clarkson et al., 1990, p. 4)

We have been instructed by the Creator to live in harmony with nature. If we destroy and misuse the water, for example, we will not be given a fine, we threaten our own existence. Oren Lyons says:

> Natural law prevails everywhere. It supersedes Man's law. If you violate it, you get hit. There's no judge and jury, there's no lawyers or courts, you can't buy or dodge or beg your way out of it. If you violate this Natural law you're going to get hit and get hit hard. One of the Natural laws is that you've got to keep things pure. Especially the water. Keeping the water pure is one of the first laws of life. If you destroy the water, you destroy life. (Wall and Arden, 1990, p. 66)

Aboriginal spirituality also plays an important role in living sustainably. Day-to-day spirituality, based on the principle of "respect," can balance off our desire for more and more material things. At the United Nations Conference on Environment and Development (UNCED) in June 1992, Oren Lyons discussed spirituality. He asked, what do we do after we have said our prayers, given our thanks, and completed our rituals and ceremonies? He answered that caring for each other is our highest calling. He said that helping each other is the short cut to spirituality. Thus, spirituality is about our personal and daily relationship with the environment and our community.

Having respect for each other and the land and showing our humanity are powerful instruments of peace. When aboriginal peoples first meet someone, they are interested in a person's humanity. Vaclav Havel is interested in somewhat the same issue — he is aware of how dehumanizing the world can be and how we are sacrificing our spirit because we have lost our balance. He thinks that human beings must have a new face, a new way of being in the postmodern world.

> A politician [leader] must become a person again, someone who trusts not only a scientific representation and analysis of the world, but also in the world itself. He must believe not only in sociological statistics, but in real people. He must trust not only an objective interpretation of reality, but also his own soul, not only an adopted ideology, but also his own thoughts; not only the summary reports he receives each morning, but also his own feelings. Soul, individual spirituality, first hand personal insights into things, the courage to be himself and go the way his conscience points, humility in the face of the mysterious order of Being, confidence in its natural direction and, above all, trust in his own subjectivity as his principle link with the subjectivity of the world — these, in my view, are the qualities that politicians of the future should cultivate. (Havel, Davos, Switzerland)

Havel goes on to say in *Summer Meditations* (1992) that, "we must build a state on intellectual and spiritual values." He describes a state that has its own history, its own specificity:

> Building an intellectual and spiritual state — a state based on ideas — does not mean building an ideological state. Indeed, an ideological state cannot be intellectual or spiritual. A state based on ideas is precisely the opposite; it is meant to extricate human beings from the straitjacket of ideological interpretations, and to rehabilitate them as subjects of individual conscience, of individual thinking backed up by experience, of individual responsibility, and with love for their neighbours that is anything but abstract. (Havel, 1992, p. 128)

I have argued here that society must learn, not only to respect the earth, but to love Mother Earth, as loving parents love their children. We have accepted a second-rate system based on cynicism and mistrust for people. Even Adam Smith said that a society built on altruism is superior to a market system based on competition. We need new systems and leaders who can instil a sense of ownership and responsibility for each other and our institutions. Aboriginal peoples have much that can be learned by western society, of what is possible. Havel says:

> A state based on ideas should be no more and no less than a guarantee of freedom and security for people who know that the state and its institutions can stand behind them only if they themselves take responsibility for the state — that is, if they see it as their own project and their own home, as something they need not fear, as something they can without shame — love, because they have built it for themselves. (Havel, 1992, p. 128)

Values are not simply what we value in our lives, friends, community, and spiritual life. All societies have environmental or earth-based values. Western society has placed a lot of attention on social values, with the result that there is an imbalance with environmental values. Today's environmental problems are not just about the scale of industrialization but also about perspective, strategy, and long-term planning. Interestingly, in a time when western society is recognizing aboriginal peoples' environmental knowledge and values, aboriginal peoples are also undergoing a deep and profound spiritual renaissance:

> A renaissance is taking place among Native American peoples. This renaissance is not of a material nature. It is a spiritual renaissance, a retrieving and reviving of our original covenant with the Creator. We are reaffirming our relationship and stewardship with our Mother the Earth. While we are inspired and directed to do this for our children and ourselves, we also realize that many, not all, of our Elders have fallen asleep, forgotten, or have never known our rightful spiritual heritage. Therefore, it is up to those of us who have, in whatever measure, the teachings, philosophy, and traditions, including the rituals, to work for their revival and continuance. (Wall and Arden, 1990, p. 50)

At the heart of the renaissance is a deep reflection on indigenous values and the need for healing between western society and indigenous peoples. Indigenous values are based on a deep respect for the environment, natural law, and everyday spirituality. These could provide a base for insight and direction for the environmental, technological, and demographic issues facing the world. At the heart of this renaissance is a new paradigm requiring an overhaul of values, ideas, norms, and actions.

INDIGENOUS TRADITIONS AND WORLD RELIGIONS

The Seventh Generation prophecy also teaches us that the peoples of the four sacred directions around the world need to find peace together on this Mother Earth. In order for people to find harmony with nature they must also find harmony among the people of the four directions. It is noteworthy that this message has been very much at the heart of the teaching of present-day prophets and religious leaders. We observe that all the world religions have original instructions on living harmoniously with the earth.

In 1986, five of the world's major religions made declarations on nature. The five declarations of Assisi were made by religious leaders of the Buddhist, Christian, Hindu, Jewish, and Moslem religions. The declarations "speak of values and ethics which challenge many of the assumptions which secular conservation has held to be true — such as the anthropocentric nature of conservation" (Assisi, 1986, p. 1). The following highlights parts of the declarations from each of the five religions.

Buddhist: His Holiness the Dalai Lama

Our ancestors have left us a world rich in its natural resources and capable of fulfilling our needs. This is a fact. It was believed in the past that the natural resources of the Earth were unlimited, no matter how much they were exploited. But we know today that without understanding and care these resources are not inexhaustible. It is not difficult to understand and bear the exploitation done in the past out of ignorance, but now that we are aware of the dangerous factors, it is very important to examine our responsibilities and our commitment to values, and think of the kind of world we are to bequeath to future generations. (Assisi, 1986, pp. 6–7)

Christian: St. Gregory of Nazianzen

God set man upon earth as a kind of second world, a microcosm; another kind of angel, a worshipper of blended nature. . . . He was king of all upon earth, but subject to heaven; earthly and heavenly; transient, yet mortal; belonging both to the visible and to the intelligible order; midway between greatness and lowliness. (Assisi, 1986, p. 11)

Hindu: Mahabharata

[E]ven if there is only one tree full of flowers and fruits in a village, that place becomes worthy of worship and respect. (Assisi, 1986, p. 18)

Hinduism believes in the all encompassing sovereignty of the divine, manifesting itself in a graded scale of evolution. The human race, though at the top of the evolutionary pyramid at present, is not seen as something apart from the earth and its multitudinous lifeforms. The Atharava Veda has the magnificent Hymn to the Earth which is redolent with ecological and environmental values. (Assisi, 1986, p. 17)

Muslim

The classical Muslim jurist, Izz ad-din ibn Abd as-Salam . . . formulated the bill of legal rights of animals in the thirteenth century. Similarly, numerous other jurists and scholars developed legislations to safeguard water resources, prevent over-grazing, conserve forests, limit growth of cities, protect cultural property and so on. (Assisi, 1986, p. 24)

Judaism: Kabbalistic Teaching

[A]s Adam named all God's creatures, he helped define their essence. Adam swore to live in harmony with those whom he had named. Thus, at the very beginning of time, man accepted responsibility before God for all of creation. (Assisi, 1986, p. 29)

The religious teachings, original instructions, and contemporary indigenous peoples all have a common and deep respect for Mother Earth. With growing populations, inefficient and polluting technologies, and real dangers to human survival, we are highly in need of a dialogue between peoples. Indigenous peoples believe we are entering a new era of peace and that this is an opportunity to learn how to live with each other and respect each other's diversity. Some believe that the first step (Clarkson et al., 1992, p. iii) is for western society to listen and learn from indigenous peoples. Indigenous peoples need to speak for themselves to break through western images and stereotypes, such as of noble savage images. We must also learn to find a balance between our notions of progress, spirituality, and technology. Culture results from the interaction between people, land, production and reproduction, and developing systems that are in harmony with the earth and each other. What indigenous peoples have learned is that there is a connection between our basic values and how we choose to use technology for production. Therefore, we can achieve the goal of eliminating pollution and poverty while maintaining a very comfortable standard of living.

ABORIGINAL ECONOMIES AND CHANGE

The traditional economy of aboriginal peoples in Canada was not one economy but many economies that evolved and adapted into sustainable systems in a variety of environments: arctic, subarctic, coastal, prairie, and forest. The traditional subsistence provided a way of life for aboriginal peoples as hunters, gatherers, fishers, horticulturists, healers, midwives, faithkeepers, storytellers, transporters, traders, scientists, leaders, and protectors.

During the fur trade era, aboriginal families adapted their economic and social systems to become trappers, hunters, fishers, traders, guides, educators, and transporters.[1] The modern North American economy emerged from the fur trade and the labour of thousands of aboriginal hunters, trappers, and traders. The North American fur trade with Indians began with the first explorers and continued as one of the major economic forces until the middle of the nineteenth century, when it declined rapidly in the face of a growing American agriculture and the newly emerging industrial sector. From its start to its decline, the American fur industry depended on Indian hunters and trappers. They knew the land, understood the behaviour of the animals, and possessed the skills and technology to capture them (Weatherford, 1991, pp. 77–78).

With the decline of the fur trade, the proliferation of agriculture, the expansion of logging, mining and fishing, aboriginal peoples found themselves on a collision course with Euro-Canadians in a competition over resources. The myth is that aboriginal peoples did not have the capacity or could not adjust to the changing economy. In reality, however, most were pushed to the margins. Studies on aboriginal farming, for example, indicate that Indians were indeed successful at farming, but were set back by Indian policy. Helen Buckley in *From Wooden Ploughs to Welfare: Why Indian Policy Failed in the Prairie Provinces* writes:

> This promising beginning does not fit the popular image of hunters who were unable to adapt to farming. It also raises a new question as to why the farming ultimately failed, having made a good start. But the answers are not long in coming for, as early as the late 1880s, farm policy moved into a new phase. This new policy, together with the continuing scarcity of equipment and working capital, defeated the efforts of the [Indian] farmers themselves. (Buckley, 1992, p. 52)

There are similar tragedies associated with competition over fishing described by Boyce Richardson in *People of Terra Nullius*. He writes that within a decade of passage of the federal Fisheries Act (1868), "commercial fish companies selling into the United States were permitted to operate on Lake of the Woods, and began a devastation of the sturgeon population that must rank as one of the worst ecological disasters in our history" (Richardson, 1993, p. 203). This phenomenon was in sharp contrast to the pre-existing sustainable fishery managed by the Ojibwa:

> For many decades the Ojibwa had maintained the harvest of sturgeon at between 250,000 and 400,000 pounds a year. In the first half of the 1880's, the commercial companies more than doubled the take to an average 864,000 pounds a year, and in the last part of that decade to 1,250,000 pounds. Naturally, the Ojibwa fishery began to collapse. In the 1894 Manitou and Long Sault, the essential centres of the Ojibwa economy reported "no fish," while great scarcity was reported from every other place invaded by the commercial fishermen. In contrast, the lakes where Ojibway remained in control — Wabuskang, Lac Seul, Wagigoon, Shoal Lake, Whitefish Bay — continued to report large catches. (Richardson, 1993, p. 203)

In general, aboriginal peoples also lost when they transformed their sustainable economic systems into trade, trapping, and primary resource harvesting because colonial policies did not allow them to keep control over their resources.

The shift from the traditional aboriginal economies to low-end employment in resource-harvesting activities, known as the primary sector, happened over a century with marked changes after the 1950s. A survey in the 1960s of aboriginal employment shows that the shift to the primary sector took place well into that decade. The report completed by H.B. Hawthorn et al., *A Survey of the Contemporary Indians of Canada*, clearly demonstrates the reliance of Indians living on reserves for employment in the primary (renewal and non-renewable resource) sector. The 1966 data from selected Indian reserves across Canada indicate that nearly 80 percent of employment was in the primary sector (see Table 13.1).

However, by the 1990s the aboriginal employment situation has dramatically changed, reflecting larger societal and global changes. Employment both on- and off-reserve has shifted from dependence on the

TABLE 13.1

SURVEY OF INDIAN EMPLOYMENT IN THIRTY-FIVE BANDS ACROSS CANADA, 1966

Industry or occupation	Percent of total jobs
Primary sector	
Forestry	
On-reserve	7.4
Off-reserve	3.6
Fishing	4.6
Trapping	14.0
Guiding	2.2
Food gathering (including making wild hay)	13.4
Handicrafts	4.1
Proprietor farm	3.7
Unskilled, casual, and farm labour[1]	27.2
Total	**80.2**
Tertiary (service) sector	
Proprietor, non-farm	2.3
Professional and technical	0.65
Clerical	2.6
Skilled[2]	14.0
Total	**19.55**

[1] *In a number of the completed questionnaires, farm labour was included in the broad category of "unskilled and casual." Only 95 were clearly defined as farm labour (not shown here).*
[2] *A number of relatively well-paid, semi-skilled workers, such as loggers in British Columbia, truck drivers, and steadily employed factory workers were included under "skilled" in this table, rather than under "unskilled, casual, and farm labour," or (in the case of loggers) "forestry," as provided in the Indian Affairs Branch Questionnaire.*

Source: Adapted from H.B. Hawthorn et al., ed., *A Survey of the Contemporary Indians of Canada: A Report on Economic, Political, Educational Needs and Policies.* Vol. I. DIAND Publication No. Q5-0603-020-EE-A-18. Ottawa: Indians Affairs Branch, 1966.

primary sector of the economy to the tertiary (service) sector. In less than three decades, the dominance of agriculture, forestry, fishing, trapping, and mining has given way to the tertiary sector. The trend is similar for the Canadian economy, but not nearly as dramatic as for the aboriginal economy.

There has been a dramatic shift in the past century for aboriginal families living a traditional lifestyle, trapping and gathering and living off the land. Within this period aboriginal peoples shifted more into the primary sector of the labour market in agriculture, forestry, fishing, and trapping. The most recent shift has been into the service sector. Another important trend is the migration of aboriginal peoples to urban centres. At present, about 75 percent of aboriginal peoples live off the reserves, in urban environments.

The employment data illustrate the shift from the primary sector to the tertiary sector today. In 1966, nearly 80 percent of the employment on the reserve was in the primary sector whereas today 83 percent of it is in the tertiary sector (see Table 13.2).

Nevertheless, some aboriginal peoples continue to live in their traditional ways on the land. They have been successful in sustainable fishing and agriculture and have adjusted to changes in the economy. As it has been argued here, external policies have interfered with aboriginal approaches to development. These barriers to traditional development approaches are still today inhibiting the potential for innovation of aboriginal peoples in production, environment, and employment creation. These must be removed, for to the surprise of some, the current unemployment in aboriginal communities and their economic development can only be controlled if aboriginal peoples regain control over their lives and are allowed to use traditional knowledge and new technologies.

ABORIGINAL SUSTAINABLE DEVELOPMENT

In a number of cases, aboriginal communities are employing traditional knowledge and new technologies to initiate sustainable development. They are developing new ways of achieving sustainable development based on their own values and knowledge. They are effectively integrating elders' advice and using consensus decision-making, participative community-based development, partnerships with stakeholders, and capacity-building for holistic ecosystem management. In the following section, a number of examples where this is taking place are presented.

The Traditional Dene Environmental Knowledge Pilot Project is based at the Dene Cultural Institute in Hay River, Northwest Territories, and was established in 1987 to preserve and promote Dene culture through research and education. Because of its link to culture and the land, traditional environmental knowledge was the focus of the project, which has been a major contributor to methods of documenting knowledge, community participation, training, and partnering with other institutions. The project has been instrumental in promoting the integration of traditional environmental knowledge with western science for future management resources.

The Inuit Circumpolar Conference (ICC) has been instrumental in promoting the use of indigenous knowledge in environmental problem-solving. In a speech to the 1992 preparatory meeting to the U.N. Conference on Environment and Development (UNCED), Mary Simon, then president of the ICC, called on UNCED to recognize "that various levels of support

TABLE 13.2

Aboriginal Employment in Canada by Industry, 1991

On-reserve

Primary Sector		
Agriculture	1 760	
Fishing and trapping	2 090	
Logging and forestry	2 850	
Mining, quarrying, and oil wells	530	
Total	**7 230**	**(11.4%)**
Secondary Sector		
Manufacturing	3 365	
Total	**3 365**	**(5.3%)**
Tertiary Sector		
Construction	4 945	
Transportation and storage	1 660	
Communication and other utility	920	
Wholesale trade	415	
Retail trade	3 995	
Finance and insurance	235	
Real estate operators and insurance agents	140	
Business services	540	
Government services	24 905	
Educational services	5 390	
Health and social services	3 810	
Accommodation, food, and beverage services	3 260	
Other services	2 385	
Total	**52 600**	**(83.2%)**
Total all industries	**63 195**	**(100%)**

Off-reserve

Primary Sector		
Agriculture	8 845	
Fish and trapping	3 330	
Logging and forestry	7 250	
Mining, quarrying, and oil wells	7 960	
Total	**27 385**	**(6.9%)**
Secondary Sector		
Manufacturing	44 330	
Total	**44 330**	**(11.1%)**
Tertiary Sector		
Construction	30 685	
Transportation and storage	17 060	
Communication and other utility	12 290	
Wholesale trade	13 645	
Retail trade	49 280	
Finance and insurance	9 225	
Real estate operators and insurance agents	4 555	
Business services	17 510	
Government services	45 260	
Educational services	22 125	
Health and social services	34 805	
Accommodation, food, and beverage services	40 180	
Other services	30 925	
Total	**327 545**	**(82.0%)**
Total all industries	**399 260**	**(100%)**

Source: Statistics Canada. "Profile of Canada's Aboriginal Population," *1991 Census*, cat. no. 94-325, Ottawa: Minister of Industry, 1995.

will be required from governments to ensure that the traditional knowledge held by indigenous peoples survives to take its rightful place as an important knowledge system" (Simon, 1992).

The Porcupine Caribou Management Board has been responsible for caribou conservation and management in the Yukon and Northwest Territories since 1985. Issues dealt with are hunting on the Dempster highway, antler sales, chemical contamination, trade and barter of caribou meat, and industrial disturbance. This is an effective co-management organization that includes both Gwich'in, Inuvialuit, and three government jurisdictions and operates on the Native principle of consensus management. The Porcupine Caribou Management Board is often referred to as a model for similar joint management organizations.

The Kluskus and Ulkatcho Bands, in the interior of British Columbia, are developing plans for holistic forestry because of their concerns that current allowable cuts are two to three times the sustainable rate. As an alternative to these practices, the bands have applied for a holistic tree farm licence that would involve traditional practices, local economies, and indefinite forest conservation. Their strategy includes a complete field-based inventory, zoning for land use, alternative timber extraction (for example, selective logging), and value-added manufacturing.

The Shuswap Nation Tribal Council has established an institute to develop plans for habitat restoration on a regional scale that would integrate forestry, mining, and agriculture. It will share information with indigenous communities and other interested parties.

All these development initiatives are founded on the belief that sustainable development will spawn prosperity, strengthen culture, and generate employment. The major institutional innovation is that aboriginal peoples are taking control over development, sharing decision-making, and building on traditional knowledge. The other factor for success is the involvement of multi-stakeholders in the process. These are but a few examples of sustainable development strategies being used by aboriginal peoples.

ABORIGINAL EMPLOYMENT PLANNING

Improving and managing the environment means increased employment. Paul Hawken, author of the *Ecology of Commerce*, affirms that environmentalists who do not talk jobs are not really serious. Since the early 1980s, research has maintained that environmental protection will create jobs. This has been true for the Clean Air Act in the United States, and where communities have developed comprehensive employment strategies around protecting nature, such as the case of the spotted owl. Thus, it appears false the widespread belief that protecting the environment will result in the loss of jobs. Of course, for these new strategies to function appropriately they must be comprehensive (focussing on all present and future opportunities), effectively networked and co-ordinated, and involve partners or stakeholders.

For aboriginal peoples, the best opportunities for future jobs will be linked to the environment, self-government, and education. Of course, aboriginal employment will be shaped by the economy, but the nature and the extent will be determined by the aboriginal community's ability to control the process. We have learned from history that aboriginal peoples can compete in the international economy based on their traditional knowledge and sustainable practices. Aboriginal peoples have learned that they must control and manage their own resources and economies.

Aboriginal peoples require a planning model that links economic development, education and training, and strategic planning. Education and training must prepare aboriginal peoples for a future built on traditional environmental knowledge and the new information based economic systems. Finally, aboriginal communities need to support an economic development strategy that builds on all the economic potentials of the community, allows economic self-sufficiency, sustainable development, and self-government.

The strategic plan must not only be environmentally sustainable, but also support cultural, social, economic, and political sustainability. This can only be done when a community is building the future vision on knowing where they have come from and based on their own values and culture.

The aboriginal employment and economic sectors can be divided into five categories:

1. local government and services,

2. local markets for goods and services,

3. regional economies, often resource harvesting and tourism,

4. traditional economies, and

5. new and emerging industries.

Each aboriginal community will have to plan and implement strategies to develop a strong, self-reliant, and self-sufficient local economy that contributes to the regional, national, and international economies. Our national response to environmental issues and international trade developments will shape the types of jobs aboriginal peoples will have in the future. Products that are safe and environmentally friendly must win world markets. Processes that rely on eliminating inefficiencies and eliminating wastes, such as pollution of any kind, must lead in the future. Part of the reason for the slow recovery from the current recession is the gradual shift from polluting and exploitive industries to sustainable development. We can expect the next Henry Ford to be part environmentalist, part entrepreneur, and part social activist.

To achieve this objective, aboriginal economic development must have the following goals:

1. To become an active player in the regional economy, focussing on the restoration of natural resources based on traditional ecological knowledge and new technologies. Two main target areas are: forestry projects, with priority placed on sustainable resource harvesting and multi-use strategies; and cultural tourism, with priority placed on those projects that involve indigenous knowledge and help strengthen local culture and educate.

2. To develop and research indigenous ecological knowledge related to the environment, resource management, and subsistence systems.

3. To develop a human resource strategy focussing on the following areas: electronic technology, resource management and sustainable production, business development and entrepreneurship, subsistence hunting and gathering, and administration and services.

4. To support the formation of enterprises to retail local goods and services (for example, retail, personal services, and government services), to reduce economic leakages and to increase employment and wealth in aboriginal peoples.

5. To develop an economic development strategy that will facilitate the management of natural resources in traditional territories and strengthen the traditional economy based on indigenous knowledge and restoration of the resource base.

6. To develop partnership(s) with post-secondary institutions for the provision of environmental, technological, administrative, managerial, and entrepreneurial education and training based on lifelong learning, capacity building, and skill development.

7. To develop technical and manufacturing capacities in new and emerging environmental fields. Development in computing, telecommunication, and remote-sensing technologies must occur early in order to generate large economic and employment gains in the future. This will involve the research of new manufacturing projects, particularly in the computer and communications industries, that can be installed in aboriginal communities.

8. To develop community-based participative planning mechanisms to ensure that the strategy reflects community needs, aspirations, and long-term objectives.

9. To continue to develop the community's ability to access capital to finance business and business development.

Today, aboriginal economic development strategies need to be comprehensive in scope to capture all available opportunities. In past decades, communities around the world tried often in vain to attract that one, large industry that would solve all their economic ills. Communities now realize that this approach has failed. In order for local economies to grow, they must use opportunities of all scope. The following sections briefly summarize the broad opportunities and discuss them in the context of self-reliance, self-government, and preparing aboriginal peoples for the future.

Resources

Forestry is arguably the most significant economic opportunity for the future of aboriginal peoples and their territories, because aboriginal peoples live in the forest regions of Canada and possess the traditional knowledge to manage them. They could participate in resource industries by adopting sustainable management systems, restoring the environment, and adding value to industrial practices. The resource strategy could include restoration plans and sustainable-yield harvesting that would also permit multiple use of forests. A mixed-use strategy could be adopted, combining sustainable forestry with hunting, tourism, recreation, and gathering. For sustainable resource planning and management, aboriginal peoples can use their traditional environmental knowledge and combine it with new technologies, such as geographic information systems (GIS), to develop databases and planning instruments. As we saw above, a number of aboriginal communities are already applying traditional knowledge in this way. In order to increase aboriginal peoples' participation, training programs must be in place and linked to business development plans for this sector at the regional level.

Tourism

Tourism, as a growth area of the Canadian economy, is another promising area that aboriginal peoples could enter. The interest in tourism is that it offers opportunities to employ aboriginal peoples on the basis of traditional knowledge and ways, and to educate Canadians and foreign tourists about traditional environmental practices and values that respect Mother Earth. Ecotourism and cultural tourism is likely to interest tourists seeking new experiences and who have an interest in the natural environment. There are plenty of employment opportunities in tourism services and operations that can generate significant jobs for aboriginal peoples. These include tourism operations, visitor centres, museums, travel agencies, services, lodges, and restaurants.

Strengthening Traditional Economies

Training should be developed to meet the needs of resource management, new technologies, processing and marketing of natural resources, resource inventories, and adoption of new technologies such as remote sensing for sustainable resource management. The basis of training would be the collection and documentation of traditional knowledge. A pilot program could be established to collect such knowledge and determine its applications to employment and business development. Traditional knowledge could be integrated with other plans such as sustainable forestry management. Finally, aboriginal peoples have identified the need for training in hunting, fishing, and trapping, and in other traditional knowledge areas.

Emerging Industries

The service sector is gradually being dominated by energy-saving information technologies. The information highway promises to save energy by reducing the need to travel (local, national, and international). Internet communications systems, e-mail, and computer-conferencing promise to be efficient and effective tools for aboriginal planning, dialogue, and communication. For example, Cultural Survival Canada is developing an internet system for indigenous peoples to undertake biological diversity research, planning, and information-sharing. The system will be available worldwide and could become a significant development tool. In this and in many other ways, the shape of our work life will be dramatically affected by information technologies in the next couple of decades. Although there are risks not to be ignored in information technology, it could also have a democratizing effect where communities control their own information. Some communities, such as Deseronto, Ontario with its First Nations Technological Institute, are tapping into the high-growth potential of the new technologies sector, particularly in the area of governance and services.

In order for aboriginal peoples to benefit from the new technologies, adequate training and education are required. Development of capacity in technology, computer, and software industries is a long-term goal; yet implementation must begin immediately.

Business Development

The provision of local goods and services for the local and band-level markets could generate many of the new jobs and wealth in the aboriginal economy in the medium term. Money circulating within aboriginal communities has a "multiplier" effect, generating further jobs and business opportunities. All indications are strong that support of business development is a good investment in job generation and economic self-sufficiency. This is a rapidly emerging area because aboriginal peoples have developed strong capacities in development, management, and business.

Band Services and Administration

At present, aboriginal governance is the major source of stable full-time employment. As government programs and services are further devolved to bands, more employment and training will be required. New fields are emerging, such as accounting, bookkeeping, project management, administration, data processing, and computer technologies. Many aboriginal peoples have had the foresight to seek training in the growing field of public administration and management. Bands should develop long-term capacity-building and training plans. In addition, plans to use energy-conserving electronic systems and software would not only protect the environment, but prepare aboriginal employees for the future economy.

CONCLUSION

In the future, all employment will be determined by our social and technological responses to environmental crises. Environmental challenges will affect production, natural resource extraction, and consumption. Production methods that produce waste and pollution will not be tolerated by society. Traditional ways teach us to use everything and always return benefits to nature. Institutions and new commercial relationships, such as fair trade, must replace transactions that exploit producers and the environment. It is noteworthy that producers and companies with a social consciousness are emerging. Corporate leaders are learning that efficient production is not wasteful and polluting, and that products that support a safe environment and do not exploit people will win in the market place.

In a sense, aboriginal peoples are completing a circle. After being hunters, fishers, scientists, and storytellers, they are now major players in resource restoration and sustainable resource harvesting. Aboriginal peoples in Canada are also playing a greater role in nation building. They are gradually regaining control and management of large tracts of territories. The natural resource industry is a major contributor to the Canadian economy and can play a major role in strengthening the aboriginal economy and employment in the future. The challenge is planning for this transformation and having the vision to confront the obstacles.

The new economy will have to be rooted in traditional knowledge combined with new and emerging technologies. Already there are examples of this occurring. The Dene Cultural Centre has demonstrated vision to use traditional knowledge applied to new areas of resource management. The First Nations Technical Institute has shown how new technology can dramatically increase employment for aboriginal peoples.

This future employment cannot occur without the commitment of aboriginal peoples, government, private sector, and educational institutions to developing employment based on sustainable development.

NOTES

1. Thomas D. Lonner (1986) identifies several economic activities: hunting, fishing, gathering, farming, herding, crafting, trading, tool-making, transportation, skill training, storage, energy development, and so on.

DISCUSSION QUESTIONS

1. Can traditional aboriginal values be applied in economic and resource development planning? For example, how can "respect for nature" inform decisions made on resource management?

2. Is there a link between future employment, environment, new technology, and sustainable development? How can we develop plans that pull all these elements together?

3. How can the barriers to sustainable development be overcome? The barriers include the lack of knowledge about traditional economies and how to strengthen them, and the link between traditional and scientific knowledge.

4. What can industrialized societies learn from indigenous peoples about the environment and sustainable development?

5. How can aboriginal communities develop strong, self-reliant, and self-sufficient economies?

6. How can aboriginal peoples capitalize on economic opportunities in new and emerging industries?

FURTHER READINGS

Clarkson, Linda, Vern Morrissette, and Gabriel Regallet. 1992. *Our Responsibility to the Seventh Generation*. Winnipeg: International Institute for Sustainable Development. This is an excellent introduction to aboriginal teachings and thinking about the environment and development. The report offers a critique of development and shows how indigenous peoples have been victims of modernization. The text provides recommendations on how to achieve sustainable development.

Hawken, Paul. 1993. *The Ecology of Commerce: A Declaration of Sustainability*. New York: Harper Business, A Division of HarperCollins Publishers. If you want a vision of the future for business, read this book. Hawken writes that the present "green" businesses are just the tip of the iceberg for the future of business. This is an inspiring book with insights on the future of enterprise.

Inter Press Service, comp. 1993. *Story Earth: Native Voices on the Environment*. San Francisco, CA: Mercury House. This book gives voice to traditional cultures and their vision of Mother Earth. Understanding traditional peoples is difficult and understanding traditional peoples' concerns about development is even more complex. This book is full of insight about indigenous peoples' teachings, reaction to development, and lessons for sustainable living.

Royal Commission on Aboriginal Peoples. 1993. *Sharing the Harvest: The Road to Self-Reliance, Report of the National Round Table on Aboriginal Economic Development and Resources*. Ottawa: Royal Commission on Aboriginal Peoples. This book provides an excellent overview of current thinking on development and natural resource models and strategies. The subjects cover the components of a comprehensive development strategy for aboriginal communities. The text also describes innovative models for community and private enterprise.

Sachs, Wolfgang. 1993. *The Development Dictionary: A Guide to Knowledge as Power*. London, England: Witsatersrand University, Zed Books. This is an excellent reference for those interested in critical analysis of twentieth-century ideas on development, aid, and progress. The editor has constructed a concise collection of short chapters to resemble a learned dictionary. This book will help clarify key ideas that are central to the themes in the Further Readings recommended for this chapter.

World Commission on Environment and Development. 1987. *Our Common Future*. Oxford and New York: Oxford University Press. *Our Common Future* is a classic, also known as the Bruntland Commission Report, which pointed the way for the Earth Summit in 1992. The World Commission on Environment and Development was set up as an independent body in 1983 by the United Nations to reexamine critical environment and development problems on the planet. The report compelled nations to act together to put the world on a sustainable path.

REFERENCES

The Assisi Declarations: Messages on Man and Nature from Buddhism, Christianity, Hinduism, Islam and Judaism. 1986. Basilica di S. Francesco, Assisi, Italy, International World Wide Fund for Nature (WWF). (September 29.)

Buckley, Helen. 1992. *From Wooden Ploughs to Welfare: Why Indian Policy Failed in the Prairie Provinces*. Montreal and Kingston, Ont.: McGill-Queen's University Press.

Clarkson, Linda, Vern Morrissette, and Gabriel Regallet. 1992. *Our Responsibility to the Seventh Generation*. Winnipeg: International Institute for Sustainable Development.

Hawthorn, H.B. et al. 1966. *A Survey of the Contemporary Indians of Canada: A Report on Economic, Political, Educational Needs and Policies*, 2 vols. Ottawa: Department of Indian Affairs and Northern Development.

Havel, Vaclav. 1992. *Summer Meditations*, tr. Paul Wilson. Toronto: Alfred A. Knopf.

———. (n.d.) *Speech at the World Economic Forum*. Devos, Switzerland.

Lonner, Thomas D. 1986. "Subsistence as an Economic System in Alaska: Theoretical Observations and Management Implications." Pp. 15–27 in *Contemporary Alaskan Native Economies*, ed. Steven J. Langdon. Lanham, MD and London, England: University Press of America.

Richardson, Boyce. 1993. *People of Terra Nullius: Betrayal and Rebirth in Aboriginal Canada*. Vancouver and Toronto: Douglas & McIntyre.

Wall, Steve and Harvey Arden. 1990. *Wisdomkeepers: Meetings with Native American Spiritual Elders*. Oregon: Beyond Words Publishing.

Weatherford, Jack. 1991. *Native Roots: How The Indians Enriched America*. New York: Fawcett Columbine.

World Commission on Environment and Development. 1987. *Our Common Future*. Oxford and New York: Oxford University Press.

CHAPTER 14

Trials of the Spirit:
The Native Social Movement in Canada

David Alan Long

INTRODUCTION

Contrary to popular conception, the history of Native–state relations in Canada suggests that our country is less than deserving of the title "peaceable kingdom." This is not to say that diversity among people living in Canada has not been an important part of this country's heritage, for appreciation of regional and socio-cultural differences have long been hallmarks of the Canadian landscape. Nonetheless, the considerable distances that separate most of Canada's 600 Native communities from other Native and non-Native communities, as well as their myriad of cultural and structural arrangements, have contributed to a considerable degree of geographical and social isolation. Consequently, it might seem surprising to find meaningful similarities of experience and perspective between Native people in Canada. That certain fundamental similarities do indeed exist is less surprising when we begin to examine them in the light of the history of colonialism in Canada. One of the most striking developments in this history has been the emergence of a Native social movement over the past 30 or so years. Court challenges, lobbying efforts, and protests of various size and intensity have involved Natives and their supporters across Canada and throughout the world. My analysis in the following chapter suggests that while there are a host of socio-cultural differences represented in the movement, at its core it represents a strategically organized, spiritual, and cultural revolution against the unjust fate shared by a majority of Native people in Canada.

My general, theoretical concern is to understand the potential problems and benefits that social differences and similarities bring to coalitions and social movements. My specific concern is to understand the ways in which spiritual, cultural, economic, and political differences and similarities interact in relation to the Native movement in Canada. The major questions that inform our analysis of this movement include:

1. What is the historical context for the contemporary movements of Native peoples in Canada?

2. How are supporters and opponents of these movements involved?

3. What reasons do those involved have for their involvement?

4. What are the internal and external obstacles for coalition formation and growth?

5. How does an examination of the formation, growth, and demise of coalitions enhance our understanding of the social movement of Native people in Canada?

Our discussion begins with an outline of the theoretical posture from which we view the movement of Native people in Canada.

THEORETICAL PERSPECTIVES ON CONTEMPORARY SOCIAL MOVEMENTS

Resource Mobilization Theory

For roughly the past quarter of a century, two theoretical perspectives have informed research on contemporary social movements. Resource mobilization theorists such as Zald and McCarthy (1987) have emphasized how social movement supporters and opponents organize their efforts. In relation to Canada's Native people, this perspective focusses on the ways in which Natives and their supporters mobilize political and organizational resources in seeking to effect social change. The movement's strategies and objectives are legitimized by effective recruiting and maintaining of support, mobilizing scarce social and material resources, and addressing divisions that threaten to fragment movement solidarity and delay or attenuate potential successes. From this perspective, the contemporary Native movement reflects the successful political apprenticeship of Native organizers from the late 1960s on. In other words, it illustrates the ability of these Native apprentices to effectively address the emerging bureaucratization of Native life through the professionalization of protest.

New Social Movement Theory

On the other hand, new social movement theorists such as Touraine (1988) and *Melucci* (1985) suggest that having the means and opportunity to mobilize are merely intervening variables in the growth of any social movement. These theorists highlight the relationship between historical, cultural, and ideological elements that embody the diverse and sometimes conflicting positions held by movement supporters and opponents. According to Alaine Touraine (1988, pp. 63–64), divisions within a given society are between those who maintain hegemonic control of principal cultural resources and those who do not. Through dialogue and social action, discrete beliefs, values, and ethical rules blend to form relatively shared models of and for social action. Social movements thus reflect the historical struggle for hegemonic control over cultural resources.

Understanding the Native movement thus requires more than acknowledging the successes and failures of professionalized lobbyists and strategically militant protesters during the late 1960s and early 1970s. It depends, rather, on careful reflection of the increasingly shared, albeit distanced, awareness by Natives and their supporters of the culturally and structurally oppressed minority status of Native people in Canada. Touraine (1988) notes that increased collective awareness serves to strengthen and solidify social movement supporters. At the same time, social movements are relatively unstable phenomena since they exist in tension with the systems of domination that in a sense gave them birth (Touraine, 1988, p. 66). Social movements thus represent and exacerbate the conflict in social life that may lead to a breakup of the larger social system or at least to institutional reform. Given that they do not emerge in a vacuum, however, understanding the ebb and flow of coalition and social movement activities means taking into account the pressures on coalition and movement participants from the past as well as the present, and from within as well as from without. The following socio-historical overview of the aspirations and actions of Native people in relation to government action and policies thus sets the stage for the case study of coalition support for the Lubicon Lake First Nation in Alberta, Canada.

THE SOCIO-HISTORICAL CONTEXT OF NATIVE–STATE RELATIONS

Precontact Aboriginal Conditions

There is substantial agreement among academics that most precontact societies of aboriginal peoples were well organized, culturally distinct, and economically viable. Indeed, it was the "intelligent manipulation of nature backed by supportive social structure that made survival possible under extremely difficult conditions" (Dickason, 1993, p. 30). The picture of life in the Americas painted by the early explorers and many historians writing before 1960 was quite different from that experienced by those already settled there. While the former wrote of a New World, the latter had for thousands of years built great civilizations, developing agriculture into a science, producing artists, mathematicians, and deeply spiritual, philosophical thinkers. The organization of Native societies in precontact

Canada varied with the conditions they faced, from the bounty of the Pacific coast, through the marginal subsistence conditions of the north-central region, to the relative stability of the eastern woodlands (Dickason, 1993, chapter 4). And although Native peoples have never been culturally or organizationally homogeneous, their long history reflects certain shared, fundamental ways of being and doing. In general, their approach to life was holistic: that is, all details of life were viewed in relation to one another (Dickason, 1993, pp. 79–80). Of course, Native systems of social control did not always work perfectly within or between bands and tribes: taboos against killing did not prevent intertribal fighting (Dickason, 1993, pp. 67–69, 79–82).

Early Postcontact Relations

Since the turn of the century, scholarly estimates regarding the size of the indigenous population of pre-Columbian North America have varied between one million and ten million; today, the general consensus is that between two million and five million people were living north of the Rio Grande by the end of the 1400s (Cornell, 1988, pp. 51–53). By 1650, 85 to 90 percent of these people had been wiped out through disease, massacre, and suicide. For those who survived this holocaust, life changed profoundly. Initially, the fur trade provided a substantial increase in goods and income in eastern and northern Canada, and many Natives benefited from their relations with the European traders who depended on their expertise in trapping, hunting, and knowledge of the territories (Rich, 1991, pp. 158–68). However, rising competition in trade also increased the divisions between tribes that were already divided (Adams, 1989, chapter 3). Moreover, when the fur trade went into decline, difficulties arose among Natives who had become dependent upon European goods (Dickason, 1993, pp. 192–96). The most profound effects of European contact, however, followed the signing of treaties.

The settling of Europeans in western and northern regions led to the making of agreements and treaties with various tribes. Although pre- and post-Confederation treaties involved different concessions, most arranged for First Nations peoples to cede their interest in large tracts of land in return for reserves along with small annuities, the right to hunt and fish on the reserves or on unoccupied crown land, the right to limited educational services, and, in treaties negotiated after Treaty Number 6 (1876), the provision of a medicine chest (Taylor, 1991, pp. 208–10). By Confederation, Canada had a fully developed Indian policy adapted from the French, British imperial, and colonial governments and already administered by the Crown Lands Department (eventually to become the Department of Indian Affairs and Northern Development [DIAND]). The last of the eleven numbered treaties was not signed until 1921, but Native people had begun to mobilize in response to problems associated with the policies and practices of the colonizers long before then.

Indeed, organized, sometimes violent, political action by Native people started well before the turn of the century, as evidenced by the Red River conflict of 1869–70 and the North-West conflict of 1885. Torrance's (1977, pp. 494–95) contention that Canadian governments have historically responded promptly and decisively to violent political actions was illustrated early on by the deployment of some 8000 troops, militia, and police to Saskatchewan during the 1885 North-West conflict (Miller, 1991, p. 252). Following the conflict, it became increasingly difficult for First Nations people to effect meaningful social and political change. Assistant Indian commissioner Hayter Reed drew up a list of fifteen recommendations that supported almost total suppression of Native political activity. While Hayter proposed that it be illegal for Indians involved in the North-West conflict to be off-reserve without a pass signed by an Indian department official, this was later applied to all Indians (Stonechild, 1992, p. 274). Eventually, it also became illegal to use band funds for political organization (Cardinal, 1969, p. 103). Moreover, any legal actions First Nations people might have wanted to initiate were undoubtedly stifled by the fact that until 1961, it was illegal for lawyers to represent Indians in actions against the crown. Nonetheless, the numerous violent and non-violent political activities during the early part of this century prepared important ground on which later activists would build. Through the 1930s and 1940s, Native tribes, bands, and communities worked to organize and develop lines of communication within and across provincial boundaries. Although the Indian Act had remained virtually intact since its enactment in 1876, increased lobbying, demonstrations, and violent confrontations on behalf of Native people served to pressure the federal government into amending the act in 1951 (Cardinal, 1969, pp. 108–9).[1]

Bureaucratization of Native–State Relations

In general, the 1950s and early 1960s saw a subsiding of violent political activity and a slowing of organized interest and pressure to effect change. Nevertheless, two developments in the late 1960s were important catalysts for the resurgence of both violent and non-violent efforts at social change on the part of Native people and their supporters. One was the establishment of the National Indian Brotherhood (NIB) in 1968, the first national organization run by and for Canada's First Nations. Although the organization's turbulent history was largely a result of contentions within and without over funding and agendas (Ponting, 1986, pp. 40–41), NIB board member Harold Cardinal (who was also president of the Indian Association of Alberta) noted that the creation of the NIB was a turning point (Cardinal, 1969, p. 107). The second occurrence that served as a focal point for organized Native interests at this time was the introduction by the minister of Indian Affairs of the 1969 white paper. For aboriginal people in Canada, the white paper served as a symbol that helped to crystallize the problem they faced. Native leaders from across Canada immediately and categorically rejected what they termed the genocidal implications of the white paper, and in 1970 adopted the Indian Chiefs of Alberta's position paper, *Citizens Plus*, as their national response. As an outspoken representative of two of the most recognized Native organizations in the country, Harold Cardinal was both hopeful and wary. He warned that failure of the NIB and other similar organizations, especially if Canadian governments were at fault, could result in aboriginal peoples' "taking the dangerous and explosive path travelled by the black militants of the United States" (Cardinal, 1969, p. 107).

Post-1970s Lobbies, Protests, and Escalation of Violence

Numerous violent political incidents during the 1970s and 1980s seemed to fulfil Cardinal's prophecy. It is important to note, however, that most of these incidents have been strategically planned: they have not been the spontaneous, unexpected occurrences that media and state representatives have often made them out to be (York and Pindera, 1992, pp. 414–18). Moreover, Native people have often initiated such action only after they have exhausted other, more legitimate means of attempting to bring about change. One such example involves the Lubicon Lake First Nations band of northern Alberta, who have been fighting for their rights with the federal and provincial governments for over 50 years. In addition to lobbying government officials, speaking to the media, and coalescing with other Native and non-Native supporters, the Lubicon have compiled a library that includes letters to and from other Native leaders and supporters, lawyers, Canadian and international politicians, and corporate executives, newspaper articles, press releases, interviews, and leaked government documents. Although the Lubicon people and their supporters have yet to engage in violent confrontation with state representatives, they have at times expressed frustration and anger at the repeated lack of good faith and effort on the part of Canadian governments to bring the dispute to resolution. According to York and Pindera (1992), the Mohawk people had followed a similar path before the crisis at Oka in the summer of 1991.

From the perspective of state representatives, a change in Native organizations during the 1970s from issue-oriented to more bureaucratic, institutionally based organizational structures increased the credibility of those organizations (Frideres, 1988, p. 282). However, the compromises that often accompany bureaucratization also led to growing frustration among aboriginal people and their supporters who had been trying to bring about radical political and social change. Increased frustration and aggression toward the state were especially apparent during the 1980s when a large number of Natives began graduating from Canadian and American universities. Armed with a rediscovered respect for their cultural traditions and histories, a number of these educated young leaders joined with others in blending and alternating legitimate and illegitimate organizational goals and techniques (Frideres, 1988, p. 269). Supporters of

Native rights could now be expected to intersperse their peaceful lobbying, negotiating, and demonstrating activities with violent, political action. And although the targets of their non-violent and violent actions have varied — including logging and other private companies, the military, non-aboriginal communities, and at times factions within their own communities — the primary concern of most politically active Native people over the past 30 years has been to challenge the policies and practices used by state representatives to gain Native consent to state rule.

Challenging the state has been both difficult and costly, however, largely because of the internal colonization that has affected every area of Native life. Among the policies and practices that have been used by the state are the following: publicly supporting Native sovereignty by negotiating treaties with First Nations peoples, while at the same time assuming the fundamental principle of crown sovereignty (Boldt, 1993, p. 5); manipulating sentiment through guilt management by painting a particular picture of Native–state relations (Boldt, 1993, pp. 18–21); the social and geographical isolation of Native people on reserves (Dickason, 1993, p. 257); political co-optation of key Native leaders (Hammersmith, 1992, p. 55); manipulation of the discourse used in Native–white relations (Jensen, 1993, pp. 350–352); and widening division between bands and tribes by sponsoring competitive, specialized funding programs for community development projects and research into specific tribal histories for land claims arguments (Frideres, 1988, p. 286). For well over a century, aboriginal people in Canada have not had meaningful control of their lands, funds, business interactions, or educational, social, community, and local government activities. Although the federal government's stated goal for its Native wards was and continues to be full and equal participation in Canadian society, the route of separate development enshrined in the Indian acts of 1876 and 1951 has continued in many ways to lock many Native communities and individuals into a structure that has done little more than perpetuate their political, legal, cultural, and social marginality (Erasmus, 1989, p. 295).

Despite their colonially enforced marginality, many Natives began lobbying government representatives and going through various legal channels during the 1970s and 1980s in order to challenge the policies, legislation, and practices of European colonization. For example, in the early 1960s, Mary Two Axe-Early was joined by other Native women in openly condemning the Indian Act for its discrimination against Native women. Continuing throughout the 1970s, these efforts resulted in the Canadian government's promise, in 1979, to remove section 12(1)(b) of the Indian Act, a promise that was finally honoured in 1985 when the act was amended and Indian women were offered official reinstatement (Silman, 1987, p. 235).[2] Aboriginal people also recognized that mass-media coverage of their activities could bring added attention to their concerns and possibly help them cultivate a broader social support base. For example, in 1993, members of the Peigan First Nation in central Alberta focussed national attention on their grievances against the provincial government and members of the local community by organizing a violent protest against the building of the Old Man River Dam. Consequently, the mayor of a nearby town cancelled a ceremony scheduled to celebrate the opening of the dam because he and others "feared for their lives."[3] Although accounts vary as to what happened and why, Native leader Milton Born with a Tooth was eventually convicted on five counts of dangerous use of a firearm. No doubt such militant, sometimes violent, political actions have often angered those whose interests they threaten, but they have also enabled Native people and their supporters to draw local, national, and international attention to their ongoing experience of colonization and their desire for change.

The most widely publicized recent occurrence of political violence involving Native people in the past 30 years was the 1990 Oka crisis. During the summer of that year, the Mohawks of Kanasetake engaged in an armed standoff with the Canadian military on the grounds that the extension of a local golf course onto their land would have broken an agreement between the government of Quebec and the Mohawk people. This confrontation received unprecedented national and international attention (York and Pindera, 1992). But it was by no means the only occasion in Canada on which police and army personnel have been dispatched to quell potential Native uprisings. Among the more newsworthy examples have been the Montagnais Indians' 1969 demonstration during which they threatened to burn down a fishing club near Montreal in protest against the provincial government's violation of their fishing rights; the Native People's Caravan of 1974, in which hundreds of Natives and their supporters travelled from Vancouver to Ottawa to protest their treatment at the opening of Parliament; the 1974 occupation of the DIAND office in Morley, Alberta by members of the Stoney band in order to bring attention to their concerns and to secure discussions with the federal minister of Indian Affairs; and the four-month occupation in 1983 of their band office by Native women of the Tobique reserve in New Brunswick in order to attract attention to the problems facing them. More recently, the Lubicon of northern Alberta lobbied, set up road blockades, and protested in various other ways throughout the 1980s to bring attention to their 50-year-old land-rights dispute and to prevent large-scale deforestation of their territory; the Dene and Métis of northern Alberta have protested and lobbied against the building of the proposed pulp mills on the Peace and Athabasca rivers; the Haida of British Columbia have stood in the path of logging machines ready to clear-cut their forests; the Lonefighters of the Peigan Indian Nation in Alberta forced an armed standoff in 1990 with local and provincial authorities because of their land-rights and environmental concerns around the proposed building of the Old Man River Dam; and the Tin Wis coalition of British Columbia, a group of Natives, labour groups, and environmentalists, has continued to use violent protest as well as international boycotts against MacMillan Bloedel for destroying the rainforest in the Clayoquot Sound region.

These and many other examples illustrate the preparedness of aboriginal people and their supporters to engage in violence when they have felt it was necessary. Various expressions of political activism also highlight the tension that has characterized Native–state relations since the arrival of the European explorers. As early as 1974, the RCMP described the Native movement as the single greatest threat to national security. Although this may now be viewed as a rather gross overstatement, what the RCMP does appear to have understood was that those with relatively little power can and do resort to violence in order to effect change (Gurr, 1970, pp. 210–12). Others, in contrast, including Prime Minister Trudeau, dismissed the early militant outbursts as insignificant actions by a small and desperate group of extremists (York, 1989, p. 251). While the Trudeau assessment may have contained a grain of truth — certainly many such incidents did reflect a degree of desperation — a more credible interpretation would have viewed Native political violence as a response to the experience of oppression resulting from social, economic, legal, and political inequality.

Most aboriginal people in Canada would undoubtedly have preferred that their social, economic, political, and legal problems were resolved in peaceful ways. However, the development of an ideological agenda that expressed itself in an often violent manner during the 1970s and 1980s was for many Native people a matter of survival (York, 1989, pp. 260–61). To continue to turn the other cheek would mean accepting the prospect of continued cultural and physical genocide of their people. Their strategic use of violent political action also served to shock other Canadians into realizing that the vision of their country as a peaceable kingdom was little more than a state-perpetuated myth (Boldt, 1993, p. 21), and that aboriginal people and their supporters would resort to political violence if their involvement in constructing a truly democratic Canada continued to be ignored or co-opted (Boldt, 1981, p. 215).

As is noted in the following section, the Lubicon Lake First Nation people of Alberta have sought to resolve their more than 50-year-old land claim with federal and provincial governments in a variety of ways. From a social movement perspective, the most noteworthy development in this scenario has been the emergence of worldwide coalition support for the Lubicon. Analysis of the recent history of this coalition highlights that counter-hegemonic and hegemonic agents rely on similar precarious resources to bolster and/or maintain their identity and position of strength.

AN OVERVIEW OF THE LUBICON COALITION

Historical Context of Coalition Support

The Lubicon coalition is a microcosm of the social movement of Native peoples throughout the world. Moreover, the coalition embodies the 500-year-old spirit and vision of those who oppose colonization. The history of relations between aboriginal and non-aboriginal peoples in Canada thus provides an essential backdrop against which the current movements of Lubicon coalition supporters and those who oppose them should be seen. Moreover, understanding the strength of coalition support for the Lubicon means taking into account how and why potential supporters identify with the people, ideas, and activities that make up the coalition in the first place. This means examining the ways in which a number of fundamental beliefs, perspectives, and interests have been drawn from the historical and cultural movements of Native people and their supporters.

There have been countless conflicts between Native and non-Native people since the days of first contact. But the willingness of people to align themselves for or against the Lubicon coalition does not merely depend on their having a clear understanding of the place of Native people in Canadian history. Even those unfamiliar with the specific history and circumstances of Native people in general and the Lubicon in particular are likely to have become aware of the presence of dissatisfied Native people in Canada during the past few decades. The growth in awareness surrounding Native issues is both a reflection and a result of media coverage of such high-profile events as the 1990 Oka crisis and the stand taken by Native member of Parliament Elijah Harper against the Meech Lake accord in 1991. Whether or not people agree with these and other actions of Native people in Canada, widespread coverage has raised the average Canadian's awareness in relation to activities and concerns of Native people in this country and around the world.

Nonetheless, Ponting notes that increased public awareness in relation to Native issues since the early 1970s has not coincided with a deepening of knowledge in relation to the demographics of the Native population. Neither has increased awareness generated support for Native peoples in Canada. In fact, Ponting (1991, p. 22) found that support for Native issues had eroded slightly between 1976 and 1986. Canadians tend to be supportive of Native aspirations for self-government and their land claims, although their support for arrangements that connote special privileges for this country's Native people has waned (Ponting 1991, p. 27). Ironically, part of the difficulty in mobilizing support for the Lubicon and other Native peoples is that Native issues now touch all areas of Canadian life. The increased complexity of issues and interests leaves grass-roots coalition supporters behind. As Hamel (1994, p. 35) notes, it is much harder to mobilize people around the Constitution than it is to mobilize them around a pipeline or a dam. Current apathy on the part of non-Native people in Canada toward Native issues also suggests that colonial attitudes die hard. The problem, however, is not merely reducible to a condition of racist apathy. While some non-Native people choose to ignore or oppose Native interests, other non-Native people actively support Native peoples in Canada. This suggests that there are factors other than one's racial or ethnic heritage that contribute to support for hegemonic visions and activities.

International Context of Coalition Support

While it is important to understand the historical contexts, political and legal interests, and spiritual or material visions that have given shape to the Lubicon coalition and the more general movement of Native people in Canada, both of these collective movements are microcosms of two global, cross-cutting, socio-historical movements — support for the rights of indigenous peoples and protection of the environment. Although the highly organized, well-targeted campaign to pressure those who oppose justice for the Lubicon emerged from within Canada, support for the Lubicon outside Canada suggests that there are similar coalitions and movements elsewhere. Again, although coalition supporters and opponents outside Canada may have little or no direct contact with members of the Lubicon Lake First Nation, they are informed by global awareness and activity networks that seek to redress the myriad of problems associated with colonialism and environmental degradation. The theoretical and political significance of these global movements is that they provide two major frames of reference that Native and non-Native people throughout the world use in relation to the plight of the Lubicon.

Supporters' Perspectives on Coalition Involvement

The problems associated with colonialism and the efforts by Native people and their supporters to address them are often understood by many in primarily political and legal terms. For example, Weaver (1981) sees it as both possible and desirable to acknowledge the special status of the original occupants of a territory in a manner that aims at restoring unique political and legal rights and entitlements of aboriginal peoples. Accordingly, she asserts that the most critical issues associated with aboriginal rights pertain to the establishment of separate political and legal jurisdictions, and of a land base. Many Lubicon coalition supporters view the problems of the Lubicon within this type of political and legal framework. Moreover, much hegemonic activity is directed against the political and legal interests of the Lubicon. The problem for Native supporters and opponents working within this perspective is an inability to address the fundamental concerns and claims of the Lubicon. Focussing on political, legal, and even land issues is vital, although the strength of coalition support for Lubicon concerns depends on coalition members' taking the spiritual and cultural dimensions of Lubicon life into account. Similarly, coalition opponents who fail to take these dimensions of Lubicon life seriously will be only partially successful in their efforts to maintain the status quo.

In contrast to those who focus on the political and legal dimensions of hegemonic struggles, Touraine (1981) has argued that historical conflicts between hegemonic and counter-hegemonic representatives is fundamentally a conflict between different visions of the state. In this respect, Long (1992) has argued that Native people have developed an alternative vision for their place in Canada by defining their political and legal concerns and activities in spiritual terms. In general, many aboriginal people acknowledge that a balanced life is one that honours the laws of both the spiritual and physical dimensions of reality (Bopp et al., 1984, p. 27). In more spiritual/political terms, McKay (1992, p. 30) notes:

> The vision that moves us in the struggle toward aboriginal sovereignty is integral to our spirituality. The elders speak to us of our need for balance between the physical and spiritual aspects of our being. They would caution our political leaders not to become so caught up in the struggle for power that they compromise the spiritual heritage that shaped our being.

McKay's comments suggest that our ability to understand the social movement of aboriginal people in Canada means acknowledging that the political struggle for aboriginal sovereignty, while undoubtedly giving a certain contour to the spiritual vision of Native people and their supporters, has itself emerged out of a spiritual vision. Comments and activities by supporters representing the Oblate Missionary Society, the United Church of Canada, the Aboriginal Rights Coalition, the Edmonton Interchurch Committee for Aboriginal Rights, the Society for Endangered Peoples, and many other similar organizations suggest that the dialogue between spiritual and political visions is vital for those whose concerns transcend mere control over physical or cultural resources. The pursuit of justice for the Lubicon is, as it were, the spiritual tie that binds many coalition members. They find that the spiritual connection enables them to build a model of what they believe about the Lubicon and a model for actions they believe ought to be taken to support the Lubicon (Geertz, 1984, p. 17).

Visions of and for social change in relation to the Lubicon can also take on quite physical contours. For example, a 1993 press release from the Rainforest Action Group (RAN) warned:

> If the Alberta government doesn't significantly modify existing agreements with Diashowa and Al-Pac — which is majority-owned by Mitsubishi — we will at the request of provincial environmental groups call for a worldwide boycott of tourism in this province until changes are made which could begin as early as 1994.

RAN support for the Lubicon in the form of an Alberta tourism boycott toward Alberta was based on their concern over the enormous area covered by logging agreements (about one-third of the province), the fragile ecosystem in the province with its shallow soil and short growing season, the fact that Al-Pac was just beginning to produce pulp and paper, and the pace of logging. The focus of RAN and similar groups is thus not primarily to protect the political, legal, or spiritual interests of the Lubicon, but to fight against abuse of the environment and to "help groups develop non-destructive, sustainable, alternatives that will provide Albertans with jobs while protecting their beautiful, vital and fragile world."

As the above suggests, inviting difference is an important aspect of the visions shared by social movement and coalition supporters. Social movement research often suggests that people in a given movement coalesce around ideas and practices representing particular interests, whether they are religious, political, or economic in nature. It is then a short theoretical step to presume that movements have homogeneous, overarching systems of belief and practice that embody the essence of the movement. No matter how the success or failure of movements is then explained (such as their historical truthfulness or illusory character, the effective mobilization of resources, the control over the contents, ways, and means of particular cultures by historical agents battling over hegemony, etc.), it is assumed that social movements manifest certain socially accepted goals, interests, and practices that can be defined and quantified by a neutral, objective observer. In contrast, Hall (1988), LaClau and Mouffe (1985), and others convincingly argue that neither social movements nor even the many coalitions that comprise them are homogeneous entities. Just as there are beliefs and practices that serve to unify coalition supporters, so there are beliefs, interests, and practices that potentially divide them. In contrast to the apparently monolithic social systems they defy, coalitions and social movements invite the inevitable cultural and structural changes that occur when differences are taken seriously.

For example, members of the Lubicon coalition such as the Rainforest Action Group, Earthkeepers, Greenpeace, Friends of the Earth, Iwerliewen, and Big Mountain Action Group align themselves philosophically or even spiritually with the Lubicon. Each of these groups shares a desire to protect the creation from the destructive, log-harvesting practices of the transnational company Diashowa. Nonetheless, the primary interest of these and many other environmental groups is to protect and preserve the natural environment for everyone's enjoyment, often through international lobbying efforts to establish parks and animal sanctuaries. In contrast, the Lubicon wish to negotiate a land-claim settlement with the provincial government of Alberta and the federal government of Canada that would essentially allow them to do as they wish with their land. Although environmentally concerned coalition members support the Lubicon, it is not difficult to envision a future clash between these same environmentalists and the Lubicon over the appropriate use of the land claimed by the Lubicon Lake First Nation.

REASONS FOR COALITION INVOLVEMENT

Differences in Beliefs, Perspectives, and Interests

Given their historical and socio-cultural differences, it is not easy to identify what it is that ties Lubicon coalition supporters together. Important in this regard is distinguishing between the discrete beliefs, overarching worldviews, and concrete interests of those involved. In general, Lubicon coalition members believe that the Lubicon deserve to be treated in a just manner by governments in Canada and that government representatives should do their part in settling the Lubicon land claims. However, coalition supporters such as the Society for Endangered Peoples, the Innu Support Groups, the Austrian Society for Endangered Peoples, the Working Circle for North American Indians, the Assembly of First Nations, the Aboriginal Rights Coalition, and the Native Women's Association of Canada see justice in terms of ensuring protection for the basic human rights of the Lubicon. Other coalition members emphasize that the injustice experienced by the Lubicon demonstrates that hegemonic agents are more concerned with economic gain than with respecting the relationship between humans and their natural environments. These environmentally focussed groups, such as the Rainforest Action Group, Earthkeepers, Greenpeace, Friends of the Earth, Iwerliewen, the Big Mountain Action Group, Synesthetics, and the rock group Syren, assert that humans should not abuse the physical environment. As Berger and Luckmann (1967) note, overarching meaning systems are often composed of such discrete beliefs. Through dialogue and action, plausibility structures enable coalition supporters to make sense of the Lubicon situation. As the preceding analysis suggests, people can interact within similar plausibility structures while making sense of their world in religious, environmental, business, philosophical, and economic terms. Nonetheless, while allowing people with different assumptions and definitions of the situation is the lifeblood of a given coalition or social movement, there are consequences to inviting such differences.

The Problem of Difference

As noted earlier, representatives of the Edmonton Interchurch Committee on Aboriginal Rights, the Aboriginal Rights Coalition, the Assembly of First Nations, and the Native Women's Association of Canada and representatives from similar organizations view what happens politically and legally to the Lubicon in spiritual terms.[4] Environmental groups may use similar language, but clearly they are more concerned about what happens to the environment when human beings ignore their responsibility toward it and their almost sacred relation to it. In contrast, businesses such as Roots Canada, Knechtel's Grocery Wholesaling, and The Body Shop assert that Diashowa's logging practices are unacceptable because they contribute to the degradation of the environment, which also occurs at the expense of the Lubicon's well-being. In a somewhat different vein, organizations such as Kentucky Fried Chicken, Maison Du Fromage, YWCA, and Now magazine offer support for the coalition boycott because they are critical of Diashowa's apparent concern to make money with little or no regard for the protection of basic human rights. A number of businesses are also a part of the coalition boycott, due in no small part to the threat of economic boycott against their businesses. For example, Pizza Pizza in Toronto initially refused to "take sides" in the Lubicon dispute, arguing that it was convinced that Diashowa was negotiating with the Lubicon and the government of Alberta in good faith. Management representatives for Pizza Pizza communicated with boycott organizers Friends of the Lubicon (FOL) for over three months during 1991 and 1992. During this time, Pizza Pizza was a target of the boycott. Although Pizza Pizza representatives eventually joined the Lubicon coalition by honouring the boycott of Diashowa, the changing tone and contents of letters from the company's president to FOL representatives indicate that Pizza Pizza's interest in doing so was primarily economically motivated.

That there are often major differences among coalition supporters has significant implications for understanding the current and future dynamics of hegemonic and counter-hegemonic perspectives and activities. One implication is the need to recognize that although coalition supporters have many different reasons and interests for being involved, such differences may or may not contribute to a weakening of coalition efforts. Nonetheless, failure to take human diversity into account can lead to distorted, even mythical, pictures of social movements. Since even the smallest coalitions give expression to a diversity of beliefs, perspectives, and interests that are themselves open to challenge and change, counter-hegemonic coalitions and the larger social movements of which they are a part are inherently fragile phenomena. We thus distort both the "inner integrity" and the social struggles of coalition supporters and larger social movements when and if we portray them as anything less than highly complex social phenomena that reflect the coming together and movement of diverse socio-cultural histories. In this regard, the crystallization of beliefs, sentiments, and activities into what we have referred to as the Lubicon coalition is much more than a collection of people fighting against injustice. Both the coalition and the larger social movement of which it is a part more fundamentally represent the dynamic movements of diverse people who have decided to contend for their alternative visions of the state.

It is equally important to note that even though hegemonic forces may appear monolithic, they are also composed of individuals and groups who hold many different beliefs, perspectives, interests, and goals. Since those in the hegemonic camp undoubtedly have different reasons for supporting the status quo, their unity and apparent immutability are potentially subject to the same disruption and change that threaten the coalitions and social movements they oppose. In short, although social movements appear to be a case of "us against them," unity among supporters or opponents of large-scale social change is a precarious phenomenon. Predicting the directions that hegemonic or counter-hegemonic activities will take in relation to the movement of Native peoples in Canada is thereby difficult for a number of reasons, including the subtlety and diversity of social action, disagreements within movement and counter-movement camps over beliefs, perspectives, tactics, and goals, and the frequent lack of predictable, concrete public support for movement or counter-movement ideas and activities.

CONCLUDING REMARKS

Native peoples in Canada have been socially and politically active for thousands of years. It is my contention that the countless incidents involving natives and their supporters are much more than idiosyncratic, knee-jerk reactions to isolated experiences of government or corporate colonialism. On the one hand, the Native social movement involves the strategic actions and reactions of those who desire to challenge ideas, policies, laws, and organized activities that perpetuate injustice against Native people in Canada. On the other hand, differences in thought and action among social movement supporters in Canada and throughout the world suggest that the type and degree of diversity in hegemonic and counter-hegemonic camps are as important to the success or failure of social movements and coalitions as is unity. The preceding analysis also suggests that people in both camps:

1. believe many different things about the nature of human life;

2. have very different perspectives on the purpose of human life and why they support or oppose a specific social movement;

3. become involved in counter-hegemonic or hegemonic activities for a wide variety of reasons; and

4. often have very different interests at stake in the success or failure of a given social movement.

Social movements and the countless coalitions that give movements much of their definition and "movement" must therefore be understood as historical phenomena in which countless factors interact with one another. Understanding why coalitions and larger social movements exist, fail, or succeed thus depends on understanding them in historical context and identifying their particular social characteristics. Of these, I suggest that a close examination of differences within hegemonic and counter-hegemonic camps, as well as the global interaction of cross-cutting movements and coalitions, is particularly important for understanding the success or failure of a given coalition or movement. Making sense of the Native social movement in Canada means placing it in the context of the complex history of Native–white relations in pre- and post-Confederation Canada, the particular beliefs, perspectives, and interests of the people involved, and the ways in which supporters and opponents are linked to those who support or oppose the more global, cross-cutting indigenous peoples and environmental protection movements.

The preceding discussion illustrates that not all Native people in Canada have chosen the same path of resistance to European colonization. As the chapters in this book attest, most aboriginal people in Canada undoubtedly would have preferred that their social, economic, political, and legal problems were resolved in peaceful ways. Nonetheless, it is evident that for much longer than the past 30 years, countless tears and much blood have been shed because of the violence involving many of Canada's aboriginal peoples. The development of a militant agenda that expressed itself in an often violent manner during the 1970s and 1980s was for many Native people a matter of survival (York, 1989, pp. 260–61). It also served as an effective means of shocking other Canadians into realizing that the vision of Canada as a "peaceable kingdom" was little more than a state-perpetuated myth (Boldt, 1993, p. 21), and that Native people and their supporters would resort to political violence if their part in reconstructing a truly democratic Canada continued to be ignored or co-opted (Boldt, 1981, p. 215).

This study also highlights the difficulty in mobilizing and maintaining large-scale support for alternative visions of the state. Given the differences among Lubicon coalition members and Native social movement supporters, it is probable that much support for the Lubicon and other Natives will wane with the settling of Native land claims. The same will undoubtedly occur as other Native concerns and interests are addressed to the satisfaction of those involved. The potential dissolving of support for the Lubicon or other Native peoples raises the important theoretical question of how social scientists ought to understand the relationships between social systems, social movements, and coalitions. It will also, we hope, prompt those who wish to prevent the violence and confrontation that has characterized much of Canada's past to reflect on and work toward a common vision for this country's future.

NOTES

1. Amendments in the 1951 Indian Act that conferred special benefits, subsidies, and exemptions, especially for Natives on reserve, quelled the concerns of some Natives for a time.

2. See Chapter 5 for more discussion of the significance of Bill C-31.

3. Reported in *The Edmonton Journal*, June 25, 1993, p. A5.

4. We must be careful not to oversimplify our analysis by suggesting that all those with spiritual (or other) perspectives share the same material visions and interests. As Hamel (1994, pp. 22–23) notes, religiously based coalitions are not exempt from experiencing intense conflict and debate from within over concrete interests and goals.

DISCUSSION QUESTIONS

1. What is the relationship between the colonization of Native peoples in Canada and the current Native social movement?

2. In what ways do resource mobilization and new social movement perspectives provide a sense of past, present, and possibly future

developments in the Native social movement? Can you think of other ways of making sense of this movement?

3. What is the relationship between the socio-economic conditions in which many Native people find themselves and the Native social movement? Do you think socio-economic conditions are the main determining factor in life satisfaction? What might be some other factors that contribute to being satisfied with life?

4. Do you think beliefs, perspectives, and interests play different roles in the development of Lubicon and other coalitions? In what ways do the beliefs, perspectives, and interests that you have make a difference in how you live your life?

5. What do you think holds social movement supporters or opponents together in the face of their often widely divergent beliefs, perspectives, experiences, and interests? Put another way, what role do you think diversity plays when even the unified front — that is little more than surface unity — begins to break down?

FURTHER READINGS

Adams, Howard. 1989. *Prison of Grass: Canada from a Native Point of View*, rev. ed. Saskatoon: Fifth House Publishers. A passionate, insightful, angry critique of colonization from one Native person's perspective.

Cornell, Stephen. 1988. *The Return of the Native: American Indian Political Resurgence*. New York: Oxford University Press. A sweeping analysis of Native American social and political activism.

Englestad, Diane and John Bird, eds. 1992. *Nation to Nation: Aboriginal Sovereignty and the Future of Canada*. Toronto: Anansi. Wide variety of thoughtful articles on points of agreement and tension between Native and non-Native peoples in Canada.

Kelly, M.T. 1987. *A Dream Like Mine*. Toronto: Stoddart. A haunting allegory of Native and non-Native worlds clashing in violent, unpredictable ways.

Silman, Janet. 1987. *Enough Is Enough: Aboriginal Women Speak Out*. Toronto: Women's Press. Loosely narrated discussion of struggles and victories of women involved with the Tobique women's political action group. Splendid example of how oral histories ought to be researched and written.

Richardson, Boyce, ed. 1989. *Drum Beat: Anger and Renewal in Indian Country*. Toronto: Summerhill Press. Collection of articles by Native and non-Native writers on current experiences and future hopes of Native peoples in Canada.

York, Geoffrey and Loreen Pindera. 1992. *The People of the Pines.* Toronto: Little, Brown and Company. Detailed analysis of the Mohawk people at Oka and Kahnawake. Provides a strong sense of the personal and socio-historical context that informed the Oka crisis of 1990.

REFERENCES

Adams, Howard. 1989. *Prison of Grass: Canada from a Native Point of View*, rev. ed. Saskatoon: Fifth House Publishers.

Berger, Peter and Thomas Luckmann. 1967. *The Social Construction of Reality.* Garden City, N.Y.: Doubleday.

Boldt, Menno. 1981. "Philosophy, Politics and Extralegal Action: Native Indian Leaders in Canada." *Ethnic and Racial Studies* 4(2): pp. 205–22.

———. 1993. *Surviving as Indians: The Challenge of Self-Government.* Toronto: University of Toronto Press.

Bopp, Judie, Michael Bopp, Lee Brown, and Phil Lane, compilers. 1984. *The Sacred Tree.* Lethbridge, Alta.: Four Worlds Development Publishers.

Cardinal, Harold. 1969. *The Unjust Society.* Edmonton: Hurtig.

Cornell, Stephen. 1988. *The Return of the Native: American Indian Political Resurgence.* New York: Oxford University Press.

Dickason, Olive Patricia. 1993. *Canada's First Nations: A History of Founding People from the Earliest Times.* Toronto: McClelland & Stewart.

Erasmus, George. 1989. "Epilogue." Pp. 295–302 in *Drum Beat: Anger and Renewal in Indian Country*, ed. Boyce Richardson. Toronto: Summerhill Press.

Frideres, James. 1988. *Native Peoples in Canada: Contemporary Conflicts*, 3rd ed. Scarborough, Ont.: Prentice-Hall.

Geertz, Clifford. 1984. "Religion as a Cultural System." Pp. 12–18 in *Religion: North American Style*, 2nd ed., ed. P. McNamara. Belmont, Calif.: Wadsworth Publishing Co.

Gurr, Ted Robert. 1970. *Why Men Rebel.* Princeton, N.J.: Princeton University Press.

Hall, Stuart. 1988. *The Hard Road to Renewal: Thatcherism and the Crisis of the Left.* London: Verso.

Hamel, Peter. 1994. "The Aboriginal Rights Coalition," Pp. 16–36 in *Coalitions for Justice: The Story of Canada's Interchurch Coalitions*, ed. Christopher Lind and Joe Mihevc. Ottawa: Novalis.

Hammersmith, Bernice. 1992. "Aboriginal Women and Self-Government." Pp. 53–59 in *Nation to Nation: Aboriginal Sovereignty and the Future of Canada*, ed. Diane Englestad and John Bird. Toronto: Anansi.

Jensen, Jane. 1993. "Naming Nations: Making Nationalist Claims in Canadian Public Discourse." *Canadian Review of Sociology and Anthropology* 30(3): pp. 337–58.

Laclau, Ernesto and Chantal Mouffe. 1985. *Hegemony and Socialist Strategy: Towards a Radical Democratic Politics.* London: Verso.

Long, David. 1992. "Culture, Ideology and Militancy: The Movement of Indians in Canada 1969–1991." Pp. 118–34 in *Organizing Dissent: Contemporary Social Movements in Theory and Practice*, ed. W. Carroll. Toronto: Garamond.

McKay, Stan. 1992. "Calling Creation into Our Family." Pp. 28–34 in *Nation to Nation: Aboriginal Sovereignty and the Future of Canada*, ed. Diane Engelstad and John Bird. Toronto: Anansi.

Melucci, Antonio. 1985. "The Symbolic Challenge of Contemporary Movements." *Social Research* 52(4).

Miller, J.R. 1991. "The Northwest Rebellion of 1885." Pp. 243–58 in *Sweet Promises: A Reader on Indian–White Relations in Canada*, ed. J.R. Miller. Toronto: University of Toronto Press.

Ponting, J. Rick, ed. 1986. *Arduous Journey: Canadian Indians and Decolonization*. Toronto: Butterworths.

———. 1991. "Public Opinion on Aboriginal Issues in Canada." Pp. 19–27 in *Canadian Social Trends*, ed. Craig McKie and Keith Thompson. Toronto: Thompson Educational Publishing.

Rich, E.E. 1991. "Trade Habits and Economic Motivation Among the Indians of North America." Pp. 158–79 in *Sweet Promises: A Reader on Indian–White Relations in Canada*, ed. J.R. Miller. Toronto: University of Toronto Press.

Silman, Janet. 1987. *Enough Is Enough: Aboriginal Women Speak Out*. Toronto: Women's Press.

Stonechild, Blair A. 1991. "The Indian View of the 1885 Uprising." Pp. 259–76 in *Sweet Promises: A Reader on Indian–White Relations in Canada*, ed. J.R. Miller. Toronto: University of Toronto Press.

Taylor, John Leonard. 1991. "Canada's Northwest Indian Policy in the 1870s: Traditional Promises and Necessary Innovations." Pp. 207–11 in *Sweet Promises: A Reader on Indian–White Relations in Canada*, ed. J.R. Miller. Toronto: University of Toronto Press.

Torrance, Judy. 1977. "The Response of Canadian Governments to Violence." *Canadian Journal of Political Science* 3: pp. 473–96.

Touraine, Alain. 1981. *The Voice and the Eye: An Analysis of Social Movements*, tr. Alan Duff. Cambridge: Cambridge University Press.

———. 1988. *Return of the Actor: Social Theory in Postindustrial Society*, tr. Myrna Godzich. Minneapolis: University of Minnesota Press.

Weaver, Sally. 1981. *Making Canadian Indian Policy: The Hidden Agenda, 1968–1970*. Toronto: University of Toronto Press.

York, Geoffrey. 1989. *The Dispossessed: Life and Death in Native Canada*. London: Vintage Press.

York, Geoffrey and Loreen Pindera. 1992. *The People of the Pines*. Toronto: Little, Brown and Company.

Zald, Mayer N. and John D. McCarthy. 1987. "Resource Mobilization and Social Movements: A Partial Theory." Pp. 15–42 in *Social Movements in an Organizational Society: Collected Essays*, ed. Mayer N. Zald and John D. McCarthy. New Brunswick, N.J.: Transaction Books.

CONTRIBUTORS

JEAN BARMAN is a professor in the Department of Educational Studies at the University of British Columbia. She is co-editor of *Indian Education in Canada*, 2 vols. (UBC Press, 1986–87) and *First Nations Education in Canada: the Circle Unfolds* (UBC Press, 1995), and author of *The West beyond the West: A History of British Columbia* (University of Toronto Press, 1991, rev. 1996). She co-edits the journal *BC Studies* and serves on the council of the Canadian Historical Association.

SIMON BRASCOUPÉ is a member of the Kitigan Zibi Anishinabeg, formerly the River Desert Indian band, Maniwaki, Quebec. He is a lecturer in the Department of Native Studies at Trent University, and an adjunct research professor in the Department of Sociology and Anthropology at Carleton University. He is currently completing his Ph.D. at State University, Buffalo, New York. Simon is an artist who has exhibited in Canada, the United States, Europe, China, and Cuba, and his work is in major corporations' and private collections. He was a member of the Canadian delegation at the United Nations Conference on Environment and Development in 1992, and more recently represented Canada at the 1995 UN Conference on Biological Diversity in Jakarta, Indonesia.

JOSEPH E. COUTURE is an Alberta Métis of Cree ancestry. His Ph.D. training and experience are in the areas of Native development, psychology, and education at all levels. His work experience includes teaching, addictions counselling, community development, and research. He has been apprenticed to Elders since 1971.

OLIVE PATRICIA DICKASON is a professor emeritus of history at the University of Alberta. She is the author of several books, including *Canada's First Nations*, *The Myth of the Savage*, and *Indian Arts in Canada* (all published in English and French). Before she began her career as a scholar, she was a journalist for the Montreal *Gazette* and *The Globe and Mail*. She holds honorary degrees from the University of Alberta and the University of New Brunswick, and is a fellow of Ryerson Polytechnic University, Toronto. Most recently, The First Nations Students Association and the Native Centre of the University of Calgary presented her with the Dr. Joseph Crowshoe Award. Throughout, she remains proud of her Métis heritage.

RUBY FARRELL, who is Ojibway, was born and raised on her father's trap line in northwestern Ontario. She is currently an assistant professor in the

Faculty of Education, and coordinator of the Native teacher education program at Lakehead University. For the past three years, she has been examining the effects of colonization on aboriginal peoples' arts and crafts forms in Canada and Australia with Rita L. Irwin.

AUGIE FLERAS is an associate professor in the Department of Sociology at the University of Waterloo. His primary interests reside in the field of race, ethnic, and aboriginal relations, with particular emphasis on aboriginal–state renewal in Canada and Aotearoa (NZ), multiculturalism and society-building, and the concept of institutional accommodation. He has published widely in these areas, and intends to continue with current research on the topic of media–minority relations and the politics of representation.

TERRY FOX is Cree and a member of the Wesley-Stoney First Nation near Morley, Alberta. She has been actively involved in bringing social, political, and economic healing and development to her people, and is currently enrolled in the Native studies program at the University of Victoria.

RITA L. IRWIN is an associate professor of curriculum studies at the University of British Columbia. For the past three years, she has been examining the effects of colonization on aboriginal peoples' arts and crafts forms in Canada and Australia with co-investigator Ruby Farrell. Her publications in the *Canadian Journal of Native Education, Journal of Cross-Cultural and Multicultural Research, Research in Art Education, Journal of the Canadian Society for Education for Art*, and her book *A Circle of Empowerment: Women, Education, and Leadership* (SUNY Press, 1995) exhibit her interest in exploring qualitatively issues related to women art educators and First Nations art.

DAVID ALAN LONG currently resides with his wife and three children in Edmonton, Alberta, and is an associate professor of sociology at The King's University College. The publishing he has done in a variety of disciplinary and interdisciplinary journals and books expresses his research interests in relations between aboriginal and non-aboriginal peoples in Canada, religion and spirituality, science, technology and society, pedagogy, gender, and deviance.

PETER McFARLANE is a Montreal-based freelance writer. His most recent book is *Brotherhood to Nationhood: George Manuel and the Making of the Modern Indian Movement*.

PATRICIA A. MONTURE-ANGUS is a Mohawk from the Six Nations community near Brantford, Ontario, and currently resides with her husband and children at the Thunderchild First Nation in Saskatchewan. Educated as a lawyer, she is currently employed as an associate professor in the Department of Native Studies at the University of Saskatchewan. Her first book,

Thunder in My Soul: A Mohawk Woman Speaks Out was published in the summer of 1995, and has been short-listed in the "Best Book" category for the awards sponsored by the Saskatchewan Writer's Guild.

MARY JANE NORRIS is a senior population analyst with Statistics Canada. She has written on aboriginal demography and migration, and recently completed the aboriginal identity population projections (1991–2016) for the Royal Commission on Aboriginal Peoples. Her interest in aboriginal issues and demography stems, in part, from her own aboriginal ancestry. Her maternal grandmother was born and raised in the Algonquin Golden Lake First Nation of the Ottawa Valley.

EVELYN PETERS is an associate professor at Queen's University, Kingston, Ontario. She teaches in the areas of urban and social geography. Her research and publications are in the areas of aboriginal self-government, the demographic characteristics of urban aboriginal peoples, and the ways in which aboriginal urbanization has been conceptualized in non-aboriginal literature.

BENJAMIN G. SMILLIE recently retired after 25 years of teaching church history at St. Andrew's College, Saskatoon, Saskatchewan. His contributions to many different books, journals, and church publications indicate his wide-ranging interests in church history, theology, and politics. His most recently completed books are *Beyond the Social Gospel: Gospel Protest in the Prairies* (Fifth House Publishers) and *Christian Ethics in a Pluralistic Canadian Society* (United Church Publishing House).

CORA J. VOYAGEUR is a Ph.D. candidate in the Sociology Department at the University of Alberta. She is a member of the Athabasca Chipewyan First Nation in Fort Chipewyan, Alberta. She has published articles on Native education, Native economic development, and Native women's issues, and is currently exploring the impact of the federal Employment Equity Act on aboriginal people in Canada.

READER REPLY CARD

We are interested in your reaction to *Visions of the Heart: Canadian Aboriginal Issues,* by David Alan Long and Olive Patricia Dickason. You can help us to improve this book in future by completing this questionnaire.

1. What was your reason for using this book?

☐ university course ☐ college course ☐ continuing education course

☐ professional ☐ personal ☐ other (specify) interest

_____

2. If you are a student, please identify your school and the course in which you used this book.

3. Which chapters or parts of this book did you use? Which did you omit?

4. What did you like best about this book? What did you like least?

5. Please identify any topics you think should be added to future editions.

6. Please add any comments or suggestions.

7. May we contact you for further information?

Name: _____

Address: _____

_____

_____

Phone: _____

(fold here and tape shut)

MAIL ➤ POSTE

Canada Post Corporation / Société canadienne des postes

Postage paid
If mailed in Canada

Port payé
si posté au Canada

**Business
Reply**

**Réponse
d'affaires**

0116870399   01

0116870399-M8Z4X6-BR01

Heather McWhinney
Publisher, College Division
HARCOURT BRACE & COMPANY, CANADA
55 HORNER AVENUE
TORONTO, ONTARIO
M8Z 9Z9